Dear Sister ☆
Lynn,
This is your year!
YEAR OF THE METAL
RABBIT
(pages 59., 60, 61)
It occurs every 60 years
Happy Birthday!
Much Love to you! ♡
XXX OOO ♡
— Annie Bones
(Sister Sheeler)
☆

CELESTIAL FORECASTER ®

2011

EVERYONE'S
DAILY ASTROLOGY GUIDE

FEATURING:

- Daily forecasts based on planetary alignments
- Monthly overview of significant aspects
- Lunar aspects guide
- Daily table of aspect influences
- Full year calendar,
- Built-in ephemeris and
- Famous birthdays

Loon Feather Publications
Box 47031 Victoria, B.C.
V9B 5T2 Canada
www.metaphysical.ca/forecaster
email: loonfeather@metaphysical.ca

Acknowledgements:

Thanks to all of you for continuing to make the Celestial Forecaster
a success. Your enthusiasm is what keeps the Forecaster going.
Thanks to Soror SSH for the great work editing,
and to Cara and Frater 72 for production.

Printing and Binding:	Data reproductions Corporation
Production & cover:	Cara & Frater 72
Editing:	Soror SSH
Inside Graphics:	Merx Toledo International
ISBN:	978-0-9731518-8-6

TABLE OF CONTENTS

TIME ZONE ADJUSTMENTS

In the *Celestial Forecaster* we show Pacific Time and Eastern Time. Most poeple in North America are familiar with adjusting to one of those two zones. If you use **Central Time**, add two hours to Pacific Time. For **Rocky Mountain Time**, add one hour to Pacific Time. To get **Greenwich Mean Time**, add 8 hours to Pacific Time (PST) or seven hours to Pacific Daylight Time (PDT). If you live outside North America, you can refer to the Time Zone Map below.

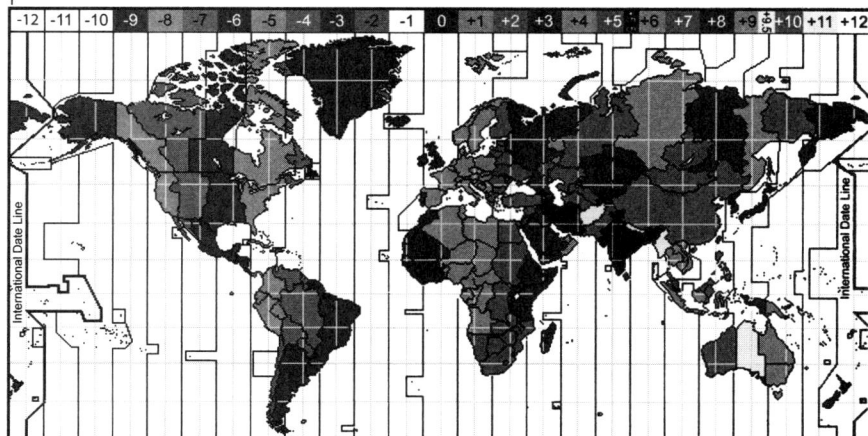

Definitions of Terms

Aspect: Planets are said to be "in aspect" with each other when their location in the sky forms particular angles with the earth which are deemed significant. The main aspects and angles used in this book are as follows:

✳ **Sextile (60°):** The sextile aspect is considered to be favorable, and opens up possibilities and opportunities to work energies out between the two planetary influences.

☐ **Square (90°):** The square aspect indicates a struggle or stress between two planetary influences. This aspect often brings obstacles, or difficulties in our ability to learn and understand. A positive way to address this aspect is to see it as a time when we need to work through our challenges. In these blocks or obstacles a great deal of energy is concentrated. If one acts with caution and care, the energy released by dealing with our challenges can be harnessed, and overcoming the obstacle becomes a personal triumph that leads to growth and the strengthening of character.

△ **Trine (120°):** The most advantageous and harmonious aspect. It is considered to bring the most positive effects. A trine aspect brings gifts, and talents are often realized and acted upon.

☍ **Opposition (180°):** The opposition is the furthest apart the two planets are able to be in their orbits. This aspect brings an acute awareness of the energies that two planetary influences have upon us. It can also bring an overwhelming effect, and handling the polarity often requires awareness and caution.

☌ **Conjunction (0°):** Conjunction is the act of joining, or the state of being joined. When two planets have reached the same degree in the sky this is called a conjunction. It represents the direct confrontation of these energies which will be positive or negative depending on the nature of the planets which are in conjunction.

The Orb: The orb is the area of influence before and after an exact aspect, measured in degrees. The smaller the orb, the closer we are to an exact aspect, and the more strongly we feel the planetary influences. Orbs are divided into two parts: applying and separating. **Applying** — the part of the orb when the planetary aspect is approaching the exact time of reaching its peak. **Separating** — the part of the orb when the planetary aspect is moving away from the peak point of the aspect. Orbs in this book have been calculated using an orb of 6° applying, and 3° separating for all aspects except the sextile, for which 4° applying and 2° separating have been used.

v/c **Void-of-course Moon:** As it travels through a zodiacal sign, the Moon is in aspect with a number of planets. The final major aspect it reaches in a sign marks the time when the Moon goes void-of-course (v/c), meaning it will undergo no further aspects while in that zodiac sign. The Moon will remain void-of-course until it enters the next zodiac sign. While the Moon is void-of-course is a time of less direction and more confusion, particularly on the emotional or mood level.

R **Retrograde:** This occurs when the orbit of a planet causes it to appear to move backward through the sky. It represents a time of moving back over old ground, and inverting influences. The section on Mercury retrograde (page 8) gives examples of how retrogrades work. The Sun and Moon, not being planets, do not go retrograde.

D **Direct:** After a period of retrograde motion, the planet ceases its backward motion and moves forward again through the zodiacal signs. It represents a time of release and forward movement, though the old ground that was just covered in retrograde fashion must be gone over again before any new progress can be made.

Glossary of Astrological Symbols

Aries	♈		Sun	☉
Taurus	♉		Moon	☽
Gemini	♊		Mercury	☿
Cancer	♋		Venus	♀
Leo	♌		Mars	♂
Virgo	♍		Jupiter	♃
Libra	♎		Saturn	♄
Scorpio	♏		Neptune	♆
Sagittarius	♐		Uranus	♅
Capricorn	♑		Pluto	♇
Aquarius	♒			
Pisces	♓			

How to Use this Book

To adjust for time zones other than Pacific or Eastern USA, use the *Time Zone Adjustments* table on page 5.

For planetary aspectarian and for the phases of the Moon: use the *Overview of Significant Aspects in 2011* found on pages 9 – 17.

For major daily influences at a glance: look at the *Table of Aspect Influences* on pages 18 - 21.

For exact zodiacal position of a planet: use the *Ephemeris* on pages 273-279.

For daily commentary and analysis: see the main section pages 37-272, including:

Sun Signs: The glyph for the current sun sign is shown in the upper right margin on each page of the daily commentary.

Headers: The date headers at the top of each day show the date, the day of the week, and a selection of notable holidays.

Moon signs and void-of-course periods: Below the date header is the Moon's sign. The Moon's void-of-course period and entry to the next sign is shown chronologically with the day's planetary aspects. The numerous lunar aspects are included this year, and are interpreted in the new *Lunar aspects guide* on pages 23 - 35.

Aspects: Below the Moon's sign in the header is a list of the day's exact planetary and lunar aspects, together with their time of occurrence. Also listed are aspects whose orb of influence is just beginning, and the aspect's date of exact occurrence. Occasionally the aspect information is followed by quotes from famous people.

Mood Watch:: Each day features a *Mood Watch:* section. This commentary examines key lunar aspects of the day, and explains their likely influence on our moods. Like our moods, these lunar aspects are generally short-lived.

Aspect Analysis: Below the *Mood Watch:* section are shown the day's main planetary aspects, the dates their orb of influence occurs, and an in-depth aspect analysis.

Mercury retrograde periods: 2011

BEGINS (Mercury goes retrograde)		ENDS (Mercury goes direct)	
March 30	in Aries	April 23	in Aries
Aug. 2	in Virgo	Aug. 26	in Leo
Nov. 23	in Sagittarius	Dec. 13	in Sagittarius

Mercury Retrograde through the Fire Signs, and through Virgo

Mercury represents how we process information and communicate. Mercury retrograde is a term that describes an orbital shift as it moves backwards through a sign. Technically it only appears to move backwards through the degrees of the zodiac from our geocentric view. Astrologically, this is a time of communication related setbacks, reiterations, or inconsistencies – particularly the first few days going into and out of the retrograde period. Mercury retrograde periods take place for an average of three weeks at a time, and will occur on the average of three times a year.

Mercury retrograde is a time of going back over various topics, and repeating or correcting a lot of information. General misinformation and absentmindedness are the most common symptoms. Be on the look-out for frequent bouts of dyslexia and other communication errors in writing, speaking, and journalism.

This year Mercury will go retrograde in the three fire signs of the zodiac: Aries, Leo, and Sagittarius. In the beginning of the second retrograde phase (Aug. 2 - 26), it will also be retrograde in the mutable earth sign, Virgo (Aug. 2 – 8).

As Mercury goes retrograde through the three fire signs – Aries, Leo, and Sagittarius – communications regarding all vital creative processes and projects will be affected. This fans the internal fires of the mind and may cause anxiety, impatience and heated turmoil when it comes to communication attempts. It is best to mind the temper when attempting to communicate during these periods. Expect to see some heat and active or brazen enthusiasm while delivering or receiving messages.

Mercury retrograde in Aries (March 30 – April 23) brings miscommunications over personal boundaries and issues of control.

While Mercury is retrograde in the Mercury-ruled earth sign, Virgo (Aug. 2 – 8), be careful not to get caught up in disputes over health matters, accounting and budgets, and be sure to double check inventories. Expect some confusion over situations involving the maintenance of resources and resale goods.

While Mercury is retrograde in Leo (Aug. 8 – 26), be cautious with ego related matters, and beware of the general hypersensitivity to the manner in which people are personally addressed.

While Mercury is retrograde in the fire sign, Sagittarius (Nov. 23 – Dec. 13), communication mistakes will be apparent in such topics as philosophy, travel, sports, and exploration, and this is an especially significant time to expect travel delays.

Overview of Significant Events in 2011

Particularly noteworthy events

JAN 4	- JUPITER CONJUNCT URANUS
JAN 2	- JUPITER ENTERS ARIES
MAR 11	- URANUS ENTERS ARIES
APRIL 4	- NEPTUNE ENTERS PISCES
JUNE 4	- JUPITER ENTERS TAURUS
JULY 7 & OCT. 28	- JUPITER TRINE PLUTO
JULY 10	- URANUS-SQUARE-PLUTO-NON-EXACT
AUGUST 4	- Retrograde NEPTUNE REENTERS AQUARIUS
OCTOBER 29	- SATURN-TRINE-NEPTUNE-NON-EXACT

JANUARY

Orbital Range

Exact Occurrence Date		BEGINS	ENDS
4	**New Moon in Capricorn** – *Solar Eclipse*		
	Venus square Neptune	Dec. 28, 2010	Jan. 7
`	Venus trine Uranus	Dec. 28, 2010	Jan. 7
	Venus trine Jupiter	Dec. 27, 2010	Jan. 7
	JUPITER CONJUNCT URANUS	Dec. 15, 2010	Jan. 26
7	Venus enters Sagittarius	Jan. 7	Feb. 3
	Sun square Saturn	Jan. 1	Jan. 10
10	Mercury sextile Neptune	Jan. 6	Jan. 12
	Mercury square Uranus	Jan. 3	Jan. 13
11	Mercury square Jupiter	Jan. 3	Jan. 14
12	**First Quarter Moon in Aries**		
	Mars sextile Uranus	Jan. 6	Jan. 14
13	Mercury enters Capricorn	Jan. 13	Feb. 3
	Mars sextile Jupiter	Jan. 7	Jan. 16
15	Mars enters Aquarius	Jan. 15	Feb. 22
17	Sun sextile Uranus	Jan.13	Jan. 19
	Mercury conjunct Pluto	Jan. 12	Jan. 20
19	**Full Moon in Cancer**		
	Sun sextile Jupiter	Jan. 14	Jan. 21
20	Sun enters Aquarius	Jan. 20	Feb. 18
22	JUPITER ENTERS ARIES	Jan. 22	June 4

JANUARY (cont'd)

Exact Occurrence Date

		Orbital Range	
		BEGINS	**ENDS**
23	Venus sextile Saturn	Jan. 19	Jan. 25
25	Saturn goes retrograde	Jan. 25	June 12
26	**Last Quarter Moon in Scorpio**		
	Mercury square Saturn	Jan. 21	Jan. 28

FEBRUARY

1	Venus sextile Neptune	Jan. 29	Feb. 3
2	**New Moon in Aquarius - Candlemas / Imbolc / Groundhog Day**		
	Venus square Uranus	Jan. 27	Feb. 4
	Mercury sextile Uranus	Jan. 30	Feb. 3
3	***Chinese New Year: Metal RABBIT***	Feb. 3	Jan. 22, 2012
	Mercury enters Aquarius	Feb. 3	Feb. 21
	Venus enters Capricorn	Feb. 3	March 26
4	Sun conjunct Mars	Jan. 9	Feb. 17
5	Mercury sextile Jupiter	Feb. 2	Feb. 6
	Sun trine Saturn	Jan. 31	Feb. 8
6	Mars trine Saturn	Jan. 29	Feb. 10
	Venus square Jupiter	Jan. 31	Feb. 9
9	Venus conjunct Pluto	Feb. 4	Feb. 12
10	**First Quarter Moon in Taurus**		
14	Mercury trine Saturn	Feb. 10	Feb. 15
16	**Full Moon in Leo**		
17	Sun conjunct Neptune	Feb. 10	Feb. 20
18	Venus square Saturn	Feb. 13	Feb. 20
	Sun enters Pisces	Feb. 18	March 20
20	Mercury conjunct Mars	Feb. 14	Feb. 23
	Mercury conjunct Neptune	Feb. 17	Feb. 22
	Mars conjunct Neptune	Feb. 12	Feb. 24
21	Mercury enters Pisces	Feb. 21	March 9
22	Mars enters Pisces	Feb. 22	April 1
24	**Last Quarter Moon in Sagittarius**		
25	Sun conjunct Mercury	Feb. 17	Feb. 28
	Mercury sextile Pluto	Feb. 23	Feb. 26
	Jupiter square Pluto	Jan. 22	March 11
	Sun sextile Pluto	Feb. 21	Feb. 27

MARCH

1	Venus sextile Uranus	Feb. 25	March 3
	Venus enters Aquarius	March 1	March 26
3	Mars sextile Pluto	Feb. 26	March 6

MARCH (cont'd)

Exact Occurrence Date		BEGINS	ENDS
4	**New Moon in Pisces**		
9	Mercury enters Aries	March 9	May 15
	Mercury conjunct Uranus	March 6	March 11
10	Venus sextile Jupiter	March 5	March 12
11	URANUS ENTERS ARIES	March 11	May 15, 2018
12	**First Quarter Moon in Gemini**		
13	*Daylight Saving Time Begins*		
	Mercury square Pluto	March 10	March 15
14	Venus trine Saturn	March 9	March 17
15	Mercury conjunct Jupiter	March 11	March 18
18	Mercury-opposite-Saturn-non-exact	March 14	March 20
19	**Full Moon in Virgo**		
20	**Vernal Equinox** – Sun enters Aries	March 20	April 20
21	Sun conjunct Uranus	March 14	March 24
26	**Last Quarter Moon in Capricorn**		
	Venus conjunct Neptune	March 21	March 29
	Venus enters Pisces	March 26	April 20
28	Sun square Pluto	March 22	March 31
	Jupiter opposite Saturn	March 9	April 7
30	Mercury goes retrograde	March 30	April 23

APRIL

1	Mars enters Aries	April 1	May 11
2	Venus sextile Pluto	March 29	April 3
3	**New Moon in Aries**		
	Mars conjunct Uranus	March 26	April 7
	Sun opposite Saturn	April 1	April 6
4	NEPTUNE ENTERS PISCES	April 4	Aug. 4
6	Sun conjunct Jupiter	March 29	April 10
8	Saturn-square-Pluto-non-exact	April 8	April 9
9	Pluto goes retrograde	April 9	Sept. 16
	Sun conjunct Mercury	April 5	April 11
11	**First Quarter Moon in Cancer**		
	Mars square Pluto	April 3	April 15
	Mercury conjunct Jupiter	April 5	April 15
17	**Full Moon in Libra**		
18	Mars opposite Saturn	April 11	April 21
19	Mercury conjunct Mars	April 14	April 22
20	Sun enters Taurus	April 20	May 21
	Sun sextile Neptune	April 16	April 22
	Venus enters Aries	April 20	May 15
	Mercury-square-Pluto-non-exact	April 19	April 21

APRIL (cont'd)

Exact Occurrence Date	BEGINS	ENDS 22
Venus conjunct Uranus	April 17	April 25
23 Mercury goes direct	April 23	Aug. 2
Mercury-opposite-Saturn-non-exact	April 9	April 30
24 **Last Quarter Moon in Aquarius**		
27 Venus square Pluto	April 22	April 29
Sun trine Pluto	April 21	April 30
30 Venus opposite Saturn	April 26	May 3

MAY

1 **Beltane / May Day**		
2/3 **New Moon in Taurus**		
9 Mercury conjunct Venus	April 27	May 25
10 **First Quarter Moon in Leo**		
11 Mars enters Taurus	May 11	June 20
Venus conjunct Jupiter	May 5	May 14
Mercury conjunct Jupiter	May 3	May 14
12 Mars sextile Neptune	May 6	May 14
15 Venus enters Taurus	May 15	June 9
Mercury enters Taurus	May 15	June 2
16 Mercury conjunct Venus	April 27	May 25
Mercury sextile Neptune	May 13	May 17
17 **Full Moon in Scorpio**		
20 Mars trine Pluto	May 12	May 24
Mercury trine Pluto	May 16	May 22
Mercury conjunct Mars	May 10	May 24
22 Sun square Neptune	May 15	May 25
21 Sun enters Gemini	May 21	June 21
Venus trine Pluto	May 16	May 23
23 Venus conjunct Mars	May 10	May 29
24 **Last Quarter Moon in Pisces**		
Sun sextile Uranus	May 20	May 27

JUNE

1 **New Moon in Gemini** – *Solar Eclipse*		
Sun trine Saturn	May 25	June 4
2 Mercury enters Gemini	June 2	June 16
3 Mercury square Neptune	May 30	June 4
Neptune goes retrograde	June 3	Nov. 9
4 JUPITER ENTERS TAURUS	June 4	June 11, 2012
Mercury sextile Uranus	June 2	June 5

June (cont'd)

Orbital Range

Exact Occurrence Date	BEGINS	ENDS
7 Mercury trine Saturn	June 4	June 8
8 **First Quarter Moon in Virgo**		
Jupiter sextile Neptune	May 20	June 18
9 Venus enters Gemini	June 9	July 3
10 Venus square Neptune	June 5	June 12
12 Venus sextile Uranus	June 9	June 14
Saturn goes direct	June 12	Feb. 9, 2012
15 **Full Moon in Sagittarius** – *Lunar Eclipse*		
16 Mercury enters Cancer	June 16	July 1
Mercury trine Neptune	June 14	June 18
17 Mercury sextile Jupiter	June 15	June 18
Venus trine Saturn	June 12	June 20
18 Mercury square Uranus	June 15	June 19
19 Mercury-opposite-Pluto-non-exact	June 18	June 20
20 Mars enters Gemini	June 20	Aug. 3
21 **Summer Solstice -** Sun enters Cancer	June 21	July 22 / 23
Mercury square Saturn	June 18	June 22
Mars square Neptune	June 13	June 26
22 Sun trine Neptune	June 16	June 25
23 **Last Quarter Moon in Aries**		
25 Sun sextile Jupiter	June 20	June 28
26 Sun square Uranus	June 19	June 29
27 Mars sextile Uranus	June 21	June 30
Sun opposite Pluto	June 21	June 30

JULY

1 **New Moon in Cancer** – *Solar Eclipse*		
Mercury enters Leo	July 1	July 28
2 Sun square Saturn	June 26	July 5
3 Venus enters Cancer	July 3	July 28
4 Venus trine Neptune	June 29	July 6
Mercury trine Uranus	July 1	July 6
5 Mercury square Jupiter	July 1	July 7
6 Mars trine Saturn	June 27	July 10
7 **First Quarter Moon in Libra**		
JUPITER TRINE PLUTO	June 7	Nov. 16
Venus square Uranus	July 2	July 10
8 Venus sextile Jupiter	July 5	July 10
9 Venus opposite Pluto	July 3	July 11
Mercury sextile Saturn	July 6	July 10
Uranus goes retrograde	July 9	Dec. 9

July (cont'd)

Orbital Range

Exact Occurrence Date	BEGINS	ENDS
10 URANUS-SQUARE-PLUTO-Non-Exact	April 7	Oct. 9
11 Mercury sextile Mars	July 6	Sept. 30
13 Venus square Saturn	July 7	July 15
14 **Full Moon in Capricorn**		
22 **Last Quarter Moon in Taurus**		
22/23 Sun enters Leo	July 22/23	Aug. 23
27 Sun trine Uranus	July 21	July 30
28 Venus enters Leo	July 28	Aug. 21
Mercury enters Virgo	July 28	Aug. 8
30 **New Moon in Leo**		
31 Venus trine Uranus	July 27	Aug. 3

AUGUST

	BEGINS	ENDS
1 **Lammas / Lughnassad**		
Sun square Jupiter	July 25	Aug. 4
2 Mercury goes retrograde	Aug. 2	Aug. 26
3 Mars enters Cancer	Aug. 3	Sept. 18
Mars trine Neptune	July 25	Aug. 7
4 Mercury sextile Mars	July 6	Sept. 30
NEPTUNE ENTERS AQUARIUS	Aug. 4	Feb. 3, 2012
Venus square Jupiter	July 30	Aug. 7
5 Sun sextile Saturn	July 31	Aug. 7
6 **First Quarter Moon in Scorpio**		
7 Venus sextile Saturn	Aug. 4	Aug. 9
8 Mercury enters Leo	Aug. 8	Sept. 8
Mercury opposite Neptune	July 24	Sept. 10
9 Mars square Uranus	July 31	Aug. 13
11 Mars opposite Pluto	Aug. 2	Aug. 15
13 **Full Moon in Aquarius**		
16 Sun conjunct Venus	July 25	Aug. 27
Mercury conjunct Venus	Aug. 13	Aug. 18
Sun conjunct Mercury	Aug. 13	Aug. 18
18 Mars sextile Jupiter	Aug. 11	Aug. 21
21 **Last Quarter Moon in Taurus**		
Venus opposite Neptune	Aug. 16	Aug. 23
Venus enters Virgo	Aug. 21	Sept. 14
22 Sun opposite Neptune	Aug. 16	Aug. 25
23 Sun enters Virgo	Aug. 23	Sept. 23
25 Mars square Saturn	Aug. 14	Aug. 30
Venus trine Pluto	Aug. 20	Aug. 28

August (cont'd)

Exact Occurrence Date	*Orbital Range* BEGINS	ENDS 28
26 Mercury goes direct	Aug. 26	Nov. 23
New Moon in Virgo		
Sun trine Pluto	Aug. 22	Aug. 31
29 Venus trine Jupiter	Aug. 25	Sept. 1
30 Jupiter goes retrograde	Aug. 30	Dec. 25

SEPTEMBER

2	Sun trine Jupiter	Aug. 27	Sept. 5
4	**First Quarter Moon in Sagittarius**		
8	Mercury opposite Neptune	July 24	Sept. 10
	Mercury enters Virgo	Sept. 8	Sept. 25
10	Venus sextile Mars	Sept. 4	Sept. 14
11	Mercury trine Pluto	Sept. 8	Sept. 13
12	**Full Moon in Pisces**		
14	Mercury trine Jupiter	Sept. 11	Sept. 16
	Venus enters Libra	Sept. 14	Oct. 8
16	Pluto goes direct	Sept. 16	April 11, 2012
17	Venus opposite Uranus	Sept. 12	Sept. 19
18	Venus square Pluto	Sept. 13	Sept. 21
	Mars enters Leo	Sept. 18	Nov. 10
20	**Last Quarter Moon in Gemini**		
23	**Autumnal Equinox** - Sun enters Libra	Sept. 23	Oct. 23
	Mars trine Uranus	Sept. 13	Sept. 27
25	Mercury enters Libra	Sept. 25	Oct. 13
	Sun opposite Uranus	Sept. 19	Sept. 28
26	Mercury opposite Uranus	Sept. 23	Sept. 28
27	**New Moon in Libra**		
28	Sun square Pluto	Sept. 21	Oct. 1
	Mercury square Pluto	Sept. 24	Sept. 30
	Sun conjunct Mercury	Sept. 21	Oct. 2
29	Mercury sextile Mars	July 6	Sept.30
	Venus conjunct Saturn	Sept. 24	Oct. 2
	Sun sextile Mars	Sept. 19	Oct. 5

OCTOBER

2	Mars square Jupiter	Sept. 24	Oct. 7
3	**First Quarter Moon in Capricorn**		
6	Mercury conjunct Saturn	Oct. 2	Oct. 8
7	Venus trine Neptune	Oct. 2	Oct. 10
8	Venus enters Scorpio	Oct. 8	Nov. 2

October (cont'd)

Exact Occurrence Date	BEGINS	ENDS
11 **Full Moon in Aries**		
12 Mercury trine Neptune	Oct. 8	Oct. 13
13 Venus sextile Pluto	Oct. 9	Oct. 14
Mercury enters Scorpio	Oct. 13	Nov. 2
14 Venus opposite Jupiter	Oct. 10	Oct. 16
Sun conjunct Saturn	Oct. 6	Oct. 17
16 Mercury sextile Pluto	Oct. 13	Oct. 17
17 Mercury opposite Jupiter	Oct. 13	Oct. 19
19 **Last Quarter Moon in Cancer**		
21 Sun trine Neptune	Oct. 15	Oct. 24
23 Sun enters Scorpio	Oct. 23	Nov. 22
26 **New Moon in Scorpio** – *Hecate's Moon*		
Mars sextile Saturn	Oct. 16	Oct. 30
Venus square Mars	Oct. 17	Oct. 30
28 Mercury square Mars	Oct. 21	Oct. 31
JUPITER TRINE PLUTO	June 7	Nov. 16
Sun opposite Jupiter	Oct. 23	Oct. 31
Sun sextile Pluto	Oct. 24	Oct. 30
29 SATURN-TRINE-NEPTUNE-Non-Exact	Oct. 29	Mar. 13, 2012
31 **All Hallows (Halloween) / Samhain / Witches' New Year**		
Venus square Neptune	Oct. 26	Nov. 3

NOVEMBER

Exact Occurrence Date	BEGINS	ENDS
1 Mercury square Neptune	Oct. 27	Nov. 3
Mercury-conjunct-Venus-non-exact	Oct. 11	Nov. 19
2 **First Quarter Moon in Aquarius**		
Venus enters Sagittarius	Nov. 2	Nov. 26
Mercury enters Sagittarius	Nov. 2	Jan. 7, 2012
3 Venus trine Uranus	Oct. 29	Nov. 5
Mercury trine Uranus	Oct. 30	Nov. 5
6 *Daylight Saving Time Ends*		
7 Mars opposite Neptune	Oct. 27	Nov. 13
9 **Full Moon in Taurus**		
Neptune goes direct	Nov. 9	June 8, 2012
10 Mars enters Virgo	Nov. 10	July 3, 2012
16 Mars trine Jupiter	Nov. 7	Nov. 21
18 **Last Quarter Moon in Leo**		
20 Sun square Neptune	Nov. 14	Nov. 23

November (cont'd)

Exact Occurrence Date	BEGINS	ENDS 23
22 Venus sextile Saturn	Nov. 18	Nov. 23
Sun enters Sagittarius	Nov. 22	Dec. 21 / 22
Sun trine Uranus	Nov. 17	Nov. 26
Mars trine Pluto	Nov. 10	Nov. 30
23/24 Mercury goes retrograde	Nov. 23	Dec. 13
24 **New Moon in Sagittarius** – *Solar Eclipse*		
Venus sextile Neptune	Nov. 21	Nov. 26
26 Venus enters Capricorn	Nov. 26	Dec. 20
Venus square Uranus	Nov. 21	Nov. 29
27 Venus trine Jupiter	Nov. 23	Nov. 29
29 Jupiter-opposite-Saturn-non-exact	Nov. 29	Feb. 3, 2012

DECEMBER

Exact Occurrence Date	BEGINS	ENDS
1 Venus conjunct Pluto	Nov. 26	Dec. 3
2 **First Quarter Moon in Pisces**		
Sun square Mars	Nov. 21	Dec. 7
4 Sun conjunct Mercury	Dec. 1	Dec. 5
Mercury square Mars	Dec. 1	Dec. 6
5 Venus trine Mars	Nov. 27	Dec. 8
9 Uranus goes direct	Dec. 9	July 12, 2012
10 **Full Moon in Gemini** – *Lunar Eclipse*		
13 Mercury goes direct	Dec. 13	Mar. 11, 2012
14 Mercury-trine-Uranus-non-exact	Dec. 8	Dec. 14
15 Mercury-square-Neptune-non-exact	Dec. 11	Dec. 17
17 **Last Quarter Moon in Virgo**		
18 Venus square Saturn	Dec. 13	Dec. 20
19 Sun sextile Saturn	Dec. 15	Dec. 21
20 Venus enters Aquarius	Dec. 20	Jan. 13, 2012
Sun sextile Neptune	Dec. 16	Dec. 22
Venus square Jupiter	Dec. 15	Dec. 23
Venus sextile Uranus	Dec. 17	Dec. 22
21/22 **Winter Solstice** –		
Sun enters Capricorn	Dec. 21	Jan. 20, 2012
22 Sun trine Jupiter	Dec. 16	Dec. 25
Sun square Uranus	Dec. 16	Dec. 25
24 **New Moon in Capricorn**		
25 Jupiter goes direct	Dec. 25	Oct. 4, 2012
28 Sun conjunct Pluto	Dec. 22	Jan. 1, 2012
31 Mercury square Mars	Dec. 25	Jan. 3, 2012

TABLE OF ASPECT INFLUENCES

JANUARY 2011

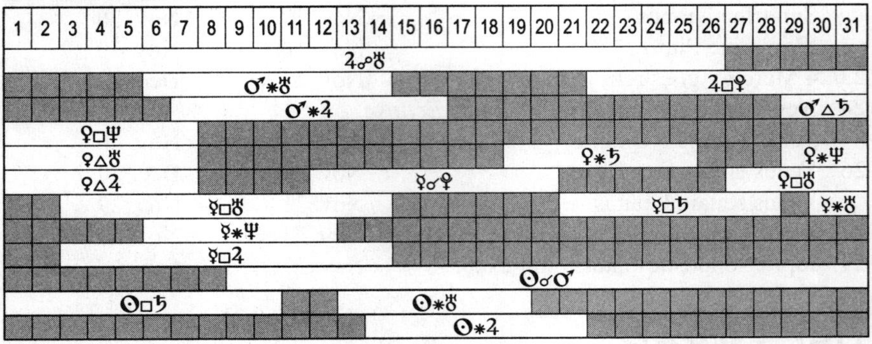

1	2	3	4	5	6	7	8	9	10	11	12	13	14	15	16	17	18	19	20	21	22	23	24	25	26	27	28	29	30	31

Aspect bars (approximate spans):
- ♃☍♅
- ♂✶♅ · ♃□♀
- ♂✶♃ · ♂△♄
- ♀□♆
- ♀△♅ · ♀✶♄ · ♀✶♆
- ♀△♃ · ☿☌♀ · ♀□♅
- ☿□♅ · ☿□♄ · ☿✶♅
- ☿✶♆
- ☿□♃
- ☉☌♂
- ☉□♄ · ☉✶♅
- ☉✶♃

FEBRUARY 2011

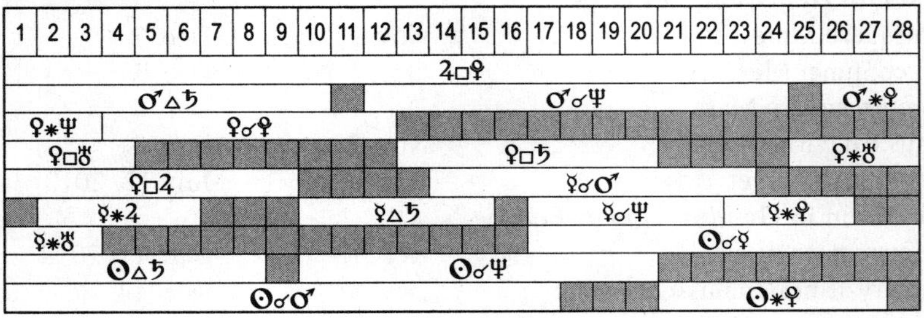

1	2	3	4	5	6	7	8	9	10	11	12	13	14	15	16	17	18	19	20	21	22	23	24	25	26	27	28

Aspect bars (approximate spans):
- ♃□♀
- ♂△♄ · ♂☌♆ · ♂✶♀
- ♀✶♆ · ♀☌♀
- ♀□♃ · ♀□♄ · ♀✶♅
- ♀□♃ · ☿☌♂
- ☿✶♃ · ☿△♄ · ☿☌♆ · ☿✶♀
- ☿✶♅ · ☉☌☿
- ☉△♄ · ☉☌♆
- ☉☌♂ · ☉✶♀

MARCH 2011

1	2	3	4	5	6	7	8	9	10	11	12	13	14	15	16	17	18	19	20	21	22	23	24	25	26	27	28	29	30	31

Aspect bars (approximate spans):
- ♃□♀
- ♂✶♀ · ♃☍♄
- ♀✶♃ · ♂☌♅
- ♀✶♅ · ♀△♄ · ♀☌♆
- ☿□♀ · ♀✶♀
- ☿☌♅ · ☉☌♅ · ☉☌♃
- ☿☌♃ · ☉□♀

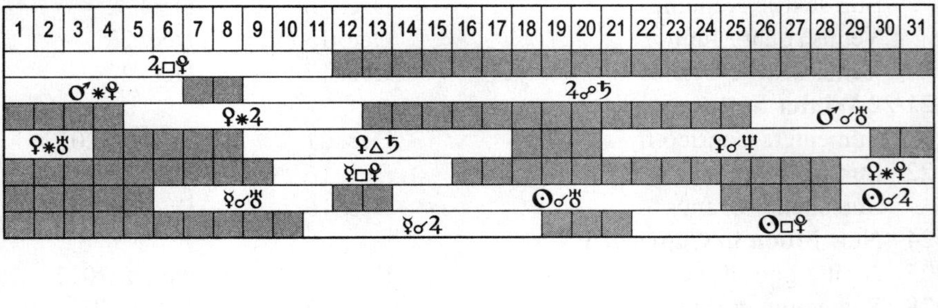

TABLE OF ASPECT INFLUENCES

APRIL 2011

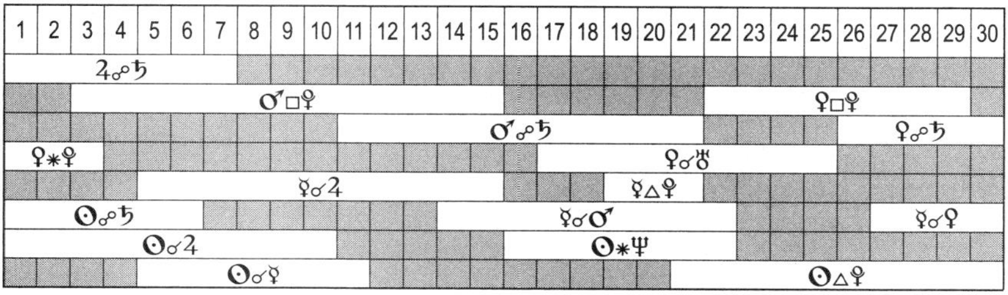

1 2 3 4 5 6 7 8 9 10 11 12 13 14 15 16 17 18 19 20 21 22 23 24 25 26 27 28 29 30
♃☍♄
♂□♇
♀□♇
♂☍♄
♀☍♄
♀✶♇
♀☌♅
☿☌♃
☿△♇
☉☍♄
☿☌♂
☿☌♀
☉☌♃
☉✶♆
☉☌☿
☉△♇

MAY 2011

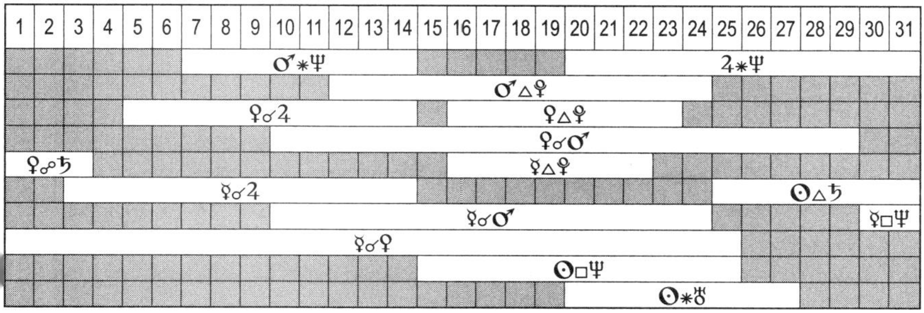

1 2 3 4 5 6 7 8 9 10 11 12 13 14 15 16 17 18 19 20 21 22 23 24 25 26 27 28 29 30 31
♂✶♆
♃✶♆
♂△♇
♀☌♃
♀△♇
♀☌♂
♀☍♄
☿△♇
☿☌♃
☉△♄
☿☌♂
☿□♆
☿☌♀
☉□♆
☉✶♅

JUNE 2011

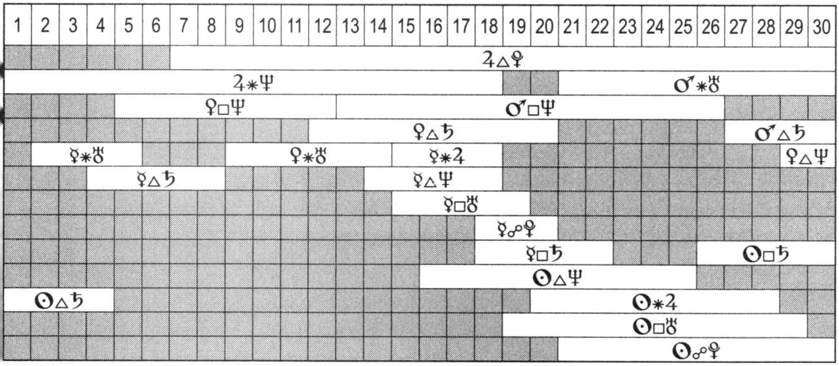

1 2 3 4 5 6 7 8 9 10 11 12 13 14 15 16 17 18 19 20 21 22 23 24 25 26 27 28 29 30
♃△♇
♃✶♆
♂✶♅
♀□♆
♂□♆
♀△♄
♂△♄
☿✶♅
♀✶♅
☿✶♃
♀△♆
☿△♄
☿△♆
☿□♅
☿☍♀
☿□♄
☉□♄
☉△♆
☉△♄
☉✶♃
☉□♅
☉☍♇

TABLE OF ASPECT INFLUENCES

JULY 2011

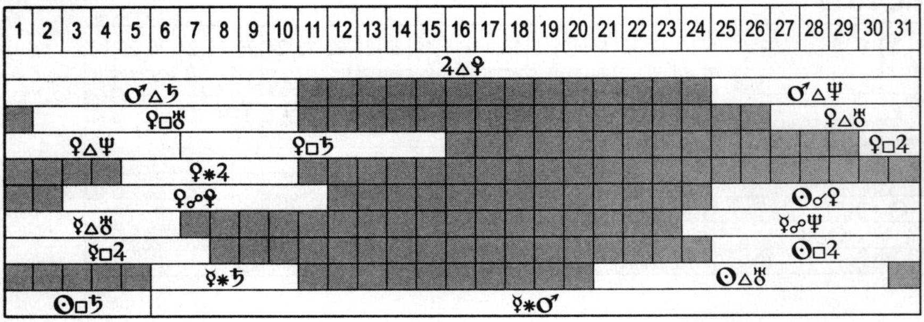
1 2 3 4 5 6 7 8 9 10 11 12 13 14 15 16 17 18 19 20 21 22 23 24 25 26 27 28 29 30 31
♃△♇
♂△♄
♂△♆
♀□♅
♀△♅
♀△♆
♀□♄
♀□♃
♀✶♃
♀☍♇
☉☌♀
☿△♅
☿☍♆
☿□♃
☉□♃
☿✶♄
☉△♅
☉□♄
☿✶♂

AUGUST 2011

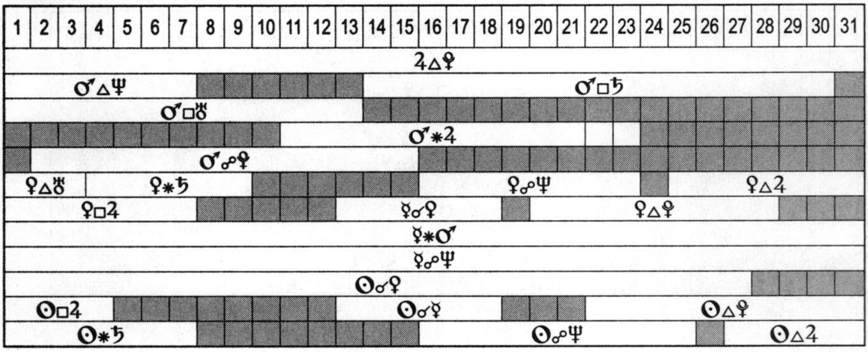
1 2 3 4 5 6 7 8 9 10 11 12 13 14 15 16 17 18 19 20 21 22 23 24 25 26 27 28 29 30 31
♃△♇
♂△♆
♂□♄
♂□♅
♂✶♃
♂☍♇
♀△♅
♀✶♄
♀☍♆
♀△♃
♀□♃
☿☌♀
♀△♇
☿✶♂
☿☍♆
☉☌♀
☉□♃
☉☌☿
☉△♇
☉✶♄
☉☍♆
☉△♃

SEPTEMBER 2011

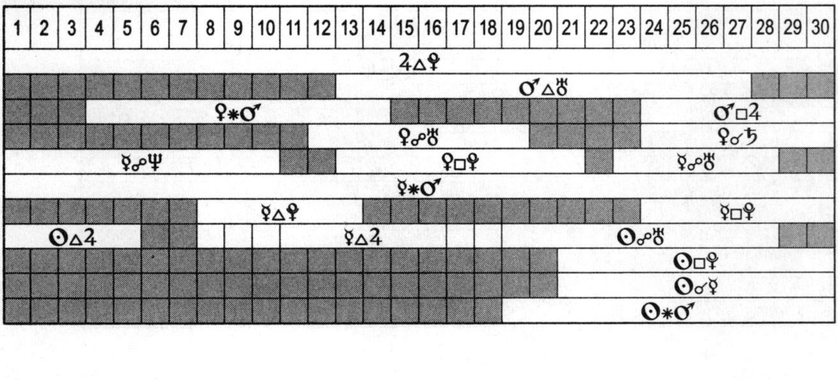
1 2 3 4 5 6 7 8 9 10 11 12 13 14 15 16 17 18 19 20 21 22 23 24 25 26 27 28 29 30
♃△♇
♂△♅
♀✶♂
♂□♃
♀☍♅
♀☌♄
☿☍♆
♀□♇
☿☍♅
☿✶♂
☿△♇
☿□♇
☉△♃
☿△♃
☉☍♅
☉□♇
☉☌☿
☉✶♂

TABLE OF ASPECT INFLUENCES

OCTOBER 2011

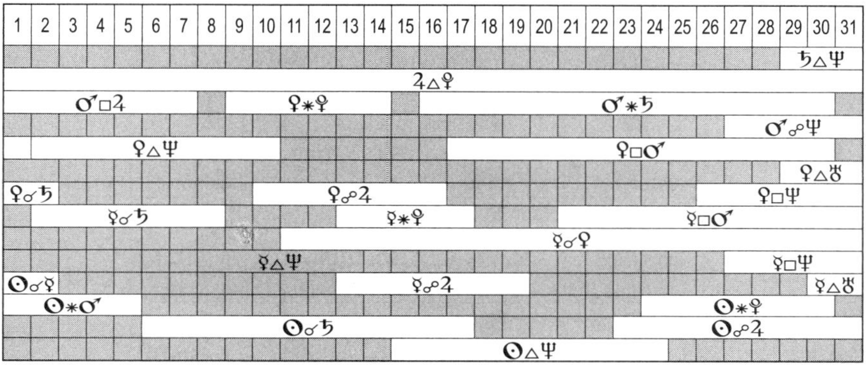
1 2 3 4 5 6 7 8 9 10 11 12 13 14 15 16 17 18 19 20 21 22 23 24 25 26 27 28 29 30 31
♄△♆
♃△♇
♂□♃
♀✱♇
♂✱♄
♂☍♆
♀△♆
♀□♂
♀△♅
♀☌♄
♀☍♃
♀□♆
☿☌♄
☿✱♇
☿□♂
☿☌♀
☿△♆
☿□♆
☉☌☿
☿☍♃
☿△♅
☉✱♂
☉✱♀
☉☌♄
☉☍♃
☉△♆

NOVEMBER 2011

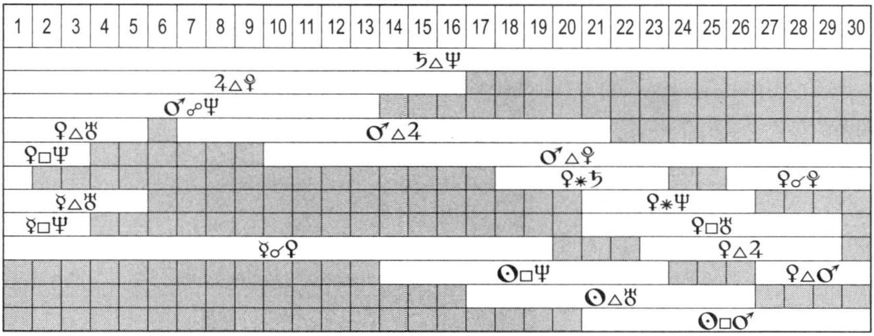
1 2 3 4 5 6 7 8 9 10 11 12 13 14 15 16 17 18 19 20 21 22 23 24 25 26 27 28 29 30
♄△♆
♃△♇
♂☍♆
♀△♅
♂△♃
♀□♆
♂△♇
♀✱♄
♀☌♇
☿△♅
♀✱♆
☿□♆
♀□♅
☿☌♀
♀△♃
☉□♆
♀△♂
☉△♅
☉□♂

DECEMBER 2011

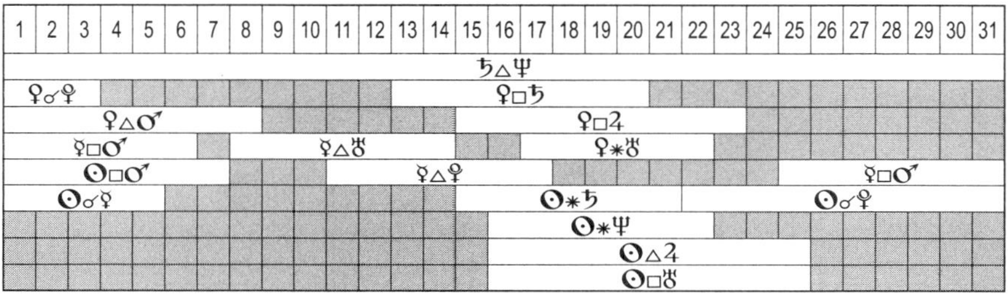
1 2 3 4 5 6 7 8 9 10 11 12 13 14 15 16 17 18 19 20 21 22 23 24 25 26 27 28 29 30 31
♄△♆
♀☌♇
♀□♄
♀△♂
♀□♃
☿□♂
☿△♅
♀✱♅
☉□♂
☿△♇
☿□♂
☉☌☿
☉✱♄
☉☌♀
☉✱♆
☉△♃
☉□♅

Phases of the Moon
Times in Pacific Time (for Eastern add 3 hours)

	● New	☽ 1st Qtr	○ Full	☾ 3rd Qtr	
January	4th 1:02AM Capricorn	12th 3:31AM Aries	19th 1:21PM Leo	26th 4:57AM Libra	
February	2nd 6:30PM Aquarius	10th 11:18PM Taurus	16th 3:31AM Leo	24th 3:26PM Sagittarius	
March	4th 12:45PM Pisces	12th 3:44PM Gemini	19th 11:10AM Virgo	26th 5:07AM Capricorn	
April	3rd 7:32AM Aries	11th 5:05AM Cancer	17th 7:43PM Libra	24th 7:46PM Aquarius	
May	2nd 11:50PM Taurus	10th 1:32PM Leo	17th 4:08PM Scorpio	24th 11:52AM Pisces	
June	1st 2:02PM Gemini	8th 7:10PM Virgo	15th 1:13PM Sagittarius	23rd 4:48AM Aries	
July	1st 1:53AM Cancer	7th 11:29PM Libra	14th 11:39PM Capricorn	22nd 10:01PM Taurus	● 30th 11:39AM Leo
August	☽ 6th 4:08AM Scorpio	○ 13th 11:57AM Aquarius	☾ 21st 2:54PM Taurus	● 28th 8:04PM Virgo	
September	☽ 4th 10:39AM Sagittarius	○ 12th 2:26AM Pisces	☾ 20th 6:38AM Gemini	● 27th 4:08AM Libra	
October	☽ 3rd 8:15PM Capricorn	○ 11th 7:05PM Aries	☾ 19th 8:30PM Cancer	● 26th 12:55PM Scorpio	
November	☽ 2nd 9:38AM Aquarius	○ 9th 9:00AM Taurus	☾ 18th 7:09PM Leo	● 24th 10:09PM Sagittarius	
December	☽ 2nd 1:52AM Pisces	○ 10th 6:36AM Gemini	☾ 17th 4:47PM Virgo	● 24th 10:06AM Capricorn	

LUNAR ASPECTS GUIDE

MOON TO SUN ASPECTS

In general, the Moon aspects to the Sun bring us a greater awareness of our feelings with regard to the season through which we are passing.

Moon sextile Sun

Moon sextile Sun brings optimism, or a brighter spirit, towards whatever seasonal activities are occurring and our moods are more likely to be encouraged by the endearing qualities of the season. This aspect helps our moods to accept and be at peace with the relevant seasonal factors, getting in tune with the seasonal pace. It assists us in making the shift from the early stage of emotional experience to the next stage of emotional development. In general, Moon sextile Sun brings positive vibrations, and acts as a catalyst in the ebb and flow of the emotions. It brings the promising potential for acceptance and reassurance and, where such moods are absent, there is the driving hope to reach a happy medium. Moon sextile Sun brings inspiration to our dreams and gives us a sense of where we are going next.

Moon square Sun (First and Last Quarter Moons)

Moon square Sun represents the First and Last Quarter stages of the Moon. It is the middle road, the half-way mark between the waxing and waning process of the Moon. It is the pinnacle of the in-between stage, and it represents the crux of what we hope to establish in our emotional process as it is affected by the Moon. The square aspect represents struggle or challenge; this tends to be the point where we exercise our emotions with diligent effort. The square of the Moon to the Sun is a time when we tend to make extra adjustments with our emotional process, and we take extra steps towards the place we have determined that our emotions are headed. This is characterized by the sign the Moon is in, and how we respond, individually, with the qualities of that sign. Moon square Sun summons some very lively and busy emotional responses in the course of our dreams.

First Quarter Moon (Waxing Quarter Moon) Halfway in between the New and Full Moon, the First Quarter Moon has built up some momentum in our emotional process. This is a positive, upbeat, anticipatory time. The sign that the Moon is in will denote the types of focuses and themes that will preoccupy us, and these are the things we will be building up and strengthening in our emotional core. As the waxing Moon reaches this First Quarter mark, this is a good time for maintaining and nurturing positive emotional vibrations.

Last Quarter Moon (Waning Quarter Moon) Halfway in between the Full and New Moon, the Last Quarter Moon breaks down the emotional momentum that was built up during the Full Moon period of the previous week. This is a time of letting go, of finishing or completing certain aspects of the emotional process. The waning Moon allows us to process and let go of emotionally taxing sensations, and from there we begin to be less weighted down by our feelings. When we struggle with letting go, it is highlighted through this stage of lunar development. As the waning Moon reaches this Last Quarter mark, this is a good time for weeding out and cleaning up emotional negativity, and for letting go of unnecessary emotional baggage.

Moon trine Sun

Overall, Moon trine Sun brings good vibes; it allows us to create or to access congenial, hopeful, and positive moods. Moon trine Sun always reminds us of the aspects of the current season that are inspiring and uplifting. Whenever the trine aspect occurs, the Moon and Sun will both (usually) be in the same element together: a fire, water, air, or earth sign. This brings synchronization and focuses the energy of our moods on positive and cohesive emotional responses. Moon trine Sun brings beautiful harmony to the mood of the day. In general, this aspect brings sunny, cheerful moods, and a positive outlook on life. Moon trine Sun influences dreams with positive vibrations, and it brings sparkling delights and gifts of happiness.

Moon opposite Sun (Full Moon)

The Full Moon represents the fruition of our emotional process. Moon opposite Sun magnifies the emotional or spiritual qualities of the season. This is a time when we access and harness a great deal of emotional energy. It's a great time to establish positive affirmations, and to celebrate the bountiful fullness of the season. Often, the Full Moon time brings a whirlwind of activity, and this represents the crescendo or climax of our emotional process as it is affected by the Moon. This climax of the Moon's luminous reflections of the Sun brings the greatest amount of light to our emotional experience, and this is a very good time to count your blessings and enjoy the wonders of your life. Moon opposite Sun brings astonishing images and rich, fulfilling, experiences to the dream world.

Moon conjunct Sun (New Moon)

The New Moon represents the beginning; a starting point, where our feelings begin their development, and where our pre-established feelings are renewed, confirmed, or re-established. This is a dark time of night, as the Moon joins forces with the daytime Sun. Through this time, our emotional process is often internalized, where it is replenished with a sense of newness. Here, newer feelings may emerge with a certain affirmation or assurance. It is here that we muster new hope, new faith, and there is a subtle – but certain – expression of re-birth in our emotional understanding. This is the time to tap into the wiser parts of the soul, to allow our older feelings to be recycled and renewed, and to open up to, and give room for, new feelings as they begin to emerge. It is also important to remember to rest, to let emotions just be, without adding complexity to them. Moon conjunct Sun brings insightful, regenerative, and profound images to the dream world.

MOON TO MERCURY ASPECTS

Moon sextile Mercury

Moon sextile Mercury brings the potential for inspiring news and communications. This lunar aspect brings clear and succinct communications which will assist us to keep business running along smoothly. It's a good time to reiterate plans, schedules, and messages and to handle communications very thoroughly. Moon sextile Mercury inspires our moods with informative talk and information but, when Mercury is retrograde, it would be wise to follow up any new information with careful research. This time brings the potential for inspiration through thoughts and ideas, and all this is possible despite the travails of Mercury retrograde periods. Moon sextile Mercury brings the potential for some intelligent brainstorming between people, and this will be a very good time to run your ideas by others. It brings intellectually stimulating dreams and reveals a lot about your thoughts and ideas.

Moon square Mercury

Moon square Mercury often brings a challenging time for communications. This may be a time when it is difficult to reassure others, and moods may be challenged by intellectual debates and discussions. It may be difficult to get the message across in the way it was intended. It may also bring uncommunicative moods, or we may find that it is difficult to describe our moods. This lunar aspect is the least ideal aspect for communications under the influence of Mercury retrograde. Moon square Mercury tends to bring moods or emotional responses which are thwarted by complex communications and difficult subjects, and defensive moods may become argumentative. This is a good time to use caution with our words and to consider the impact that harsh statements may have on others. Moon square Mercury adds mental nervousness to the course of our dreams, and may contribute to nightmarish feelings and thoughts about our dreams.

Moon trine Mercury

Moon trine Mercury brings moods in harmony with communications. This is an excellent time to talk, relay thoughts, and communicate with greater ease. Moon trine Mercury brings the gift of thoughtfulness, making communications very harmonious. This aspect brings pleasantly talkative and mindful moods, leading to discussions that may clarify misinterpreted facts. It will assist us to communicate more clearly during Mercury retrograde periods. Moon trine Mercury brings a superb time for us to communicate amicably and effectively. As a general rule, this is the time to promote positive thoughts. As the day closes, Moon trine Mercury brings a helpful time to rest the mind, but for those who are awake, this may seem like an excellent time to think matters through more easily. Moon trine Mercury brings positive thoughts to our dreams.

Moon opposite Mercury

Moon opposite Mercury brings a deeper sense of awareness – or curiosity – while we are communicating. This lunar aspect inspires a surge of thoughts and discussion, and it may be necessary to comprehend a lot of things at once. This is a time when we tend to be overwhelmed or overloaded by communications or the communication process. Our feelings are more readily challenged by our thoughts. Sometimes this lunar aspect gives us the feeling that there is a great deal more to be communicated. Beware of exhausting arguments. Moon opposite Mercury brings an intense need to communicate, to reiterate on complex messages, and to set the record straight when Mercury retrograde periods have brought havoc to our communications. Moon opposite Mercury brings complex nervous responses and complex thoughts with regard to what we are feeling or sensing. As for dreams, this aspect brings very nervous or restless kinds of dreams which may seem overwhelming and possibly loaded with too much information.

Moon conjunct Mercury

Moon conjunct Mercury brings mental clarity and acuity, inspiring thoughtful and communicative moods – this is a great time to catch up on journals, research, and correspondence. Moon conjunct Mercury brings a pensive time, and our moods will be as clearly succinct as our thinking. It engages us in mindful and resourceful planning. Moon conjunct Mercury invites us to take some time to explain various matters very carefully, especially when Mercury is retrograde. This aspect reminds us of our need to pay attention to what is being communicated, and to stay on top of communications. It allows us to drop nervous tension in our sleep, and lets those who can't sleep think clearly and relevantly through their mental processes. Moon conjunct Mercury affects our dreams and moods with the desire to connect to brilliance and intelligent ideas.

MOON TO VENUS ASPECTS

Moon sextile Venus

Moon sextile Venus brings moods inspired by beauty and there are opportunities for our moods to tune into the power of love and affection. This aspect brings moods inspired by kind and attractive feminine influences, finding us easily captivated by the law of attraction. Moon sextile Venus brings the potential for very pleasurable, affectionate, and beautiful feelings to occur. It holds the potential to bring moods that will be responsive to love, affection and gentle kindness. It also brings the potential for positive vibes between loved ones, but a definite effort to create those positive vibes will have to be made. Moon sextile Venus brings pleasant dreams touched by infinite beauty.

Moon square Venus

Moon square Venus brings moods challenged by matters of love and attraction. It's also bound to bring some challenging weather between loved ones, and this may be a good time to avoid making idealistic promises that could possibly go unfulfilled. Our moods are likely to be strained by the effort to maintain beauty and comfort. Moon square Venus tests our affections and our ability to feel and express love, and may cause unpleasant moods due to a lack of kindness or love wherever it is needed. This lunar aspect may be a difficult time for us to find the kind of affections we need, but it's best to patiently persevere through love related challenges. Moon square Venus brings dreams that may seem particularly unpleasant, and dreams that may leave us feeling abandoned, torn asunder, or separate from the things to which we are attached.

Moon trine Venus

Moon trine Venus is the most receptive and advantageous time to spread loving energy. This lunar aspect generally brings moods which will be pleasant and easily prone to affection. Moon trine Venus brings gentle, beautiful, and harmonious moods and vibrations. It often blesses our moods with kindness, and increases our fondness and appreciation for beauty. Moon trine Venus brings the strong urge for love, and loving energy won't be too hard to find. This lunar aspect helps to smooth over chaotic energies with loving and kind moods. Moon trine Venus puts us in the mood for love and for all those things that bring us comfort, inspiring especially beautiful, alluring, and relaxing dreams.

Moon opposite Venus

Moon opposite Venus brings moods that will make us acutely aware of our affections – both the giving of, and the desire for, all kinds of affection. This aspect will draw relationships and love related situations into focus, and it may be especially difficult to try to please everyone, especially our loved ones. Moon opposite Venus may bring overwhelming or obsessive desires for beauty and pleasure. This aspect implies that our moods may be dominated by feminine expression or demands. Lady Justice is blind, but that doesn't mean that her logic is not sound. Sometimes, Moon opposite Venus brings obsessive or agitating moods with regard to love. Here, we often find that our affections have been spread too thin. We may feel overwhelmed by compelling attractions. This lunar aspect brings dramatic moods and dreams about our needs for affection and beauty.

Moon conjunct Venus

Moon conjunct Venus brings gentleness, kindness, and love to our moods. It puts us directly in touch with those things we are attracted to. This lunar aspect can bring deeply affectionate and sometimes very intense loving moods. Different levels and expressions of affection occur, depending on the sign in which the Moon and Venus are conjunct. Moon conjunct Venus brings moods that will be instantly drawn to beauty and love wherever it exists. This is a good time to seek pleasure and to appreciate beauty to the fullest. Moon conjunct Venus brings dazzling beauty and pleasure to the scope of our dreams.

MOON TO MARS ASPECTS

Moon sextile Mars

Moon sextile Mars tends to bring energetic moods which are motivated by force and activity, and inspired by high energy levels. Incisive action and the affirmation of will infuse our moods. Moon sextile Mars brings moods that may point to the need to take action, but this inclination is not always acted upon. Generally, Moon sextile Mars brings positive energy, strength and courage to our moods. It brings strong impulses and urges, and our dreams will seem triumphant, although somewhat martial and headstrong in attitude.

Moon square Mars

Moon square Mars suggests our moods will be challenged by invasive forcefulness, our patience levels will be tested, and it may be difficult to get amicably motivated. This aspect brings offensive and maddening challenges to our moods where abrupt energies and unbalanced temperaments will seem like bullying martial forces. Moon square Mars – this is a recipe for accidents, fights, headaches – and many people will find that they are being especially defensive as well as impatient. This lunar aspect may lead to difficulty or conflict when one is attempting to take initiative to do things, and it often tests our temper, strength, and willpower. Moon square Mars usually brings challenging moods with regard to masculine energies. While we sleep, cruelty or mad aggression may be evident in our dreams.

Moon trine Mars

Moon trine Mars brings moods that will be gifted with lots of vibrant, positive energy and our moods are often in harmony with masculine energies and courageous activities. This aspect invites optimism that inspires action. For some, this aspect brings vibrant emotional and physical energy, positive strength and might. It's an advantageous time to build on our strength, get motivated, and to get things rolling. Moon trine Mars harmoniously energizes our dreams, often making us stronger than we ever imagined.

Moon opposite Mars

Moon opposite Mars brings moods which are opposed to offensive kinds of pressures. Some may find that they are opposed to, or overwhelmed by, masculine force. In general, it brings moods at odds with some disharmonizing force. Forcefulness and brazen activity are highlighted, and Moon opposite Mars brings exceedingly energetic and feisty moods which are sometimes offensive. A surge of emotional heat may lead to anger for some. This lunar aspect is known for its extreme force, and may stimulate alarming kinds of offensive and defensive behavior. Some folks may be overwhelmed or affronted by the activities and actions occurring around them. Without a doubt, Moon opposite Mars motivates us, and brings a sharp awareness of martial forces and masculine energies. Some folks may appear to be obsessed by or preoccupied with aggressive forces. This may also be an accident prone time. Moon opposite Mars may bring pushy, impatient, or overly defensive moods, and it can bring bloody battles to the forefront of our dream world.

Moon conjunct Mars

The sign where the Moon and Mars are conjunct will have a strong bearing on the type of energy conjured by this lunar conjunction. Moon conjunct Mars activates our moods with a feeling of get-up-and-go, stirring our moods with energy and adrenaline that may seem refreshingly positive for some and overly aggressive for others. While Moon conjunct Mars occurs, our moods are active, hot, and eager to take action. Energized moods may lead to incredulous force. Moon conjunct Mars may bring moods activated by complex and reactionary kinds of aggression. Sometimes, this conjunction puts us in touch with our anger issues. Moon conjunct

Mars impresses our moods with the need to take action on some level, and to get in touch with our true will. It's bound to stir up raw energy and action in our dreams.

MOON TO JUPITER ASPECTS

Moon sextile Jupiter
Moon sextile Jupiter brings the potential for our moods to be inspired by a sense of joviality, prosperity, travel, and adventure. It also brings moods inspired by opportunity, generosity, and extravagance. This lunar aspect invites moods which are generally hopeful and optimistic, inspired by promising prospects and propositions. It brings the potential for a warm and generous spirit, and sets the tone of the day with the potential for positive, upbeat feelings, and a sense of wellbeing and prosperity. Moon sextile Jupiter brings adventurous dreams.

Moon square Jupiter
Moon square Jupiter may cause our moods to be less generous than usual. We may find we are less willing to extend ourselves beyond our limits. Moon square Jupiter often brings moods challenged by matters of expenses and wealth. This lunar aspect may bring some apprehension with regard to the need to prosper, and this often leads to prudent or unreceptive moods. Jupiter's influence represents joy, and some folks may be prone to depression as they struggle with their ability to find joy or to express it. Many people may be irritated by rising costs or hidden expenses. We may find difficulty in handling large productions. Sometimes, our moods are challenged by travel related expenses, inconveniences, and delays. Our dreams may appear like a gambler's losing streak. Moon square Jupiter brings moods that are challenged by overextension — or perhaps, overexertion — especially in the dream world. The events in our dreams are often reflected by the fear of loss.

Moon trine Jupiter
Moon trine Jupiter brings moods that will be very generous, joyous, and gregarious, and it tops our experience with optimistic and prosperous moods. This aspect is an excellent time to appreciate good fortune, and to enjoy parties, fund raisers, and social affairs. Good luck, happiness, and positive vibes, often ensure a sense of wellbeing, bringing a healthy desire to prosper. Moon trine Jupiter harmonizes our moods with an outgoing spirit and an enthusiastic sense of adventure. Generally speaking, this aspect brings especially pleasant moods, and our dreams are bound to lead us into a pot of gold.

Moon opposite Jupiter
Moon opposite Jupiter brings moods that may be overwhelmed by abundance and rapid growth. People may be put off by, or suspicious of, extreme generosity. Moon opposite Jupiter brings deeply involved moods, especially with regard to our livelihoods, our fortunes, and our sense of wellbeing. This aspect brings an acute awareness of the need to excel and to prosper, and there may be something very tempting calling out to us at this time. Our moods could seem overwhelmed by overextension, either on a financial or a psychological level. Moon opposite

Jupiter brings a bit of a roller coaster ride on the collective wheel of fortune, which in turn brings a lot of excitement with regard to our expenditures and our sense of wellbeing. Beware of a tendency towards compulsive gambling. In some cases, this lunar aspect puts us in touch with the feeling of greed, as Jupiter brings the compulsory need to gain, profit, and get ahead of all the financial commotion. Moon opposite Jupiter brings a tendency to overindulge, and there may be a lot of defensiveness over expenditures. In the dream world, we may get lost, or find that we have gone too far out on a limb, leaving us with the feeling of overextension.

Moon conjunct Jupiter

For those who are willing to tap into it, this lunar aspect impresses our moods with rich and prosperous feelings. Moon conjunct Jupiter brings abundant enthusiasm. Moods are especially extravagant and optimistic, connecting us with a sense of joy, wealth, joviality, prosperity, and wellbeing. This is a good time to count your blessings. Moon conjunct Jupiter puts us in touch with our visions and our hopes. It's a great time to enjoy feasts and epicurean delights. This is also an excellent time to exercise, travel, and to explore new territory. With this lunar conjunction, our dreams are often gratifyingly joyous and prosperous in nature.

MOON TO SATURN ASPECTS

Moon sextile Saturn

Moon sextile Saturn opens up our moods to employment opportunities. This is a great time to instill discipline and a sense of duty, to teach, and to work. Moon sextile Saturn inspires discipline and focus, but this usually only starts to occur when some effort towards work is made. In other words, just do the work, and the inspiration to carry on will follow. Our moods tend to be expressed a little more seriously, or with greater expectation towards seeing results. Here, seeing others apply discipline can often inspire us to do the same, making this a great time to set an example, and to focus on getting things done rather than putting them off. The Moon sets the tone of the mood, the sextile aspect brings raw potential and opportunity, and the influence of Saturn gets things done. Moon sextile Saturn brings serious dreams that inspire a sense of duty and discipline.

Moon square Saturn

Moon square Saturn brings moods which are tested by deadlines, responsibilities, and limitations. It often causes challenges with our ability to concentrate, stay focused and handle pending deadlines. Sometimes, Moon square Saturn infringes on the comfort zones of our moods which may seem overshadowed by a foreboding kind of seriousness. Moon square Saturn brings another dimension to our moods, as many folks will be troubled by the burdensome responsibility of difficult work, adding a feeling of being restricted. Moon square Saturn sometimes brings moods challenged by authority. Sometimes, time is warped, or we may find ourselves wishing that time would go by a little faster. While we sleep, Moon square Saturn slips into the night and into our dreams, bringing moods often irritated by the need for discipline; with any luck, this is a time to rest and not to worry. Moon square Saturn may bring troublesome dreams about our struggles over having control, or not having it. Sleeplessness is usually filled by obsessions over career challenges, troublesome work, or burdensome responsibilities. Hang in there – stay on course with your efforts.

Moon trine Saturn

Moon trine Saturn often inspires an amicable work mood. It is a superb time to practice disciplines and to work on things that require perfect timing, allowing for a greater sense of control, precision, and focus. Moon trine Saturn brings harmonious moods with regard to our approach to discipline, or to work in general, and this usually results in more effective teamwork. It also brings moods that are likely to be in harmony with our responsibilities and, as a result, basic duties and tasks may be carried out much more smoothly than expected. This favorable aspect assures us that time is the healer. Moon trine Saturn brings dreams that allow us to feel in control, and to go beyond our limitations, possibly accomplishing the impossible.

Moon opposite Saturn

Moon opposite Saturn is a very challenging time for our moods to stay the course of our work, and it may seem tedious to fulfill our responsibilities. These are times when we may feel overworked. Moon opposite Saturn brings moods which may appear opposed to — or overwhelmed by — restrictions and limitations. This will be a good time to keep work schedules light and to anticipate serious or reluctant moods with regard to work tasks. This is usually not an easy time to hold people's attention for very long, or to get them to perform tasks beyond their usual pace. Difficult jobs will seem that much harder and may take longer than usual to do. Moon opposite Saturn brings a serious tone to our dreams and we may tend to overextend ourselves, even in the dream world. In general, this aspect puts us in touch with our limitations and reminds us of the mortal side of ourselves.

Moon conjunct Saturn

Moon conjunct Saturn brings serious moods in general, and there is often a strong sense of determination present. We also tend to be guarded, cautious, and work oriented. This conjunction occurs once a month, and it is therefore a good time to reiterate on personal goals and achievements. Moon conjunct Saturn brings moods that will be inclined towards discipline and responsibility, and will appeal to our protective instincts as well. It brings moods that awaken us to the awareness of our limitations. The act of completion is an important part of the Moon/Saturn conjunction, and this is a good time to recognize what level of completion has been achieved in the various stages of our lives. It's also a good time to count blessings as well as setting goals.

MOON TO NEPTUNE ASPECTS

Moon sextile Neptune

Moon sextile Neptune brings peaceful moods, responsive to spiritual expression. It can bring a calmness that allows us to pace ourselves comfortably, and our moods will be pleasant for the most part. This aspect brings moods inspired by spiritual perspectives. This time holds the potential for us to experience more accepting and flexible kinds of moods. Here, forgiveness is possible. Whenever it's convenient, this is a good lunar aspect to seek the comfort of a sanctuary and to enjoy some tranquility. Moon sextile Neptune brings moods that are influenced strongly by our beliefs. It inclines our moods towards simplicity or the path of least resistance. People tend to respond more intuitively to many situations. Moon sextile Neptune brings spiritual hope and reassuring beliefs. It assists us by bringing peaceful rest and calming dreams.

Moon square Neptune

Moon square Neptune brings struggles with regard to our beliefs and in spiritual matters. Our moods may be challenged by passivity, resignation, or perhaps even laziness, and they are often nebulous or vague. Moon square Neptune brings difficult spiritual forces into the picture, challenged by inactivity and passiveness. Moon square Neptune brings moods which may seem troubled by a lack of spiritual harmony, or possibly by addictions, temptations, and a lack of resistance. This aspect brings less tolerance of the beliefs of others and quite a bit of spiritual doubt. People may be questioning the burdening imposition or inconvenience of some beliefs. This is a time when people may be more susceptible to illusion. In general, Moon square Neptune brings disquieting moods, and many folks may have an insatiable urge to find a peaceful sanctuary away from the complexities of emotional clamor. This lunar aspect brings spiritually disturbing moods and dreams, and it may haunt our dreams with deceptive misconceptions.

Moon trine Neptune

Moon trine Neptune blesses our moods with spiritually uplifting vibrations. It settles our moods with a calm, cool acceptance of the way things are and brings the blessing of peacefulness. Moon trine Neptune brings our moods into perfect harmony with the spiritual energies around us, bringing tranquil and passive energy that is positive in nature. People will be inclined to kick back, relax and to accept their beliefs as they stand. This aspect adds calmness to the astrological atmosphere, and helps to smooth over the sting of any conflicting aspects that are simultaneously occurring. It also brings positive inspiration to our moods and is a superb time to apply, or enjoy, artistic expression. This is a great lunar aspect to share in spiritual ceremonies and customs with others. Moon trine Neptune brings relaxing and enchanting dreams filled with blessed tranquility and divine pleasures.

Moon opposite Neptune

Moon opposite Neptune brings moods that will be strongly stimulated by spiritual encounters and experiences, often challenging, and overwhelmed by doubt. This lunar aspect invites weakness with regard to our addictive tendencies. Moon opposite Neptune brings an especially strong awareness of our spiritual needs, but our feelings tend to be at odds with our beliefs. This lunar aspect brings moods that may be opposed to, or overwhelmed by, spiritualism. Moon opposite Neptune brings a strong and compelling awareness of the art, poetry, music, and spiritual beliefs that shape and form who and what we are in spirit and at heart. This lunar aspect awakens our spiritual nature and impresses upon us the need to apply our faith. It could be challenging for some folks to feel comfortable or spiritually in tune with others. Moon opposite Neptune may bring escapist tendencies and the potential for overindulgent moods, and we may be more easily susceptible to life's little deceptions. This aspect brings remarkable and impressionable subliminal images to our dreams.

Moon conjunct Neptune

Moon conjunct Neptune connects our moods with our beliefs and our spirituality. It brings a stronger spiritual awareness of life and there is the general feeling of connectedness among people. Moon conjunct Neptune brings moods that will be responsive to the need for tranquility and peacefulness, and our moods are able to merge easily with spiritual awareness. It brings us closer to a sense of spiritual oneness with the universe, and the common bonds that connect us are felt beyond the physical realms. This lunar conjunction brings peaceful and comforting dreams.

MOON TO URANUS ASPECTS

Moon sextile Uranus

Moon sextile Uranus brings lively and outgoing expressions of mood as well as the potential for wild and disorderly moods. As a general rule, it inspires us to let loose and feel free. When Moon sextile Uranus rolls around, our moods are more prone towards, or sympathetic to, reckless activity or behavior. It helps us to embrace the unusual and to find freedom from the mundane. Moon sextile Uranus brings freedom-loving rebelliousness and our dreams are likely to be explosive and colorful, reflecting a feeling of liberation.

Moon square Uranus

Moon square Uranus is often very challenging, as unexpected outbursts and radical surprises create chaotic moods complicated by explosive conflict. This aspect often brings disruptive disorder; moods may be intensified by undisciplined forces and by radical attitudes. During this time, many people tend to be less forgiving, particularly around unusual behavior and unconventional tones of expression. Moon square Uranus brings chaos – the kind of chaos which requires extra clean up work. It also brings confused and difficult dreams. To some folks, these dreams may seem more like explosive nightmares.

Moon trine Uranus

Moon trine Uranus brings crazy, fun-loving, and unusual kinds of moods and focuses. There's a feeling of wild and reckless abandon, and all is in harmony with the forces of chaos. Moon trine Uranus brings a sense of freedom and our moods will be carefree, or blithely reckless, but not with malicious intent. This lunar aspect can also inspire brilliance and spontaneous inventiveness. Moon trine Uranus brings very exciting and liberating dreams often in harmony with chaos and disorder.

Moon opposite Uranus

Moon opposite Uranus brings discordant sounds, disruptive energies, and explosive distractions. This lunar aspect ignites a strong urge for freedom from oppression, and makes us acutely aware of – and sensitive to – disruption of any kind. Our moods are agitated with an overwhelming feeling of chaos and disorder. Explosively contradictory moods shaken up by extreme or disruptive actions and expressions of thought are common. Moon opposite Uranus brings alarming dreams and unsettled feelings.

Moon conjunct Uranus

Moon conjunct Uranus brings moods that may seem out of the ordinary. It aligns us with the need for freedom, and we may find ourselves being somewhat counterproductive.   Beware of the tendency towards irrational or unusual behavior; rules may be broken. Moon conjunct Uranus may bring a feeling of acceptance for disorder, or it may inspire us to tackle disorder with unabashed determination. Either way, chaotic fortitude will be the energy of our mood. This lunar aspect animates our moods and our dreams with turbulent emotions.

MOON TO PLUTO ASPECTS

Moon sextile Pluto

Moon sextile Pluto brings moods inspired by vigilant efforts in the face of intensity and strife often affected by life's unchangeable circumstances. Our moods may be preoccupied with the need for trouble-shooting and problem solving. Moon sextile Pluto brings moods inspired by the opportunities that are shaped by fate and intensified by powerful and variable situations. This aspect allows us to be receptive to the inevitable factors of life, and many folks will feel as though they can tolerate just about anything. Moon sextile Pluto brings moods that are influenced by the deeds of superpowers, and gives us the incentive to look for solutions to the troubles they generate. It also brings positive moods geared towards the necessity to find ways to change our apparent destiny. Moon sextile Pluto brings dreams that are open to helping us work out our individual struggles.

Moon square Pluto

Moon square Pluto brings moods challenged by the unforeseeable factors of life, by matters of fate and by perplexing transformations. This may be a difficult time to collaborate with people of another generation or those of a different cultural background. Our moods may be challenged by our hidden fears, particularly with regard to those irreversible processes of life. We may find that our moods are oppressed by dramatic losses, hopelessness, and troublesome realities. Moon square Pluto brings dramatic complexity to our moods, which very often ends up affecting everyone. It can bring troublesome and sometimes fearful moods and dreams.

Moon trine Pluto

Moon trine Pluto brings moods that will be inspired by transformation and permanent change. It gives us the strong incentive to tackle problems and find solutions and brings harmonious and therapeutic strength to our moods, especially with regard to matters of fate and the unchangeable factors of life. It also brings moods that will be attuned to the influences of superpowers. This lunar aspect promotes accordance among generations, and those with difficult realities will feel more in tune with the sympathies of others. Moon trine Pluto brings moods enriched with the acceptance of hardships and allows us to confront hardship with a lot less difficulty. This lunar aspect helps the process of healing wounds, and it brings moods that will lean amicably towards therapeutic methods of easing pain. Moon trine Pluto inspires a profound sense of renewed hope and brings a cathartic, as well as therapeutic, breakthrough in our dreams.

Moon opposite Pluto

Moon opposite Pluto makes us conscious of the troubles and the transformations occurring in our lives, especially those likely to be opposed by the influences of superpowers. This aspect causes moods which will be strongly affected by the generation gaps or the cultural gaps that exist between different folks. It also may be the cause of relentless kinds of obsessions, bringing moods that will inspire awareness of life's more intense qualities and hardships. There's a potential for dramatic, rocky moods. Moon opposite Pluto may be the cause of some sleepless energy for various folks, and there may be some overwhelming intensity to the scope of our dreams.

Moon conjunct Pluto

Moon conjunct Pluto brings intensity and extraordinary perspectives to our moods. It leads to an awareness of the influence of superpowers and how these forces affect everyone. Moon conjunct Pluto also brings moods which will be at one with a sense of acceptance of those things which we cannot change. It puts us in touch with world events, and our moods may be surprised by the peculiar ways in which destiny evolves. Moon conjunct Pluto puts our moods and dreams in tune with the relevance and importance of world events, which are busily shaping our individual lives and our lifestyles forever.

Table of Planetary Dignities

Planet	Sign of Rulership	Sign of Detriment	Sign of Exaltation	Sign of Fall
Sun	Leo	Aquarius	Aries	Libra
Moon	Cancer	Capricorn	Taurus	Scorpio
Mercury	Gemini, Virgo	Sagittarius, Pisces	Aquarius, Virgo	Leo, Pisces
Venus	Taurus, Libra	Scorpio, Aries	Pisces	Virgo
Mars	Aries	Taurus, Libra	Capricorn	Cancer
Jupiter	Sagittarius	Gemini	Cancer	Capricorn
Saturn	Capricorn	Cancer	Libra	Aries
Uranus	Aquarius	Leo	Scorpio, Aquarius	Taurus, Leo
Neptune	Pisces	Virgo	Cancer	Capricorn
Pluto	Scorpio	Taurus	Pisces	Virgo
Moon's North Node			Gemini	Sagittarius
Moon's South Node			Sagittarius	Gemini

Table of Planetary Associations

Planet	Day	Incense	Metal	Body Part
Sun	Sunday	Frankincense	Gold	Heart
Moon	Monday	Jasmine	Silver	Eyes
Mercury	Wednesday	Storax	Mercury	Nerves
Venus	Friday	Rose, Benzoin	Copper	Skin
Mars	Tuesday	Tobacco	Iron	Muscles
Jupiter	Thursday	Cedar	Tin	Diaphram
Saturn	Saturday	Myrrh	Lead	Bones
Uranus				
Neptune				
Pluto				

CAPRICORN

Key Phrase: "I USE"

Cardinal Earth Sign

Symbol: The Goat

Ruling Planet: Saturn

December 21st, 2010

through January 19th, 2011

Aspects currently in effect:

Venus trine Jupiter (Dec. 27, 2010 – Jan. 7, 2011)
Venus trine Uranus (Dec. 28, 2010 – Jan. 7, 2011)
Venus square Neptune (Dec. 28, 2010 – Jan. 7, 2011)
- see January 4 for a detailed explanation of these aspects.

January 1st Saturday

New Year's Day

Moon in Sagittarius	**PST**	**EST**	
Moon sextile Saturn	11:21 PM	2:21 AM	(Jan 2)
Sun square Saturn begins (see January 7)			

Birthday: Vern Troyer 1969

Mood Watch: A Sagittarius Moon day is a great way to start off the New Year, as this brings a sense of adventure, enthusiasm, and an overall positive attitude. Our moods will be adaptable, generally upbeat, ever changing and – for the most part – energetic. This is a great time to set a visionary course for the month and year to come. A good motto for today: "Look down the road."

January 2nd Sunday

Moon in Sagittarius / Capricorn	**PST**	**EST**	
Moon conjunct Mercury	6:01 AM	9:01 AM	
Moon sextile Neptune	5:44 PM	8:44 PM	
Moon square Jupiter	5:49 PM	8:49 PM	
Moon square Uranus goes v/c	6:07 PM	9:07 PM	
Moon enters Capricorn	11:38 PM	2:38 AM	(Jan 3)

Birthday: Cuba Gooding, Jr. 1968

Mood Watch: The day begins with Moon conjunct Mercury in Sagittarius. This brings the urge to reach out and communicate, to speak about something profound, enlightening, or thought provoking. Throughout the day, the waning Sagittarius Moon brings insights, and it's a perfect time to internalize them! Take a walk in the park of your insightful imagination, get some exercise, and explore. Tonight's lunar aspects may invite us to intuit openly at first, but as the Moon squares with Jupiter and then Uranus, there may be a less generous spirit and the possibility of volatile energies abounding. There's an emphasis on material complications, thievery, confusion, and chaos. This evening's moods may appear distant, careless, or spacey. The Capricorn Moon comes late, but it will bring a grounding spirit nonetheless – enough to get some rest in preparation for the first work week of the New Year.

January 3rd Monday

Moon in Capricorn

	PST	EST
Moon conjunct Pluto	9:41 AM	12:41 PM
Mercury square Jupiter begins (see January 11)		
Mercury square Uranus begins (see January 10)		

Birthday: J.R.R. Tolkien 1892

Mood Watch: The Capricorn Moon wanes through the darkest hours of the lunar cycle; the New Moon Eve is here. Tomorrow's New Moon in Capricorn also brings a solar eclipse. The metaphoric winter's chill lurks in our moods, as this Moon sets a serious tone to our need to be diligent, and to persevere through the darkness. Ominous feelings often come with the conjunction of the Moon with Pluto. This is the time to get in touch with the inner soul survivor, and to persevere with gusto.

January 4th Tuesday

NEW MOON in CAPRICORN– *Partial Solar Eclipse*

Moon in Capricorn

	PST	EST
Venus square Neptune	12:27 AM	3:27 AM
Moon conjunct Sun	1:02 AM	4:02 AM
Jupiter conjunct Uranus	4:53 AM	7:53 AM
Venus trine Uranus	5:33 AM	8:33 AM
Venus trine Jupiter	5:39 AM	8:39 AM
Moon square Saturn	7:00 AM	10:00 AM
Moon conjunct Mars	3:49 PM	6:49 PM

Birthday: Dyan Cannon 1931

Mood Watch: The **New Moon in Capricorn** (Moon conjunct Sun) brings down-to-earth determination to our moods. This Moon brings a powerful defiance in the face of adversity, and we must not let dark feelings affect our senses of pragmatism and dignity. Go easy on people and use your protective emotional shields to combat the harsh attitudes of others. Expect services to run slowly at times, and take note that co-workers may appear preoccupied by external events. Venus is square dancing with Neptune while doing a trine dance with today's conjunction of Jupiter and Uranus. Our affections and our beliefs may be stunned by an acceptance of explosive new approaches to marketing and multi-media enterprises. Beware of the tendency for employers and leaders to expect too much, or to be disappointed in the way business goes today. No matter what

– be positive!

A **Solar Eclipse in Capricorn** brings an emphasis on the need for stability and security. For some, the act of gaining the upper edge and exceeding in business may be overshadowed by the solar eclipse energy. This is a good time to pace ourselves through the motions of this shadowy time.

Venus square Neptune (occurring Dec. 28, 2010 – Jan. 7) This may be a difficult – or extra busy – time to be drawn to or to meditate on spiritual matters or activities. Art with a spiritual approach may appear more phony than ethereal. Feminine expression may be set back by antiquated beliefs. Love matters could be rocky due to a conflict of beliefs. Venus is in Scorpio, where the art of attraction often occurs on the emotional plane, while Neptune is in Aquarius, formulating a new spiritual outlook for humankind. Venus influences beauty, attraction, and magnetism. Neptune is the higher spiritual vibration of the feminine spirit, the higher octave of Venus herself – the imperfect yet alluring mortal versus the perfect and irresistible goddess. When these two planets are in conflict, it is a time when women are being sent mixed messages about how to live up to a higher standard of the self. This aspect will reoccur on June 10 and October 31.

JUPITER CONJUNCT URANUS (occurring Dec. 15, 2010 – Jan. 26, 2011) Jupiter represents prosperity, social advancement, opportunities towards growth – to name a few – while Uranus's influence symbolizes revolution, chaos, and disruption. This conjunction of these two highly influential planets will affect absolutely everyone, and it is likely to bring an economic shift that, for some, may seem especially alarming, as the course of great economic change will be inevitable. For some folks, this dynamic shift will be the beginning of a whole new economic revolution. While these two planets are conjunct in Pisces, big chaos brings the illusion of economic growth on the international market, while the market may also grow aggressively in hidden or unseen places. This conjunction will bring unforgettable dealings in large corporations and many people may consciously choose to override the economic mistakes of the previous generations by radically investing in futuristic markets. At first, it may seem as if we've all been sold on a future vision, but hidden behind the scenes, there is a strong incentive for big profiteers to stay ahead of international markets.

Jupiter and Uranus are conjunct at the twenty-seven degree mark of Pisces, implying not only large scale, chaotic changes in economics, but especially intuitive, instinctual, and creative investments. Pisces opens us up to the necessity to act intuitively with regard to economic turmoil, and large scale markets are now on the brink of making large scale conversions in their manufacturing efforts. There are likely to be struggles regarding market control, and the volatile theme of unstable markets will continue to alarm us. Where there is uncertainty, there must be faith, and this is a time of hopefulness and, in many cases, blind faith. This theme of a battered and prolonged Jupiterian road to success is all part of an outer planet conjunction series.

There are three outer planets, Uranus, Neptune, and Pluto and when Jupiter is in conjunction with these purveyors of godhood and fate, there is bound to be an economic alteration of historical proportions. This century, Jupiter has been busily conversing with all three of the outer planets, starting with Jupiter conjunct Pluto in Capricorn, which occurred in December 2007; it silently kicked off the first impressive round of economic distresses. This is the point at which this century's first recession began and some of the most influential economic indicators started to plummet, beginning with the US housing market. Then in May, July, and December of 2009, Jupiter was conjunct with Neptune in Aquarius. This conjunction ended on January 7, 2010, and it was responsible for a very necessary, quintessential boost for our morale in the midst of our economic plight. People needed faith in the financial system. People also needed faith in their dreams in order to persevere through the financial hardships that erupted in 2008.

In the autumn of 2003, Jupiter was in the *opposition* to Uranus, a time when the US - Iraq war was taking hold at a great expense to US taxpayers. This revolutionary money machine has cost Americans trillions of dollars.

The Jupiter – Pluto conjunction commenced the transformation of our economy. The Jupiter – Neptune conjunction established the spiritual tone of our economic revolution. Now, Jupiter conjunct Uranus represents the revolution itself. Jupiter first came into this conjunction with Uranus on June 8, 2010 (occurrence range: Apr. 25 – Oct. 27, 2010), a time when the news was swarming with concerns over the BP corporation's Gulf of Mexico oil spill. This prompted a serious discussion about the crude oil industry and the North American economic dependency on petroleum products. Jupiter represents the health and expansive outreach of our economic growth, while Uranus is the explosive catalyst for creating chaos and destruction. In order for the obscenely wealthy profiteers and corporations to progress in the future, they must address the widespread concerns of the people. Jupiter conjunct Uranus moves our economic wellbeing to challenging and uncomfortable places so that we may address the imbalances caused by our misplaced priorities.

With Jupiter conjunct Uranus, it is here we will begin to see the radical twists of our economic future. This year's conjunction is occurring in Pisces, therefore we must expect some explosive emotional roller coasters on the stock market. The theme of economic havoc and destruction is likely to be based on something that resembles an amazingly controversial pipe dream.

It is not advisable to play the market until the Jupiter – Uranus conjunction has passed. Some may argue this revolution is bringing nothing but opportunity. Jupiter always represents opportunity, and the necessity to find joy and exuberance in life. As a social planet, Jupiter represents our social duty to instill optimism and hope. Jupiter also represents the pursuit of happiness, and Uranus represents revolutionary, chaotic, irrevocable worldwide change. Opportunity is bound to occur through change, but it is wise to only gamble that which one can afford to lose. We can all afford to invest in hope and a positive attitude, but we cannot afford to surrender to disparity. Uranus's mysterious and abrupt evolutionary lessons are inevitable.

Venus trine Uranus (occurring Dec. 28, 2010 – Jan. 7, 2011) Venus in Scorpio is trine Uranus in Pisces. Dynamic and passionate kinds of love and attraction (Venus in Scorpio) will bring positive breakthroughs (the trine aspect) through a radical spiritual outreach (Uranus in Pisces). This is a time of freedom fighters and rebel love, and youth is easily attracted to the spirit of rebellion. Dangerous love and taking chances become common occurrences. This aspect creates an attraction to the unusual, yet it allows a harmony to exist in love related matters while chaotic occurrences are taking place. Love at first sight is explosive at this time, but not necessarily long lasting. This aspect will occur on July 31 and November 3.

Venus trine Jupiter (occurring Dec. 27, 2010 – Jan. 7, 2011) Valuable and inspiring gifts of love and affection come with this aspect. Love (Venus) is harmoniously placed with prosperity and opportunity (Jupiter). Venus in Scorpio trine Jupiter in Pisces brings intense and ecstatic expressions of love and affection, which may lead to enterprising and elaborate displays of richness and prosperity. This is a great time to give gifts of love, and for many, it offers an expansive outlook of love's power. Getting ahead in life, in this case, has everything to do with appreciating and loving those areas of life in which we want to expand and prosper. A positive outlook can help make this happen. This aspect will reoccur on Aug. 29 and Nov. 27.

January 5th Wednesday

Moon in Capricorn / Aquarius	PST	EST
Moon sextile Uranus	2:29 AM	5:29 AM
Moon sextile Jupiter	2:42 AM	5:42 AM
Moon sextile Venus goes v/c	4:15 AM	7:15 AM
Moon enters Aquarius	8:07 AM	11:07 AM

Birthday: Robert Duvall 1931

Mood Watch: Early this morning, the newly waxing Capricorn Moon goes void-of-course for a few hours. There may be a need for some folks to put off the usual chores, or they may feel out of sync with the progress of their morning workload. Yesterday's planetary events, coupled with the ecliptic Moon, may have slowed us down a little, but it's really just a matter of processing and adjusting to the strong shift of energies. Some early morning obstacles may seem out of hand, but the Capricorn spirit keeps us diligent nonetheless. It isn't long before the Moon enters Aquarius, and the day really begins to shine intelligently. Our moods are inclined to be interactive and open to suggestions, with a strong emphasis on community spirit, pooling ideas together, and experimenting with technological systems. Apply knowledge, seek answers!

January 6th Thursday

Moon in Aquarius	PST	EST
Moon trine Saturn	4:59 PM	7:59 PM
Mercury sextile Neptune begins (see January 10)		
Mars sextile Uranus begins (see January 12)		

Birthday: Rowan Atkinson 1955

Mood Watch: This is the time to look for answers to the unsolved puzzles of our lives. The waxing Aquarius Moon brings out human interest stories. Here is where intelligent questions are pondered, and the answers and responses to these questions are rapidly absorbed and examined. Multi-media communication has reached a very effective pinnacle, allowing special interest groups to act swiftly and with astonishing results. This is an excellent time to support a group for a good cause. This evening, Moon trine Saturn tunes us into our capabilities and gives us the edge to organize and focus on important goals.

January 7th Friday

Moon in Aquarius	PST	EST
Venus enters Sagittarius	4:30 AM	7:30 AM
Sun square Saturn	6:00 AM	9:00 AM
Moon sextile Mercury	6:43 AM	9:43 AM
Moon conjunct Neptune goes v/c	12:50 PM	3:50 PM
Moon enters Pisces	6:56 PM	9:56 PM
Mars sextile Jupiter begins (see January 13)		

Birthday: Nicolas Cage 1964

Mood Watch: Despite the squaring of the Sun with Saturn, the morning starts out well with an accommodating, well-mannered quality of mood. Many will head off into the day with a cheerful outlook, but as the Moon goes void-of-course this afternoon, moods may appear anywhere from spacey to overly complex. People may resort to pretending that they know what they're doing when, in fact, they don't have a clue. It may take a little longer to get the right service, to work through line ups, and to get around traffic related congestion. To make up for the dysfunctions of the day, this evening's Moon in Pisces brings playful, intuitive, and artistic expressions of mood.

Venus enters Sagittarius (Venus in Sagittarius: Jan. 7 – Feb. 3) Now the planet of love and of the expression of affection is enhanced by the inspired character of Sagittarius. Venus in Sagittarius brings out a love of the arts, travel, philosophy, cultural exploration and sports achievements. With this comes a positive and optimistic spirit of camaraderie among people in general, and the effort to take affections beyond the usual bounds is certainly present. Philosophical theories help to ease and justify love matters. Venus in Sagittarius will help to boost the love life and affections of our Sagittarius friends. This is your time, Sagittarius people, to reaffirm your visions of how to enhance the beauty and the love you are enjoying in your lives.

Sun square Saturn (occurring Jan. 1 – 10) This occurrence of Sun square Saturn especially affects Capricorn people who are celebrating birthdays January 1 – 10. These folks may be experiencing some personal challenges such as impatience, loss of control, a poor sense of timing, or difficulty identifying with current obligations. The challenge is, therefore, to overcome those obstacles that intrude on one's control of discipline and accuracy. These challenges will pass, and for those folks who have uplifting and positive things occurring in their lives, these (Saturn square natal sun) challenges may seem insignificant. Either way, you can bet these people are driven by their goals. They will have a good look at what really matters in life, and hopefully, they will honor and appreciate it. Saturn represents those things in life that we are willing to work for and maintain. Don't give up, birthday folks – conserve your energies and take losses and difficulties in stride! Through the tests, a stronger human being emerges to take on future tests with greater ability. This aspect will repeat on July 2, affecting the Cancer birthday folks of that time.

January 8th Saturday

Moon in Pisces

	PST	EST
Moon sextile Pluto	6:09 AM	9:09 AM

Birthday: David Bowie 1947

Mood Watch: The waxing Pisces Moon brings a wide range of fluctuating moods. Pisces Moon can take us to some exceedingly high or low places and, depending on which end of the scale one occupies, their quality of mood may seem magnified or accentuated in some way. Our feelings tend to run easily to the surface, and with some keen observation, this may be a particularly revealing time to learn about the true feelings of others. The attraction of escape – or indulgence in fantasies – runs strongly on this Saturday night. Intuitive senses are strong, and it is wise to apply some precaution or moderation when indulging in temptations and curiosities.

January 9th Sunday

Moon in Pisces

	PST	EST	
Moon sextile Sun	9:19 AM	12:19 PM	
Moon sextile Mars	10:25 PM	1:25 AM	(Jan 10)
Sun conjunct Mars begins (see February 4)			

Birthday: Richard Nixon 1913

Mood Watch: A little bit of imagination goes a long way with the waxing Moon in Pisces. Here we are drawn to the world of mutable feelings, to the sanctuary of the soul where the imagination can run free and our hopes and dreams are stirred. Pisces Moon is a good time to reaffirm beliefs, and to maintain those beliefs with positive mottos and catchphrases. Leisurely hobbies, crafts, and artistic endeavors are sure bets for fun and enjoyment on a waxing Pisces Moon Sunday. Pisces Moon moods can easily fluctuate, and it's often best to keep those moods moving in a positive direction.

January 10th Monday

Moon in Pisces / Aries	PST	EST
Moon square Mercury	12:20 AM	3:20 AM
Moon conjunct Uranus	1:43 AM	4:43 AM
Moon conjunct Jupiter goes v/c	3:12 AM	6:12 AM
Moon enters Aries	7:23 AM	10:23 AM
Mercury sextile Neptune	12:03 PM	3:03 PM
Moon trine Venus	2:27 PM	5:27 PM
Mercury square Uranus	4:12 PM	7:12 PM
Moon square Pluto	6:54 PM	9:54 PM

Birthday: Rod Stewart 1945

Mood Watch: Early this morning the void-of-course Pisces Moon brings spacey moods, particularly for those who were caught up in the restlessness of the night. As morning progresses, the mood shifts into a much more determined spirit as it enters Aries. The waxing Aries Moon brings eager, anticipatory, and ambitious moods. This afternoon's Moon trine Venus entices us to go after the things we find ourselves attracted to. This evening's Moon square Pluto calls for some extra effort to smooth over the difficult adjustments that the big transitions of life often bring.

Mercury sextile Neptune (occurring Jan. 6 – 12) Mercury in Sagittarius sextile Neptune in Aquarius reassures us that communicating our philosophies and our beliefs also empowers our belief in humanity. This is an opportunistic time to cautiously attempt communication with regard to beliefs and spiritual matters. Mercury is in Sagittarius placing a philosophical emphasis of talk on such Neptune related subjects as spiritual growth, guidance, and inspiration. Take this opportunity to transmute thoughts and beliefs into a workable understanding and to share it with others in a way that encourages them. Prayers, channeling, and spells are all very effective with Mercury sextile Neptune. This aspect will reoccur on May 16.

Mercury square Uranus (occurring Jan. 3 – 13) This aspect creates excessive disruptions in communications. Mercury square Uranus brings communications that may appear troubled and challenged by unusual or explosive circumstances. Mercury in Sagittarius emphasizes the need to communicate about the need for expansion and prosperous growth, while Uranus in Pisces emphasizes the need to deal with the revolutionary process of moral and spiritual beliefs, and with challenging or demanding new environments. The two focuses are creating a tension between people as they discuss their need for change and rapid adjustment. This aspect will reoccur June 18.

January 11th Tuesday

Moon in Aries	PST	EST
Mercury square Jupiter	12:36 PM	3:36 PM
Moon opposite Saturn	5:47 PM	8:47 PM

Birthday: Samuel Liddell MacGregor Mathers 1854

Mood Watch: The Aries Moon brings a courageous and warrior-like spirit to brave the toils of winter. The warrior spirit is usually in an offensive or defensive mode, as many folks may seem to be on the defense with Mercury square Jupiter (see below). Those who feel as though they've been stretched to their limit aren't likely to budge very far, and they won't be too hard to spot. Sun in Capricorn and Moon in Aries classically brings an eagerness to succeed. However, today's Aries Moon spirit will tend to go further if it doesn't require the additional labor or financial help of others. It may be a better time to design or mastermind a group project than to try to enlist the help of others.

Mercury square Jupiter (occurring Jan. 3 – 14) Mercury in Sagittarius is square to Jupiter in Pisces. Philosophical conversations are likely to complicate our cultural activities. With this aspect, it is best to beware of negative views that discourage prosperous growth, as deceptive words, lies – and even the truth – are easily misconstrued on a much larger scale. During this aspect, it may be best to hold off on a job request, asking for a raise, or signing any binding contracts concerning long term investment and payment schedules. It may be an especially difficult time to communicate during travels, and it may be best to double check travel schedules. This aspect has a tendency to create expensive misunderstandings when it comes to large scale investments. This may also be a difficult time to raise money for charities. Dig harder and investigate more thoroughly the details associated with long term investments. This aspect will reoccur on July 5.

January 12th Wednesday

FIRST QUARTER MOON in ARIES	PST	EST
Moon in Aries / Taurus		
Mars sextile Uranus	2:29 AM	5:29 AM
Moon square Sun	3:31 AM	6:31 AM
Moon sextile Neptune	1:51 PM	4:51 PM
Moon square Mars	2:59 PM	5:59 PM
Moon trine Mercury goes v/c	6:46 PM	9:46 PM
Moon enters Taurus	7:36 PM	10:36 PM
Mercury conjunct Pluto begins (see January 17)		

Birthday: The Amazing Kreskin 1935

Mood Watch: The **First Quarter Moon in Aries** (Moon square Sun) energizes our moods, and inspires an upbeat, outgoing, and forward manner. Aries Moon is a superb time to get in tune with your own personal levels of energy, strength, and vitality. It may mean that this is the time to build on the courage to find inner strength. The First Quarter Moon is a good time to apply diligence and inspired ability to your work. Aries Moon brings on an expression of courageous vigor, as well as a sense of bold adventure. As a general rule, moods are marked by confidence, and sometimes by cantankerous forcefulness and the drive to make a lasting impression.

Mars sextile Uranus (occurring Jan. 6 – 14) Mars in Capricorn is sextile to Uranus in Pisces. Serious forces of combat are ignited in unanticipated ways.

Mars governs all activities and forces of action. The sextile aspect puts this exalted Capricornian Mars energy into a position of opportunity and hope with regard to the explosive, unpredictable and chaotic energies of Uranus in Pisces. Both of these planets are charged with forceful energy and vitality as well as being violent and unsettled at times. Masculine forces are forging ahead abruptly and loudly right now. The overall qualities of Mars sextile Uranus are very fiery, although not necessarily completely destructive. It is important to look for the opportunity and potential in all sources of raw masculine energy. This aspect will reoccur on June 27.

January 13th Thursday

Moon in Taurus	PST	EST
Mercury enters Capricorn	3:24 AM	6:24 AM
Moon trine Pluto	6:59 AM	9:59 AM
Mars sextile Jupiter	4:34 PM	7:34 PM
Sun sextile Uranus begins (see January 17)		

Birthday: George Ivanovich Gurdjieff 1866

Mood Watch: The Taurus Moon waxes favorably today as it kicks off this day with a trine to Pluto. This is the time for healing and for drawing strength from beauty and pleasure. Our moods are comforted by the resolve to do well with whatever life presents to us. This bullish attitude brings the practical things that give us the edge to proceed. In another couple of days, Mercury square Jupiter (see Jan. 11) will completely fade away, and there will be a much more open approach to some of the financial binds and limitations facing us.

Mercury enters Capricorn (Mercury in Capricorn: Jan. 13 – Feb. 3) While Mercury travels through Capricorn, communications tend to be more serious and to the point, although not necessarily less complex. In negotiations, there is an emphasis on enterprise. While this versatile planet goes through Capricorn, our realms of communications have a determined and persistent quality of expression, like a demanding voice waiting to be heard and received with hospitality. This fits with the solar days of Capricorn, when the harsh realities of winter demand clarity of purpose in our communications. Communication is one of the tools of survival, and this is an important time to use those skills wisely and sensibly. Mercury in Capricorn also focuses talk on such issues as commercial and corporate progress, market control, the attainment of goods and resources, and the necessity for discipline.

Mars sextile Jupiter (occurring Jan. 7 – 16) Mars in Capricorn is sextile Jupiter in Pisces. Determined and enterprising actions, when taken, have the opportunity to go profoundly far and be very successful in the long run. It will also help if we apply our instincts with regard to market trends while Jupiter is in Pisces. Those who act on specific urges and impulses to achieve their heart's desire are more likely to make a breakthrough during this aspect. This is a time to make true efforts to promote career skills or to enhance a career move. Remember – action is required; mere good intentions will get you nothing while this aspect is in full force. This is a good time to go adventuring and exploring while Mars sextile Jupiter promotes opportunities. This aspect will reoccur on August 18.

♑

January 14th Friday

Moon in Taurus

	PST	EST
Moon trine Sun	7:15 PM	10:15 PM
Sun sextile Jupiter begins (see January 19)		

Birthday: LL Cool J 1968

Mood Watch: The waxing Taurus Moon gives us the edge to proceed through the material world. Sun in Capricorn and Moon in Taurus brings a strong focus on accounting, business, and financial matters. There is also the element of cleaning, perfecting, and beautifying our surroundings. All of that work isn't for nothing, as the Taurus Moon is especially known for bringing out our need for pleasure and enjoyment. Whether a quiet, cozy evening by the fire or a sparkling social affair with friends is preferred, this Taurus Moon Friday puts us in the mood for some comforting pleasures.

January 15th Saturday

Moon in Taurus / Gemini

	PST	EST	
Moon square Neptune	12:05 AM	3:05 AM	
Moon sextile Uranus	12:25 AM	3:25 AM	
Moon sextile Jupiter	3:01 AM	6:01 AM	
Moon trine Mars goes v/c	4:46 AM	7:46 AM	
Moon enters Gemini	5:22 AM	8:22 AM	
Mars enters Aquarius	2:41 PM	5:41 PM	
Moon opposite Venus	10:07 PM	1:07 AM	(Jan 16)
Moon opposite Neptune	11:21 PM	2:21 AM	(Jan 16)

Birthday: Don Van Vliet (Captain Beefheart) 1941

Mood Watch: Early this morning the Taurus Moon goes void-of-course for a brief spell, causing a bit of Saturday morning laziness – or just plain stubborn reluctance. However, this doesn't have time enough to be a problem, as the Moon enters Gemini and our moods shift into a much more curious and interactive quality of expression. Gemini Moon keeps us busy working through the essential details. Thoughts and conversations are brought on by busy minds and thought provoking patterns of mood.

Mars enters Aquarius (Mars in Aquarius: Jan. 15 – Feb. 22) As Mars, the red warrior planet, moves through Aquarius, a surge of energy and vitality takes place in the lives of Aquarius people. Aquarians, no matter how hot it gets for you, energy and strength are there to be claimed. Now the fixed signs of the zodiac go into an activity mode, for as Mars goes through Aquarius, Scorpio and Taurus people will experience Mars squaring with their natal Sun signs, causing their lives to be more prone towards accidents, fights, fevers, and unyielding activities of great challenge. Mars in Aquarius will be opposing the fixed sign Leo, making our Leo friends realize that the activities in their lives are a challenge to keep up with;

occasional bouts of exhaustion may occur. Leos, you may be good at handling the heat, but don't punish yourself! Mars in the air sign of Aquarius shows that activities will emphasize science, technology and computer data banks, as well as humanitarian endeavors. Watch out for the potential for electrical equipment to overheat and fry during this time of Mars in Aquarius.

January 16th Sunday

Moon in Gemini	PST	EST
Moon trine Saturn	12:45 PM	3:45 PM

Birthday: Kate Moss 1974

Mood Watch: The waxing Gemini Moon is a good time to get organized, particularly while Moon trine Saturn gives us the edge we need to stay focused and to complete tasks in a timely manner. Versatility is the name of the game. In general, Gemini Moon keeps us talkative and inquisitive as it waxes brightly towards fullness. It's a good time to make connections with people, and to enjoy the company of others, especially those folks who are interesting to be around and are full of entertaining information.

January 17th Monday

Dr. Martin Luther King, Jr. Day *(born January 15, 1929)*

Moon in Gemini / Cancer	PST	EST	
Moon trine Neptune	6:40 AM	9:40 AM	
Moon square Uranus	6:59 AM	9:59 AM	
Moon square Jupiter goes v/c	9:57 AM	12:57 PM	
Moon enters Cancer	11:28 AM	2:28 PM	
Sun sextile Uranus	1:55 PM	4:55 PM	
Mercury conjunct Pluto	9:50 PM	12:50 AM	(Jan 18)

Birthday: Michelle Obama 1964

Mood Watch: The Gemini Moon brings inquisitive thoughts with a fair share of ups and downs. Moon trine Neptune starts off the day with positive, open, trusting vibes that quickly dissolve into an internal process as Moon square Uranus brings chaotic, explosive, or unusual energy. Then the heavily waxing Gemini Moon goes void-of-course while it is square to Jupiter; at this point, it may seem difficult to negotiate in business or to work around the shortcomings of a financial network. For a brief time, some folks may seem a little less generous or they may be especially unwilling to put themselves on the line for others. As the Moon enters Cancer, our deeper feelings begin to surface. The Cancer Moon is waxing up towards fullness, when folks openly seek encouragement and support. A little encouragement goes a long way.

Sun sextile Uranus (occurring Jan. 13 – 19) This occurrence of Sun sextile Uranus particularly affects those Capricorn folks celebrating birthdays January 13 – 19. These birthday people are being given an opportunity to blow off some chaotic steam, and to reach for qualities of freedom that may have been absent in their recent past. This will be your time to make radical breakthroughs, birthday

Capricorn; your natal Sun is currently sextile Uranus for a good reason – to find a liberating balance in the midst of the chaos, and to use the chaos in your life to your advantage. Once you've done this, you'll be ready to take the next step. Right now, there is no holding back, so go for it; discover your freedom. The victory of creative change will bring a more optimistic outlook on life. This aspect will repeat on May 24, affecting the lives of Taurus/Gemini people whose birthdays fall between May 20 – 27.

Mercury conjunct Pluto (occurring Jan. 12 – 20) Mercury conjunct Pluto raises issues of power. The areas of our lives that have required challenge, struggle, sacrifice and transformation now bring us to a place where we can talk about them. With Mercury and Pluto in the sign of Capricorn, a very strong sense of duty is instilled in the delivery of messages. This is a time when people instinctively know their own fate. Mercury conjunct Pluto in Capricorn allows us to voice our hardships, and to contemplate and deliberate over the powerful occurrences that challenge and change our lives. There will be a great deal of intensity in our conversations at this time, especially with regard to the fate of the world and our ongoing efforts to end hardship and suffering.

January 18ᵗʰ Tuesday

Moon in Cancer	PST	EST
Moon square Saturn	4:53 PM	7:53 PM

Birthday: Robert Anton Wilson 1932

Mood Watch: It's the Full Moon eve; the Cancer Moon brings out deep feelings of compassion, desire, or perhaps loneliness, and may lead some people to seek motherly advice or attention. Many folks will feel that the need for care and nurturing is essential. This afternoon's Moon square Saturn may cause some frustration, or people may find that certain things are taking a longer time than usual to handle. Concentration and focus will get us through the afternoon despite the distraction of strong feelings. The Moon rules Cancer, and when it's in its

home sign, it rarely fails to bring out a particularly moody quality of interaction among people. Some feelings are difficult to hide; patience and understanding will help.

January 19ᵗʰ Wednesday

FULL MOON in CANCER	PST	EST
Moon in Cancer / Leo		
Moon trine Uranus	10:08 AM	1:08 PM
Moon opposite Sun	1:21 PM	4:21 PM
Moon trine Jupiter goes v/c	1:25 PM	4:25 PM
Moon enters Leo	2:15 PM	5:15 PM
Sun sextile Jupiter	2:38 PM	5:38 PM
Moon opposite Mars	7:35 PM	10:35 PM
Venus sextile Saturn begins (see January 23)		

Birthday: Alexander Woollcott 1887

Mood Watch: The **Full Moon in Cancer** (Moon opposite Sun) emphasizes Mom and maternal energy, and people may be moody or especially preoccupied with their feelings. Nurturing activities and emotional support are the best ways to approach the Full Cancer Moon. Be careful not to overeat, but be sure to enjoy heartwarming, delicious, and nourishing foods. For a short time this afternoon, as the Full Cancer Moon goes void-of-course, beware of the tendency for strong emotional responses to dominate the course of events. It may take a little time to get a clear picture of matters. The emotional stress of the Full Cancer Moon's events has taken its toll on some people. Tonight's Moon in Leo brings out the urges to seek entertainment, engage in family activities, and to reflect on the day's events with friends.

Sun sextile Jupiter (occurring Jan. 14 – 21) Capricorn/Aquarius people celebrating birthdays this year from January 14 – 21 are now being brought into a favorable natal Sun position to Jupiter. It's a time of opportunity and expansion for these birthday folks if they act on their desires and work towards their goals. Skills learned throughout this year will support their overall plans for career advancement and fortune building. It's a good time to make the most of it Capricorn/Aquarius birthday folks! This aspect will reoccur on June 25.

AQUARIUS

Key Phrase: "I KNOW"

Fixed Air Sign

Ruling Planet: Uranus

Symbol : The Water Bearer

January 20th through February 18th

January 20th Thursday

Moon in Leo

	PST	EST
Sun enters Aquarius	2:18 AM	5:18 AM
Moon trine Venus	1:16 PM	4:16 PM
Moon sextile Saturn	6:25 PM	9:25 PM

Birthday: George Burns 1896

Mood Watch: Though still very full, the newly waning Leo Moon brings lots of energy that, for some, may have an overwhelming affect. The Leo Moon brings a strong sense of self-awareness as it focuses on our personal needs. The overall moods of the day are friendly, outgoing, and playful, particularly with Moon trine Venus. This Leo Moon brings an atmosphere of acceptance, with an emphasis on

50

public recognition, encouragement, and appreciation. Be aware of the tendency for people to tackle too much at once. Waning Moon reminds us to let go of overtaxing aspirations and desires, and to center in on the self in a way that protects vital energy levels.

 Sun enters Aquarius (Sun in Aquarius: Jan. 20 – Feb. 18) Aquarius is ruled by the enigmatic planetary force of Uranus, the often strange villain who forges new clarity and hope through the storms of chaos and disruption. Freedom fighters will remind us always that we must find a solution to every great atrocity that dampens the human spirit. We must take measures to prevent tomorrow's health crisis and to ensure the perpetuity of our species. Aquarius is the "fixed air" sign which represents the sum of human knowledge. It is an old world oppression that we must address in this Aquarian time – through knowledge we will succeed. This is a time for opening up new ideas and possibilities. Aquarians are usually very clever people who love a good challenge.

January 21st Friday

Moon in Leo / Virgo	PST	EST
Moon opposite Pluto	1:31 AM	4:31 AM
Moon opposite Mercury goes v/c	11:45 AM	2:45 PM
Moon enters Virgo	3:10 PM	6:10 PM
Mercury square Saturn begins (see January 26)		

Birthday: Benny Hill 1924

Mood Watch: Today's Moon shifts from Leo to Virgo, but there's more than three hours of void-of-course Leo Moon energy, which slows down the entire process of attempting to get things done. After a Full Moon week (see Wednesday), some rest may be required. The void-of-course Leo Moon brings distractions, particularly due to a tendency for most folks to be completely absorbed in the self. Everyone's beckoning for something – a little more attention, a bit of "alone time," the V.I.P. service, a moment in the limelight, a microphone. By the time the Moon enters Virgo, the primary focus of the mood is to get something practical done, and to enjoy simplicity, refinement and, if at all possible, relaxation.

January 22nd Saturday

Moon in Virgo	PST	EST
Moon trine Pluto	1:00 AM	4:00 AM
Jupiter enters Aries	9:11 AM	12:11 PM
Moon trine Mercury	10:42 AM	1:42 PM
Moon opposite Uranus	1:19 PM	4:19 PM
Moon square Venus goes v/c	5:47 PM	8:47 PM
Jupiter square Pluto begins (see February 25)		

Birthday: Grigori Rasputin 1869

Mood Watch: The waning Moon in Virgo focuses our attention on seed counting. Virgo puts us into a rhythmic pattern of moving, shifting, and accounting for the physical things of our lives. We are naturally inclined to clean, organize, pull apart, recombine, and rearrange things. We may find that everything has to be done in a particular order, so as to make sense of the cleaning and organizing process. This mind-set includes the disassembling of something, which often requires the keen observations of how it will need to be reassembled. It might get too complex if we try to disseminate our feelings in this manner, but the mood is clear – the energy of this week requires a real clean up job. Waning Virgo Moon keeps us busy simplifying, observing, and cleansing our space. In the most literal sense and on every proverbial level, Virgo Moon reminds us we need to take out the trash. Tonight's void-of-course Virgo Moon is initiated with Moon square Venus; take it easy on loved ones.

Jupiter enters Aries (Jupiter in Aries Jan. 22 – June 4) Today Jupiter, the planet of joy, luck, and fortune, enters the constellation Aries. Since September 8/9, 2010, Jupiter has been traveling through the mutable water sign Pisces, bringing imaginative and emotionally responsive efforts towards economic growth and prosperity. Jupiter in the cardinal fire sign Aries begins an era of new enterprises, independent business, and bold risk taking. Jupiter in Aries brings a pioneering spirit to the economic trends of our life. Jupiter is the planet where a sense of advancement is achieved and Aries, the first sign of the zodiac, emphasizes the need for leadership, independence, and enthusiastic confidence.

Here in Aries, Jupiter will boost our morale in an effort to regain our identity in the economic world. This will be seen in such Aries like businesses as metalworking, engineering, arms manufacturing, mechanics, and the automobile industry. Take note how these industries change and develop. Jupiter in Aries brings an enthusiastic effort to spend energy and time in the establishment of new enterprise. This is also the place where independence is asserted in business, as Jupiter in Aries demands enterprising advancement towards a sense of self-actualized fulfillment.

Aries has an integral, pioneering spirit that is hard to deny; however, not all new enterprising businesses of this time will be wise investments, since Aries also has an impulsive, reckless, and domineering quality that is sometimes overconfident and won't necessarily inspire wise decisions with large expenditures.

Jupiter doesn't always represent money, business, and economy. It is the social pulse beat of our collective conscience which determines how and where we derive our sense of joy, happiness, and hope. Wherever we instill a sense of optimism and enthusiasm, there is often a growth pattern of interest which eventually expands into prosperous gain. Aries demands the freedom to act independently and competitively. The self-reliant Aries says, "I AM," and demands alert, incisive, and resourceful growth. The economic state of affairs is not likely to stagnate during this time of Jupiter in Aries, as it will certainly undergo a fiery, bold and courageous level of change and innovative establishment.

Aries people will be able to enjoy some abundant opportunities and joyous personal experiences while Jupiter crosses over their natal Sun. They will also have a strong influence on the wave of the economic future, undoubtedly through many forms of new enterprise. The other fire signs of the zodiac, Leo and Sagittarius, will enjoy the fruits of Jupiter being trine to their natal Sun signs. This will bring the potential for travel or financial boons of some kind for the early born Leo and Sagittarius people. Libra folks would be wise to use their sensibilities and take precautions with their expenditures while Jupiter opposes their natal Sun. They may also find that the effort to handle massive volumes of business or a large inheritance may be overwhelming. Cancer and Capricorn people may discover that it will be especially difficult to keep up with expenses and opportunities in their lives while Jupiter squares to their natal Sun signs. Aquarius and Gemini people's natal Sun signs will be in the sextile position to Jupiter, and this will bring the potential for business or career opportunities in those areas of life where these people have already been working hard, or where they have made some genuine effort to succeed over time. Jupiter will remain in Aries from today until June 4, when it proceeds into Taurus.

January 23rd Sunday

Moon in Virgo / Libra	PST	EST	
Venus sextile Saturn	11:18 AM	2:18 PM	
Moon enters Libra	3:58 PM	6:58 PM	
Moon opposite Jupiter	4:22 PM	7:22 PM	
Moon trine Sun	10:24 PM	1:24 AM	(Jan 24)

Birthday: Django Reinhardt 1910

Mood Watch: Prudent resourcefulness comes in handy during waning Virgo Moon. People may tend to stick to their own affairs and be somewhat withdrawn in the early part of the day. This morning's mood may be a bit skeptical – perhaps even cynical at times. The Virgo Moon is void-of-course throughout most of the day, and it's not a time to test people's patience. As the Moon heads on into Libra, our moods enter into the need for harmony in relationships and for a sense of balance. Libra Moon emphasizes the need to clear up any troubling imbalances that exist between friends. This is a good time to drop grudges and attempt diplomacy with others.

Venus sextile Saturn (occurring Jan. 19 – 25) Venus is in Sagittarius sextile to Saturn in Libra. Venus in Sagittarius invites an attraction to traveling, adventurous love play, and uplifting social encounters. Venus sextile Saturn brings the opportunity for us to gain some control of our love relationships, and to better understand our boundaries and limitations. Saturn in Libra brings an even tempered and civil minded attempt to apply discipline in relationships. It is through this aspect that love relationships are given an opportunity for stronger levels of commitment and responsibility. This is the time to protect loved ones with guidance, and to teach them about discipline. Perfect timing brings pleasure. Venus sextile Saturn teaches us how to hold onto and maintain the things we love – those places, people, and things that matter to us. True love has a binding and lasting affect, and this aspect often shows us the ways in which love stands the test of time. This aspect will reoccur on August 7 and November 22.

January 24th Monday

Moon in Libra	PST	EST	
Moon square Pluto	2:06 AM	5:06 AM	
Moon trine Mars	2:59 AM	5:59 AM	
Moon square Mercury	5:19 PM	8:19 PM	
Moon conjunct Saturn	8:35 PM	11:35 PM	
Moon sextile Venus	11:21 PM	2:21 AM	(Jan 25)

Birthday: John Belushi 1949

Mood Watch: The waning Libra Moon emphasizes the need for harmony. Our moods go through a balancing act. The focus of this Moon is on the decision making process. We all have our own ways of weighing out different factors and drawing together conclusions. This is a good time to encourage others, to apply effective team-work practices, and to enjoy quality time with friends and loved ones. This evening's Moon square Mercury brings complexity to the thought process, and communications may get messy. Later, Moon conjunct Saturn brings a sense of completion and fruition. It may also indicate a time for commitment or affirmation of goals. Much later, Moon sextile Venus brings beauty to the scope of our dreams.

January 25th Tuesday

Moon in Libra / Scorpio	PST	EST	
Moon trine Neptune goes v/c	2:03 PM	5:03 PM	
Moon enters Scorpio	6:15 PM	9:15 PM	
Saturn goes retrograde	10:09 PM	1:09 AM	(Jan 26)

Birthday: Virginia Woolf 1882

Mood Watch: Sun in Aquarius and Moon in Libra emphases the need to apply ourselves intelligently. Later in the day, Moon trine Neptune brings tranquil and somewhat passive moods as we head into a void-of-course Moon period for a few hours. Line ups and delays may be evident here and there. A bit of absentmindedness may be the cause of some of those delays. Tonight's Moon in Scorpio brings clarity and a sharp edge to the feel of our moods. Waning Scorpio Moon reminds us of the value of our hidden perceptions, and of our instinct to survive and stay vital. This is the time to purge the emotional baggage that distracts us from our true feelings.

Saturn goes retrograde (Saturn retrograde: Jan. 25 – June 12) Saturn represents discipline, responsibility, and the tenacity required to get the job done. Sacrifices may be necessary in order to complete important projects, and discipline and perseverance are essential. Saturn, currently at the seventeen degree mark of Libra, will return to the ten degree mark. Saturn retrograde in Libra requires extra work to maintain the due process of the justice system, as well as the maintenance of relationships and friendships. For some folks, this will be a time of completion, of ending the treadmill of old cycles, and of learning to let others take responsibility for themselves. During Saturn retrograde, there will be a lot of work to do, retracing steps in the areas of life that need restructuring. It may be difficult, although not impossible, to begin new endeavors that require structure and the investment of time or commitment. We may be haunted by incomplete projects, and unsolved problems of the past could dominate the stage. Being careful of what we commit to at this time may prevent the need to drop other unfulfilled commitments midstream. If we haven't already dropped a few unnecessary responsibilities, we may have to do so soon. Learn how to delegate your tasks fairly to those who can handle them. Keep a steady check on quality control while Saturn is retrograde today through June 12.

January 26ᵗʰ Wednesday
LAST QUARTER MOON in SCORPIO PST   EST

	PST	EST
Mercury square Saturn	1:57 AM	4:57 AM
Moon sextile Pluto	4:57 AM	7:57 AM
Moon square Sun	4:57 AM	7:57 AM
Moon square Mars	8:47 AM	11:47 AM

Birthday: Paul Newman 1925

Mood Watch: The **Last Quarter Moon in Scorpio** (Moon square Sun) occurs very early this morning, and it focuses our attention on issues of passion and compassion. It is likely the dark secrets of our life will be touched on somehow. This Moon urges us to release stored up tension, and to find release for our emotional baggage without imposing it on others. Physical workouts are excellent for this Moon, provided safety consciousness is maintained. Safety consciousness of any kind is particularly important during Scorpio Moon. Don't forget to keep an eye out for suspicious activity – beware of thieves, smooth talkers, and the potential for aggressive outbreaks. Scorpio Moon brings out the daring side of our moods. This can also be an incredibly creative time for some folks. Last Quarter Scorpio Moon is a time for healing; everyone has a place in their life that needs some good healing energy.

Mercury square Saturn (occurring Jan. 21 – 28) Mercury in Capricorn square Saturn in Libra may be a difficult time to ask for favors, or to make requests of others in a way that they don't feel as if they're being used or taken advantage of. It may be a challenging time to communicate instructions or to inform someone of the end of something. It may also be challenging to sell someone on a product, or to successfully request a raise or promotion. Whatever the desired effect may be, it is wise to use caution when attempting communications during Mercury square Saturn. The retrograde Saturn is in Libra, creating limitations and structural changes in matters of law, justice, marriage, and relationships. This aspect makes it difficult to put a message out there and be taken seriously – or sometimes, we are taken *too* seriously. Some people may become very tongue-tied and feel quite off track. Mercury square Saturn will reoccur on June 21.

January 27th Thursday

Moon in Scorpio / Sagittarius	PST	EST	
Moon sextile Mercury	2:50 AM	5:50 AM	
Moon square Neptune	6:38 PM	9:38 PM	
Moon trine Uranus goes v/c	7:00 PM	10:00 PM	
Moon enters Sagittarius	10:54 PM	1:54 AM	(Jan 28)
Venus square Uranus begins (see February 2)			

Birthday: Lewis Carroll 1832

Mood Watch: The waning Scorpio Moon puts a focus on the powerful and astonishing quality of the 21st century's events up to date. These are dangerous times in the world and quite often the waning Scorpio Moon puts us in touch with our sensibilities, our suspicions and our deeper concerns. There's a surreal sense of mood-play occurring, giving the occasional impression that this dangerous world is utterly incompetent. We may feel constantly affronted by mini-dramas and the audacity of life's unexpected surprises. Our moods instinctively will rise to the occasion of every real life encounter with a sense of Scorpio-like urgency. Be cautious while the Scorpio Moon is void-of-course this evening.

January 28th Friday

Moon in Sagittarius	PST	EST
Moon trine Jupiter	12:48 AM	3:48 AM
Moon sextile Sun	2:34 PM	5:34 PM
Moon sextile Mars	5:33 PM	8:33 PM

Birthday: Jackson Pollock 1912

Mood Watch: Today's lunar aspects are positive and upbeat, and although waning, the Sagittarius Moon brings hope and optimism. The waning Sagittarius Moon is an excellent time for the internal, philosophical part of the self to be reinforced with an affirmation of vision. It is particularly important to let go of the things that thwart or get in the way of that vision. What in your life would you like to see thrive and grow? Catch the vision. Make room for that growth!

January 29th Saturday

Moon in Sagittarius	PST	EST
Moon sextile Saturn	6:16 AM	9:16 AM
Moon conjunct Venus	7:17 PM	10:17 PM
Venus sextile Neptune begins (see February 1)		
Mars trine Saturn begins (see February 6)		

Birthday: Oprah Winfrey 1954

Mood Watch: The waning Sagittarius Moon brings insightfulness and contemplative moods. This morning's Moon sextile Saturn brings moods of strong intent, and there is determination in the air. This evening's Moon conjunct Venus in Sagittarius brings a love for adventure as well as feelings of longing, and there's a quality of attraction, like a magnetic effect, to the things that catch our eye. Be it on an internal – or external – level, Sagittarius Moon invites us to explore, to grow, to mature, and to take on more skills and capabilities.

January 30th Sunday

Moon in Sagittarius / Capricorn	PST	EST
Moon sextile Neptune	1:46 AM	4:46 AM
Moon square Uranus goes v/c	2:10 AM	5:10 AM
Moon enters Capricorn	6:03 AM	9:03 AM
Moon square Jupiter	8:53 AM	11:53 AM
Moon conjunct Pluto	6:02 PM	9:02 PM
Mercury sextile Uranus begins (see February 2)		

Birthday: Z. Budapest 1940

Mood Watch: This morning the waning Moon enters Capricorn; our moods are likely to be dominated by a serious phase of expression throughout the day. Capricorn Moon keeps our moods focused on important matters and relentlessly reminds us to get a handle on our unfinished business. For some, the important "task" may be the job of resting, but if that's not the case for you, don't use this as an excuse! Whatever you do, enjoy the work while the atmosphere invites success.

January 31st Monday

Moon in Capricorn	PST	EST
Moon square Saturn	2:40 PM	5:40 PM
Venus square Jupiter begins (see February 6)		
Sun trine Saturn begins (see February 5)		

Birthday: Minnie Driver 1971

Mood Watch: The waning Capricorn Moon brings an emphasis on completion. This makes sense, since it's the end of the month. The spirit of this Moon focuses our moods on toning down emotional clamor and distractions. A serious tone sets the stage; it's time to get to work. The month's end tasks could be arduous, and the ever popular stiff upper lip may be required. This afternoon's Moon square Saturn brings trials, a tricky task, and some extra work to wade through – then there's the necessity to tackle these big jobs with greater gusto.

February 1st Tuesday

Moon in Capricorn / Aquarius	PST	EST	
Moon conjunct Mercury	8:41 AM	11:41 AM	
Moon sextile Uranus goes v/c	11:31 AM	2:31 PM	
Moon enters Aquarius	3:21 PM	6:21 PM	
Moon sextile Jupiter	7:11 PM	10:11 PM	
Venus sextile Neptune	11:34 PM	2:34 AM	(Feb 2)

Birthday: Clark Gable 1901

Mood Watch: Throughout the first part of the day, the darkly waning Capricorn Moon brings serious moods, with an industrious intent to get things done on this first day of a new month. However, as the Moon goes void-of-course, chaos and rebellious feelings begin to surface. Work may seem arduous and tasks may take longer than planned. Later on, Moon in Aquarius brings a brighter outlook. The New Moon Eve has arrived. This evening's Aquarius Moon brings a new approach to overcome the doldrums of life. It is the eve of Candlemas, and the desire for light must be satiated. This is the time to bring light and intelligence into the picture.

Venus sextile Neptune (occurring Jan. 29 – Feb. 3) Venus in Sagittarius sextile Neptune in Aquarius brings inspirational and creative love to the art of spirituality. The sextile of Venus to Neptune brings the opportunity for us to find spiritual enhancement in the adventure of love, and to spread its healing power around for all to share. This serves as an excellent time to reach out spiritually to those we love as well as to our spirit guides. This aspect will reoccur on May 16 and November 24.

February 2nd Wednesday

Candlemas / Groundhog Day

NEW MOON in AQUARIUS

	PST	EST
Venus square Uranus	4:47 AM	7:47 AM
Mercury sextile Uranus	8:15 AM	11:15 AM
Moon conjunct Sun	6:30 PM	9:30 PM
Moon conjunct Mars	7:16 PM	10:16 PM
Mercury sextile Jupiter begins (see February 5)		

Birthday: Stan Getz 1927

Mood Watch: The **New Moon in Aquarius** (Moon conjunct Sun) is a good time to begin social and philanthropic endeavors, and to gain fresh knowledge by learning something new about ourselves or our ever changing world. Moods created by this New Moon may be bold or daring, with a flair for experimenting with life. This is the time to open up to a greater comprehension of the science and technology of these changing times, adding to our power.

Venus square Uranus (occurring Jan. 27 – Feb. 4) Venus is in Sagittarius squaring to Uranus in Pisces. A love for travel may be stifled by chaotic changes. This aspect tends to put obstacles between love and freedom. Be careful not to become too personally affronted by explosive or radical love matters. This influence may be testing the power of love to withstand chaos. Be assured in self-love and empower affection with personal integrity and a strong loving vision. People are changing at a rapid rate and it is essential to let love take its course with regard to issues of personal freedom. This aspect will reoccur on July 7 and November 26.

Mercury sextile Uranus (occurring Jan. 30 – Feb. 3) Mercury is in Capricorn, placing a determined emphasis on our efforts to communicate. Uranus is in Pisces, stirring up chaos in the arts, religion, and perhaps even in our collective struggle with substance abuses. Mercury sextile Uranus gives us the opportunity to freely speak our minds and to address the turmoil that exists in our lives. Sensationalism may be played up in the news during this aspect. Mercury in an earth sign focuses talk, information and news on such practical matters as the value and cost of things, while Uranus in Pisces is blowing all practicality right out of the water. This aspect will reoccur on June 4.

February 3rd Thursday

Chinese New Year: RABBIT (Year 4709) – Metal Rabbit

Moon in Aquarius	PST	EST	
Moon trine Saturn	12:56 AM	3:56 AM	
Mercury enters Aquarius	2:18 PM	5:18 PM	
Venus enters Capricorn	9:58 PM	12:58 AM	(Feb 4)
Moon conjunct Neptune goes v/c	10:11 PM	1:11 AM	(Feb 4)

Birthday: Norman Rockwell 1894

Mood Watch: Our moods are open to new discoveries and to social events and galas. This is a time when our moods are one with our thoughts and we are not likely to spend too much time explaining what we already intuitively know. This Moon gives us the inclination to exercise our knowledge and our expertise. Scientific knowledge and innovative breakthroughs are often highlighted during Aquarius Moon. Explore new ideas and share them with others.

Mercury enters Aquarius (Mercury in Aquarius: Feb. 3 – 21) Today, Mercury enters Aquarius, the fixed air sign of the zodiac which represents humanity's knowledge. As the force of communication (Mercury) travels through the constellation of fixed thought and meditation (Aquarius), there are great opportunities for us to share and to empower each other through our knowledge. This is a splendid time to communicate ideas and investigate the latest in technology, science, and the world of invention. Mercury in Aquarius is also a special time to speak out on humanitarian issues and the rights of freedom. Eccentric talk and unusual subjects will fill the airwaves while Mercury is in Aquarius.

Venus enters Capricorn (Venus in Capricorn: Feb. 3 – March 26) Now Venus will be grounded in the stoic and serious focuses of Capricorn. Venus in Capricorn brings out an attraction for the staunch and ardent duty of accomplishing goals as well as a love of predictability. This type of expression creates stable ground for the development of relationships, and the general course of affections will be oriented towards making impressions, with a hard and ambitious drive towards providing well for loved ones. This is the time when the general populace is attracted to getting in shape. Venus in Capricorn will certainly bring out a more serious approach to love matters in general. It is important to have respect and maturity in matters of love if we are to be taken seriously by loved ones while Venus is in Capricorn.

Happy Chinese New Year! – Year of the Rabbit (occurring Feb. 3, 2011 *Metal RABBIT* – Jan. 22, 2012 - Next year's animal will be *Water DRAGON*). Chinese New Year happens on the New Aquarius Moon in China, which means it usually occurs within a day of the Aquarius New Moon in North America. In the Chinese calendar, we have reached the year 4709, and this time marks the *Year of the Metal Rabbit*. Every twelve years, the Year of the Rabbit rolls around, and every sixty years, we come to the specific Rabbit year known as the Metal Rabbit. Metal Rabbits of the 20th century were born from February 4, 1951 to February 5, 1952.

As for **Metal Rabbits (1951 & 2011)**, the metal element makes these folks particularly resilient, and perhaps not as quiet as the other Rabbit personalities. Metal rabbits are very determined and motivated and they often get what they want. They incorporate their ambitions into everything they do and they also put their emotions into their carefully crafted intent to get things done. Metal rabbits are often fully immersed in their projects, both business and personal, revealing spunk and strong aspirations. If they exhibit any sign of aggression, which is not a character trait of the rabbit, they are likely to be a passive-aggressive personality, subtly manipulative and persuasive. These rabbit personalities are not malicious or ill willed, and their harmful tendencies are by no means intended. They sincerely believe they have everyone's best interest in mind. Metal Rabbits want to be accepted and to have some input towards creating a better environment. They are not afraid of work and enjoy seeing the fruits of their labors.

As for all rabbits, people born under the **Year of the Rabbit (or Hare)** can be quite Venusian. They are generally merciful, elegant, and they adore beauty. They are also very kind and loving. Rabbits are particularly offended by – and sensitive to – hostility and hatred. They may appear very gentle or delicate, with soft or subtle features, but they are often quite strong minded and strong willed. They enjoy the pursuit of a lifestyle filled with precision and orderly conduct. They are generally cautious and like to take things slowly.

Rabbits are not aggressive, but they are not exactly docile either. They are quite keen and observant when they want to be but, because they're prone to being calm and serene, they can sometimes miss things. They may appear high strung or nervous, but they know how to relax when they feel safe. They have an astute sense of style, sophistication, and class. They can be very attractive and endearing. Rabbits can be wise and considerate, but on the downside they are sneaky and obsessive. Overall, the tranquil quality of the rabbit's personality often sets people at ease and rabbit folks are good at avoiding harm to themselves. Rabbit people are generally good listeners, hence, they represent the classic animal totem with the surprisingly elongated ears! However, Rabbits are very independent and they are not necessarily inclined to apply the advice or suggestions they're listening to. You might say that they use their listening skills to hear what they want to hear, and to pick out what they need to hear. It is the rabbit's ability to hear approaching predators that contributes to their survival skills.

Stress and conflicts can be especially harmful to the rabbit personality and it is wise if they choose careers that contribute to easing their stress levels rather than challenging them. Rabbits generally do better in positions of management, a place where they can use their excellent organizational skills and control the level of demand their job places upon them. Rabbits make excellent teachers, counselors, therapists, artists, musicians, actors, fashion designers, and massage therapists. They love to spend their money on homes, cars, and furniture. They appreciate art, crafts, and beautiful things and they are intrigued by beautiful and practical antiques. As a general rule, rabbits make sound investments, and it is good for them to invest in things that appreciate over time, especially since they are not always good at hanging on to cash.

If you know of Rabbit people who do not fit these personality descriptions, bear in mind that systems such as Western or Chinese Astrology are multifaceted parts of an intricate and complex human makeup. Sometimes the vast combination of celestial traits in humans can bring surprising results, and sometimes, through sheer persistence of will – as well as environmental and cultural influences – people change completely from their inherent nature into something phenomenally different. This is why it is not wise to blithely accept every probability predicted in this book. You have the power to change what's around you!

Famous Rabbit People: Anaïs Nin (water 1903), Bing Crosby (water 1903), George Orwell (water 1903), Frank Sinatra (wood 1915), Edith Piaf (wood 1915), Muddy Waters (wood 1915), Billie Holiday (wood 1915), Gina Lollobrigida (fire 1927), Marvin Gaye (earth 1939), Francis Ford Coppola (earth 1939), Judy Collins (earth 1939), Tina Turner (earth 1939), John Cleese (earth 1939), Jane Seymour (metal 1951), Anjelica Huston (metal 1951), Huey Lewis (metal 1951), John Cougar Mellencamp (metal 1951), Drew Barrymore (water 1963), Helen Hunt (water 1963), Natasha Richardson (water 1963), Brad Pitt (water 1963), Angelina Jolie (wood 1975), Tiger Woods (wood 1975), Tobey Maguire (wood 1975), Kate Winslet (wood 1975).

February 4th Friday

Moon in Aquarius / Pisces	PST	EST
Moon enters Pisces	2:23 AM	5:23 AM
Moon sextile Venus	2:51 AM	5:51 AM
Sun conjunct Mars	8:40 AM	11:40 AM
Moon sextile Pluto	3:23 PM	6:23 PM
Venus conjunct Pluto begins (see February 9)		

Birthday: Alice Cooper 1948

Mood Watch: Overnight, the newly waxing Moon enters Pisces and our moods are met by a calm, curious, and flirtatious spirit. Positive vibrations are often qualities of the youthfully waxing Pisces Moon, though sometimes Pisces Moon puts us in touch with our addictive tendencies. Temptations abound, yet they also empower us when we resist them. This is not a good time to side with old habits that aren't beneficial. Pisces Moon reminds us that everything we do in our life is special, no matter how insignificant an action or task may seem. We must, therefore, make an art out of all of our movements, and find within ourselves the special qualities of each waking hour. Moon sextile Pluto puts us in touch with the many aspects of power and fate that exist in our lives. Pisces Moon assists us to find the calm in every storm.

Sun conjunct Mars (occurring Jan. 9 – Feb. 17) Sagittarius folks celebrating birthdays Jan. 9 – Feb. 17 are undergoing a Mars conjunction to their natal sun. Mars stirs up newness and extreme energy into the lives of these birthday people. If you were born during this time, obvious and genuine changes are occurring, and there is heat in most facets of your life. Positive Mars changes involve the breaking down of old structure and the creative reconstruction of one's personal desires and environment. Negative Mars changes often involve accidents, breakups, fevers and the collapse of overheated internal organs, as well as bouts of impatience and anger. Bursts of energy now fill your life, birthday Sagittarians. This may be the most energy and action you'll have to contend with all year. Use it wisely and creatively while you've got it, and allow the activities of your days to infuse you with rich, enthusiastic vigor. Attempt as best you can to use the heat of anger to be constructive, as opposed to destructive.

February 5th Saturday

Moon in Pisces

	PST	EST	
Mercury sextile Jupiter	7:29 AM	10:29 AM	
Sun trine Saturn	10:40 PM	1:40 AM	(Feb 6)

Birthday: William Burroughs 1914

Mood Watch: Something intrinsically special and often incommunicable touches the heart in the newly waxing inspiration of Pisces Moon. This is the time to recognize an inherent gift that exists within, and to visualize the ways in which that gift can manifest. Spiritual moods put us in touch with our ability to withstand adversity and to accept how we feel.

Mercury sextile Jupiter (occurring Feb. 2 – 6) Mercury brings news and talk, while Jupiter brings wealth and prosperous advancement. The money flows where our attention goes. Communicating our knowledge (Mercury in Aquarius) brings opportunities and the potential for success (the sextile aspect) in typical Aries endeavors. These include the growth of new businesses and the mechanical and engineering sciences, as well as the expansion of self-reliance, motivation, and entrepreneurship (Jupiter in Aries). Opportunity exists for both the employer and the employee. This is a good time to advertise. Mercury sextile Jupiter brings joyful and mind expanding conversations. This aspect will reoccur on June 17.

Sun trine Saturn (occurring Jan. 31 – Feb. 8) This aspect particularly affects Aquarius people celebrating birthdays January 31 – February 8. This is a positive time for these folks to get a handle on their lives, and it may be easier for them to take on their responsibilities with fewer complications and less difficulty in the year to come. These birthday people may notice more acceptable forms of control, responsibility and work occurring in their lives. Now is your time (birthday people) to successfully work on putting some structure into your life; the kind of structure you've needed and wanted awaits you in the coming year. It is possible that time (Saturn) is on your side to make that move you've wanted to make towards achieving your goals. This aspect will reoccur June 1, affecting the Gemini people of that time.

February 6th Sunday

Moon in Pisces / Aries

	PST	EST
Mars trine Saturn	9:15 AM	12:15 PM
Moon conjunct Uranus goes v/c	11:13 AM	2:13 PM

	PST	EST	
Venus square Jupiter	11:39 AM	2:39 PM	
Moon enters Aries	2:45 PM	5:45 PM	
Moon conjunct Jupiter	8:50 PM	11:50 PM	
Moon square Venus	9:38 PM	12:38 AM	(Feb 7)

Birthday: Babe Ruth 1895

Mood Watch: The waxing Pisces Moon brings tranquil Sunday morning feelings. As the Moon goes void-of-course, our moods become, classically, spacey and easily distracted. High expectations are not likely to be easily met. This is a good time to take it easy and to enjoy creative and artistic endeavors. Later today, the Aries Moon kicks up the dust of our ambitions. Tonight, outgoing and energetic moods inspire a determined outlook for the week to come.

Mars trine Saturn (occurring Jan. 29 – Feb. 10) Mars in Aquarius trine Saturn in Libra is an ideal time to research, facilitate, and take action with humanitarian projects. In general, large scale projects can expect to move ahead, although it may not necessarily occur on time. Our actions bring gifts with this aspect, provided there is an application of discipline and timing. This may be a good time to apply diligent practice with one's favorite sport, especially those physical activities which demand precision and perfect timing. The timely gift of willpower and discipline brings rewards and positive results. To fully benefit from this aspect, one must use the energy (Mars) responsibly (Saturn). This is usually a time of harmonious transitions, when endings and new beginnings are easily merged. This aspect will reoccur on July 6.

Venus square Jupiter (occurring Jan. 31 – Feb. 9) This aspect brings love and attraction (Venus) into difficulty or hard work (the square aspect) over the need for prosperity, growth and jubilation (Jupiter). Venus in Capricorn square Jupiter in Aries brings a love for practical goal setting at a pressing time when the need to handle escalating economic obligations or personal debts may be hard. Some folks may be experiencing challenges with their senses of appreciation, enjoyment, or fulfillment. Our experiences of beauty and affection may be tested by the difficulty of attracting or acquiring prosperity and joy. Some might say that the act of appreciating beauty is a form of prosperity in itself, but at times like this, a great deal more effort and support is required. This aspect may create an obstacle to acknowledging the expenses incurred by our attractions and love-needs. It reminds us that something more than love's blindness is required in order for us to fully realize our riches and the value of what we care about most. This aspect will reoccur two more times, on August 4 and December 20.

February 7th Monday

Moon in Aries

	PST	EST
Moon sextile Mercury	1:51 AM	4:51 AM
Moon square Pluto	4:04 AM	7:04 AM

Birthday: Chris Rock 1965

Mood Watch: Aries Moon invokes the powers of initiation and newness as an essential part of regenerative force. This is a time to generate and promote inspiration and happiness. Aries is the sign of the warrior. The fight to sustain love on Planet Earth calls for many courageous battles, and now is an excellent time to actively initiate new projects and endeavors that will help to serve one's sense of well-being. The Aries Moon of winter sometimes brings a restless spirit, and many folks may find themselves feeling somewhat agitated by the monotonous setbacks of winter. Aries Moon will either test our patience or inspire us to get out and do something productive.

February 8th Tuesday

Moon in Aries

	PST	EST	
Moon opposite Saturn	12:26 AM	3:26 AM	
Moon sextile Mars	4:15 AM	7:15 AM	
Moon sextile Sun	6:09 AM	9:09 AM	
Moon sextile Neptune goes v/c	11:30 PM	2:30 AM	(Feb 9)

Birthday: Eliphas Levi (Alphonse Louis Constant) 1810
"Life isn't about finding yourself. Life is about creating yourself."
– George Bernard Shaw

Mood Watch: The Aries Moon brings moods that are notably more alert, high spirited, and a great deal more direct. Throughout the day and into the evening, our moods may be measured by the efficiency with which tasks and deeds are carried out, and by how much self-assurance and self-confidence can be felt in the course of our actions.

February 9th Wednesday

Moon in Aries / Taurus

	PST	EST	
Moon enters Taurus	3:22 AM	6:22 AM	
Moon trine Venus	4:32 PM	7:32 PM	
Moon trine Pluto	4:39 PM	7:39 PM	
Venus conjunct Pluto	5:51 PM	8:51 PM	
Moon square Mercury	11:40 PM	2:40 AM	(Feb 10)

Birthday: Ziyi Zhang 1979

Mood Watch: The Taurus Moon inspires us to face big endeavors with a practical, positive, down-to-earth spirit. This Taurus Moon is favorably waxing, and our enthusiastic stubbornness to get the job done will make the difference. This afternoon, the Moon is trine to both Venus and Pluto. These positive lunar trine aspects suggest that we are open to the good attributes of the Venus-Pluto conjunction (see below). Beauty and strength are combined to boost our morale.

Venus conjunct Pluto (occurring Feb. 4 – 12) This conjunction often places affections and love right where they are needed most: the areas of life that are deeply challenging and sometimes traumatic. It also intensifies love related efforts and, at times, our affections may seem overpowering or daunting in some way. Venus represents love and beauty, while Pluto (in Greek myth) represents the god of the underworld, who lured the goddess of love, Persephone, away from heaven with the rich scent of a narcissus flower. This single act of peculiar passion led the youthful goddess into a fateful entanglement that would later force her to descend into the depths of Earth every autumn to join the underworld god until spring. She represents the life of spring and summer, and when she is absent, planet Earth remains barren or dormant. Venus (Persephone) conjunct Pluto (Hades) represents the union of beauty and strength. In the end, there is always a rich price to pay for the pursuit of passion, but true love and beauty are everlasting. This is a time when the intensity or hardship of love and attraction create richly striking images and perspectives of which we must eventually let go completely in the hope that love and beauty will transform our lives once again. Love and beauty are far richer experiences when they are met by the transformation demanded by Plutonian tests. Pluto brings loss through illness, death, and decay. Venus brings love that is renewed through all hardships, even loneliness. This is a time of deep confessions and secrets revealed. One of the powers of love is that we can always find it, even when we are alone, or in a barren or dormant state of being. Venus conjunct Pluto is occurring in Capricorn. This emphasizes the sobering awareness that is taking place with regard to the transformation process of love and attraction. This is a good time to find love's powers and unite them within. This conjunction will reoccur on December 1.

February 10th Thursday

FIRST QUARTER MOON in TAURUS

	PST	EST	
Moon square Mars	8:13 PM	11:13 PM	
Moon square Sun	11:18 PM	2:18 AM	(Feb 11)
Sun conjunct Neptune begins (see February 17)			
Mercury trine Saturn begins (see February 14)			

Birthday: Jimmy Durante 1893

Mood Watch: The **First Quarter Moon in Taurus** (Moon square Sun) brings the pressure to take care of essential needs. Taurus is the *fixed earth* sign, and the nature of Taurus Moon leads many folks to watch their pocketbook, and make sure they're getting the most value possible out of all expenditures. There is also a need to let the beauty of our surroundings be accented and appreciated. Somewhere in between the processes of earning and reaping rewards, a happy medium is struck. The Moon is *exalted* in the place of Taurus, and positive harmony brings satisfaction. However, tonight's Moon square Mars may bring agitation to some folk's moods. Some simple patience may be required.

February 11th Friday

Moon in Taurus / Gemini

	PST	EST	
Moon square Neptune	10:49 AM	1:49 PM	
Moon sextile Uranus goes v/c	11:26 AM	2:26 PM	
Moon enters Gemini	2:20 PM	5:20 PM	
Moon sextile Jupiter	10:04 PM	1:04 AM	(Feb 12)

Birthday: Sheryl Crow 1963

Mood Watch: Throughout the morning, the waxing Taurus Moon emphasizes the need for comfort and functionality. Moon square Neptune may bring moods that are particularly challenged by discordant noises or unpleasant surroundings. As the Moon goes void-of-course, it is sextile to Uranus, bringing with it a brief period of impractical distractions and chaos. Then the Moon enters Gemini, and our moods enter into a period of curiosity and wonder. Gemini says: "I think," and the Gemini Moon brings talkative, thoughtful, and communicative expressions of mood. The Sun and Moon are both in air signs; it's a good time to communicate with others and to share thoughts and ideas.

February 12th Saturday

Moon in Gemini	PST	EST	
Moon trine Mercury	6:08 PM	9:08 PM	
Moon trine Saturn	10:09 PM	1:09 AM	(Feb 13)
Mars conjunct Neptune begins (see February 20)			

Birthday: Abraham Lincoln 1809

Mood Watch: Trivia Question: What are the two most common things in the universe?* Sometimes the whirling universe is bursting with more great mystery than one can comprehend. Sometimes the vastness of knowledge cannot be stored with so much detail overloading the system. Sometimes the mind is full and the chattering world won't cease. Gemini Moon playfully waxes and loves to play tricks on the mind. Don't overdo the caffeine and take it easy on the nervous system. When in doubt, apply humor.

*Trivia Quiz Answer: Did you guess hydrogen and oxygen? You were close! Comedy dictates that hydrogen and *stupidity* are the two most common things in the universe! Aquarius Sun and Gemini Moon indicate the need to act with knowledge and to think matters through. There are a lot of things we don't know, but sometimes ignoring the things we do know is a sign of stupidity.

February 13th Sunday

Moon in Gemini / Cancer	PST	EST	
Moon trine Mars	8:31 AM	11:31 AM	
Moon trine Sun	12:27 PM	3:27 PM	
Moon trine Neptune	6:41 PM	9:41 PM	
Moon square Uranus goes v/c	7:19 PM	10:19 PM	
Moon enters Cancer	9:48 PM	12:48 AM	(Feb 14)
Venus square Saturn begins (see February 18)			

Birthday: Peter Gabriel 1950

Mood Watch: The Moon in Gemini brings a curiosity to our moods, with lively conversation and interaction. Sun in Aquarius and Moon in Gemini is often a time when research is highlighted and innovative new approaches to problem solving are available. This is a particularly good time to study, to memorize, to examine important decisions more closely, and to investigate the well-being of the working systems that we depend on. However, this evening our ability to multi-task and think matters through may not appear as keen as our daytime pursuits.

Moon square Uranus occurs as the Moon goes void-of-course. Beware of the possibility of explosive reactions to potentially confusing and chaotic situations. Our evening moods may be challenged by malfunctions, thoughtless attempts at communicating, and a tendency towards uncertainty. Later, the Moon in Cancer brings out the true expression of our emotions.

February 14th Monday

Saint Valentine's Day

Moon in Cancer	**PST**	**EST**
Mercury trine Saturn	12:48 AM	3:48 AM
Moon square Jupiter	5:51 AM	8:51 AM
Moon opposite Venus	7:33 PM	10:33 PM
Mercury conjunct Mars begins (see February 20)		

Birthday: Jack Benny 1903

Mood Watch: A nearly full Moon in Cancer is always certain to put us in touch with how we feel. On this Valentine's Day, the waxing Moon in Cancer is generally considered a good time for loved ones to interact. However, the lunar aspects suggest that the feelings may be somewhat overpowering. This morning's Moon square Jupiter brings a less than generous spirit. There may also be a strong need for some folks to acquire crucial resources. One thing that is certain – for most this will seem like a moody day. This evening's Moon opposite Venus generally brings the feeling of pressure with regard to the things and people we love. Whether there is a greater pressure for commitment to love, or an overwhelming pressure to find love, it may be tricky to find – and be appeased by – the people and the things that usually bring pleasure. On the other hand, the Moon opposite Venus can also produce the affect of unabashed, passionate, outgoing love.

Mercury trine Saturn (occurring Feb. 10 – 15) Mercury is in Aquarius where the emphasis of information is placed on science, technology and the need for knowledge and know-how. Saturn is in Libra where new laws are forged and there is a strong emphasis on the need to protect ourselves and our civil rights. Mercury in Aquarius trine Saturn in Libra brings favorable communication which tells us how – and where – to intelligently draw the lines for ourselves. This is a good time to make an impression, to teach, and to communicate to others those important matters that must be clarified. This is a great time to study or practice memorization skills. Timely information and news represents a gift or blessing. This aspect will reoccur on June 7.

February 15th Tuesday

Moon in Cancer	**PST**	**EST**	
Moon square Saturn	3:10 AM	6:10 AM	
Moon trine Uranus goes v/c	11:06 PM	2:06 AM	(Feb 16)

Birthday: Richard Payne Knight 1750

Mood Watch: In the early hours of the morning, Moon square Saturn places an emphasis on how we're feeling about our limitations. We are often challenged with the idea that we could do better than we're actually doing. The waxing Cancer Moon is brilliantly bright, and this marks the eve of the Full Moon, which is set to be full tomorrow in Leo. This is a good time to combat fear. Cancer Moon is no time to obsessively worry. The act of worry serves no purpose, and if not properly thwarted, it can sometimes act like a self-fulfilling prophecy to make things go wrong. Fight worry with confidence and positive thoughts. Tonight's Moon trine Uranus occurs as the Moon goes void-of-course. Rebellious feelings can be quite liberating. Restlessness often comes with a very full void-of-course Cancer Moon.

February 16th Wednesday
FULL MOON in LEO

Moon in Cancer / Leo	PST	EST
Moon enters Leo	1:14 AM	4:14 AM
Moon opposite Sun	3:31 AM	6:31 AM
Moon trine Jupiter	9:29 AM	12:29 PM

Birthday: Sonny Bono 1935

Mood Watch: The **Full Moon in Leo** (Moon opposite Sun) captivates our moods with a wild and instinctual push. It reaches its peak early this morning, creating a day of playful, imaginative, and creative expressions of mood. Most of us are easily drawn towards the need to find warmth and affection, or just plain attention. There may be an opportunity here to enhance and harmonize friendships and family situations in a fulfilling and enriching manner. Moon in Leo puts us in touch with those places, people, and things to which we feel loyal. Many folks may find themselves feeling somewhat courageous and confident. As a general rule, warmth and vitality is generated in our moods, especially since the Leo Moon puts us in touch with the Sun. Leo is ruled by the Sun, and the Full Leo Moon reminds us of the much more noticeable light and the lengthening of days when the solar light uplifts our spirits in preparation for spring.

February 17th Thursday

Moon in Leo	PST	EST
Sun conjunct Neptune	1:55 AM	4:55 AM
Moon sextile Saturn	4:35 AM	7:35 AM
Moon opposite Pluto goes v/c	7:06 AM	10:06 AM
Mercury conjunct Neptune begins (see February 20)		
Sun conjunct Mercury begins (see February 25)		

Birthday: Paris Hilton 1981

Mood Watch: The charge of yesterday's Full Leo Moon has taken its toll on our energy levels. Moon opposite Pluto strikes this morning with a strong jolt of reality. We are reminded that sometimes the powers of fate take precedence over our plans. At times, the long void-of-course Leo Moon day brings spacey, selfish, and unaccommodating moods. This may be a difficult day to get some good service, to get people's attention, and to find satisfaction where high expectations are concerned. Laziness and tiredness may also be the culprits of this endless void-of-course Moon day. The energy that has been running so high all week has reached a definitive low level. Relaxation and rest are a good way to go.

Sun conjunct Neptune (occurring Feb. 10 – 20) This occurrence of Sun conjunct Neptune particularly affects Aquarius/Pisces cusp born people celebrating birthdays February 10 – 20 with intuitive inclinations and spiritual desires. Your visions (Aquarius/Pisces birthday folks) will inspire great feats, and the higher, more spiritually refined parts of the soul are going to be speaking to you throughout the upcoming year. Listen! This may be a time to let go of personal attachments and outmoded desires that appear to be going nowhere. Your highly complex Aquarian idealism, or your keenly adaptable Piscean intuition, will work up your spiritual beliefs into a kind of peak performance level, even if you don't believe you have such a thing as spiritual beliefs. Birthday Aquarians and early born Pisces, you will continue to encounter a kind of spiritual catharsis and, by the time you've come through this, you'll know what that means. Integrate a istening pattern concerning the Great Spirit in your life; focus on the spiritual part of the self (or higher self) that rules over personal destiny and guides the true desires of the soul. Can you handle that, birthday folks?

PISCES

Key Phrase: "I Believe"

Mutable Water Sign

Ruling Planet: Neptune

Symbol : The Fishes

February 18th through March 20th

February 18th Friday

Moon in Leo / Virgo

	PST	EST
Moon enters Virgo	1:38 AM	4:38 AM
Venus square Saturn	11:21 AM	2:21 PM
Moon trine Pluto	12:31 PM	3:31 PM
Sun enters Pisces	4:25 PM	7:25 PM

Birthday: Yoko Ono 1933

Mood Watch: Early this morning, the Moon enters Virgo. Practical matters now come to the surface. The waning Virgo Moon keeps us cautious, suspicious, and

69

carefully poised. This is a good time to concentrate on the cleansing process of the soul. Virgo Moon emphasizes the need to focus on such things as spa activities, accounting, dieting, research and analysis. Sun in Aquarius and Moon in Virgo bring out the need to get the technical world of communications in order. Don't put off till tomorrow what you can do today; tomorrow's long void-of-course Moon is not likely to be very productive.

Venus square Saturn (occurring Feb. 13 – 20) Venus in Capricorn is square to Saturn in Libra. Romances may appear overly serious and the limitations, or restrictions, may have too high a price. It may seem as if something is always getting in the way of basic pleasures. Perhaps it is best not to get bent out of shape over some people's need to create restrictions in order to protect their own sense of security while love related troubles are being worked out. No matter how much one prioritizes a focus on love, it is still likely to be misinterpreted on some level during Venus square Saturn. Love related dramas may be taken too seriously. Give it your best – keep singing the praises of love and applying the law of attraction, but expect some challenges and high demands for discipline nonetheless. This aspect will reoccur on July 13 and December 18.

Sun enters Pisces (Sun in Pisces: Feb. 18 – March 20) Out of Aquarius we take the extraordinary knowledge and experience of humanity, and in Pisces we purify that experience and seek further insight by getting in touch with divinity. Pisces is the last sign of the zodiac, representing the completion of a cycle. This mutable water sign is adaptive, and Pisceans can absorb all kinds of influence. However, if bogged down by oppressive influences, the Piscean becomes burnt out, oversensitive, and depressed; it's important to find ways to vent heavy feelings of oppression. Pisces people are very psychic as a general rule, and they are also quite artistic and imaginative. The Pisces time of year is a good time to get in touch with personal beliefs and divinity.

February 19th Saturday

Moon in Virgo

	PST	EST
Moon trine Venus goes v/c	5:27 AM	8:27 AM

Birthday: Nicolaus Copernicus 1473

Mood Watch: Early this morning the waning Virgo Moon goes void-of-course as it trines with Venus. Pleasant moods fade into spacey moods. The waning Virgo Moon is often a time when we are especially aware of how clean our surroundings are, and we are especially prone to the need for cleanliness and order. While perfectionism is emphasized, laziness abounds. Void-of-course Virgo Moon is no time for high expectations, but it is also a time when a certain standard of excellence will be demanded. Beware of the tendency for people to be skeptical, suspicious, or nit-picky. Try as you may, you can't please everyone in this highly sensitive atmosphere. Rest and relaxation may be the best recourses for today's activities.

February 20th Sunday

Moon in Virgo / Libra	PST	EST
Moon enters Libra	1:00 AM	4:00 AM
Moon opposite Jupiter	10:23 AM	1:23 PM
Moon square Pluto	12:01 PM	3:01 PM
Mercury conjunct Mars	2:43 PM	5:43 PM
Mercury conjunct Neptune	5:06 PM	8:06 PM
Mars conjunct Neptune	8:17 PM	11:17 PM

Birthday: Kirt Cobain 1967

Mood Watch: The waning Libra Moon emphasizes our need to create harmony and to put a sense of balance into our lives. This is a good time to encourage others, apply good teamwork practices, and to enjoy quality time with friends and loved ones.

Mercury conjunct Mars (occurring Feb. 14 – 23) This conjunction brings the forces of communication (Mercury) together with the forces of action (Mars). It's not a very good time to bluff, especially with regard to technical equipment or scientific experiments while these two planets are in Aquarius. This conjunction brings words and deeds together, and in this case, the greatest action occurs with knowledge and is empowered in the expression of the message. This is an excellent time to get others motivated through speech. It may be a time of angry words being spoken. Some might say the best way to win an argument is to begin by being right; taking this approach now is likely to win you favors but not friendship. Take caution with your words; if they are intended to incite a battle, this is the time to put on your boxing gloves. Note: due to Mercury retrograde (March 30 – April 23), this conjunction will reoccur on April 19 and May 20.

Mercury conjunct Neptune (occurring Feb. 17 – 22) This year's only conjunction of Mercury and Neptune inspires communications on the hypersensitive issues of people's belief systems. Aquarius represents humanity, and Neptune in the late degrees of Aquarius focuses on the essential need for belief in humankind; that is, we must believe in ourselves and our own capabilities in order to survive spiritually. Mercury in Aquarius focuses news, talk, and discussion on human rights issues. Many people, especially Aquarians, are deeply moved to speak about their convictions. This conjunction also presents a good time to learn from the news and talk concerning humanitarian issues and to pray, meditate on, and connect with that higher spirit that dwells within.

Mars conjunct Neptune (occurring Feb. 12 – 24) Mars, the planet of activity and action, is conjunct Neptune, the planet of mysticism and spiritual bounty. This planetary conjunction generally brings action to a fondness for the arts, and magnifies generosity, spiritual activity, and enthusiasm. There is mysticism, romance, and adventure in the air with this conjunction, which will also add a special and very spiritual quality to the activities of late winter. Mars comes on very strong, directing the forces of our actions, while Neptune evokes a deeper, more dramatic spiritual awareness. This is a time to be especially careful not to overindulge in strong beverages, rich fatty foods, drugs, chemicals, anesthetics,

71

etc. It's an important time to ensure one has the proper nutrients. Mars conjunct Neptune can also create busy activity in temples, churches or any kind of spiritual retreat. On the down side, there may be a militant flare of energy brewing in the sanctuaries of holy places. However, on a more positive note, it is an active time for folks on spiritual quests as well as artists, musicians, choreographers and designers. Mars conjunct Neptune in Aquarius activates an openness to rise above mundane concerns with heightened awareness and newly inspired spiritual strength.

February 21st Monday

President's Day, USA (observed)

Moon in Libra	PST	EST	
Moon opposite Mercury	2:09 AM	5:09 AM	
Moon conjunct Saturn	3:36 AM	6:36 AM	
Moon square Venus	9:18 AM	12:18 PM	
Mercury enters Pisces	12:53 PM	3:53 PM	
Moon trine Neptune	11:06 PM	2:06 AM	(Feb 22)
Sun sextile Pluto begins (see February 25)			

Birthday: Anaïs Nin 1903

Mood Watch: The waning Libra Moon puts the focus on our need to feel in accord with the people around us. Early in the day, Moon square Venus challenges our sense of pleasure and esthetics. People may be less inclined to show affection at this time. Libra is the Venus ruled sign emphasizing harmony, and it isn't too long before we work out our incongruities with each other. The Libra Moon reminds us that love conquers all. Later tonight, Moon trine Neptune brings spiritual harmony.

Mercury enters Pisces (Mercury in Pisces: Feb. 21 – March 9) Today Mercury enters Pisces and this brings the emphasis of news, media, and communications on our beliefs, spiritual growth, cultural expression, and our tendencies towards escapism and drug use. Today through March 9, Mercury in Pisces brings out the mystic in all of us and adds quite a bit of color and flair to the imagination in relayed messages. This is also a good time to immerse oneself in creative writing and music or to open up the channels to the spirit world. Listen and learn from the priests, holy teachers, loved ones, and spirit guides of your choosing. Sometimes the voice of sense and reason needs to surrender to the simplicity of just listening in silence.

February 22nd Tuesday

♓

Washington's Birthday (President's Day observed, Feb. 21)

Moon in Libra / Scorpio	PST	EST	
Moon trine Mars goes v/c	12:34 AM	3:34 AM	
Moon enters Scorpio	1:28 AM	4:28 AM	
Moon trine Mercury	3:16 AM	6:16 AM	
Moon trine Sun	7:33 AM	10:33 AM	
Moon sextile Pluto	1:06 PM	4:06 PM	
Mars enters Pisces	5:05 PM	8:05 PM	
Moon opposite Neptune	11:31 PM	2:31 AM	(Feb 23)

Birthday: Sybil Leek 1917

Mood Watch: Sun in Pisces and Moon in Scorpio bring clear perception and put us in touch with our emotions. Waning Scorpio Moon emphasizes the need for release of tension and emotional buildups. This is a good time to work on allowing emotional expression to flow, however harsh it may appear on some levels, and trust that the release will bring a greater sense of healing.

Mars enters Pisces (Mars in Pisces: Feb. 22 – April 1) Mars represents the heated energy in our lives. Force, vitality, energy, and action are influenced by Mars. While Mars traverses Pisces, much activity is taking place with regard to music and the arts, not to mention some heated action concerning the politics of our spiritual and religious beliefs. As Mars crosses over their natal Sun during this time, Pisceans will feel lots of hot and busy energy entering their realm. The nature of Pisces is fluid, passive, and dreamy – this is the spiritual realm of the zodiac. Mars in Pisces opens the gates to active visions and dreams. Intuitive strength is realized. This is a time to activate our creativity, and to work out hot feelings, such as anger, in an artful and healthy manner. Mars is also the famed god of war, reminding us to be especially cautious given the fact that hatred, violence, aggression and strife are often touching on the pulse of our belief structures (Pisces).

February 23rd Wednesday

Moon in Scorpio	PST	EST
Moon sextile Venus	4:10 PM	7:10 PM
Mercury sextile Pluto begins (February 25)		

Birthday: George Frederic Handel 1685

Mood Watch: The Sun and Moon in a water sign often bring wet weather, especially in winter. The waning Scorpio Moon is a good time to purge unnecessary – or false – feelings. Scorpio Moon encourages us to confront important matters with a sense of urgency. Sometimes we don't know how we feel about others until we test them. As soon as we have tested them, we will discover that our keen observations reveal a lot, but in the end, the heart knows what the mind doesn't notice. Later on, positive and optimistic moods are generated through Moon sextile Venus. Kind and loving feelings bring healing.

February 24th Thursday

LAST QUARTER MOON in SAGITTARIUS

Moon in Scorpio / Sagittarius	PST	EST
Moon square Neptune	2:22 AM	5:22 AM
Moon trine Uranus goes v/c	3:14 AM	6:14 AM
Moon enters Sagittarius	4:45 AM	7:45 AM
Moon square Mars	6:57 AM	9:57 AM
Moon opposite Uranus	7:25 AM	10:25 AM
Moon square Mercury	2:45 PM	5:45 PM
Moon square Sun	3:26 PM	6:26 PM
Moon trine Jupiter	4:58 PM	7:58 PM

Birthday: Billy Zane 1966

Mood Watch: Our moods and attitudes may tend to lash out in the early part of the morning. This is brought on by the void-of-course Scorpio Moon, coupled with the fact that the Moon squares with Mars a little later. The **Last Quarter Moon in Sagittarius** (Moon square Sun) is a good time to internalize your new wishes and thoughts about the upcoming spring season. The best course of action centers on healing disruptive feelings and makes a sporting effort to let go of unsatisfactory habits. The lunar aspects are somewhat challenging today, but fortunately, the Sagittarius Moon keeps us vigilant to find the silver lining. In general, the Sagittarius Moon focuses our attention on such things as fitness, philosophy and travel. Despite whatever hardships have soiled our travels, once we have cleared the path for our dreams to unfold, the Sagittarius Moon energies will inspire us to take bold and creative steps towards making life brighter and more positive. This is the time to broaden the mind and allow yourself to go further than anticipated in realizing your vision for the future.

February 25th Friday

Moon in Sagittarius	PST	EST
Sun conjunct Mercury	12:47 AM	3:47 AM
Mercury sextile Pluto	9:06 AM	12:06 PM
Moon sextile Saturn	10:19 AM	1:19 PM
Jupiter square Pluto	12:40 PM	3:40 PM
Sun sextile Pluto	4:17 PM	7:17 PM
Venus sextile Uranus begins (see March 1)		

Birthday: Zeppo Marx 1901

Mood Watch: In the face of adversities or trials, the spirit of the Sagittarius Moon encourages us to look beyond what's in front of us. The Sun is in Pisces and the Moon is in Sagittarius, and both of these signs are mutable, focusing our energies on completion, adaptability, and change. Sagittarius Moon brings the energy and vitality that make room for change to occur in our hearts.

Sun conjunct Mercury (occurring Feb. 17 – 28) This conjunction will occur half a dozen times this year – it is a common occurrence due to the closeness

74

of Mercury to the Sun. It will create a much more thoughtful, communicative, and expressive year ahead for Aquarius and Pisces people celebrating birthdays from February 17 – 28. This is your time (birthday folks) to record ideas, relay important messages, and pay close attention to your imaginative thoughts as they are touched by Mercury, creating the urge to speak and be heard. Birthday folks, your thoughts will reveal a great deal about who you are, now and in the year to come.

Mercury sextile Pluto (occurring Feb. 23 – 26) Communications and discussions are facilitated, with an opportunity to get your message across in negotiations with those in positions of power. Mercury is now in Pisces, ensuring the strong belief behind our topics of communication, while Pluto in Capricorn is forcing us to acknowledge our resources and to use them wisely. Vital information regarding treatments for illness or disease may frequent the news, and news in general may well have some critical impact. This is a good time to reach out to those of another generation and make an attempt to communicate something essential. This aspect will reoccur on October 16.

Sun sextile Pluto (occurring Feb. 21 – 27) Sun in Pisces sextile Pluto in Capricorn brings opportunities that appear both vast and demanding to Pisces born people celebrating birthdays February 21 – 27. These birthday people are experiencing the sextile aspect of their natal sun to Pluto, giving them opportunities to take charge, to step into positions of power, and to accept and embrace permanent change in their lives. These are powerful transformations which provide opportunities to embody what has been learned from the personal trials of the past. Conquer, master Pisceans! Persist with diligence to resolve the conflicts of your life with self-respect and assurance. Your time to triumph is always available when your will to achieve is balanced by knowledge and hard work. This holds true for all signs of the zodiac. This aspect will reoccur on October 28, affecting some of the Scorpio born folks of that time.

Jupiter square Pluto (occurring Jan. 22 - March 11) The enterprising Jupiter in Aries is now square to the power mongering Pluto in Capricorn. Jupiter represents expansion, prosperity, and social advancement – to name a few – while Pluto represents transformation, power, and fate. This aspect is likely to bring an economic shift that, for some, may seem rather hellish. This has already proved to be the case since we began to feel a taste of this aspect from May 28 to September 10, 2010 when it last occurred. Strong power plays are at work on the international market at this time. Jupiter square Pluto brings the difficulty of facing up to the economic haunts and crises of previous generations and corporate actions. The BP oil spill crisis may well have been influenced by this aspect, as it has caused quite a stir in the economic and environmental quality of North American life. There are likely to be struggles regarding inheritance. Jupiter in Aries square Pluto in Capricorn ensures the demand for new enterprises will be in conflict with institutional powers. Beware of the potential for large scale deception in business.

Once again, the powers that be are likely to exhibit too much greed. Through this aspect, there will probably be many sacrifices, and there will be many power struggles over the fortunes that are made. Avoid heavy gambling, new credit lines, risky and hasty expenditures, and expect a few rounds of difficult transformation with regard to economics over this tricky period of Jupiter square Pluto. There is a great effort going on between generations and various power structures to secure a prosperous future.

February 26th Saturday

Moon in Sagittarius / Capricorn	PST	EST
Moon sextile Neptune	9:09 AM	12:09 PM
Moon square Uranus goes v/c	10:08 AM	1:08 PM
Moon enters Capricorn	11:31 AM	2:31 PM
Moon sextile Mars	5:30 PM	8:30 PM
Mars sextile Pluto begins (see March 3)		

Birthday: William "Buffalo Bill" Cody 1846

Mood Watch: There may be a little bit of confusion, or lack of direction, as the waning Sagittarius Moon goes void-of-course. This soon passes, and as the Moon enters Capricorn, a much more determined and down-to-earth set of moods begin to surface. Capricorn Moon brings out a serious effort to tackle big jobs. Waning Capricorn Moon is the time when we tend to set strong feelings aside, to subdue emotional tides with sober intent. Many folks may seem to be intolerant of emotional weakness. This is a time when we commonly deal with our problems through stalwart labor and persistent effort.

February 27th Sunday

Moon in Capricorn	PST	EST
Moon conjunct Pluto	12:54 AM	3:54 AM
Moon square Jupiter	1:30 AM	4:30 AM
Moon sextile Sun	3:40 AM	6:40 AM
Moon sextile Mercury	7:47 AM	10:47 AM
Moon square Saturn	6:35 PM	9:35 PM

Birthday: Chelsea Clinton 1980

Mood Watch: Today's sun in Pisces, coupled with the waning Moon in Capricorn, brings clarity and adaptability to the mood. This is the time to work on completion, to prepare for (or clean up after) late winter storms. There is a need today to get things done, to face up to unfinished business and to handle whatever comes along with strict effort. This evening's Moon square Saturn may bring a demanding quality of mood, as there tends to be a struggle to get through serious or arduous conditions. Capricorn gives us what it takes to push past our limitations.

February 28th Monday

Moon in Capricorn / Aquarius	PST	EST	
Moon conjunct Venus	6:57 PM	9:57 PM	
Moon sextile Uranus goes v/c	8:03 PM	11:03 PM	
Moon enters Aquarius	9:14 PM	12:14 AM	(Mar 1)

Birthday: Rae Dawn Chong 1961

Mood Watch: The end of the month brings a time of completion and deadlines. Today's Capricorn Moon brings a serious intent to complete projects and to prepare for the transition of the lively days of March. Waning Capricorn Moon produces some very focused and stern qualities of mood, which are easily satiated with the accomplishment of tasks. This evening's Moon conjunct Venus focuses our attention on the value of what we have. A little later, Moon sextile Uranus brings the void-of-course Moon for an hour or so, and at this point, a little chaos breaks up the energy with interesting distractions. As the Moon enters Aquarius, we are drawn to the things that fascinate and interest us, especially the thought provoking interests that excite our curiosity.

March 1st Tuesday

Moon in Aquarius	PST	EST
Venus sextile Uranus	6:49 AM	9:49 AM
Moon sextile Jupiter	12:53 PM	3:53 PM
Venus enters Aquarius	6:38 PM	9:38 PM

Birthday: Glen Miller 1904

Mood Watch: The darkness of this waning winter Moon brings internal reflection, and now is certainly a time to preserve our energies. The need for preparation calls to us. March has arrived and the days will get lighter at a steady pace. Aquarius Moon tunes us into the experiences of those around us, and the ways we can enhance our own experience through observing them. This may be an excellent time for researchers, and for scientific studies to lead to important discoveries and lessons.

Venus sextile Uranus (occurring Feb. 25 – March 3) Venus in Capricorn is sextile to Uranus in Pisces. Radically serious types of love and aesthetics can be very uplifting at this time, particularly while extreme types of tests are occurring and being stretched beyond the limits in love related matters. Eccentric love may erupt with this aspect. This is the time to work on pent up frustrations with loved ones and to reconcile differences by loving and accepting variation, giving freedom and slack to our loved ones. This aspect will reoccur on June 12 and December 20.

Venus enters Aquarius (Venus in Aquarius: March 1 – 26) Venus in Aquarius creates a fondness for invention, eccentric pleasures, and social life. It puts the focus of attraction and adoration on illuminating types of knowledge and on brilliant humanitarian causes and exploits. There is an especially strong attraction to invention – all types of invention – and to new technologies. It is likely to be a beneficial time for the love life of Aquarius people, whose affections and aesthetic pleasures can be enhanced now. By contrast, Scorpio and Taurus people may notice that love related focuses are causing tension in their personal lives – too many complex issues. Leo people, as a general rule, can never get enough love and affection, and they may be particularly aware of their own personal needs for love and beauty while Venus is opposing their natal Sun. Venus in Aquarius is a prime time to perfect and enhance our love of humanity, and to break down the barriers of useless and destructive prejudice and stereotyping.

March 2nd Wednesday

Moon in Aquarius	**PST**	**EST**
Moon trine Saturn	5:10 AM	8:10 AM

Birthday: Lou Reed 1944

Mood Watch: The only aspect of the day, Moon trine Saturn, kicks off the day with clarity and purpose. Moon in Aquarius affects our moods with a sense of humanitarian openness, while a scientific sense of proceeding with caution reminds us to apply our knowledge in all dealings with others. This is a good time to try experimenting with one's way of life, and to apply new methods of living more boldly and freely. With the sun in Pisces, the characteristic dreamy quality of life, coupled with the Moon in Aquarius, makes for a very imaginative and interesting time.

March 3rd Thursday

Moon in Aquarius / Pisces	**PST**	**EST**	
Moon conjunct Neptune goes v/c	6:36 AM	9:36 AM	
Moon enters Pisces	8:46 AM	11:46 AM	
Mars sextile Pluto	6:52 PM	9:52 PM	
Moon sextile Pluto	11:09 PM	2:09 AM	(Mar 4)
Moon conjunct Mars	11:27 PM	2:27 AM	(Mar 4)

Birthday: Alexander Graham Bell 1847

Mood Watch: This morning the Aquarius Moon goes void-of-course for a couple of hours. This is classically a time when technology goes haywire and complexities take awhile to work out. As the Moon enters Pisces, it casts a spell of frequent daydreaming and long moments of internal reflection. Tendencies towards escapism may be strong. As we approach tomorrow's New Moon in Pisces, internal reflection brings rebirth.

Mars sextile Pluto (occurring Feb. 26 – March 6) Mars, the planet of action, is in a favorable position to Pluto, the planet of the generations. Mars in Pisces sextile to Pluto in Capricorn brings the opportunity for adaptable and swift action. This is a superb time to take up activities with people of a different culture, or with someone who is of a different level of maturity or experience. This is also potentially a good time to reconcile differences. Those who are not in accordance with others at this time are likely to stand out – quite obviously. This may be a beneficial aspect for successfully recuperating from an illness. Mars represents the masculine push of our personal lives, the area where we activate our will, strength, and vitality; this brings opportunity, optimism, and the added boost to face otherwise tense situations and predicaments. The activities of Mars sextile Pluto will teach us about hardships and what we can learn from other generations.

March 4th Friday

NEW MOON in PISCES	PST	EST
Moon conjunct Sun	12:45 PM	3:45 PM

Birthday: Miriam Makeba 1932

Mood Watch: The **New Moon in Pisces** (Moon conjunct Sun) focuses our attention on the need to get in touch with our own beliefs, and to inspire those beliefs with devotion and renewed faith. Tendencies towards escapism may be strong today, particularly for those who are unwilling to let go of the past. The New Moon in Pisces inspires a new outlook on our moods. This is a time of emotional as well as spiritual purging. The spirit of what is now emerging and showing through our moods is a sense of renewed faith in something divine and omnipotent. The world of magic exists in the melding mutable water of the Piscean expression.

March 5th Saturday

Moon in Pisces / Aries	PST	EST	
Moon conjunct Mercury	4:55 AM	7:55 AM	
Moon conjunct Uranus goes v/c	8:33 PM	11:33 PM	
Moon enters Aries	9:13 PM	12:13 AM	(Mar 6)
Venus sextile Jupiter begins (see March 10)			

Birthday: Andy Gibb 1958

Mood Watch: Ever so new is the light of the waxing Pisces Moon. Crisp new psychic and intuitive inclinations lead to a spark of inspiration that carries us through the dwindling days of winter towards the renewed light of Spring Equinox, set to occur March 20. Let the intuitive and creative process begin! Let the spirit of renewed faith cleanse our beliefs. This is the time to allow for new inspiration to come through in such Piscean kinds of things as art, music, poetic thought and prose, as well as spiritual reverie and meditation.

March 6th Sunday

Moon in Aries	PST	EST
Moon sextile Venus	8:08 AM	11:08 AM
Moon square Pluto	11:49 AM	2:49 PM
Moon conjunct Jupiter	3:42 PM	6:42 PM
Mercury conjunct Uranus begins (see March 9)		

Birthday: Elizabeth Barrett Browning 1806

Mood Watch: It's March; the Moon is waxing in Aries. We're now counting down to the end of winter season and a restless fervor captures our moods. Aries Moon activity breaks the sleepy winter lull with a sudden propensity to cut through the grey areas of life. As a general rule there is very little tolerance for vagueness or uncertainty going around. To be uncertain is to get pushed aside or perceived as being unworthy by the public. Stand up or stand out today, otherwise you might be overlooked. Unless, of course, you wish to lay low, at which point you're bound to be less noticeable.

March 7th Monday

Moon in Aries	PST	EST
Moon opposite Saturn	5:20 AM	8:20 AM

Birthday: Maurice Ravel 1875

Mood Watch: Early this morning, Moon opposite Saturn alerts us to the necessity to get out into the world and get things done. The newly waxing Aries Moon is encouraging us to take the initiative to do things rather than put them off. This is a good time to start projects and to spread some enthusiasm. Aries says, "I am," and this represents the personal inclination to act on the things that will enhance a sense of personal welfare and triumph.

March 8th Tuesday

Moon in Aries / Taurus	PST	EST
Moon sextile Neptune goes v/c	8:03 AM	11:03 AM
Moon enters Taurus	9:51 AM	12:51 PM

Birthday: Mickey Dolenz 1945

Mood Watch: The Aries Moon goes void-of-course this morning, which may bring a bit of a rough start for some folks as there will be a tendency towards impatience or intolerance. However, the Taurus Moon soon turns around the false starts of the day. Waxing Moon in Taurus brings pleasure seeking moods. Many folks will be focused on their finances and on practicalities. Our moods enter into the need for beauty and – just as important – the need for comfort, too. This is a good time to tackle physical projects and to begin spring cleaning.

March 9th Wednesday

Moon in Taurus	PST	EST
Moon trine Pluto	12:26 AM	3:26 AM
Moon square Venus	3:22 AM	6:22 AM
Mercury conjunct Uranus	8:05 AM	11:05 AM
Moon sextile Mars	9:05 AM	12:05 PM
Mercury enters Aries	9:47 AM	12:47 PM
Jupiter opposite Saturn begins (see March 28)		
Venus trine Saturn begins (see March 14)		

Birthday: Bobby Fisher 1943

Mood Watch: The newly waxing Moon in Taurus fixes our moods on the need to stay grounded and practical. Many of us will have our eyes set on new things we need or want to have in our life. For that very reason, this is an excellent day to indulge in some early spring cleaning. This is a good time to seek beautiful and pleasurable things that will enhance our experience of life. Now is the time to look for something that will get us in the mood for spring.

Mercury conjunct Uranus (occurring March 6 – 11) Mercury and Uranus are conjunct in Pisces, giving birth to radical, bright, inspired and intuitive ideas. This may raise some very interesting and unusual questions about what we choose to believe in. Consciousness raising talk is prevalent. Mercury conjunct Uranus magnifies the volume of shocking or question-raising news, and stirs the minds and mouths of rebels and nonconformists who are inspired to speak out. Everyone is crying for some kind of freedom! This is the only time this year Mercury and Uranus will be conjunct.

Mercury enters Aries (Mercury in Aries: March 9 – May 15) Mercury now enters Aries, bringing a focus of communications on selfhood, initiation, new projects, and new ways of seeing and experiencing life. We are all perpetually in the process of being initiated into some aspect of selfhood, particularly given that we are constantly learning, acquiring new skills, growing and aging. Mercury in Aries brings some lively heat to our communications and discussions. Mercury is the messenger, activating information, and Aries is the warrior and the force of nature that takes on life with fearless vigor and aggression. Communications possess a quality of command and a pioneering spirit. Now through May 15, while Mercury is in Aries, talk, news and discussions will be actively focused on the challenging and demanding enterprises and battles that await us.

March 10ᵗʰ Thursday

Moon in Taurus / Gemini	PST	EST	
Moon sextile Sun	12:42 AM	3:42 AM	
Venus sextile Jupiter	4:25 AM	7:25 AM	
Moon square Neptune	7:56 PM	10:56 PM	
Moon sextile Uranus goes v/c	9:25 PM	12:25 AM	(Mar 11)
Moon enters Gemini	9:31 PM	12:31 AM	(Mar 11)
Mercury square Pluto begins (see March 13)			

Birthday: Sharon Stone 1958

Mood Watch: While many desire comfort and practicality with the Taurus Moon, practical needs require effort. There is a determined, almost stubborn, effort on the part of many folks to get to the place of comfort and to feel a sense of security. Meanwhile, our finances demand attention, and so does our physical environment. Count on Taurus Moon to get us in the mood to address the physical issues in our life. Today is as good a time as any to beautify and simplify the value of our surroundings. Tonight's void-of-course Moon brings the potential for a great deal of laziness, and there may be a tendency for things to be misplaced. After the hard drive to achieve results, tonight would be a good time to kick back and relax.

Venus sextile Jupiter (occurring March 5 – 12)Venus is in Aquarius, the place of science, politics, and unusual love play. Jupiter is in Aries, bringing a direct, resourceful and candid outreach for fulfillment and a joyful effort towards getting in touch with the things we love. Humanitarian – as well as socially active – attractions and pleasures (Venus in Aquarius) lead us to possible opportunities in new enterprises, mechanical engineering, psychology, and professional sportsmanship (Jupiter in Aries). This is an excellent time to shower loved ones with gifts and compliments in a way that uplifts their spirits. This is the time to allow expansion to occur in love matters, and to take the next step towards enlivening and enhancing the beauty of life. A greater opportunity for increasing skills or augmenting your livelihood is available, especially if your focus remains on doing what you love most. This aspect will reoccur on July 8.

March 11ᵗʰ Friday

Moon in Gemini	PST	EST	
Moon sextile Mercury	3:55 AM	6:55 AM	
URANUS ENTERS ARIES	4:49 PM	7:49 PM	
Moon sextile Jupiter	5:30 PM	8:30 PM	
Moon trine Venus	8:38 PM	11:38 PM	
Moon square Mars	11:50 PM	2:50 AM	(Mar 12)
Mercury conjunct Jupiter begins (see March 15)			

Birthday: Lawrence Welk 1903

Mood Watch: Gemini Moon often focuses our attention on those areas of life where we have mixed feelings and there is a tendency to mull things over that have been on our minds. This evening's Moon sextile Jupiter is a good time to openly seek opportunities, particularly in light of Uranus now entering Aries (see below). Moon trine Venus is a great time to tune in with loved ones. Later, Moon square Mars may bring some hot tempered moods, and since it's late enough, a good night's sleep may be the best way to combat the anxiety of this time.

URANUS ENTERS ARIES (Uranus in Aries: March 11, 2011 – May 15, 2018) Last year, for two and a half months (May 27 – Aug. 13, 2010), we observed the initial entry of Uranus into the cardinal fire sign, Aries. On August 13, 2010 the retrograde Uranus reentered the tail end of Pisces, and today it completes its full cycle in Pisces which began in March, 2003.

This icy planet with its frozen gases is one of the three outer planets, and it has come to be associated by astrologers as the planet of insurrection. Radical and explosive change is associated with Uranus' influence. Its orbit around the Sun takes 84 years to complete, which gives Uranus an average of seven years through each sign of the zodiac.

ASTROLOGICAL HISTORY OF URANUS

Radical change is the status quo of Uranus' expression in our world. From 1988 – 1996 Uranus was in Capricorn, shaking up the operations and standards of the old, stoic institutions. From this we got strip malls and chain stores galore. Then from 1996 – 2003 Uranus graced the skies in Aquarius, the sign it rules, as radical change took place in humanitarian issues and in the world of invention and

82

technology. The internet, cell phones and compact discs took the spotlight with massive production, and competition soared in the technology world.

Out of the creation of those strip malls and chain stores came the need to fill them up with innovative electronic gadgetry and tools for humanity. Technology has been mass produced to the point of inundating the market. Radical change has come in the Aquarian areas of biological technology, scientific discoveries, biological warfare issues, and the mass marketing of pharmaceuticals.

Uranus in Pisces has revealed much about our need to change and evolve. As production dropped off, companies downsized, and the recession moved in; the radical increase of a hunger for change has left us with technological chaos and far-reaching market fluctuations.

Uranus in Pisces has been testing our faith and our beliefs. It has ripped apart our false dreams and nonconstructive patterns. All kinds of beliefs are tested: beliefs in science, in the existence of global warming, in the world's complex religious concepts, in our government, in our own capacities as an influence on the world, and the overall conduct of the world at large. The explosive and drastic energies of Uranus now move from the last sign of the zodiac, Pisces, into the initiator of new causes and new exploits – the pioneer's territory, Aries, the first sign of the zodiac.

URANUS IN ARIES

Uranus in Aries marks an era of new enterprise. If Uranus had a motto for this transition it would be, "out with the old and in with the new." This will mark a new era of energy and power systems. It will be a whole new era for robotics, engineering, digital technology, and international corporate business. Many new technologies will involve the necessity to use explosives, as Uranus is famous for blowing things up in general, and Aries will lend the pioneering spirit to process technological breakthroughs. There will be new policies set for world economy, global warming, and international commerce.

Uranus is the higher octave of the god of war, Mars, and Aries is ruled by Mars. Uranus in Aries will be creating the need for explosive kinds of change in such Aries-like things as war tactics and war technology. Could this be the time for martial law? Uranus in Aries affects radical change in such fields as psychology, psychiatric studies, surgical procedures and techniques, the metallurgic sciences, exploration, artificial entities (robotics), engineering, firefighting, arms manufacturing, trade union policies, mechanical sciences, dentistry, and professional sportsmanship. Over the course of the next seven to eight years, we can expect to see the newest and latest versions of the extraordinary things to come in the 21st century.

Aries represents the exploration of new territory and Uranus represents radical breakthroughs in humankind. We might expect to see some unprecedented types of global change that will radically alter the operations of world politics. Since Uranus takes a long time to travel through a sign, we can expect to see some radical events that will alter our overall outlook on the development of the future. However, not all of these events will be unwelcome.

Uranus's traverses through the zodiac represent mankind's urges to take the big steps towards evolution. These changes are not easy to endure, but they do eventually allow us to overcome our ignorance and our prejudices. The biggest thing we can expect to notice is the shape of free enterprise. There will be a new world order of enterprises with Uranus in Aries. Since Aries is associated with competition and leadership, radical change of a competitive and authoritative nature can be expected.

HISTORY REPEATS

We might anticipate some hardships in the form of mass riots and protests, resembling the time of the late 1960s, when Uranus was in Libra, the polarized opposite of Aries. We might also expect some hardships that resemble the hard economic times of 1926 into the early 1930s when Uranus traveled through Aries in the 20th century. The Uranus square Pluto aspect was a reality at that time also. Uranus in Aries was square to Pluto in Cancer (1933 to 1934), a time of financial hardship for many people, and a time when there was a pressing need to regenerate the morale and livelihood of so many hard hit Americans. We are bound to repeat history, but not in the same way as we did in the 1930s. This transformation requires a systems overhaul to suit the temperament of the future, and that is bound to bring the classic Uranus-like effects of chaos and disorder long before the newness of Aries concepts can take hold as workable and useful global systems.

Quite simply, Uranus represents the need for freedom and revolution, without which we would not evolve. Uranus clears away the obstacles that prevent us from evolving, while Pluto, the planet of the generations, sees us through our various stages of consciousness as the generations of humankind. We must learn the Tao of chaos and find a way to get used to the disarray of our future pandemonium. From this revolutionary process comes the freedom of movement that allows us to regenerate brilliantly. Uranus rules Aquarius and this is the Age of Aquarius. The lessons of this planet may seem volatile, but without it we would stagnate to the point of extinction.

March 12th Saturday
FIRST QUARTER MOON in GEMINI

	PST	EST
Moon trine Saturn	3:29 AM	6:29 AM
Moon square Sun	3:44 PM	6:44 PM

Birthday: Jack Kerouac 1922

Mood Watch: The **First Quarter Moon in Gemini** (Moon square Sun) brings the necessity for our moods to be changeable and adaptable. Our moods are easily affected by the busy buzz of intellectual focuses and pursuits. The emphasis of covering many details at once becomes the primary objective, but not necessarily the answer to our insatiable curiosity. The act of processing information becomes essential. Do not let gossip and idle chatter be the cause of disruption in your day – thoughtlessness is also a symptom of the Gemini Moon atmosphere. The Gemini Moon puts us in touch with how we feel about our thoughts. If you don't like how you feel about your thoughts, endeavor to alter your way of thinking. Omit thoughts which attempt to defeat your sense of purpose; encourage thoughts that uplift and inspire your spirit. Be careful not to overdo the caffeine.

March 13th Sunday

DAYLIGHT SAVING TIME BEGINS

Turn clocks ahead one hour at 2:00 a.m.

Moon in Gemini / Cancer	PDT	EDT	
Moon trine Neptune goes v/c	6:10 AM	9:10 AM	
Moon enters Cancer	7:29 AM	10:29 AM	
Moon square Uranus	7:39 AM	10:39 AM	
Mercury square Pluto	10:31 AM	1:31 PM	
Moon opposite Pluto	8:49 PM	11:49 PM	
Moon square Mercury	10:22 PM	1:22 AM	(Mar 14)

Birthday: Mircea Eliade 1907

Mood Watch: For awhile this morning the Gemini Moon goes void-of-course which may make it confusing to try to keep track of a number of details. The main thing we need to remember is that the North American time has been changed and although we lose an hour, we gain some extra evening light. As the Moon enters Cancer, a shift of moods allows us to adjust to the changes. The Sun and Moon are in water signs, commonly bringing wet weather throughout most of North America. Cancer Moon keeps our moods focused on personal comfort zones, the nurturing spirit of motherly energies, and on the shifts taking place on the emotional level.

Mercury square Pluto (occurring March 10 – 15) Mercury in Aries is square to Pluto in Capricorn. Selfishness will make it difficult to communicate with those of another generation. This is a particularly difficult time to deal with burdensome issues and discuss them in a manner that relieves tension. Mercury square Pluto often brings harsh and sometimes fatal news. Talk revolves around the corruption of superpowers and the setbacks caused by this corruption. This may be an especially difficult time to discuss matters involving permanent change. This aspect will begin to reoccur as a non-exact aspect from April 19 to 21 (see April 20) but it will not reach a full peak due to Mercury's next retrograde period (March 30 – April 23). It will also repeat, for the last time this year, on September 28.

March 14th Monday

Moon in Cancer	PDT	EDT
Moon square Jupiter	3:12 AM	6:12 AM
Moon square Saturn	11:14 AM	2:14 PM
Moon trine Mars	11:31 AM	2:31 PM
Venus trine Saturn	6:34 PM	9:34 PM
Sun conjunct Uranus begins (see March 21)		
Mercury-opposite-Saturn-non-exact begins (see March 18)		

Birthday: Michael Caine 1933

Mood Watch: Cancer Moon Monday can be most moody, particularly as the Moon squares to Jupiter and Saturn. Fortunately, Moon trine Mars brings some positive pep to our step. Throughout the day, the waxing Moon in Cancer brings out our maternal instincts, and focuses our moods and feelings on the desire to nurture emotional needs.

Venus trine Saturn (occurring March 9 – 17) Venus in Aquarius trine Saturn in Libra brings very attractive humanitarian efforts to stabilize our relationships through balanced and responsible action. Here is where we easily devote ourselves to the thing(s) that attract us most, but with Venus in Aquarius, devotion alone is not enough – intelligence is required. While Saturn is in Libra, a commitment to trustworthiness, compromise, and teamwork becomes equally important. Where love and attraction have withstood the test of time, this aspect is bound to remind us of who – and what – matters most. Venus trine Saturn often brings the gift of responsive and enduring love. This aspect may assist in bringing some peace to the structure or the closure of a love relationship. This is good time to initiate or enhance a love vow or oath, and to apply the values of devotion and responsive caring intelligently. Love is a gift and a responsibility. Use this time affectionately and wisely; it often makes an impression. This aspect will reoccur on June 17.

March 15th Tuesday

Moon in Cancer / Leo	PDT	EDT
Moon trine Sun goes v/c	3:05 AM	6:05 AM
Moon enters Leo	12:32 PM	3:32 PM
Moon trine Uranus	12:54 PM	3:54 PM
Mercury conjunct Jupiter	6:26 PM	9:26 PM

Birthday: Sly Stone 1944

Mood Watch: Moon in Cancer is a typical time of moodiness, particularly as the Moon goes void-of-course and remains this way all morning and into the afternoon. A warm bubble bath, cosmetic pampering, massage, and delicious nourishing foods are just some of the many delightful ways to soothe one's morning ills. This afternoon, the Leo Moon puts a much more cheerful glow on the quality of our moods; sit back, take it easy, and enjoy some good clean fun to help ease the emotional flow. Moon trine Uranus kicks up our rebellious and adventurous heels. The Leo Moon focuses our attention on family, friends, and the need for affection.

Mercury conjunct Jupiter (occurring March 11 – 18) Mercury and Jupiter are conjunct in Aries, and this brings an excellent time to explore a pioneering spirit. News and discussions (Mercury) revolve around our joys, our prosperity, and our wealth (Jupiter) – particularly relating to fulfilling our desires and abiding by our deep passions in life. This aspect creates expansive talk which spreads quickly with news about the economic state of affairs. Thoughts and information (Mercury) with regard to a prosperous and visionary breakthrough (Jupiter) will be highlighted. It's a great time to boost the morale of others by complimenting them on their skills. Due to Mercury's next retrograde cycle (March 30 – April

23), this conjunction of Mercury and Jupiter will repeat two more times, on April 11 and May 11.

March 16ᵗʰ Wednesday

Moon in Leo	**PDT**	**EDT**
Moon trine Jupiter	7:40 AM	10:40 AM
Moon trine Mercury	9:04 AM	12:04 PM
Moon sextile Saturn	2:00 PM	5:00 PM
Moon opposite Venus goes v/c	6:05 PM	9:05 PM

Birthday: Bernardo Bertolucci 1940

Mood Watch: The lunar aspects are most inviting today, starting off with Moon trine Jupiter and then Mercury. This is a good time to focus on what makes us happy and to communicate with others. This afternoon's Moon sextile Saturn brings an agreeable work pace and it's also an excellent time to get organized or to finish up, as well as to begin, personal projects. The waxing Leo Moon puts us in touch with personal and family related needs and desires. Tonight's Moon opposite Venus could be a passionate time. The Moon will be void-of-course all evening, and this is classically a very lazy time – it's not a good time to hold expectations of others.

March 17ᵗʰ Thursday

Saint Patrick's Day

Moon in Leo / Virgo	**PDT**	**EDT**
Moon enters Virgo	1:53 PM	4:53 PM

Birthday: Nat King Cole 1919

"I showed my appreciation of my native land in the usual Irish way by getting out of it as soon as I possibly could." - George Bernard Shaw (1856 – 1950)

Mood Watch: The day may have a slow start due to the fact that the void-of-course Leo Moon brings a lazy time when our less ambitious qualities will tend to surface. Ego related problems or issues of self-confidence may be the cause of some hesitation, or reluctance, to do much this morning. This afternoon, as the Moon enters Virgo, our moods may appear somewhat reserved. Except for the completely unabashed Irish patrons of Saint Patrick's Day activities, many folks may seem rather shy or retiring. Virgo Moon brings out the skeptic in all of us, but that won't stop a proud Irishman from standing out in the crowd. This is the day when Patrick was tricked into thinking he drove the "snakes" out of Ireland. Those snakes were actually Druids, a breed of solar rites practitioners, whose ideas and activities are alive and well throughout the world today. Some folks affectionately call this day, "All Snakes Day."

March 18th Friday

Moon in Virgo	PDT	EDT
Moon trine Pluto	1:36 AM	4:36 AM
Moon opposite Neptune	3:56 AM	6:56 AM
Moon opposite Mars	7:50 PM	10:50 PM
Mercury-opposite-Saturn-non-exact (see below)		

Birthday: Manly Palmer Hall 1901

Mood Watch: The Full Moon Eve has arrived. The scrutinizing qualities of the Virgo Moon atmosphere will direct us toward a more compelling need to organize, purify, and apply some cleanliness to our existence. Efficiency, thoroughness, and the need for communication are the keys to this lunar energy. Be aware of the tendency towards doubtfulness and skepticism.

Mercury-opposite-Saturn-non-exact (occurring March 14 – 20) Today is as close as we come – within a one degree orb – of Mercury reaching a full opposition to Saturn. Today Mercury is in Aries and Saturn is in Libra. This aspect brings a very strong awareness of the need to speak out on serious and important subjects. News, talk, discussions and media tend to revolve around matters of closure, deaths, endings, and the establishment of control. There may be an overwhelming tone of command or restriction in some of the more serious subjects being communicated. While Mercury opposes Saturn, be careful where you choose to draw the lines. Mercury is in Aries, where articulate precision is succinct, forthright, and uninhibited. Saturn is in Libra, where it emphasizes the perimeters and security of our relationships and other such Libra-like issues as the need to create balance and diplomacy in all serious dealings. We may be especially aware of the delicate subject of how rules and laws are affecting our wellbeing. This non-aspect will come much closer to occurring again on April 23.

March 19th Saturday

FULL MOON in VIRGO	PDT	EDT
Moon in Virgo / Libra		
Moon opposite Sun goes v/c	11:10 AM	2:10 PM
Moon enters Libra	1:03 PM	4:03 PM
Moon opposite Uranus	1:44 PM	4:44 PM

Birthday: Glen Close 1947

Mood Watch: The **Full Moon in Virgo** (Moon opposite Sun), which reaches its peak this morning, reminds us of the need to organize, analyze, and constructively criticize our health and cleanliness practices. Virgo also puts the focus on organization, filing, accounting, preparing taxes, and handling all of life's mundane necessities. Virgo Moon energy purges and purifies our surroundings with sound resourcefulness and simple logic. Virgo rules the intestines of the body and represents the process of elimination. Now is an excellent time to focus on eliminating toxins and purifying the body. This is also a good time to purge the useless, destructive, or outmoded habits of our life. Celebrate your existing health, and do something good for your body on this Full Virgo Moon.

ARIES

Key Phrase: "I AM"

Cardinal Fire Sign

Ruling Planet: Mars

Symbol: The Ram

March 20th through April 20th

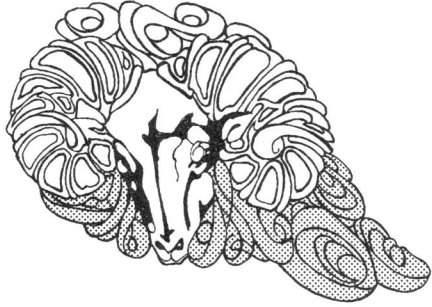

March 20th Sunday

Vernal Equinox

Moon in Libra	PDT	EDT
Moon square Pluto	12:36 AM	3:36 AM
Moon opposite Jupiter	8:22 AM	11:22 AM
Moon conjunct Saturn	12:27 PM	3:27 PM
Sun enters Aries	4:20 PM	7:20 PM
Moon opposite Mercury	5:46 PM	8:46 PM

Birthday: Spike Lee 1957

Mood Watch: The effects of a post-full Virgo Moon still ring with a buzz, and with the Moon now in Libra, we act with a great deal more subtlety and poise. There may be some resistance this morning with Moon opposite Jupiter reminding us how expensive life has become. Libra Moon balances our doubting insecurities with the need to apply teamwork and a bit more of a caring attitude. Moon conjunct Saturn brings serious and focused moods, which are handy moods to have wherever there's the cooperative spirit of Libra Moon. Later, Moon opposite Mercury makes us acutely aware of the need to communicate and think matters through. Spring season brings a lot to think about.

Sun enters Aries (Sun in Aries: March 20 – April 20) Today, the event classically called **Vernal Equinox**, also known as Spring Equinox, marks the start of a new season and the beginning of the zodiac. This is the time when the daylight hours are equal in length to the hours of the night. Spring arrives when the earth is tilted so the Sun is directly over the equator. In the northern parts of the world, the first day of spring is on or about March 20. In the northern hemisphere we are on the side of the Equinox that returns toward the light, as opposed to Autumnal Equinox when the Sun enters Libra, the opposite of Aries. With Daylight Savings Time already underway since March 13, we now celebrate the continued lengthening of the days.

The Sun in Aries inspires courageous and bold new beginnings, as well as instilling confidence and forcefulness. Many Aries folks have an inherent desire to not only survive, but to exceed, and to make a lasting impression. Aries is the cardinal fire sign that doesn't give up easily. Some Aries folks love to start up businesses, but continue into other ventures once the business has been established and requires the dull monotony of upkeep and maintenance. The Aries character typically expresses quality of leadership in the fiery realm of the cardinal signs, and is ruled by the active and vital planet, Mars. Aries boasts of being the first, and works earnestly to defy all who would mock, criticize, or misunderstand their drive to reach a certain self-appointed plateau of excellence. Sun in Aries serves as a good time to initiate new projects and apply diligence with inspired ability. The youthful vigor that is characteristic of Arians is reflected in the season, and this spring-like sprouting and growth is inspiration for us all.

March 21st Monday

Moon in Libra / Scorpio	PDT	EDT
Moon trine Venus	12:54 AM	3:54 AM
Sun conjunct Uranus	5:24 AM	8:24 AM
Moon trine Neptune goes v/c	11:34 AM	2:34 PM
Moon enters Scorpio	12:16 PM	3:16 PM
Venus conjunct Neptune begins (see March 26)		

Birthday: Matthew Broderick 1962

Mood Watch: It's the first full day of the Sun in Aries, bringing the Vernal Equinox to its fruition. The waning Libra Moon brings internal equilibrium, and there is the potential for us to balance energies interactively. Libra Moon emphasizes relationships, and a good part of this morning's focuses will be based on our ability to enhance our lives through the act of finding the happy medium with those whom we love and admire. This afternoon, the Moon in Scorpio brings a good time to seek solutions to pressing concerns. Instinctual, clairvoyant, and resilient expressions of mood will show us the way.

Sun conjunct Uranus (occurring March 14 – 24) This one time annual occurrence of Sun conjunct Uranus especially affects Pisces and Aries people celebrating birthdays March 14 – 24. There may well be a healthy dollop of disruption and chaos in the lives of these folks. Radical breakthroughs that create a sense of freedom will be apparent. Sun conjunct Uranus causes strong rebellious tendencies. Pisces and Aries folks will have stronger than usual desires to roll with change and take life at a different pace, to fight oppression and injustice, possibly even with an entirely off-the-wall approach to deal with calamity. Where there is knowledge to back this radical new approach, there's a way to achieve a sense of freedom with a good chance to make an impression in the year to come. This will be your year (birthday folks) to express yourselves and your innovative desires and ideas. This is the most beneficial time to learn to live with chaos.

March 22nd Tuesday

Moon in Scorpio	PDT	EDT
Moon sextile Pluto	12:13 AM	3:13 AM
Sun square Pluto begins (see March 28)		

Birthday: Chico Marx 1887

Groucho: "Do you want to become a public nuisance?" Chico: "Sure. How much does the job pay?"

Mood Watch: Today's moods are awakened by our sense of perception. Scorpio Moon brings out our desires and our creative sensibilities. The waning Scorpio Moon reminds us to keep a handle on self-criticism, as well as the tendencies towards jealousy, suspicion and crimes of hate. Intense moods can be worked out through all kinds of therapy. Dealing with personal truth is important.

March 23rd Wednesday

Moon in Scorpio / Sagittarius	PDT	EDT
Moon trine Mars	12:41 AM	3:41 AM
Moon square Venus	6:08 AM	9:08 AM
Moon square Neptune goes v/c	1:07 PM	4:07 PM
Moon enters Sagittarius	1:45 PM	4:45 PM
Moon trine Uranus	2:54 PM	5:54 PM
Moon trine Sun	7:02 PM	10:02 PM

Birthday: Chaka Khan 1953

Mood Watch: The waning Scorpio Moon morning brings eagerness and passion. However, Moon square Venus may focus our energies on the conflicts in relationships. Interactive and profound moods delight our senses with the desire to participate in all kinds of activity. Moon square Neptune may bring some doubtfulness as the Moon goes void-of-course. Later today, Moon in Sagittarius invites our explorative moods to come out and play. Moon trine Uranus brings fun loving rebellion. Moon trine Sun puts us in touch with the season.

March 24th Thursday

Moon in Sagittarius	PDT	EDT
Moon trine Jupiter	12:57 PM	3:57 PM
Moon sextile Saturn	3:14 PM	6:14 PM

Birthday: Harry Houdini 1874

Mood Watch: The sun and moon are in fire signs and a lively feeling brings ambition and exploration. It's all good as the waning Sagittarius Moon entices us to hone in on our philosophical perspectives of life. Internal reflection brings a spirited outlook. Moon trine Jupiter is a splendid time to seek opportunity, haggle in the market, and enjoy life's riches. Moon sextile Saturn is a good time to get organized and to make some progress with getting a handle on matters. The Sagittarius Moon shows us the way and brings enthusiasm to our viewpoint.

March 25th Friday

Moon in Sagittarius / Capricorn	PDT	EDT
Moon trine Mercury	5:22 AM	8:22 AM
Moon square Mars	8:08 AM	11:08 AM
Moon sextile Venus	4:01 PM	7:01 PM
Moon sextile Neptune goes v/c	6:24 PM	9:24 PM
Moon enters Capricorn	6:57 PM	9:57 PM
Moon square Uranus	8:26 PM	11:26 PM

Birthday: Elton John 1947

Mood Watch: Sun in Aries and Moon in Sagittarius bring a very fiery, active, and creative time. From Greek mythology, the Centaur is the symbol of Sagittarius. Centaurs are a race of creatures that are half human and half horse. They are famous in children's books for being stargazers, foretellers of the future, and they are also considered to be benevolent and wise, loyal to the very end. Throughout the course of the day, our moods are touched by the need to look ahead and to apply the wisdom and moral self-discipline to overcome the troublesome limitations of a treacherous and uncertain new century. Even when life's continuing difficulties seem insurmountable, the wisdom of the centaur reminds us to hold an optimistic outlook, no matter what. Tonight's Capricorn Moon brings reserved feelings, particularly as Moon square Uranus brings some conflicting chaos to our moods.

March 26th Saturday

Earth Hour – Lights Out from 8:30 pm to 9:30 pm, at participants' respective local time.

LAST QUARTER MOON in CAPRICORN

	PDT	EDT	
Moon square Sun	5:07 AM	8:07 AM	
Moon conjunct Pluto	8:48 AM	11:48 AM	
Venus conjunct Neptune	6:39 PM	9:39 PM	
Moon square Jupiter	9:00 PM	12:00 AM	(Mar 27)
Moon square Saturn	10:03 PM	1:03 AM	(Mar 27)
Venus enters Pisces	11:52 PM	2:52 AM	(Mar 27)
Mars conjunct Uranus begins (see April 3)			

Birthday: Joseph Campbell 1904

Mood Watch: The **Last Quarter Moon in Capricorn** (Moon square Sun) is here. This Moon emphasizes issues of control – whether that means taking control or letting go of it where needed. The waning Capricorn Moon reminds us not to give up, to persist as the mountain goat does, and to find a way to overcome the steep and rocky roads. Capricorn Moon gives moods a serious undertone of needing and wanting to take hold of our goals and create results. Saturn ruled Capricorn emphasizes time and the timeliness of important events. This may be a time to address impending deadlines. Life is so serious with Capricorn Moon in its last quarter state; it reminds us that in order to be in control we must let go of that which we can't control. Attached to success? How important is success to you? Persistence wins overall where there is a stubborn drive to excel.

Venus conjunct Neptune (occurring March 21 – 29) Venus represents love, magnetism, and attraction, while Neptune (the higher octave of Venus) represents spiritual love and the melding of spiritual energies. Venus is conjunct with Neptune in the sign of Aquarius right at the cusp of Pisces. Here the cohesive and melding forces of Venus and Neptune manifest with original, idealistic, and inventive expressions. There is also a strong element of feminine intuition at work with these two planets at the cusp of Pisces. Beauty and art (Venus) are linked

92

with spirituality and belief (Neptune), much of it focused around humanitarian causes and issues (Aquarius). Science and technology are given more acceptable and aesthetic appearances with this conjunction. Venus conjunct Neptune can be utilized to reach a higher vibration of feminine, spiritual love. This allows beauty, femininity, and personal attraction to be connected with the higher spiritual vibrations of the universe. This is an ideal time to connect with one's own guardian angel and spirit guide. Venus conjunct Neptune, if utilized, will bring great wisdom.

Venus enters Pisces (Venus in Pisces: March 26 – April 20) Venus, the planet of magnetism and love, will focus our attention on recreational endeavors. While Venus is in Pisces, music, poetry, the arts, psychic phenomena, and spiritual and religious practices will all be endearing and lively pursuits. As Venus crosses over their natal Sun sign, it will touch the personal realms of our Pisces friends with an awareness of the need for love and beauty in their lives. Venus is the feminine planet of love, and Pisces is an extremely feminine, dreamy, and spiritual placement for the love force of Venus. Matters of the heart will emphasize passivity, tenderness, sensitivity and the need for a gentle approach towards love's expression.

March 27th Sunday

Moon in Capricorn	PDT	EDT
Moon square Mercury	3:59 PM	6:59 PM
Moon sextile Mars goes v/c	8:17 PM	11:17 PM

Birthday: Sarah Vaughan 1924

Mood Watch: The feeling of importance is hatching – springtime is here! The Capricorn Moon gives some folks the feeling they could create or crush a whole universe, while the courageous days of Aries lead us fearlessly onward. Capricorn Moon keeps us on the straight and narrow. A determined world of doers sets a busy, but steady, pace. This weekend Capricorn Moon invites us to do some spring cleaning and organizing, to get a handle on our surroundings, and to be useful and resourceful. Tonight, as the Moon goes void-of-course, laziness settles in.

March 28th Monday

Moon in Capricorn / Aquarius	PDT	EDT
Moon enters Aquarius	3:59 AM	6:59 AM
Sun square Pluto	5:12 AM	8:12 AM
Moon sextile Uranus	5:50 AM	8:50 AM
Jupiter opposite Saturn	2:54 PM	5:54 PM
Moon sextile Sun	7:51 PM	10:51 PM

Birthday: Julia Stiles 1981

Mood Watch: Before we know it, the Moon enters Aquarius, and our moods will be especially thoughtful and innovative. The Aquarius Moon atmosphere enlivens our outlook in unusual and dynamic ways. Aquarius Moon challenges us to overcome the impossible with brilliant solutions.

Sun square Pluto (occurring March 22 – 31) This aspect particularly affects March born Aries people celebrating birthdays this month from March 22 – 31. Pluto squaring the natal Sun of these people brings disruptive changes and many challenges to overcome, such as the pain of loss and the severity of transformation. Trying to hold onto the regrets and the pain of the past will only bring greater destruction later. This is the time to persevere through the obstacles of hardship. Yet, the hardships that are taking place now will resurface in time, so do take note of the struggles going on in the lives of the people who are directly affected by Pluto's tests. Realize this trend will be repeated, and so necessitates finding methods of release and attitude changes in order to survive the anxiety and stress. Take it one day at a time and do not let fear and worry rule this condition. Move steadily through the required transformation, as stagnation and fear will only bring extended suffering. This aspect will reoccur again this year on September 28, affecting some of the Libra people of that time.

Jupiter opposite Saturn (occurring March 9 – April 7) Jupiter and Saturn are the two social planets of our solar system. Jupiter represents, joy, attainment, expansion, wealth, increase, and the place wherever growth happens, or wherever a surplus of supply is found. Saturn is the guard at the edge of time, and represents the work, discipline, timing, focus, restriction, limitation, and the responsibility that comes with the prosperous attainment of growth here on planet Earth. They are considered the social planets because here in North America, our value as individuals is often measured by how much we earn and by how many achievements and goals we have accomplished. With each bountiful step of attainment, there is always the restriction imposed to maintain it, and the duty of labor required to keep it growing or expanding in value and quality. Jupiter in Aries opposes Saturn in Libra. Both of these social-monger planets are in cardinal signs signifying a time of great leadership, exploration, and establishment in commerce.

Jupiter in Aries brings a wealth of experimental exploits and expenditures based on new enterprise, which leads to tenuous accounting, budgetary tasks and, eventually, a sure regrowth of new business enterprises. Saturn in Libra emphasizes our need to draw the line with regard to civil laws, the courts, and the institution of marriage. Saturn in Libra tests the boundaries of our justice system, and represents the need to defend, get to work on, or place limitations upon the things that matter most to us – those areas of life where we hope to see responsible growth and prosperity.

When Jupiter opposes Saturn, there is an acute awareness of our incessant need to spend at the same time we need to place some serious limitations on those expenditures. Does all this sound familiar with the global money crunch that has developed in the past few years? Now more than ever, this realization requires balance (Saturn in Libra). Nonetheless, through this aspect we can expect to see rapid growth, and the control of that expansion, occur at an expedited pace (Jupiter in Aries).

There will be greater opportunities, for those folks who apply a discerning focus on their strengths and skills, to reinforce a sense of security and control with regards to our economic focuses. Jupiter opposite Saturn is saying be diligent and seize all opportunities with persistence, but also take joy and have faith in the work of assessing all avenues of resource and wealth. This is the time to be especially responsive and loyal to the important things in life that must matter to everyone, such as environmental sensitivity. Here, the demand for earth friendly products and alternative sources of power will become more prevalent. It is through this process of loyal persistence to the things that matter that we can find peace where there is economic hardship, or wherever there is restriction due to budgetary measures or the conversion of old systems of commerce. Opportunities are arising out of the act of applying what needs to be done, especially with regard to establishing new forms of prosperity and growth. Work that is yet to be realized and assessed, as well as accepted and approved, can lead to a powerful resource of jobs and business. Jupiter opposite Saturn brings alarming breakthroughs towards social and economic security. This aspect will begin reoccurring, as a *non-exact-aspect*, on November 29, and it will dissipate on February 19, 2012 before it reaches another oppositional peak.

March 29ᵗʰ Tuesday

Moon in Aquarius	PDT	EDT
Moon trine Saturn	8:11 AM	11:11 AM
Moon sextile Jupiter	8:39 AM	11:39 AM
Venus sextile Pluto begins (see April 2)		
Sun conjunct Jupiter begins (see April 6)		

Birthday: Pearl Bailey 1918

Mood Watch: Aquarius Moon brings out our conceptual ways of thinking and allows us to look at problems with innovative solutions. The morning aspects are bright and promising. Moon trine Saturn inspires an amicable work mood, allowing for a greater sense of control, precision, and focus. Moon sextile Jupiter brings the potential for our moods to be inspired by a sense of joviality, prosperity, and optimism. Creative problem solving will allow us to move ahead with greater confidence and inspiration. Mercury is about to go retrograde (see tomorrow), and this is often a time when our thoughts are challenged by stillness or a lack of mental agility. The Aquarius Moon will help us to stay on track. Meanwhile, it's okay to take a moment to collect your thoughts!

March 30ᵗʰ Wednesday

Moon in Aquarius / Pisces	PDT	EDT
Moon sextile Mercury	4:16 AM	7:16 AM
Mercury goes retrograde	1:47 PM	4:47 PM
Moon conjunct Neptune goes v/c	3:21 PM	6:21 PM
Moon enters Pisces	3:38 PM	6:38 PM

Birthday: Eric Clapton 1945

Mood Watch: The Aquarius Moon often brings out the scientific, knowledgeable, and sometimes unusual qualities of our moods. This is the Moon that puts us in touch with our sense of humanity, or lack of humanity. Moral and ethical issues are often at the forefront of our intellectual pursuits, and this gives the overall mood a quality of irony or incongruity. How can we think freely if we are bound to ethical principles? The answer is simple: people change. Morals and ethics change, and this especially occurs through the ways we choose to think. Nonetheless, the rules of society must be applied and the laws must be obeyed, yet even these laws will change. Aquarius Moon gives us the impetus to keep an open mind and this is how we eventually evolve. By afternoon everything changes – the Moon goes void-of-course and enters Pisces within minutes. Pisces Moon opens up our psychic abilities. We're going to need that as Mercury goes retrograde!

Mercury goes retrograde (Mercury retrograde: March 30 – April 23) As of today, Mercury goes retrograde at the twenty-four degree mark of Aries and it will return back to the midpoint of Aries at the twelve degree mark on April 23. Mercury retrograde in Aries is likely to bring a great deal of communication disruption to issues around beginning new projects or enterprises. In Aries, the retrograde Mercury often causes communication mix ups with regard to such Aries-like things as fire fighting, surgery, metal workers, engineering, arms-manufacturing, trade-unions, dentistry, and professional sports. Despite rational and fair minded attempts to spontaneously articulate important subjects, Mercury retrograde in Aries will often leave us impatient, dissatisfied, and tongue tied. Establishing a clear understanding will be the most important part of engaging in various kinds of agreements. It is also important to get a handle on the temper while Mercury is retrograde in Aries. We are likely to see a bit of head butting, some arguments, and a lot of disputes. Expect to repeat yourself more than once or twice, and to be persistent as well as patient during this time. Whatever you agree on, if it's very important, get it in writing! For more information on Mercury retrograde, see the section in the introduction about *Mercury retrograde periods*.

March 31st Thursday

Moon in Pisces	PDT	EDT
Moon conjunct Venus	1:28 AM	4:28 AM
Moon sextile Pluto goes v/c	6:43 AM	9:43 AM

Birthday: Al Gore 1948

Mood Watch: The Moon wanes in Pisces bringing an intuitive and introspective time. Our Thursday morning moods may seem dreamy, idealistic and, at times, unrealistic, especially since the Moon will be void-of-course all day and night. Nonetheless, our moods may also be fairly accommodating, charming, and imaginative. This is a good time to tap into artistic methods of releasing pent up energies. It is also a time to be aware of addictive behavior patterns and weakness in abstinence. This is no time to have high expectations for the day. The void-of-course Pisces Moon is about as spacey as it gets, especially since Mercury just went retrograde as of yesterday.

April 1ˢᵗ Friday

♈

April Fool's Day

Moon void-of-course in Pisces	**PDT**	**EDT**	
Mars enters Aries	9:51 PM	12:51 AM	(Apr 2)
Sun opposite Saturn begins (see April 3)			

Birthday: Debbie Reynolds 1932

Mood Watch: Well, well, well – it doesn't get any more comical than this: it's **April Fool's Day**, the Moon is void-of-course in Pisces *ALL DAY and NIGHT*, and Mars enters the place it rules, Aries! Like the Fool, we charge in the darkness to the depths of Pisces, the place of belief, the mutable waters. We are pioneering, brave, and forthright. There's an especially fine line between bravery and stupidity. Happy **April Fool's Day**, also known as *All Fools' Day*. This is a holiday of uncertain origin, but just about everybody knows it as the day for practical joking. Before the adoption of the Gregorian calendar in 1564, April 1ˢᵗ was observed as New Year's Day by many cultures from the Roman to the Hindu. This holiday is considered to be related to the festival of the Vernal Equinox, when the Sun enters Aries, on or about March 20ᵗʰ.

Mars enters Aries (Mars in Aries: April 1 – May 11) Mars, the planet of action and masculine drive and force, is at home in Aries, the sign it rules, where it initiates activities in the most forward and direct manner possible. Mars is the god of war in mythology; often Mars related experience is generated through our impulses, our anger and rage, our fear and compulsion, our need to confront and bring forth the primal force of energy and zeal that is our ability to take action – it's our spark of life. Mars now in Aries boosts the lives of Aries people and gives them both the energy and the incentive to take action in their lives, and there are undoubtedly heated matters going on in their lives as well. Mars' influence generates activity and heat which can often appear explosive under pressure. Aries people are reminded to keep a cool sense of control at all times, and to build on their crucible of energy with a direct sense of clarity and purpose. Aries folks can strike now while the iron is hot, but use caution: be aware of fires, potential accidents, and fevers. Capricorn and Cancer folks need to be especially cautious as Mars now squares to their natal Sun sign, causing the events around them to seem personally abrasive and particularly maddening at times. Libra people may be aware of extreme fiery activity in their lives with Mars opposing their natal Sun sign. Leo and Sagittarius people are experiencing the favorable trine of Mars to their natal Sun signs; this gives our fire sign friends a boost of energy, some hot and some all too hot. Fire signs have within them the means to naturally identify with the forces of Mars activity in their lives. However, even when one is in one's element, the relentless spirit of Mars must be carefully tempered in people's busy lives, or they'll burn out. Mars in Aries places an emphasis on the courage, initiative, drive, energy, willpower, and strength necessary to take action. This kind of force forms the hot lava pools of *Pele* – the Hawaiian volcano goddess of fire, lightning, and dance (to name a few of her attributes). A lot goes on with Mars in Aries, so when the strain becomes too absorbing, remember to rest now and then.

April 2nd Saturday

Moon in Pisces / Aries	PDT	EDT
Moon enters Aries	4:15 AM	7:15 AM
Moon conjunct Mars	4:42 AM	7:42 AM
Venus sextile Pluto	5:30 AM	8:30 AM
Moon conjunct Uranus	6:44 AM	9:44 AM
Moon square Pluto	7:25 PM	10:25 PM

Birthday: Giovanni Casanova 1725

Mood Watch: There is eagerness in our moods, and an aggressive desire to launch into new patterns of life. This morning's Moon conjunct Mars puts us in touch with our strengths. Moon conjunct Uranus empowers our need to break routine. It's the New Moon Eve, a good time for internal reflection, particularly a reflection on personal strength and vitality. This evening's Moon square Pluto brings intensity, particularly in areas of life that seem too powerful to expediently change.

Venus sextile Pluto (occurring March 29 – April 3) Venus sextile Pluto means business when it comes to making proposals of love. Venus is in Pisces where the law of attraction is irresistible, easy going, and artistically uplifting. Pluto in Capricorn brings dutiful allegiance to matters of fate. Venus sextile Pluto implies that even in the midst of hardship, opportunities are arising with regard to the things we treasure and are attracted to, and also in matters of love and affection (Venus). These opportunities often are born out of fate or destiny (Pluto), or sometimes are a result of an unpredictable factor. For some, this aspect may be teaching them the lessons of acceptance, of learning to let go of attachments, as well as finding liberation through the transformative process of acceptance, particularly in matters of love. This aspect will reoccur on October 13.

April 3rd Sunday

NEW MOON in ARIES	PDT	EDT
Moon opposite Saturn	7:17 AM	10:17 AM
Moon conjunct Sun	7:32 AM	10:32 AM
Moon conjunct Jupiter	12:08 PM	3:08 PM
Mars conjunct Uranus	1:51 PM	4:51 PM
Moon opposite Neptune	2:51 PM	5:51 PM
Sun opposite Saturn	4:56 PM	7:56 PM
Mars square Pluto begins (see April 11)		

Birthday: Doris Day 1924

Mood Watch: The **New Moon in Aries** (Moon conjunct Sun) invokes the powers of initiation; it is the essential part of regenerative force to take the initiative and to start anew. This is the time when the new parts of the self begin to emerge, and our moods are encouraged by confidence, motivation, courageousness, and fiery intent. Now is the time to generate and promote inspiration and happiness. In general, the spirit of our moods brings a strong sense of newness and a great deal of activity.

Mars conjunct Uranus (occurring March 26 – April 7) Every couple of years the Mars/Uranus conjunction occurs. Activity and force of action (Mars) is in direct alignment with the explosive and chaotic energy of the rebel (Uranus). Both of these planets are charged with force, energy, and vitality, and are known for creating disruptive and unsettled energy. Masculine forces are erupting abruptly and loudly. The outlook is very fiery, especially now that as these two dominant forces are magnified in the masculine element of the cardinal fire sign, Aries. This may be a time of violence, accidents and upheaval in the world of weaponry and martial encounters. Activities are likely to be explosive over issues touching on gun control, arms manufacturing, racing and competitive sports, and those hypersensitive war issues currently plaguing our planet. The combat of war could be especially damaging, or for some, liberating. Volcanic energies may be particularly explosive. New territory could be marked in the realm of chaotic forms of destruction. Anger and frustration can be stifling at times, causing the fierce desire for freedom and the need for a definite revolution or revolt. Take caution with your own actions, and be aware of the potential for accidents and outbreaks of chaotic energy from others. This conjunction of Mars and Uranus is most advantageous for success in demolition projects and wherever strong force is needed to make a total breakthrough.

Sun opposite Saturn (occurring April 1 – 6) This annual occurrence of Sun opposite Saturn particularly affects those Aries people celebrating birthdays from April 1 – 6. These birthday folks are undergoing personal challenges with regard to patience, leaving them strongly aware of who and what is in control. They are mindful of the crucial factors of time, limitations, and timing. Work demands may be overwhelming, and these Aries folks will have to apply discipline and determination in order to achieve success. Work that requires self-motivation may be the most challenging part of applying discipline while Saturn is in Libra. Aries birthday folks, this is a most important time in your life to persist! Endure! Keep up the Great Work! Take heart, as this may well be your year to accomplish something astounding.

April 4ᵗʰ Monday
Moon in Aries / Taurus

	PDT	EDT
Moon conjunct Mercury goes v/c	3:04 AM	6:04 AM
NEPTUNE ENTERS PISCES	6:50 AM	9:50 AM
Moon enters Taurus	4:45 PM	7:45 PM
Moon sextile Neptune	4:47 PM	7:47 PM

Birthday: Muddy Waters 1915

Mood Watch: The newly waxing Aries Moon goes void-of-course early this morning and for most of the day it remains void in Aries. On this moody Monday we are likely to see a lot of impatience, annoyance, and irritation at the repetitive incompetence of others. Avoid the murky waters; stick with *Muddy Waters*! This evening, as the Moon enters Taurus, our focuses are inclined towards the need for security, a pooling of resources, and for rest and relaxation.

NEPTUNE ENTERS PISCES (Neptune in Pisces: April 4 – Aug. 4) For the next four months, we will observe the initial entry of Neptune in the mutable water sign, Pisces. Pisces is the place where Neptune is at home, the twelfth sign of the zodiac.

Neptune has been going through the sign of Aquarius since January 28, 1998 (thirteen years), and today the planet we attribute to spiritual bounty enters the sign of Pisces for the first time in this cycle. Once Neptune re-enters Pisces next year, on February 3, it will remain there for the long run – fourteen years – until January 26, 2026. Perhaps now you're getting the picture that this planet has a long cycle through each sign of the zodiac – yes it's true, and this is the nature of the slow moving outer planets, which are also referred to by some as the "modern planets."

A REVIEW OF NEPTUNE IN AQUARIUS

January 28, 1998 – April 4, 2011 & August 4, 2011 – February 3, 2012)

Neptune teaches us about our spiritual path as a species. It illuminates our understanding of ourselves through the power of dissolving all doubt and embracing the unknown, and through the general principles of our beliefs. Aquarius is the sign of the knower so, naturally, the spiritual personality of the Aquarian has risen to shocking and astonishing heights, moving through the unknown with unusual faculties of knowledge and speculation. Ironically, while Aquarius represents knowledge, Neptune deals with the unknown and our capacity for intuitive and psychic sensibility. Aquarius is the sign of the scientist, the eccentric, the genius, and the experimenter; through these channels of thought, our beliefs have been greatly debated and challenged over the past thirteen years.

Neptune has melded our visions of utopia into the Aquarian nature that has involved unexpected, controversial, and outrageous levels of brilliance. It is through this time period that we have encountered religious conflicts, wars, and an amazing evolution of drug discoveries, drug demands, and massive drug production. Neptune's subtle but very powerful nature envelops our sense of receptivity, and through its compelling and slow moving qualities of dissolving our struggles into complete resignation, eventually we recognize those areas of our evolution where "resistance is futile." This is not necessarily a "Borg" science where we lose our sensibilities, identity, and urge to fight. This is a sanctuary where we give our prayers, hopes, meditations, and spells – whatever you wish to call them – to the divine. We do this in the wake of our rapidly growing knowledge and technology. We have formed a stronger bond with our global kinsfolk through this technology. There is always a place where we can *do no more*, where we must surrender all of our mortal efforts to the hands of God, the gods, divine Spirit, and the sublime powers that be. It is that place where we resign to the compelling force of Neptune's mysterious and miraculous function: to carry our prayers beyond, to give up our futility, to recognize our shortcomings and our weaknesses as humans. Through this process of surrender, something divine occurs, as we realize that our greatest strengths and our ability to heal, to find ecstasy, and to take delight in the arts and the sciences, comes with the letting go process.

Although the western and eastern paths of magic, myth, religion, and mystery are inherently different, the underlying truth to which these paths are leading is the same. Neptune has been busily dissolving the boarders of our many belief systems to slowly – ever so slowly – unravel the great mystery that human beings either run from or embrace. Aquarius people have been growing spiritually and, while Neptune has been transiting through their natal sun sign, an existential understanding of life has blossomed. Through Neptune in Aquarius we have discovered that knowledge is power, but (and this is a big *but* here) that power is only temporary. Today's iPhone, iPod, and transportable data systems of technology are tomorrow's landfill materials. Neptune demands the necessity for us to realize that we are spiritual beings having a physical experience. What we accomplish here on Earth is left by the mark of our spirit, that infallible urge to create and leave something behind that speaks for who we are. Neptune in Aquarius has been busily reminding us that there is a reason we are always striving for more, and never satisfied with what we know, or what we *think* we know. Spirituality moves in mysterious ways and this is the nature of Neptune. For more information on Neptune in Aquarius, *see August 4*, when the retrograde Neptune re-enters Aquarius.

THE HISTORY OF NEPTUNE'S LAST PHASE IN PISCES

Neptune last traveled through Pisces between 1847 – 1861. The American Secession crisis was going strong, and it was the closure of this Neptune in Pisces era that lead to the commencement of the Civil War (1861 – 1865). In those days, slavery in America was just beginning to come to its end. In 1851, the first blood was spilled over slavery. Many slaves were escaping through the underground railroad. The first National Women's Convention occurred in the USA in 1850, the same year of the Great Fire in San Francisco. Also, California was admitted as a State of the Union with Neptune in Pisces. Canada was going through the final throes of shaking itself from British control which ended in 1867. This was a time for people to stand up for what they believed in, to address the illusion that all Americans were living a life of freedom. Strong commands for equality were being addressed. Neptune focuses on our beliefs, as well as illusion, confusion, dreams, the mystical arts, inspirations, and transcendental occurrences. This is the planet that brings us enlightenment, acceptance, compassion, and mercy. Neptune also represents the domain of the arts, and it was at the close of this particular Neptune in Pisces cycle that the popularity of Impressionism was born (1860 – 1900). People like Monet and Cezanne began a new era for art and took the late 19th and early 20th centuries by storm. History indicates that the phase of Neptune in Pisces is a strong one for addressing the need for acceptance, tolerance, truth, and religious freedom. Undoubtedly, these themes will be the core of some of our biggest 21st century battles, with Neptune in Pisces over the next fourteen to fifteen years. Interestingly enough, the planet Neptune was first discovered in 1846, the year it began its shift from Aquarius to Pisces. That means we have officially come full circle since the time of its discovery.

NEPTUNE IN PISCES: April 4– August 4, 2011

The Long Run: February 3, 2012 – January 26, 2026

As it goes with slow moving planets, Neptune's effects will be far too subtle for most of us to notice at first, as ever so delicately the collective dreamscape is shifting. Eventually, the fluid nature of this highly attuned energy infiltrates our spiritual outlooks with a broader sense of how our beliefs are evolving. In the sign Pisces, Neptune will teach us a lot about what we truly believe in. It is here we discover the truth behind our beliefs, and those beliefs are likely to undergo a great deal of change through this time of Neptune in Pisces. As Somerset Maugham once said, "If you don't change your beliefs, your life will be like this forever. Is that good news?"

Neptune is associated with some very important elements in our modern society. These include religion, drugs, alcohol, elixirs, poisons, gas (as in fossil fuels and petroleum products), anesthetics, prisons, hospitals, institutions, art, music, mimicry, poetry, dance, fantasy, escapism, magic, myths, symbology, legends, psychic phenomena, and the thalamus gland of the body. Neptune deals with illusion and all that is nebulous and difficult to explain. A keyword for Neptune is cloudiness. Pisces mirrors much of what Neptune represents. It is, after all, the place of Neptune's domain – so naturally, Pisces characteristics also mimic Neptune's traits, governing the lymphatic system, the feet and the lachrymal glands. Neptune rules the thalamus, which receives and sorts sensory impulses. Pisces also rules the feet – that place on which we stand. Pisces says: "I believe," and it represents the place where we stake our beliefs and our way of life.

Since Pisces is the last sign of the zodiac, it symbolizes the summation of all of human experience, particularly when a human life nears the end. On the positive side, Neptune and Pisces focus on the realm of the imagination; they typify the subtle, sensitive, and hypersensitive parts of our being. This gives us great powers of perception and intuition. The negative side of this planet and sign emphasize deception, carelessness, sentimentality, impracticality, idleness, and changeability. However, adaptability is one of the keys to Piscean success. The mutable waters may absorb the poisons of the world, but they are also capable of dissolving them through the miraculous ability to let go of negative influences. This is probably why holy people, a long line of priests and kings, are associated with Pisces. Jesus Christ is a figurehead of the age of Pisces, and one of the symbols of Christianity is the fish.

Neptune in Pisces will not only test our faith and our spiritual outlook on life, but it will also establish a new outlook on all those things that Neptune represents, such as drugs, alcohol, natural resources, and institutions. In the next four months, it will be useful for us to observe the signs of the times, particularly all those things that represent Neptune's domain. It is from those observations that we will get a pretty good idea what the next fourteen years will be like in the realm of our spiritual evolution.

April 5th Tuesday

Moon in Taurus	PDT	EDT
Moon trine Pluto	7:47 AM	10:47 AM
Moon sextile Venus goes v/c	4:02 PM	7:02 PM
Mercury conjunct Jupiter begins (see April 11)		
Sun conjunct Mercury begins (see April 9)		

♈

Birthday: Algernon Charles Swinburne 1837

Mood Watch: The newly waxing Taurus Moon brings a bustling energy in the marketplace, and a firm sense of enterprising gaiety. The waxing Taurus Moon inspires our sense of beauty, entices us to have new supplies, and puts us in touch with down-to-earth focuses. This is the time to organize finances, to shop for practical needs, and to be resourceful. It is best to focus on completing as many tasks as possible early in the day since the Moon goes void-of-course later on, and remains void throughout the evening, as well as the *entire* day tomorrow. The void-of-course Taurus Moon may seem arduous and troublesome at times. Remember to pace yourself throughout tonight and tomorrow.

April 6th Wednesday

Moon void-of-course in Taurus	PDT	EDT
Sun conjunct Jupiter	7:40 AM	10:40 AM

Birthday: Baba Ram Dass 1931

Mood Watch: The Moon is void-of-course in Taurus the entire day and night, a somewhat rare and very arduous condition, especially while Mercury is retrograde (March 30 – April 23). This may be a stubborn time for our moods, and people may seem somewhat distant as they will tend to keep to themselves. Laziness – or a downright spacey attitude – may be common behaviors to encounter, and this is no time to have high expectations on the outcome of the day. Laborious conditions will be most tedious. Pace yourself and keep an eye on your pocketbook. This is often a time when people tend to lose things and misplace essential articles. Your motto today: *stay focused*!

Sun conjunct Jupiter (occurring March 29 – April 10) This conjunction brings those Aries folks celebrating birthdays March 29 – April 10 into an especially favorable position of their natal sun to Jupiter. This represents a time of gifts and expansion for these birthday folks, and there are good times in the works for these people. Financial or career advancement as well as skill building, exploration, travel, inheritance – and perhaps just plain happiness – become a bonus for these folks. Be sure to count your blessings, birthday Aries; you may find there are a great deal more blessings opening up for you this year than you might have expected! As a general rule, this conjunction usually only occurs once a year.

April 7th Thursday

Moon in Taurus / Gemini	PDT	EDT
Moon enters Gemini	4:21 AM	7:21 AM
Moon square Neptune	4:31 AM	7:31 AM
Moon sextile Uranus	7:18 AM	10:18 AM
Moon sextile Mars	12:55 PM	3:55 PM
URANUS-SQUARE-PLUTO-NON-EXACT begins (see July 10)		

Birthday: Jackie Chan 1954

Mood Watch: The waxing Gemini Moon will assist us to straighten out the details of yesterday's laborious void-of-course Taurus Moon events. Talkative expressions of mood bring numerous details for us to think about. Curious and thoughtful moods will keep us talking. Gemini is ruled by Mercury, and Mercury is currently retrograde (March 30 – April 23), creating complexity and confusion around our attempts to communicate. Gemini Moon focuses our attention on those areas of life where we have mixed feelings, and there is a tendency to mull over those things that have not settled just right in our minds. Take a deep breath and avoid hasty decisions. It will take awhile to adjust to the perplexity of our easily misunderstood mental processes.

April 8th Friday

Holy Day of Thelema (Nuit)

Moon in Gemini	PDT	EDT
Moon trine Saturn	6:40 AM	9:40 AM
Moon square Venus	9:21 AM	12:21 PM
Moon sextile Jupiter	1:20 PM	4:20 PM
Moon sextile Sun	4:47 PM	7:47 PM
Moon sextile Mercury goes v/c	7:23 PM	10:23 PM
Saturn-square-Pluto-non-exact (see below)		

Birthday: Julian Lennon 1963

Mood Watch: Moon trine Saturn is a productive and useful way to start off this waxing Gemini Moon day. Curious and upbeat moods abound, but we might have to work a little harder to please friends and loved ones while Moon square Venus occurs. This afternoon's Moon sextile Jupiter is an excellent time to explore and search for deals. Moon sextile Sun puts us in touch with the joys of the season. Tonight, as Moon sextile Mercury occurs, the Moon goes void-of-course; our thoughts may seem clear, but there isn't much attention being paid to them. The Gemini Moon time focuses on communications, and while Mercury is retrograde (March 30 – April 23), this is an important time to pay careful attention to how our communications are being interpreted. A good laugh will come in handy when a thought is misinterpreted.

Saturn-square-Pluto-non-exact (occurring April 8 – 9) This large and long winded aspect is currently biding farewell. Off and on throughout the past couple of years, it has been a primary player in our efforts to get a handle on large scale challenges and big transformations. It has already done its work and it will not reach an exact peak this time. Perhaps it is here just to remind us of the trials and tribulations that we have weathered in recent years. The last few times Saturn square Pluto reached an exact peak was on August 21 and January 21 of 2010, and it also occurred on November 15, 2009. Saturn and Pluto are both in cardinal signs (Libra and Capricorn) bringing lawfully sanctioned and physically enduring types of permanent change.

Now that Saturn and Pluto have been spending this time in the unfavorable square position to one another, it is up to us to determine how we will survive and grow stronger through this transformation process. This is a time for us to apply a careful approach to lawmaking, and for us to be cautious with our sense of control, particularly with regard to the current channels of power occurring in the world at large. It is through the square aspect that we will take great pains in our efforts to redefine our responsibilities and to shift our goals and priorities to suit the rapidly changing ways of the 21st century. The trials that we will encounter will dramatically shape our ideas of how power operates, and we will eventually acquire the knowledge and the survival tools to see us through closure of this difficult time. Restrictive laws and corruption in corporate circles point to a struggle that is being played out on the world stage through this aspect. Saturn in Libra intensifies judicial affairs while Pluto in Capricorn transforms the ways in which we go about the attainment of power. Limitations have been imposed on a variety of relationships while Saturn has been in the square position to the harsh and unrelenting forces of Pluto. This aspect is likely to bring great change in our attitudes, especially with regard to how we adapt to the structure of our rapidly changing environment within the confines of its stringent laws.

When Saturn tangos with Pluto, our lives undergo change in remarkable and notably demanding ways. As Saturn now finalizes its challenging square position to Pluto, we are bound to steadily undergo riveting transformational change which reflects our sense of stamina as well as our senses of reason and wisdom. This change occurs across the board in political, ethical, social, religious, theosophical, and moral arenas of thought and human conduct. As Saturn continues through Libra, laws and judicial standards will be constituted to reflect these changes in order to meet the long-term conditions that the 21st century lifestyle will effectively continue to establish. Through the trials we have already endured, we can reclaim our strength and begin to come full circle in our understanding of what this process of Saturn square Pluto has meant.

April 9th Saturday

Holy Day of Thelema (Hadit)

Moon in Gemini / Cancer	PDT	EDT
Sun conjunct Mercury	12:36 PM	3:36 PM
Moon enters Cancer	2:01 PM	5:01 PM
Moon trine Neptune	2:18 PM	5:18 PM
Moon square Uranus	5:06 PM	8:06 PM
Mercury-opposite-Saturn-non-exact begins (see April 23)		

Birthday: Charles Baudelaire 1821

Mood Watch: Throughout the morning and well into the afternoon, the void-of-course Gemini Moon coupled with Mercury retrograde makes this a tricky time to engage in clear communications. People may seem preoccupied, and this is undoubtedly a hard time to get them to listen. As the Moon enters Cancer, our emotional patterns will surface in much more clear and distinct ways. Moon trine Neptune brings pleasant moods. Later on, Moon square Uranus may be a somewhat chaotic time for our moods, as many folks will tend to dump a lot of frenzied feelings. No matter – a comforting atmosphere with some delicious foods will set the tone right for a fulfilling evening.

Pluto goes retrograde (Pluto retrograde: April 9 – Sept. 16) Processes governed by Pluto take the longest time to go through since, from our perspective, Pluto appears to move the slowest of all the planets because it's the furthest away from us. Pluto goes retrograde today and when it resumes a forward moving course late this summer, it will have traveled only a few degrees in the sky, which is average for a Pluto retrograde period. This means the types of hardships that have been created and brought to our attention in the past five months must be addressed all over again, and that we must acknowledge the evolution of humankind's current condition in order to survive the changes that are occurring on Earth. Pluto is currently at 7 degrees in Capricorn and it will be retrograde back to the 4 degree mark of Capricorn. A few degrees at a time is plenty enough for us to handle and to physically and emotionally process.

Pluto deals with the changes that occur in attitude according to the overall group consciousness of each of the generations. Each generation has its own insight as to what hardship represents. This is a time to make life better by consciously transforming fear into determination and despair into belief in oneself, no matter what condition of fate surrounds you. The destructive habits, prejudices, sufferings and haunts of previous generations must be acknowledged and addressed – and of course – altered to enable us to tackle the world of the future. We will all face greater challenges and tests of epic proportions, and outdated concerns must be dealt with so that we may find solutions to the new problems in front of us.

With Pluto's changes we must face tragedies, diseases, losses, poisons, shattered dreams, and altered or unexpected doses of reality. Pluto very slowly, but surely, sweeps away the decay of human tragedy. Last year's Gulf Coast oil spill was a tragic dose of reality. This tragedy occurred the month Pluto went retrograde. The epic proportion of this tragedy has classically resembled many qualities of Pluto's tests. Pluto represents the power struggles of transformation. The consequences of the actions and reactions of a corporation can be brutal; too much power is a force to be reckoned with, and this is the nature of Pluto. Pluto retrograde forces us to look within; this is a good time to confirm our greatest strengths by directing abusive patterns into constructive and useful disciplines and ways of thinking which will reshape and bring hope to the emerging outlook on life.

Pluto represents the forces of power and control, which are always in a state of flux due to our mortal tango with fate. Pluto retrograde is a time of readdressing universal human problems that take decades to fix. Pluto, newly in the sign of Capricorn (since Jan. 25, 2008), will continue to influence such Capricorn related focuses as corporate growth, architectural feats, monumental achievements, industrial capitalization, environmental control, and many unprecedented forms of success and goal attainment. It is through the retrograde process that Pluto in Capricorn will shape and cause us to reexamine our views and perspectives on the large scale changes occurring on our planet.

Sun conjunct Mercury (occurring April 5 – 11) This conjunction will create a much more thoughtful, communicative and expressive year ahead for those Aries folks celebrating birthdays April 5 – 11. This is your time (birthday Aries) to record ideas, relay important messages, and pay close attention to your imaginative thoughts as they are touched by Mercury, creating the urge to speak and be heard. Birthday Aries, your thoughts will reveal a great deal about who you are, now and in the year to come.

April 10th Sunday

Holy Day of Thelema (Ra-Hoor-Khuit)

Moon in Cancer	PDT	EDT	
Moon square Mars	1:52 AM	4:52 AM	
Moon opposite Pluto	7:08 AM	10:08 AM	
Moon square Saturn	2:44 PM	5:44 PM	
Moon square Jupiter	10:25 PM	1:25 AM	(Apr 11)
Moon trine Venus	11:15 PM	2:15 AM	(Apr 11)

Birthday: Linda Goodman 1925

Mood Watch: Challenging lunar aspects make this waxing Cancer Moon day a little trying at times and, fortunately, it doesn't all come at once. Cancer Moon puts us in touch with our truer feelings, and it's most beneficial when we address them with positive affirmations and reassurance. The Cancer Moon time brings impressionable feelings. It's important to master the art of focusing on the best case scenarios, rather than dwelling on – or worrying about – life's unruly hardships and infringements. Much later, Moon trine Venus brings the kiss of love and it's a good time to count blessings.

April 11th Monday

FIRST QUARTER MOON in CANCER

Moon in Cancer / Leo	PDT	EDT	
Moon square Mercury	12:03 AM	3:03 AM	
Moon square Sun goes v/c	5:05 AM	8:05 AM	
Mars square Pluto	1:40 PM	4:40 PM	
Moon enters Leo	8:37 PM	11:37 PM	
Mercury conjunct Jupiter	8:59 PM	11:59 PM	
Moon trine Uranus	11:43 PM	2:43 AM	(Apr 12)
Mars opposite Saturn begins (see April 18)			

Birthday: Louise Lasser 1939

Mood Watch: The **First Quarter Moon in Cancer** (Moon square Sun) urges us to share our feelings and take care of emotional needs, particularly in our home. Home focused activities bring warm expressions of contentment. With First Quarter Cancer Moon, the emotional current tends to be magnified. Nutritional foods and trustworthy company are important components of today's activities. This is all especially true as the First Quarter Moon goes void-of-course early this morning and remains void most of today. Emotional obsessions or distractions will be commonplace. Treating ourselves and others in a nurturing way becomes the key to enhancing or cleansing our emotional perspective. Be careful not to push the buttons of sensitive people and use words wisely while considering the feelings of yourself and others. Later tonight, the Leo Moon is a superb time to reinforce a positive affirmation towards self-confidence and personal needs.

Mars square Pluto (occurring April 3 – 15) Mars in Aries square Pluto in Capricorn brings recklessly domineering battles over the seemingly unchangeable realities of global power structures. Mars emphasizes all forms of action, while Pluto represents the transformational powers of destiny. These two planets in the square position spell out the potential for trouble with regard to our actions. Strong disputes and war related action between generations, and among those of different cultures, are likely to occur. This aspect does imply a more likely time for an attack from groups seeking to take power, but with such attacks there will be struggles. These actions against or conflicts with higher powers are likely to backfire – it is best not to bluff those of a higher or unanticipated authority at this time, as taking action in an attempt to create a transformation may be very dangerous. This may be a particularly difficult time to fight addiction, disease, and war related stress – it is also the most crucial time not to give up the fight. Thankfully, this is the only time this year we will have to endure Mars square Pluto.

Mercury conjunct Jupiter (occurring April 5 – 15) Mercury and Jupiter are conjunct in Aries, and this brings an excellent time to explore a pioneering spirit. News and discussions (Mercury) revolve around our joys, our prosperity, and our wealth (Jupiter). Thoughts and information (Mercury) with regard to a prosperous and visionary breakthrough (Jupiter) will be highlighted. Due to Mercury's current retrograde cycle (March 30 – April 23), this conjunction of Mercury and

Jupiter may not be as effective as when Mercury is direct. However, we will have ♈ another chance next month to make use of this conjunction's beneficial qualities. Mercury conjunct Jupiter last occurred on March 15 and it will repeat once more with Mercury direct on May 11.

April 12th Tuesday

Moon in Leo	PDT	EDT
Moon trine Mars	10:53 AM	1:53 PM
Moon sextile Saturn	7:27 PM	10:27 PM

Birthday: Tiny Tim 1930

Mood Watch: Leo Moon moods are energetic and openly focused on identity. The sun and moon are both in fire signs, and archetypes abound with tales of the self, bursting with character and ego. A waxing Moon in Leo uplifts our moods with entertainment, magnetism and stimulation. It's good time to do something special for yourself, and to reinforce your own integral outlook on the importance of living life according to will-power. Get in touch with a sense of personal vitality and call it your own.

April 13th Wednesday

Moon in Leo / Virgo	PDT	EDT	
Moon trine Mercury	1:48 AM	4:48 AM	
Moon trine Jupiter	3:50 AM	6:50 AM	
Moon trine Sun goes v/c	12:58 PM	3:58 PM	
Moon enters Virgo	11:40 PM	2:40 AM	(Apr 14)

Birthday: Thomas Jefferson 1743

Mood Watch: Encouraging lunar aspects set the right tone for a joyous, exuberant Leo Moon morning. The trine aspects of the Moon to Mercury, Jupiter, and later, Moon trine Sun, are positive and uplifting. Despite the travails of Mercury retrograde (March 30 – April 23), our challenging communications and our miscommunications will give us the opportunity to brush up on our patience, tolerance, and wisdom. This afternoon, the waxing Leo Moon goes void-of-course and remains void throughout the evening. This may bring restless energy and what may seem to be an aggressive attempt at going in circles. When laziness sets in, family members don't cooperate, personal projects are set back due to delays, or self-doubt clouds the brain, know that these are just the symptoms of a void-of-course Leo Moon. Beastly moods will soon pass.

April 14th Thursday

Moon in Virgo	PDT	EDT
Moon trine Pluto	11:56 AM	2:56 PM
Mercury conjunct Mars begins (see April 19)		

Birthday: Julie Christie 1941

Mood Watch: Virgo Moon moods bring ingenuity and the desire for cleanliness and keenness of spirit. Since Virgo is ruled by Mercury, we must not forget that there is a certain degree of willingness to debate, deliberate, and argue for the sake of our ideals or principles. In the midst of all this scrutiny, there is a shyness or prudence in our demeanor that allows for some dignity and discernment. Not everything in the universe is worth debating, particularly while the retrograde Mercury in Aries (March 30 – April 23) has us up in arms over misinterpreted words. We must not forget our ignorance, as it is still quite impossible to know it all. The Virgo Moon keeps us curious and this is why we question so much. Keep a cool head and your day will be rewarding. It is sometimes easier to admit what you don't know than it is to argue what you do.

April 15th Friday

Moon in Virgo / Libra	PDT	EDT	
Moon opposite Venus goes v/c	1:14 AM	4:14 AM	
Moon enters Libra	11:58 PM	2:58 AM	(Apr 16)

Birthday: Leonardo da Vinci 1452

Mood Watch: Throughout the morning, the heavily waxing Virgo Moon is void-of-course. There may be some confusion, doubt, and a fair bit of skepticism as we encounter a wide range of reluctance, hesitance, delays, and stalls due to uncertainty. Some patience will be required as the nervous or awkward undertones of the mood may appear contagious at times. In some cases, people may appear more poker faced than usual, or they may be prone to depression and narcotics. If you're the type of person who requires your "alone time," this may be one of the better times to seek the hermitage. It's important to focus on making healthy choices.

April 16th Saturday

Moon in Libra	PDT	EDT	
Moon opposite Uranus	3:07 AM	6:07 AM	
Moon square Pluto	11:48 AM	2:48 PM	
Moon opposite Mars	6:08 PM	9:08 PM	
Moon conjunct Saturn	8:17 PM	11:17 PM	
Moon opposite Mercury	10:49 PM	1:49 AM	(Apr 17)
Sun sextile Neptune begins (see April 20)			

Birthday: Charlie Chaplin 1889

Mood Watch: This Full Libra Moon Eve encourages us to reach out to others, and to collaborate in a way that helps to make the troublesome parts of the day go more smoothly. This morning's lunar aspects are daunting and challenging on some levels, but we are also reminded of our need for each other, and for some diplomacy and tact. Tonight's lunar aspects keep us charged with energy, focused and serious about matters, and intent on the need to get the facts straight. Full Libra Moon invites us to enjoy the fruits of our labors with the people we love.

April 17ᵗʰ Sunday   ♈

Palm Sunday
FULL MOON in LIBRA

Moon in Libra / Scorpio	PDT	EDT	
Moon opposite Jupiter	6:05 AM	9:05 AM	
Moon opposite Sun goes v/c	7:43 PM	10:43 PM	
Moon enters Scorpio	11:18 PM	2:18 AM	(Apr 18)
Moon trine Neptune	11:53 PM	2:53 AM	(Apr 18)
Venus conjunct Uranus begins (see April 22)			

Birthday: William Holden 1918

Mood Watch: The **Full Moon in Libra** (Moon opposite Sun) brings events that revolve around such things as law, the justice system, friends, and marital partners. Relationships are a balancing act. Friends will share their strengths as well as their weaknesses. Troubled times can strengthen even the weakest links in friendship. Refuse to contribute to the weakness of a friend; nurture friendship with patience, understanding, and encouragement. Use this Full Libra Moon energy to empower your relationships. Diplomacy, peace and goodwill can be achieved among loved ones, but a definite effort is required. As the Full Moon reaches its peak this evening, it also goes void-of-course for a few hours. Don't let forgetfulness, irritating attitudes, or minor disagreements impinge on the quality of your relationships. Later, as the Moon enters Scorpio, emotional intensity captures the importance of what we are feeling. It's a good time to focus on healing and to begin a purging process wherever it may be needed.

April 18ᵗʰ Monday

Moon in Scorpio	PDT	EDT
Mars opposite Saturn	10:47 AM	1:47 PM
Moon sextile Pluto	11:13 AM	2:13 PM

Birthday: Leopold Stokowski 1882

Mood Watch: Emotions run high as this post-full Scorpio Moon Monday keeps us on the defense. Today we are feeling the tiring brunt of a full Moon weekend and the most sensible way to combat the emotional strain is to get into a cool, calm, collected pace. While it may be important to vent some penned up emotion now and then, professionalism demands that we get a handle on our intensity by controlling our impulses and desires wisely. Destructive tendencies may require some vigilant care. This is a good time to keep the guard up and to conserve our energies.

Mars opposite Saturn (occurring April 11 – 21)Mars opposite Saturn always makes us aware of the timeliness of our actions and the importance of acting in a timely manner – for example, doing something about a problem before it's too late. Medical emergencies often crop up with this particular aspect. There will also be an awareness of the dynamic polarity between offensive and defensive forces. For opposing forces in battle, this aspect often brings fiery and sometimes tragic endings. Mars in Aries is opposing the retrograde Saturn in Libra, which accentuates bold attacks on the structure of our established rules and protocol. Saturn has been retrograde since January 25, and will go direct on June 12. Saturn is the restrictive discipline behind every effort to contain, guard, and hold onto what matters to us. Mars in Aries brings swift and intrepid action to all modes of attack. Saturn in the place of Libra emphasizes the need to face our responsibilities in a timely manner, particularly with regard to law, justice, and the courts. This is the time to act wisely and responsibly, or suffer the consequences. Pay attention to those aspects of life that hold active potential for accidents. The popular old adage of "look before you leap" is a good meditation to apply during this crucial time of Mars opposite Saturn.

April 19th Tuesday

Passover

Moon in Scorpio / Sagittarius

	PDT	EDT	
Mercury conjunct Mars	7:58 AM	10:58 AM	
Moon trine Venus goes v/c	9:53 PM	12:53 AM	(Apr 20)
Moon enters Sagittarius	11:49 PM	2:49 AM	(Apr 20)
Mars conjunct Jupiter begins (see April 30)			
Mercury-square-Pluto-non-exact begins (see April 20)			

Birthday: Tim Curry 1946

Mood Watch: The waning Scorpio Moon keeps us vigilant, as those who are in tune with their emotions will instinctively know to act on their suspicions or intuitive hunches. With Mercury retrograde, there is a greater potential for critical misunderstandings, and it is wise not to fan the fires of emotional dramas or fear. Persist with a careful review of the facts. This is a good time to concentrate on healing and easing emotional pressures and illness. We are also reminded of the necessity to place some trust in others. Sometimes we must take chances, and it's always wise not to gamble more than you can afford to lose. In most cases, with a great deal of keen observation, you will see the real side of someone, and once you've done that you can usually trust that person to be who you know them to be. It is futile to expect people to change, as we can only encourage them if it is their will to do so. Watch their actions *not* just their words.

Mercury conjunct Mars (occurring April 14 – 22) The Retrograde Mercury (March 30 – April 23), is now in a conjunction with Mars. The Mercury retrograde effect of this conjunction brings the potential for greater misunderstanding in the face of actions and commands. This could definitely mean a punch in the face when a thing is wrongly interpreted about serious matters. This may be a time of angry words being spoken. Now is the time to proceed with absolute caution and vigilance. Stay on the defense for awhile. Mercury conjunct Mars in Aries emphasizes the need for swift action upon command. It also emphasizes the need to actively communicate about issues of new enterprise, leadership, authority, competition. There is also an emphasis on self-motivation. This conjunction last occurred on February 20 and it will reoccur on May 20.

112

TAURUS

Key Phrase: "I HAVE"

Fixed Earth Sign

Ruling Planet: Venus

Symbol: The Bull

April 20th through May 21st

April 20th Wednesday

Moon in Sagittarius	PDT	EDT	
Moon square Neptune	12:30 AM	3:30 AM	
Sun enters Taurus	3:17 AM	6:17 AM	
Moon trine Uranus	3:29 AM	6:29 AM	
Sun sextile Neptune	1:42 PM	4:42 PM	
Moon sextile Saturn	8:59 PM	11:59 PM	
Venus enters Aries	9:06 PM	12:06 AM	(Apr 21)
Moon trine Mercury	9:52 PM	12:52 AM	(Apr 21)
Mercury-square-Pluto-non-exact (see below)			

Birthday: Napoleon III 1808

Mood Watch: The waning Sagittarius Moon brings moods of internal reflection as well as internal exploration. Philosophical perspectives and growing points of interest remind us that life is always expanding and evolving into new plateaus of understanding. The Sagittarius Moon is generally a good time to explore the outdoors, to seek more flexibility and versatility in life, and to spread encouragement and optimism. Don't put off today what you think you can do tomorrow; Thursday's all day void-of-course Moon is likely to bring spacey moods and misdirected efforts, especially while Mercury is retrograde (March 30 – April 23).

Sun enters Taurus (April 20 – May 21) Taurus is a Venus ruled sign whose attraction to beauty is second nature. As a general rule, Taurus energy promotes a strong desire to keep physically fit, and to keep possessions and personal effects shining and looking good. Taurus has a very matter-of-fact way of looking at life, and likes to keep the surroundings neat and functional, as well as aesthetically pleasing and socially acceptable. This is not to say that Taurus folks are orderly according to the rest of the world! They have a very sensitive and often sentimental side, and find it difficult to change and adapt swiftly when their lives seem to be in perfect order. Taurus loves stability and security. Taurus folks have a knack for smelling money and for finding the value in all things. Taurus says, "I have," and Taurus folks are interested in preserving and enhancing what they have attained and acquired in the course of their lives.

Sun sextile Neptune (occurring April 16 – 22) This occurrence of Sun sextile Neptune creates an opportunistic time for those Aries and Taurus people celebrating birthdays from April 16 – 22. These folks are experiencing an opportunity to awaken in the realm of spirituality and creativity. There is an awareness of the self that goes deep here, and these birthday people are likely to appear distracted and difficult to reach while this phenomenon of great depth is occurring. This will be your year, birthday folks, to explore personal opportunities of spiritual growth. It may be a time to get away from it all, and find a sanctuary in which to meditate and open up to some valuable answers to old questions. These folks are in a place that gives them an opportunity to better understand the work of their path, but this is probably only true if they act on their own intuitive sensibilities, without the influences of others. That shouldn't be too hard for the enterprising and self-motivated Aries natures among us, as well as the (cusp born) practical minded Taurians. This will be your year (birthday people) to enhance and strengthen your intuition and primal instincts by tapping into them while they are easily available. This may also be the time to overcome addictions and disruptive patterns. This aspect will reoccur on December 20, affecting some of the Sagittarius and Capricorn (cusp born) people of that time.

Venus enters Aries (Venus in Aries: April 20 – May 15) As Venus enters Aries ,the expression of beauty, love and attraction assumes a fascination for the warrior spirit. Venus represents magnetic draw and attraction, and now the planet of love and beauty focuses our attention on the force and fire of Aries related interests. This brings sheer love of and appreciation for such activities as competition, rights (or rites) of selfhood, and initiation into new endeavors. Venus in Aries brings out the warrior and conqueror quality in people, and a new sense of life and vitality will be evident. Venus in Aries emphasizes ardent, open and forthright expressions and proposals of love, especially from our Aries friends who may be blinded by the lust for beauty. New hobbies, crafts and talents will spring forth. In Aries, Venus is in the place of detriment. Remember, Aries rules the head; there are numerous ways you can use your head before plunging head first into love matters. Try not to be too impulsive, impatient, or militant in the expression of true feelings, affection, and love. New and ardent love is inspired with Venus in Aries.

Mercury-square-Pluto-non-exact (occurring April 19 – 21) Today is as close as we come, within six orbital degrees, of a very brief interlude with Mercury square Pluto. Due to the retrograde cycle of Mercury (March 30 – April 23), this aspect begins to occur but doesn't reach a peak. Although it is not as pronounced, the energy of this aspect is still present. For a recap of the story of Mercury square Pluto, see March 13 when it last occurred in full. Mercury square Pluto will repeat one more time on September 28.

April 21st Thursday

Moon in Sagittarius	PDT	EDT
Moon trine Mars	12:48 AM	3:48 AM
Moon trine Jupiter goes v/c	9:56 AM	12:56 PM

Sun trine Pluto begins (see April 27)
Birthday: Queen Elizabeth II 1926

♉

Mood Watch: Positive lunar aspects start the day off nicely; however, as the waning Sagittarius Moon goes void-of-course, there may be a tendency for people to be spacey, indiscreet, flippant, rash, or erratic. The void-of-course Sagittarius Moon can be a troublesome time to travel, with transportation delays, miscommunications, and sometimes there's a tendency for people to get lost. Mercury retrograde (March 30 - to April 23) doesn't help matters either. You can't always trust a navigation system to get to where you're going. For example, if you use a satellite navigation system to get to my home address, it leads you to a road that hasn't been built yet. It's a good time to arm yourself with more than one resource of information to get where you need to go. Despite the spacey moods, Sagittarius Moon keeps our outlook positive! Keep it light and humorous.

April 22ⁿᵈ Friday

Earth Day / Good Friday

Moon in Sagittarius / Capricorn	PDT	EDT
Moon enters Capricorn	3:24 AM	6:24 AM
Moon sextile Neptune	4:13 AM	7:13 AM
Moon square Venus	6:24 AM	9:24 AM
Moon trine Sun	7:10 AM	10:10 AM
Moon square Uranus	7:32 AM	10:32 AM
Moon conjunct Pluto	4:50 PM	7:50 PM
Venus conjunct Uranus	7:28 PM	10:28 PM
Venus square Pluto begins (see April 27)		

Birthday: Charles Mingus 1922

"Here's what I think the truth is: We are all addicts of fossil fuels in a state of denial, about to face cold turkey, our leaders are now committing violent crimes to get what little is left of what we're hooked on." – Kurt Vonnegut

Mood Watch: A serious tone strikes our moods with the waning Moon in Capricorn on this **Earth Day / Good Friday**. We are likely to see a great deal of emphasis placed on corporations and their accountability, or lack of, to responsible environmental management. The waning Capricorn Moon is not generally considered a good time to explore people's feelings. During Sun in Taurus and Moon in Capricorn, people tend to be staunch, distant, guarded, or preoccupied with their work. This may be the time to talk dollars and cents, to cover material matters, and to get some serious business done.

Venus conjunct Uranus (occurring April 17 – 25) It's no wonder that love matters seem wild or chaotic – this conjunction brings an element of shock value to the expression of love. Venus conjunct Uranus in Aries creates the potential for lively encounters with ardent and exciting love and affection, wherein there is sometimes an exceedingly abrupt, and often unusual, counsel of love. A radical or explosive attraction or fascination may occur with this conjunction, opening our senses to a more amicable understanding of chaos. For those who are strongly affected, mischievous, brilliant, and unusual modes of love and affection now occur. Hang in there. Chaos is often considered a true test of love. Be positive and open to the challenge of love with chaos.

April 23rd Saturday

Moon in Capricorn	PDT	EDT
Moon square Saturn	1:55 AM	4:55 AM
Moon square Mercury	2:47 AM	5:47 AM
Mercury goes direct	3:03 AM	6:03 AM
Moon square Mars	9:42 AM	12:42 PM
Moon square Jupiter goes v/c	5:13 PM	8:13 PM
Mercury-opposite-Saturn-non-exact (see below + March 18)		

Birthday: Shirley Temple Black 1928

Mood Watch: Capricorn Moon focuses our moods on the importance of diligence, persistence, and discipline. There is a need to get things done, to finish business, and handle whatever comes along with serious intent. There is great potential to accomplish much today as long as everyone remains focused on their tasks and watches their time. Drop fears concerning financial security. Risk becomes greater when nothing is done to change one's condition. Hope comes with diligent effort.

Mercury goes direct (Mercury direct: April 23 – Aug. 2) Since March 30, Mercury retrograde in the sign of Aries may be the cause of a lot of head butting, arguments, and disputes, and fortunately, it's almost at an end. Now we can breathe a greatly needed sigh of relief as Mercury, the planet governing the realms of communication, becomes stationary and will soon begin to move forward. Take note that our faculties and manner of communicating will definitely improve within the next few days. Although perhaps not today – when the stationary Mercury often freezes communication efforts – but very soon, our communications will run more smoothly; this will be a good time to begin clearing up various misunderstandings that have occurred over the past few weeks. For more information on this recently completed phase of Mercury retrograde, see March 30 when it first began. For more on Mercury retrograde patterns throughout this year, see the introduction on *Mercury retrograde periods.*

Mercury-opposite-Saturn-non-exact (occurring April 9 – 30) Due to Mercury going direct today, this is as close as we come – within minutes – of Mercury reaching a full opposition to Saturn. This near opposition also reached a close peak on March 18. For a recap on the story of how Mercury in Aries and Saturn in Libra affects us, *see March 18.*

April 24th Sunday

Easter Sunday
LAST QUARTER MOON in AQUARIUS

Moon in Capricorn / Aquarius	PDT	EDT	
Moon enters Aquarius	10:58 AM	1:58 PM	
Moon sextile Uranus	3:39 PM	6:39 PM	
Moon square Sun	7:46 PM	10:46 PM	
Moon sextile Venus	8:12 PM	11:12 PM	

ᛜ

Birthday: Barbara Streisand 1942

Mood Watch: The **Last Quarter Moon in Aquarius** (Moon square Sun) brings humanitarian focuses to the scope of our experience. A kind word or sympathetic ear has great healing power and oftentimes promotes peace. This Moon beckons to us to find solutions, however temporary, to human problems, and it connects us with the dichotomies and ironies of the human experience. This is a time when the work of genius is ever present, but often goes undetected.

April 25th Monday

Moon in Aquarius	PDT	EDT	
Moon trine Saturn	10:45 AM	1:45 PM	
Moon sextile Mercury	12:27 PM	3:27 PM	
Moon sextile Mars	11:13 PM	2:13 AM	(Apr 26)

Birthday: Ella Fitzgerald 1917

Mood Watch: This is the time when many will be making social connections. The signs of the times are all around us, applying some very interesting twists and turns in the ventures and knowledge of humankind. On some level, the desire for freedom or personal breakthrough calls out to some folks. The restlessness of spring season stirs our hearts. Sun in Taurus and Moon in Aquarius is an important time to banish fear and test the realms with one's own sensibilities. There's enough love and beauty to go around for everyone.

April 26th Tuesday

Moon in Aquarius / Pisces	PDT	EDT	
Moon sextile Jupiter goes v/c	4:27 AM	7:27 AM	
Moon enters Pisces	9:57 PM	12:57 AM	(Apr 27)
Moon conjunct Neptune	11:04 PM	2:04 AM	(Apr 27)
Venus opposite Saturn begins (see April 30)			

Birthday: Carol Burnett 1933

Mood Watch: Just as our communications begin to notably improve now that Mercury is direct since Saturday, a long void-of-course Aquarius Moon day disrupts our moods with technical glitches, complex problem solving, and unexpected delays. Human foibles are as common as ever, especially under these lunar conditions. Resolve to fix whatever problem might come your way, but don't get hung up on how long it will take to solve the problem. There is much to be learned about ourselves and the systems we use when they're not working. Much later, the Moon entering Pisces will bring a more tranquil mood.

April 27th Wednesday

Moon in Pisces	PDT	EDT
Venus square Pluto	12:21 AM	3:21 AM
Moon sextile Sun	12:24 PM	3:24 PM
Moon sextile Pluto goes v/c	12:52 PM	3:52 PM
Sun trine Pluto	5:59 PM	8:59 PM
Mercury conjunct Venus begins (see May 9)		

Birthday: Ulysses S. Grant 1822

Mood Watch: The waning Pisces Moon brings curious, artistic, and deeply spiritual moods. It all goes somewhat smoothly this morning with reflective, adaptable, and abstract perspectives at work. However, as the Pisces Moon goes void-of-course this afternoon, temptation sets in. This is a time when addictive tendencies are strong. Spacey moods cloud the brain as we fall under the spell of an extraordinarily long void-of-course Moon phase set to take place throughout this evening, all of tomorrow, and into a fair portion of Friday. It is important to hold fast to the strongest and most positive principles, especially at a time when our faith and beliefs are generously tested.

Venus square Pluto (occurring April 22 – 29) Venus in Aries is square to Pluto in Capricorn. The energetic, swift and intrepid qualities of our affections are likely to take a pretty good beating. Our concepts of beauty may be challenged as the corruption of superpowers prompts action which threatens or alters the beauty and pleasure in our lives. There may be environmental destruction that intrudes on our sense of natural aesthetics. Venus square Pluto often involves such difficulties as loss or death of a loved one, the obstacles of rejection, and general oppression for those aspects of life to which we are undeniably attached and which we hold dear. If something of this nature is occurring for you, it is best to recognize that love will triumph in every dimension, despite the pain of separation, or the disease and strife of the beloved. While Pluto is in Capricorn, the square of Venus in Aries may create the sense that loving efforts are unreciprocated. Some people may feel used, unappreciated, or disadvantaged. Be both strong and gentle in matters of love. Let the obstacles of love's pain become the building blocks of a better outlook, and a stronger love will supersede these current trials of the heart. Venus square Pluto will repeat on September 18.

Sun trine Pluto (occurring April 21 – 30) Positive, life altering changes are occurring, particularly in the lives of those Taurus born people celebrating birthdays this year from April 21 – 30. These folks are currently undergoing the favorable trine aspect of Pluto to their natal Sun, bringing out experiences that involve transformation, and encounters with greater powers and with fate. For some of these birthday folks, the concept of receiving gifts and empowerment in the midst of fateful events may seem rocky and not particularly advantageous. Have no fear; this is a time to get in touch with your power, birthday Taurus! It is wise to remember Pluto moves slowly in our cosmos, and powerful encounters that seem deadly or harsh are actually a necessary process. Though unavoidable, matters involving fate can be positive, and the trine aspect does represent a gift being bestowed. Taurus birthday people, be grateful this is the trine aspect that brings power issues into your life in a more positive fashion with Pluto, and the work of destiny will bestow untold gifts this year. Sun trine Pluto will reoccur August 28, affecting the Leo and Virgo cusp born people of that time.

♉

April 28th Thursday
Moon void-of-course in Pisces
No Exact Aspects
Birthday: Terry Prachett 1948

Mood Watch: It's uncommon but it does happen – the waning Pisces Moon is void-of-course throughout this entire day. The complexity of our emotions may be difficult to mask at times, as we find ourselves wading in a sea of delays, time warps, sloppy excuses, and some all around spacey moods. On the other hand, this is a splendid time for frivolity, creativity, artistry, wizardry, and magic. Meditation, prayer, and calming sanctuaries provide helpful avenues of release and fortification. If you don't have the advantage of taking time off from strong mental focuses, let humor, acceptance, and a happy-go-lucky pace provide some relief. An evening reading Terry Prachett could be just the ticket to a fun filled getaway. Beware of the tendency for many folks to overdo addictive substances. Moderation is especially important at a time when we are prone to hypersensitivity.

April 29th Friday

Moon in Pisces / Aries	PDT	EDT	
Moon enters Aries	10:33 AM	1:33 PM	
Moon conjunct Uranus	3:58 PM	6:58 PM	

Birthday: Duke Ellington 1899

Mood Watch: Out of the deep bog of our spaced out minds, the last of the void-of-course Pisces Moon brings a slow start to the day. However, by the time the Moon enters Aries many folks will appear anxiously raring to go in order to make some week's end progress. A hustle and bustle spirit greets us this afternoon. Aries Moon reminds us of the importance of going out and getting what we need from life. Moon conjunct Uranus brings a restless spirit and allows us to identify with a temporary sense of wild abandon. Spring is here!

April 30th Saturday

Moon in Aries	PDT	EDT	
Moon square Pluto	1:31 AM	4:31 AM	
Moon conjunct Venus	9:53 AM	12:53 PM	
Moon conjunct Mercury	5:13 PM	8:13 PM	
Venus opposite Saturn	5:14 PM	8:14 PM	
Mars conjunct Jupiter	9:25 PM	12:25 AM	(May 1)

Birthday: Willie Nelson 1933

Mood Watch: Waning Aries Moon is an excellent time to reiterate personal affirmations and to prepare for the reinventing process of the self. This means weeding out and dropping the old tendencies and habits that are holding back the emergence of the new self. Most importantly, this is a time of abolishing self doubt.

Venus opposite Saturn (occurring April 26 – May 3) Venus in Aries opposes Saturn in Libra, and this brings daring, assertive, and sometimes impetuous expressions of love at odds with the even-tempered scrutiny of restrictive types of discipline. While there is a very strong need to attain a sense of beauty, there is also a constantly compelling and obsessive compulsion to press on with work and vital responsibilities. This may be a difficult time for some to feel in tune with loved ones, and career related disciplines may be impeding on recreational needs and desires. This may be particularly so because Saturn is currently retrograde (Jan. 25 – June 12). Love matters – and the things we are attracted to – are subjected to unavoidable trials and restrictions. There will be folks among us thrust into the challenges of facing jealousy, guilt, offensive outbreaks, anguish, oppression, defeat or despair. There are always lessons where our not so sheltered passions lie. We must be careful how our passions are stirred or handled. Hold steadfast to all principles of wisdom. Be careful not to bite off more than you can chew, especially with regard to irresistible attractions laden with restrictive laws.

Mars conjunct Jupiter (occurring April 19 – May 6) Mars is conjunct with Jupiter in Aries. Strong actions will occur – possibly even warlike or defensive actions with regard to the distribution and management of large sums of wealth and revenue. While Mars and Jupiter are conjunct in Aries, these active shifts of revenue will occur around such Aries related things as psychiatric centers, surgical activities, metal workers, explorers, engineers, fire fighting, arms-manufacturing, military leaders, trade-unions, mechanical services, dentists, and professional sports. Mars represents action as it occurs, while Jupiter symbolizes expansion and matters of skill building, investing, joviality, vision quests, and achievement. This could be a time of exceedingly active breakthroughs with great wins or losses in economic endeavors. This is an especially active time for war related events. Market mergers will bring great fortune where great losses may have otherwise occurred. Opportunities to enhance or perfect talents or skills make this a good time to activate a business or career, especially in such Aries related activities as new enterprise. This is the only time this planetary conjunction will occur in 2011. It's an excellent time to attempt to prosper, and to act on personal and community needs.

May 1st Sunday

Beltane / May Day

Moon in Aries / Taurus	PDT	EDT	
Moon conjunct Jupiter	7:50 AM	10:50 AM	
Moon conjunct Mars goes v/c	8:20 AM	11:20 AM	
Moon enters Taurus	10:58 PM	1:58 AM	(May 2)

Birthday: Judy Collins 1939

Mood Watch: The Moon wanes darkly in Aries on this May Day Sunday of the

New Moon eve. Our moods are met by our need for courage, self-reliance, and a logical course of action. People will need incentives, praise, and room for self-expression. Where these freedoms are not met, there will be oppression, conflict, and aggressive tension. The Sun in Taurus with a darkly waning Aries Moon often brings stubbornness and strife, particularly while the moon is void-of-course. On a positive note, these are the struggles that allow us to grow stronger and more independent. Take heart – this is the time of spring flower glory, unabashed beauty and strength!

Happy **May Day!** This is a traditional old world solar holiday, also known as **Beltane**. We have now reached the half-way mark – and the height – of the spring season. This holiday celebrates the dance of the Maypole and fertility, beauty, rapturous love, and the various kinds of youthful play and frolic appropriate to spring. May Day is a celebration of the fruition and beauty found in nature. It represents the awakening of the passion and youthfulness in all of life. This time calls to us all to take joy in the fertilization of those parts of ourselves and our lives that need to be brought to fruition.

May 2nd Monday
NEW MOON in TAURUS

	PDT	EDT	
Moon sextile Neptune	12:16 AM	3:16 AM	
Moon trine Pluto	1:38 PM	4:38 PM	
Moon conjunct Sun goes v/c	11:50 PM	2:50 AM	(May 3)

Birthday: Dwayne "The Rock" Johnson 1972

Mood Watch: The **New Moon in Taurus** (Moon conjunct Sun) emphasizes the acquisition of new possessions, or it could mean there is a need to restore, replenish, and maintain the old ones. Personal contentment counts with new possessions. Search for the value of what you need and want. The Moon in Taurus is exalted and calls to us to enjoy the beauty that surrounds us. Taurus is ruled by Venus, the architect of the arts.

May 3rd Tuesday
Moon void-of-course in Taurus   **PDT**   **EDT**
Mercury conjunct Jupiter begins (see May 11)

Birthday: James Brown 1933

Mood Watch: Keep your spirits high and your expectations low. Just when we thought we were over the effects of the April 28 all day void-of-course-Moon – pop! – a new endless void-of-course Moon day strikes. It's nothing really; it's just a slower paced, easy going, lazy, stubborn sort of day. On a positive note, the newly waxing Moon is exalted in the place of Taurus, and our moods are more in tune with nature, as well as our practical needs and desires. While banking matters may seem to take forever today, a little spending and sensible splurging will go a long way for the morale.

May 4th Wednesday

Moon in Taurus / Gemini	PDT	EDT
Moon enters Gemini	10:09 AM	1:09 PM
Moon square Neptune	11:29 AM	2:29 PM
Moon sextile Uranus	3:48 PM	6:48 PM

Birthday: Audrey Hepburn 1929

Mood Watch: A somewhat lazy, lethargic, and stubborn morning occurs as the void-of-course Moon completes its cycle in Taurus. Creature comforts and basic necessities are an important part of starting the day off right. As the Moon enters Gemini, a curious, playful, and talkative quality of expression strikes our moods. Gemini Moon puts us in a communicative spirit. Moon square Neptune brings a challenging time for our beliefs, and it may also emphasize our struggles with escapism or unfulfilled dreams. Moon sextile Uranus brings the opportunity for us to kick up our heels, blow off some steam, and have fun!

May 5th Thursday

Cinco de Mayo

Moon in Gemini	PDT	EDT	
Moon trine Saturn	8:37 AM	11:37 AM	
Moon sextile Venus	9:08 PM	12:08 AM	(May 6)
Moon sextile Mercury	10:49 PM	1:49 AM	(May 6)
Venus conjunct Jupiter begins (see May 11)			

Birthday: Ann B. Davis 1926

Mood Watch: The youthfully waxing Gemini Moon fills our moods with an intrusion of mutable thoughts and busy ideas. Springtime frenzy is changing the rate at which we are able to plan and keep track of matters. Getting an earful of everyone else's affairs can seem tedious, but it's just a way for folks to vent that extra nervous energy. Gemini Moon reminds us to filter through all the trivia and take it in stride. Prioritize the important things in life. As if it were a game, learn to enjoy setting straight all the minor details.

May 6th Friday

Moon in Gemini / Cancer	PDT	EDT
Moon sextile Jupiter	7:29 AM	10:29 AM
Moon sextile Mars goes v/c	1:12 PM	4:12 PM
Moon enters Cancer	7:31 PM	10:31 PM
Moon trine Neptune	8:53 PM	11:53 PM
Mars sextile Neptune begins (see May 12)		

Birthday: George Clooney 1961

Mood Watch: Spring is in the air and talkative moods abound. Moon sextile Jupiter brings optimism and open mindedness. Don't be fooled by those who are not talkative – they undoubtedly have a lot on their minds. Gemini Moon focuses our attention on those areas of life where we have mixed feelings, and there is a tendency to mull over those things that have not settled just right in our heads. Moon sextile Mars brings opportunities, as our moods will be bursting with fiery force and energy. However, the Moon goes void-of-course in the afternoon, and although there's a lot of useful information going around, there is not a whole lot of attention being paid to it. Traffic, delays, and various other distractions may be the common symptoms of this time. Information overload could be another reason people aren't paying attention. This evening's Cancer Moon brings the need for nurturing, a yearning for love, and intimacy. Moon trine Neptune brings a greater chance for acceptance, peace, and spiritual harmony.

May 7ᵗʰ Saturday

Moon in Cancer	PDT	EDT
Moon square Uranus	1:11 AM	4:11 AM
Moon opposite Pluto	9:10 AM	12:10 PM
Moon square Saturn	4:55 PM	7:55 PM

Birthday: Johannes Brahms 1833

Mood Watch: Today's lunar aspects are challenging. If someone reaches out to you, it sometimes means they trust you, or sometimes manipulative motivation is at work. When the Moon is in Cancer and someone is opening up to you, it is potentially dangerous to ignore them. Cancer Moon brings out our need for nurturing reassurance and, sometimes, motherly affection and advice are needed. It is an honor to be trusted by someone, and it is even more honorable when we do not break that trust. Sometimes we need to learn how to just listen, not judge, and give our advice only when it is asked of us. There are many ways to care, and since people are often complex, it may take awhile before we learn how to care in a way that is helpful. Don't buy guilt – it's far too expensive!

May 8ᵗʰ Sunday

Mother's Day

Moon in Cancer	PDT	EDT	
Moon sextile Sun	4:00 AM	7:00 AM	
Moon square Venus	10:51 AM	1:51 PM	
Moon square Mercury	11:10 AM	2:10 PM	
Moon square Jupiter	4:04 PM	7:04 PM	
Moon square Mars goes v/c	11:52 PM	2:52 AM	(May 9)

Birthday: Melissa Gilbert 1964

Mood Watch: Mother Moon is in Cancer, her home base. The earliest part of the morning starts off well with Moon sextile Sun. The beauty of the season abounds, but the Cancer Moon is lined up for a number of square aspects throughout the rest of the day. The challenges of Cancer Moon require emotional stamina, and the ability to let go when the pressure builds. It's Mother's Day and this is the time to honor all those who have acted as a mother. This doesn't just include the amazing act of giving birth, although that's completely awesome. Motherhood includes the provision of shelter, protection, nourishment, guidance, teaching, discipline, and unconditional love. In the face of conflict mothers often worry, but the act of worrying is a useless tendency under so many challenging emotional conditions. Visualize the things you do want. Honor Mother today with love and pay no mind to those worries. Don't worry, be happy. Let your motherly vibrations be filled with confidence and reassurance.

May 9th Monday
Moon in Cancer / Leo

	PDT	EDT	
Moon enters Leo	2:35 AM	5:35 AM	
Moon trine Uranus	8:10 AM	11:10 AM	
Mercury conjunct Venus	8:44 AM	11:44 AM	
Moon sextile Saturn	10:46 PM	1:46 AM	(May 10)

Birthday: Billy Joel 1949

Mood Watch: Leo Moon puts us in touch with personal and integral needs and desires. Today will be a good day to pursue a taste of personal pleasure. Courageous moods abound. Take pride in the things you do!

Mercury conjunct Venus (occurring April 27 – May 25) Even though it's been awhile since Mercury went direct (April 23), this conjunction will reach two peaks this month. First, it happens today, with Mercury conjunct Venus in Aries. These two planets conjunct in the compelling and naturally buoyant sign, Aries, will bring a very convincing – or perhaps even competitive – quality to our communications. This will carry a strong, sometimes challenging quality to the communication of love. Any words of love or adoration uttered now will come across with a fervent intent – and with clear reception – particularly if this expression of love is very sincere and genuine. Mercury conjunct Venus in Aries brings a demanding tone to discussions among loved ones, and it may create an urgent quality in negotiations over such prized items as art and valuables. Communications are received best when they are delivered with considerable care. Be sure to let those whom you love know it; sometimes it's what isn't said that disquiets the heart. Hold no expectations in the expression of love, and take no offense if your attempts to express love are poorly interpreted. Know that there is a need to communicate love occurring now, and that the most simple and direct way to express love might be best. Mercury conjunct Venus will reach another peak on May 16, with Mercury conjunct Venus at the zero degree mark of Taurus. While Mercury is retrograde (Aug. 2 – 26), Mercury and Venus will also be conjunct in Leo on August 16. On November 1, there will be a non-exact conjunction of Mercury and Venus in Scorpio.

May 10th Tuesday
FIRST QUARTER MOON in LEO

	PDT	EDT	
Moon square Sun	1:32 PM	4:32 PM	
Moon trine Mercury	8:47 PM	11:47 PM	
Moon trine Venus	9:06 PM	12:06 AM	(May 11)
Moon trine Jupiter goes v/c	9:52 PM	12:52 AM	(May 11)

Venus conjunct Mars begins (see May 23)
Mercury conjunct Mars begins (see May 20)

♉

Birthday: Sid Vicious 1957

Mood Watch: The expression of a **First Quarter Moon in Leo** (Moon square Sun) places our moods in states of playfulness, self-indulgence, and the need for expression and adoration. Today's attractions tend to be towards those areas of life that we identify with the most. With the Sun in Taurus, the Moon in Leo is most likely expressed by the act of flashing around our best toys. Moods reflect on the contest of who has the best, the biggest, the shiniest, and the most expensive toys, cars, clothes, house and garden. Entertainment value and quality of presentation are just as important. Bonus points go out to those who not only have the finest trimmings, but know how to use what they have in an imaginative, original, and creative manner. Cool is always "in," and requires the assurance of the proper attitude.

May 11ᵗʰ Wednesday

Moon in Leo / Virgo

	PDT	EDT
Mars enters Taurus	12:03 AM	3:03 AM
Moon enters Virgo	6:58 AM	9:58 AM
Moon trine Mars	7:22 AM	10:22 AM
Venus conjunct Jupiter	7:42 AM	10:42 AM
Moon opposite Neptune	8:10 AM	11:10 AM
Mercury conjunct Jupiter	12:56 PM	3:56 PM
Moon trine Pluto	7:14 PM	10:14 PM

Birthday: Irving Berlin 1888

Mood Watch: The Leo Moon is void-of-course in the earliest part of the day and we may find ourselves getting off to a somewhat lazy start. Soon enough the Moon enters Virgo, and the quality of our moods will become curious, engaging, and communicative. This is a good time to focus on organization, investments, cleaning, maintenance, and the management the material world.

Mars enters Taurus (Mars in Taurus: May 11 – June 20) Mars represents all modes of action. In the fixed earth sign of Taurus, Mars' action is particularly worked out through the physical realm, making this a primary time to work active energy through the body, or to take affirmative action in the physical world, moving or activating it to change. This is a time when many of us will take strong actions with our financial and material welfare. Mars (the ruler of Aries), is considered in the detrimental position – while in Taurus – for the warrior planet. Mars in Taurus from May 31 – July 11, 2009 brought some concern when North Korea launched a number of missiles, which caused South Korean's president to visit the USA's White House for support. Meanwhile, there was still a monumental attempt to overcome the recession. There was not a happy ending for Michael Jackson who lost his life during that time. When Mars was in Taurus from July 27, 2005 to February 18, 2006, we were forced to take action with the physical world due to hurricane Katrina, which was followed by more hurricanes and immense fund raising efforts to resolve the mess they caused. Mars' energy enlivens such Taurus related activities as bargain hunting, buying and selling, bidding, investing, banking, decorating, and creating a practical work space. Mars in Taurus boosts the life energy of Taurus people and gives them the incentive to take action. Mars generates heat which can often appear explosive under pressure. Taurus people are reminded to keep a cool sense of control at all times and to be aware of the tendency towards temper tantrums when events get overheated. Taurus folks can strike while the iron is hot but they must use caution and be aware of fires and fevers. Aquarius and Leo folks also need to be especially cautious as Mars now squares to their natal Sun, causing actions around them to seem abrasive to them personally. Scorpios may be particularly aware of fiery activity in their lives at this time with Mars opposing their natal Sun.

Venus conjunct Jupiter (occurring May 5 – 14) The influence of beauty, love and attraction (Venus) blends and melds with the powers of production, expansion, and prosperity (Jupiter). In the sign of Aries, these two planets are stirring up experiences which are very active and aggressive in nature. Aries is associated with new enterprise, self-expression, and determination. This is a time to enhance love relationships and realize the precious value of love in its most limitless sense, since the influence of Jupiter reminds us that the resources of love in the universe are inexhaustible and love's great bounty is designed to be shared. A love for expansion, and the growth of skill (or personal economy), comes out with the conjunction of Venus and Jupiter. Love is infectious. The more love is disseminated the more there is to share and expound on.

Mercury conjunct Jupiter (occurring May 3 – 14) Thoughts and information (Mercury) with regard to a prosperous and visionary breakthrough (Jupiter) will be highlighted. Due to Mercury's last retrograde cycle (March 30 – April 23), this conjunction is occurring in Aries for a third time this year. For a recap on the story of this beneficial conjunction, see March 15, when it first occurred.

May 12th Thursday

Moon in Virgo	PDT	EDT
Mars sextile Neptune	1:27 AM	4:27 AM
Moon trine Sun goes v/c	7:51 PM	10:51 PM
Mars trine Pluto begins (see May 20)		

Birthday: George Carlin 1937

Mood Watch: Virgo Moon brings vigilant, cautious, and observant moods. There will be a lot to take in, and a lot to assess emotionally as well. Virgo Moon helps to get us in touch with the physical world in a way we can feel good about. Sun in Taurus and Moon in Virgo place an emphasis on practical, down-to-earth, necessary types of money management. This is also the time to tackle spring cleaning and organization. As the Moon goes void-of-course, our moods may seem more withdrawn.

Mars sextile Neptune (occurring May 6 – 14) Mars in Taurus is sextile to Neptune in Pisces at the zero degree mark. Physical initiative – when taken –

brings the potential for an intuitive and spiritual awakening. Mars sextile Neptune is a splendid time to *act* on our *beliefs*. This aspect brings the vitality of Mars' energy into a favorable position with the spirit-awakening influence of Neptune. This is a place where we can safely dump our anger and can potentially make a connection with a spiritual healing process. Those who act on their visions and on the ceremonies of their particular belief systems will have an opportunity to connect with a very profound spiritual experience. This aspect makes the active work of artists, poets, and musicians into unique and very powerful statements about being in an endowed and sacred state of awareness. Mars is active and masculine, while Neptune has a very nebulous and passive guise that affects our deeper inner sense of beliefs and spirit. When these two planets are placed in a favorable position to each other, personal spiritual breakthroughs can be made. This is the only time this aspect occurs this year.

May 13th Friday

Moon in Virgo / Libra	PDT	EDT
Moon enters Libra	8:56 AM	11:56 AM
Moon opposite Uranus	2:20 PM	5:20 PM
Moon square Pluto	8:41 PM	11:41 PM
Venus sextile Neptune begins (see May 16)		
Mercury sextile Neptune begins (see May 16)		

Birthday: Arthur Seymour Sullivan 1842

Mood Watch: Doubt and skepticism may be the cause of this morning's delays. As the Moon enters Libra, our moods become more focused on teamwork and the need for harmony and cooperation from others. Moon opposite Uranus is likely to bring especially chaotic energies. Much later, Moon square Pluto puts us in tune with the bigger problems we face in life. The waxing Libra Moon gives us the incentive to work through life's inconsistencies, and to find creative solutions to develop a greater sense of harmony.

Why is **Friday the 13th** considered such a bad omen? Friday the 13th in October of the year 1307 was a really bad day in the life of Jacques DeMolay, fearless leader of the Knights Templar. By sundown on that fateful day nearly all the Knights Templar throughout France were seized and thrown into dungeons. Thousands of men who were at one time considered nobles had their properties seized, and many suffered torture and inhumane conditions. The French King and the Pope conspired against the Templars to plunder their wealth; the Templars were then discarded as heretics and banned from the power they had held for so long. Seven years after the Friday the 13th incident, DeMolay was executed. The fall of the Templars left such a bitter mark on the soul of Europe that Friday the 13th has held a notorious reputation. Friday the 13th is often considered unlucky; however, there are some people who think of thirteen as an auspicious number, and to them this day is considered to be a lucky time. These people naturally tend to have a better experience of this day, by virtue of their more positive outlook. On a positive note, the Knights Templar is still a fascination to many and a fraternally honored memory to this day. Perhaps their fortunes will yet revive.

May 14th Saturday

Moon in Libra	PDT	EDT
Moon conjunct Saturn	3:06 AM	6:06 AM

Birthday: Cate Blanchett 1969

Mood Watch: The earliest part of the morning has a serious tone to it, while Moon conjunct Saturn tunes us into the necessity to focus on responsibilities. The waxing Libra Moon atmosphere is studious, congenial, and interactive. With Libra Moon it is best to avoid excesses, to seek objectives, and to give some ample time to others to make decisions and plan events. Libra Moon activity tips its scales back and forth between the facts and figures of life while we find ourselves searching for wisdom, truth, and justice. This is a good time to find joy in partnership and friendship, and to create balance wherever it is needed.

May 15th Sunday

Moon in Libra / Scorpio	PDT	EDT	
Moon opposite Jupiter	2:28 AM	5:28 AM	
Moon opposite Mercury	8:51 AM	11:51 AM	
Moon opposite Venus goes v/c	9:01 AM	12:01 PM	
Moon enters Scorpio	9:31 AM	12:31 PM	
Moon trine Neptune	10:52 AM	1:52 PM	
Moon opposite Mars	3:08 PM	6:08 PM	
Venus enters Taurus	3:12 PM	6:12 PM	
Mercury enters Taurus	4:18 PM	7:18 PM	
Moon sextile Pluto	9:07 PM	12:07 AM	(May 16)
Sun square Neptune begins (see May 22)			

Birthday: Brian Eno 1948

Mood Watch: The Libra Moon opposes Jupiter, Mercury, and lastly Venus before going void-of-course this morning. Wherever relationships are challenged by money, this morning's activities are likely to be especially alarming. Fortunately, the void-of-course phase of the Moon doesn't last long, and the heavily waxing Moon in Scorpio brings some theraputic intensity and depth to the scope of our moods. This would be a good time to let go of unnecessary emotional baggage and to drop those unproductive resentments, grudges, and vendettas.

Venus enters Taurus (Venus in Taurus: May 15 – June 9) Venus in Taurus is the time of an extraordinary attraction to beauty. Here in Taurus, Venus is at home nurturing us with sensual pleasure and enhancing our appreciation of nature and earthly bounty, as well as our appreciation for quality and specialty craftsmanship. Venus in Taurus brings out aesthetic awareness, and places a greater emphasis on the love of having valuable items, wealth, and abundance. Venus attracts and draws, and Taurus emphasizes the need for material acquisition, attainment, and beauty. Taurus people will be touched by the need for love and affection in their lives as Venus crosses over their natal Sun. Now is the time to acquire, polish, clean, and beautify things that give a sense of truly having something. To create beauty around oneself is to enhance one's sense of wellbeing. Simple pleasures are the best – an effort to enjoy the beauties of life is not necessarily expensive. ♉

Mercury enters Taurus (Mercury in Taurus: May 15 – June 2) Mercury moves into the sign of Taurus, and communications will focus on manifesting sales and generating economic growth. It is a good time to clarify matters involving valuables, and to focus on documents, contracts, speeches, and business procedures. Mercury is the messenger, the speaker and the director of the subject matter at hand. Mercury is also classically known as "The Merchant," "The Trickster," and "The Thief." In the fixed earth sign of Taurus, Mercury inspires the inclination to buy, sell, trade, and barter. Issues of ownership and, undoubtedly, a "steal of a deal" will appear in the arena of barter. Resourceful thinking, advertising, and information processing can lead to the extra buck. This is a time to accurately record practical matters and events, and to communicate about finances.

May 16th Monday

Moon in Scorpio	PDT	EDT
Mercury conjunct Venus	2:24 AM	5:24 AM
Mercury sextile Neptune	7:16 AM	10:16 AM
Venus sextile Neptune	7:51 AM	10:51 AM
Mercury trine Pluto begins (see May 20)		
Venus trine Pluto begins (see May 21)		

Birthday: Pierce Brosnan 1953

Mood Watch: The Full Moon Eve is upon us. There will be an emphasis today on facing challenges, finding solutions, keeping active, and on winning. It's a good time to be cautious, to watch for the signs of thievery, deception, and violence. Adventurous and daring moods may lead to trouble, but Scorpio Moon also brings intuitive and psychic abilities which can assist people in navigating their way through rough waters. Creative frolic will inspire our passions. The Full Scorpio Moon is a good time for garden lovers to transplant flowers and shrubs. Safe physical exercises and activities are excellent avenues of release.

Mercury conjunct Venus (occurring April 27 – May 25) Today's conjunction of Mercury and Venus takes place in the down-to-earth, material conscious realm of Taurus. This is often a time when intimate and loving thoughts are best reciprocated in an atmosphere of luxury, comfort, and beauty. Where these things are not present, there is much talk about the desire for them. This is the time to speak up for the things we love and to appreciate beauty with loving words. Communications are received best when they are delivered with considerable care. Be sure to let those whom you love know it; sometimes it's what isn't said that disquiets the heart. This conjunction first reached its peak in Aries on May 9. Next time Mercury is retrograde (Aug. 2 – 26), Mercury and Venus will be conjunct in Leo on August 16. Also, on November 1, there will be a non-exact conjunction of Mercury and Venus in Scorpio.

Mercury sextile Neptune (occurring May 13 – May 17) Mercury in Taurus sextile Neptune in Pisces brings practical, attractive, and enlightening messages that inform us of opportunities for spiritual growth. This is an opportunistic time to cautiously attempt communication with regard to beliefs and spiritual matters. Mercury is in Taurus, adding a cautious and systematic approach to the question of how to face such Neptune related subjects as spiritual strength, guidance, and inspiration. Address addiction problems with helpful instruction. Mercury sextile Neptune allows us to verbalize and share beliefs in a way that encourages people. This aspect last occurred on January 10.

Venus sextile Neptune (occurring May 13 – 17) Venus is at home in Taurus where it brings love, attraction, beauty, and the nature of feminine expression into prominence. Neptune is at home in Pisces and it brings a time to awaken human spirituality and to excel in creative expression through music, art, and spiritual expression. Spread this healing power around for all to share! This time also holds the potential for one to realize the profound beauty and the depths of which true love is capable. This aspect last occurred on February 1 and will reoccur November 24.

May 17th Tuesday
FULL MOON in SCORPIO

Moon in Scorpio / Sagittarius	PDT	EDT
Moon opposite Sun goes v/c	4:08 AM	7:08 AM
Moon enters Sagittarius	10:22 AM	1:22 PM
Moon square Neptune	11:47 AM	2:47 PM
Moon trine Uranus	4:07 PM	7:07 PM

Birthday: Dennis Hopper 1936

Mood Watch: The **Full Moon in Scorpio** (Moon opposite Sun) reaches its peak early this morning and was certainly busy affecting us last night. With this Moon our moods are – for lack of a better word – intensified. As this lunar fullness builds to a crescendo of emotional dramas, our emotional patterns are being played out in interesting ways. Intense desires – and what provokes them – reveal a lot about who we are and what we need to appease the satisfaction-hungry inner child. Entertaining fun, and off-the-cuff kinds of play and humor are good medicine. The Sagittarius Moon tempers the intense aftermath of the Full Scorpio Moon with a focus on the need to expand, seek opportunity, and to continue actively moving through disruptive energies while keeping a positive outlook.

May 18th Wednesday

Moon in Sagittarius	PDT	EDT
Moon sextile Saturn	4:41 AM	7:41 AM

Birthday: Perry Como 1912

Mood Watch: Early this morning, Moon sextile Saturn brings a better sense of control to our focuses. Moon in Sagittarius boosts our energy levels, and our social awareness moves in a much more amicable direction. The Sagittarius Moon, although waning, is still very full, and this is a good time to work off excess emotional baggage by becoming physically active or by exploring. Genuine rest might also be appealing to some folks today, while some philosophical exploration will be sure to inspire. Besides this morning's Moon sextile Saturn, there are no lunar aspects occurring today – a peaceful time for the brilliantly gleaming Sagittarius Moon.

May 19ᵗʰ Thursday

Moon in Sagittarius / Capricorn	PDT	EDT	
Moon trine Jupiter goes v/c	7:17 AM	10:17 AM	
Moon enters Capricorn	1:15 PM	4:15 PM	
Moon sextile Neptune	2:47 PM	5:47 PM	
Moon square Uranus	7:29 PM	10:29 PM	
Moon trine Venus	10:26 PM	1:26 AM	(May 20)

Birthday: Kyle Eastwood 1968

Mood Watch: Optimistic moods start the day with Moon trine Jupiter. However, as the waning Sagittarius Moon goes void-of-course, there may be a tendency for people to get spaced out, or to get lost easily. Later on, as the Moon enters Capricorn, our moods become a bit more industrious and goal oriented. This past week of strong lunar influences brings us to a serious and determined time for our moods. Some seriously seek rest and others seriously want to get on top of the busy events in their lives and to be in control of the bustling buzz of spring.

May 20ᵗʰ Friday

Moon in Capricorn	PDT	EDT
Moon trine Mercury	12:05 AM	3:05 AM
Moon trine Mars	1:11 AM	4:11 AM
Moon conjunct Pluto	1:46 AM	4:46 AM
Moon square Saturn	8:32 AM	11:32 AM
Mars trine Pluto	11:22 AM	2:22 PM
Mercury trine Pluto	2:54 PM	5:54 PM
Mercury conjunct Mars	6:19 PM	9:19 PM
Sun sextile Uranus begins (see May 24)		
Jupiter sextile Neptune begins (see June 8)		

Birthday: Joe Cocker 1944

Mood Watch: The basic objective of the Capricorn Moon places an emphasis on our sense of control. However, this morning's Moon square Saturn brings complex obstacles, and there may be a great effort to maintain the feeling of being in control. Patience and diligence are required. For the most part, today's lunar aspects are positive in nature. Capricorn Moon sees us through hardship. Sun in Taurus and Moon in Capricorn sets us to the task of putting the physical world into order. A sure, steady pace gets the job done.

Mars trine Pluto (occurring May 12 – 24) Mars is now in Taurus trine Pluto in Capricorn. Discerning, cautious, and practical action leads to positive, monumental, and powerful transformations. Actions taken now are more likely to have favorable results or to be influential with higher powers. This is a good time to resolve personal aggression directed towards the views and differences

131

of another generation or of established powers. This is also a good time for vital discoveries in the fight against diseases. Mars trine Pluto brings opportunity for favorable, direct action that may well make a powerful and impressionable impact. Youthful or strong new influences will reach places of power. Mars, the god of war, and Pluto, the underworld god (or hell raiser), may actually be reaching some favorable kind of truce. This aspect will reoccur November 23.

Mercury trine Pluto (occurring May 16 – 22) Mercury in Taurus trine Pluto in Capricorn brings resourceful thoughts and communications that will have powerful results. This aspect brings hope like a gift, and the myth of Pandora's Box shows us that hope regenerates our senses and fills us with the potential for triumph over difficulties. Mercury in Taurus gives a very practical and logical quality to our methods of communicating. This would be a good time to share tales of triumph, spreading those miraculous stories that remind us of the great potential of winning against all odds. This positive aspect aids communication with regard to struggles with fate, major financial losses, and fatal illnesses. This aspect will reoccur on September 11.

Mercury conjunct Mars (occurring May 10 – 24) This conjunction brings the forces of communication (Mercury) together with the forces of action (Mars). This is not a very good time to bluff, especially with regard to banking or sentimental subjects while these two planets are in Taurus. This conjunction brings words and deeds together, and in this case, the greatest action occurs with honest toil and is empowered in the expression of the message. This is an excellent time to get others motivated through speech. This may be a time of angry words being spoken. Some might say the best way to win an argument is to begin by being right; taking this approach now is likely to win you favors but not friendship. Take caution with your words; if they are intended to incite a battle, this is the time to put on your boxing gloves. This conjunction last occurred on February 20 and April 19.

GEMINI

Key Phrase: "I THINK"

Mutable Air Sign

Ruling Planet: Mercury

Symbol: The Twins

May 21st through June 21st

♊

May 21st Saturday

Moon in Capricorn / Aquarius	PDT	EDT
Sun enters Gemini	2:21 AM	5:21 AM
Venus trine Pluto	11:03 AM	2:03 PM
Moon square Jupiter goes v/c	2:04 PM	5:04 PM
Moon enters Aquarius	7:31 PM	10:31 PM
Moon trine Sun	8:55 PM	11:55 PM

Birthday: Fats Waller 1904

Mood Watch: The waning Capricorn Moon carries us into the day with a sense of duty as the Sun enters Gemini, followed by Venus trine Pluto (see below). This afternoon, Moon square Jupiter brings a void-of-course Capricorn Moon; budget cuts, financial mayhem, or less than generous tendencies are just some of the reasons there are traffic problems, delays and minor setbacks. This evening's Aquarius Moon gives us the momentum to try to make some sense of it all.

Sun enters Gemini (Sun in Gemini: May 21 – June 21) Gemini people love to think. They're often thinking of ways to change the picture and to make it brighter and more detailed. The mutable and adaptable mind must be free to roam with different concepts and ideas that haven't been fully integrated into the big picture. Gemini weaves tapestries of thought; great storytellers, Gemini people are often articulate and eloquent speakers, captivating audiences with details and keen observations. Duality is the key factor that shapes the Gemini perspective, and there is always a need to explore the two sides of life.

Venus trine Pluto (occurring May 16 – 23) Venus in Taurus is trine to Pluto in Capricorn. Practical beauty, the value of nature, and efforts to make the planet greener are enhanced and made stronger as we wade through the hardships of a vast landscape of irreversible change and transformation. Now is the time to let our ecological wishes be known, as those who are in positions of power are a little more likely to acknowledge the value of land preservation for the sake of delicate ecosystems. Beauty can be found in all aspects of existence. Venus trine Pluto represents a love or fascination for the workings of fate and power. This aspect often allows a breakthrough to occur for those who are under stress from hardship. There is hope yet that we will acquire an appreciation for the not-so-glamorous aspects of existence. This is also an aspect that allows for adoration and loving energy to flow more easily between generations, despite all the differences that have separated us in these fast changing times. This aspect will reoccur on August 25.

May 22nd Sunday

Moon in Aquarius	PDT	EDT
Sun square Neptune	12:31 AM	3:31 AM
Moon sextile Uranus	2:21 AM	5:21 AM
Moon square Venus	11:11 AM	2:11 PM
Moon square Mars	11:45 AM	2:45 PM
Moon square Mercury	2:52 PM	5:52 PM
Moon trine Saturn	4:00 PM	7:00 PM

Birthday: T. Boone Pickens 1928

Mood Watch: On some level, the desire for freedom or personal breakthrough calls out to some folks, but this may difficult with the Moon squaring to Venus, Mars, and Mercury. The day will have its struggles and minor cat fights here and there, but it will pass. The restlessness of spring season stirs our hearts. People we haven't seen in some time are starting to come out in droves. Untested theories and certain types of knowledge can sometimes be illusions; this is an important time to banish fear and test the realms with one's own sensibilities. With the Moon and Sun both now in air signs, there will be a lot on our minds and much to talk about. Moon trine Saturn is an excellent time to concentrate.

Sun square Neptune (occurring May 15 – 25) This occurrence of Sun square Neptune especially affects those Taurus and Gemini people celebrating birthdays from May 15 – 25. Neptune, in the square position to these folk's natal Sun, brings a perception that obstacles are getting in the way of Spirit, the spiritual path, or the acknowledgment of one's beliefs. Beware of the potential for drug related problems or self-delusion. The challenge for these folks is to overcome the doubts and confrontations that interfere with their beliefs. Over the next year, there will undoubtedly be some spiritual adjustments, and perhaps a change of belief is required for those encountering birthdays at this time. Taurus change? Never! Well, unless it suits them, of course. As for the cusp born Gemini folks – get used to it, my friends – Neptune is in Pisces (see April 4), and your spiritual challenges will be evident for some time to come. This aspect will reoccur on November 20, affecting the lives and beliefs of some of our Scorpio and Sagittarius friends.

May 23rd Monday

Victoria Day, Canada

Moon in Aquarius	PDT	EDT
Venus conjunct Mars	1:25 AM	4:25 AM

Birthday: Scatman Crothers 1910

134

Mood Watch: Our intelligence – or lack of it – always stands out on an Aquarius Moon day, especially during the busy spring days of Sun in Gemini. The Aquarius Moon brings clever, innovative, and gifted perspectives. The Sun and Moon are in air signs, and this is the time to compile data and research, and to integrate it into spring projects and social endeavors. Aquarius Moon is a good time to socialize, work with large groups of people, and to learn about the things that get people excited. Experimental moods lead to amazing discoveries. This evening's Moon trine Sun brings harmonious intelligence. Use this time wisely: educate yourself.

Venus conjunct Mars (occurring May 10 – 29) This conjunction brings together the feminine and the masculine in the sign of Aquarius. Venus conjunct Mars in Aquarius brings activity in relationships, proposals of marriage, and it brings masculine and feminine counterparts together in humanitarian ways. Those who are actively working to help humanity in some way are likely to fall in love with what they're doing. This conjunction puts us in touch with the power of love in action and active attraction. Here, we are easily seduced by love. This may serve as a good time to express love ardently and sincerely, and to receive love just as well. This is also a good time for an individual to get in touch with both the masculine and feminine aspects of the self, and to create peace between those active and passive parts of the personality. Venus and Mars conjunct in Aquarius will bring a strong interest in such Aquarius-like things as technology, science, research, humanitarian efforts, and social endeavors. This is a time of integration between the feminine and masculine forces – it is best done in stride and with care. Empower love relationships with the greatest respect.

May 24th Tuesday
LAST QUARTER MOON in PISCES

Moon in Aquarius / Pisces	PDT	EDT	
Moon sextile Jupiter goes v/c	12:40 AM	3:40 AM	
Moon enters Pisces	5:23 AM	8:23 AM	
Moon conjunct Neptune	7:10 AM	10:10 AM	
Moon square Sun	11:52 AM	2:52 PM	
Moon sextile Pluto	7:19 PM	10:19 PM	
Sun sextile Uranus	11:47 PM	2:47 AM	(May 25)

Birthday: Tommy Chong 1938

Mood Watch: The **Last Quarter Moon in Pisces** (Moon square Sun) brings a dreamy sort of atmosphere. Waning Pisces Moon tends to keep us entranced by those areas of our life that bring depth and meaning. This is a good time to cleanse the spiritual cobwebs from our own lives. Reinforce personal fortitude with the strength to overcome addictions by using sheer willpower and belief.

Sun sextile Uranus (occurring May 20 – 27) This occurrence of Sun sextile Uranus particularly affects those Taurus/Gemini folks celebrating birthdays May 20 – 27. These birthday people are being given an opportunity to blow off some chaotic steam and to reach for qualities of freedom that may have been absent in their recent past. This will be your time to make radical breakthroughs, birthday folks; your natal Sun is currently sextile Uranus for a good reason – to find a

135

liberating balance in the midst of the chaos. Right now, there is no holding back, so go for it; discover your freedom. The victory of creative change will bring a more optimistic outlook on life. This aspect last occurred on January 17, affecting the Capricorn birthday people of that time.

May 25th Wednesday

Moon in Pisces	PDT	EDT
Moon sextile Mars	2:21 AM	5:21 AM
Moon sextile Venus	4:31 AM	7:31 AM
Moon sextile Mercury	11:14 AM	2:14 PM
Sun trine Saturn begins (see June 1)		

Birthday: Ralph Waldo Emerson 1803

Mood Watch: The mutable air days of Gemini coupled with the mutable water Moon of Pisces brings bubbly, exuberant, intuitive, interactive, artistic, curious, thoughtful and busy expressions of mood. Not everyone does well in this sort of climate, and if that's the case, Pisces Moon can be a splendid time to seek rest, quiet, and a favorite sanctuary. Overall, Moon in Pisces brings numerous kinds of intuitive responses to the language of our moods.

May 26th Thursday

Moon in Pisces / Aries	PDT	EDT
Moon opposite Saturn goes v/c	6:45 AM	9:45 AM
Moon enters Aries	5:36 PM	8:36 PM

Birthday: Miles Davis 1926

Mood Watch: This morning, Moon opposite Saturn awakens us to a sense of duty and responsibility while the waning Pisces Moon goes void-of-course. As much as we'd like to get a handle on matters, the void Pisces Moon is a rough atmosphere for making any sense. This is the best time to be creative, humorous, and positive. Spacey attitudes are likely to be everywhere and this is no time to expect everything to go perfectly. This evening's Moon in Aries will awaken our sensibilities, and it will give us the incentive to proceed with a better feeling of clarity and purpose.

May 27th Friday

Moon in Aries	PDT	EDT
Moon conjunct Uranus	1:19 AM	4:19 AM
Moon sextile Sun	5:31 AM	8:31 AM
Moon square Pluto	7:40 AM	10:40 AM

Birthday: Isadora Duncan 1878

Mood Watch: The morning will have its rough spots with Moon square Pluto. Aries Moon often brings out a spirit of competitiveness. The waning Aries Moon brings restlessness and forces numerous folks to rustle up some energy around special interest activities. Aries Moon encourages us to act on aggressive moods while we still have the volition and the courage to fight the battles that are calling to us. It is also a time to have some fun. Don't let this precious Aries Moon time go uncelebrated.

May 28th Saturday

Moon in Aries / *No Exact Aspects*
Birthday: Gladys Knight 1944

Mood Watch: Springtime Gemini Sun and a waning Aries Moon can sometimes bring hastiness, impetuosity, and a brazen spirit. It's an up, ready, and rarin'-to-go kind of mood set. Our moods are geared toward working off energy and letting out aggression. Those candid and often satirical quips are usually not intended to hurt feelings; in some cases, it is just a childish attempt to raise a few eyebrows. Spring is in the air and the testosterone levels are running strong. It may be best just to push past it all and let the energy go.

May 29th Sunday

Moon in Aries / Taurus	PDT	EDT
Moon conjunct Jupiter goes v/c	3:27 AM	6:27 AM
Moon enters Taurus	6:01 AM	9:01 AM
Moon sextile Neptune	7:52 AM	10:52 AM
Moon trine Pluto	7:45 PM	10:45 PM

Birthday: John F. Kennedy 1917

Mood Watch: The void-of-course Aries Moon may be a troublesome time to try to get along with others, or to get motivated first thing this morning. Fortunately, it doesn't last long, and the Moon enters Taurus with a more practical and comfortable quality of mood. Taurus Moon reminds us to get a better handle on our physical world. The Moon is exalted in Taurus and this is a great time to bring practical, useful, and esthetically pleasing material goods into your life.

May 30th Monday

Memorial Day, USA

Moon in Taurus	PDT	EDT
Moon conjunct Mars	10:43 AM	1:43 PM
Moon conjunct Venus	6:22 PM	9:22 PM
Mercury square Neptune begins (see June 3)		

Birthday: Benny Goodman 1909

Mood Watch: The Moon wanes in Taurus, and this means that it is essential to clean away items in your life that are no longer of use and appear to be taking up space. If you are one of the people who cannot appreciate the power of the statement, "less is more," then now's the time for you to seek an empty, clean, Zen atmosphere, and plant yourself in the center. If the emptiness that surrounds you doesn't enliven your senses then nothing ever will. Useless junk collects dust. Polish and clean your world and you will appreciate it a whole lot more. Taurus Moon is the time to determine what is valuable to you and what is not.

May 31st Tuesday

Moon in Taurus / Gemini	PDT	EDT
Moon conjunct Mercury goes v/c	8:37 AM	11:37 AM
Moon enters Gemini	4:56 PM	7:56 PM
Moon square Neptune	6:43 PM	9:43 PM

Birthday: Walt Whitman 1819

Mood Watch: Throughout a good portion of the day and into the evening, the void-of-course Taurus Moon wanes steadily. This is a time when we are prone to laziness and distraction. Financial matters call to us, but long lines and basic delays often slow down the money management process. As the Moon enters Gemini, the New Moon eve unfolds. Complex subjects and discussions captivate our moods. There may also be a fair bit of introspective thinking and contemplation.

June 1st Wednesday

NEW MOON in GEMINI– *Partial Solar Eclipse*

Moon in Gemini	PDT	EDT
Moon sextile Uranus	12:34 AM	3:34 AM
Sun trine Saturn	2:15 AM	5:15 AM
Moon trine Saturn	1:07 PM	4:07 PM
Moon conjunct Sun	2:02 PM	5:02 PM
Moon opposite Neptune	8:08 PM	11:08 PM

Birthday: Marilyn Monroe 1926

Mood Watch: The **New Moon in Gemini** (Moon conjunct Sun) allows for novel thoughts and ideas to flow, and new feelings about the way we are thinking will begin to emerge. New Moons are like clean slates. It's time to begin a process of strengthening and celebrating your energy and planning new vistas for growth, particularly in the area of emotional wellbeing. Pay attention to those newer thoughts, ideas and caprices in the wind. This would be a good time to initiate a round of creative writing, or to apply a mental discipline in a manner which will eventually become more personally beneficial. Making an attempt to reach out to an old friend or to open up communications with a new circle will bring great insights to one's field of knowledge at this time.

A **Solar Eclipse in Gemini** brings an emphasis on the need for detailing and reviewing important information. For some, the act of thinking comprehensively may be overshadowed by the solar eclipse energy. Many folks may wish to reach out to others, but they may also discover that they're not particularly up to the task of catching up on communications, or they may be distracted by other things. This is a good time to pace ourselves through the motions of this shadowy time.

Sun trine Saturn (occurring May 25 – June 4) This aspect particularly affects

Gemini people celebrating birthdays May 25 – June 4. This is a positive time for these people to get a handle on their lives, and it may be easier for them to take on the responsibilities of life. These birthday folks may notice more acceptable forms of control occurring in their lives. Now is your time (birthday people) to successfully work on putting some structure into your life; the kind of structure you've needed and wanted awaits you in the coming year. It is possible that time (Saturn) is on your side to make that move you've wanted to make towards accomplishing and achieving your goals. This aspect last occurred on February 5, affecting the Aquarius people of that time.

June 2nd Thursday

Moon in Gemini

	PDT	EDT
Mercury enters Gemini	1:02 PM	4:02 PM
Mercury sextile Uranus begins (see June 4)		

Birthday: Alessandro Cagliostro 1743

Mood Watch: Spontaneous and random tidbits of information will draw our attention and highlight the need for correspondence and communication. The waxing Gemini Moon is a good time to bounce ideas off others. This is also an important time to pace ourselves on the mental level and not to overtax our nervous systems with too much sugar or caffeine, especially in those instances when we're under mentally challenging pressure. The waxing Gemini Moon keeps us busily observing the details of life.

Mercury enters Gemini (Mercury in Gemini: June 2 – 16) When in Gemini, Mercury is known to increase our attention to detail and to cover a wide range of interesting topics. Mercury is at home in Gemini and it directs information – like food for the brain – in an interesting and captivating way. Mercury in Gemini is the best time to inspire a storyteller who is often looking for ways to make the story more interesting. Talk, discussion, stories, gossip, and the news media all generate flashes designed to captivate one's interest. Mercury in Gemini brings out the two sides of every story. Pay heed to the message if the storyteller happens to be telling *your* story while Mercury is in Gemini.

June 3rd Friday

Moon in Gemini / Cancer

	PDT	EDT
Mercury square Neptune	12:05 AM	3:05 AM
Neptune goes retrograde	12:27 AM	3:27 AM
Moon sextile Jupiter goes v/c	1:07 AM	4:07 AM
Moon enters Cancer	1:36 AM	4:36 AM
Moon trine Neptune	3:19 AM	6:19 AM
Moon square Uranus	9:03 AM	12:03 PM
Moon square Saturn	8:55 PM	11:55 PM

Birthday: Anderson Cooper 1967

Mood Watch: The waxing Cancer Moon of June encourages growth in the

139

garden, and this is a superb time to transplant and add new plants. The same concept could be applied symbolically to our moods. The seeds and flowers of our heartfelt encouragement will be greatly appreciated in this time of need. Some lunar aspects are troublesome today; Moon square Uranus early in the day brings struggles with disruption, and later, Moon square Saturn brings a struggle with limitations and restrictions. Cancer Moon reminds us to nurture the heart.

Mercury square Neptune (occurring May 30 – June 4) For the first time in our lifetime, Mercury in Gemini is square to Neptune in Pisces. There may be complication with the effort to logically explain spiritual endeavors and phenomenon. This aspect often brings difficulty in communications with the spirit world, and with understanding and accepting spirituality and beliefs. As a result, talk and discussion concerning what we believe in may be greatly misunderstood. Neptune is newly in Pisces (see April 4) at the zero degree mark, stirring up the issue of spiritual divinity. Deep subjects must not be treated lightly while Mercury squares Neptune. The square represents struggle and difficulty, so whatever sort of trouble you may be having with regard to the relaying of spiritual messages, this is the time to work through it with a thorough effort, and to be patient and considerate of the hypersensitivity levels of others. Anticipate the possibility of religion related arguments and disputes. By June 16, Mercury will be trine Neptune and the effort to communicate spiritual messages will be easier and more beneficial. This aspect will reoccur on November 1, and it will also have a non-exact appearance on December 15.

Neptune goes retrograde (Neptune retrograde: June 3 – Nov. 9) Like clockwork, every year the planet Neptune goes retrograde for about five months. Today, for the first time in our lifetime, Neptune goes retrograde in Pisces at the zero degree mark. Neptune entered Pisces for the first time this year on April 4, and now that it has gone retrograde, it will re-enter the tail end of Aquarius on August 4, where it will remain for its final fling in Aquarius until February 3, 2012. Neptune governs the spiritual dimensions and, when in Pisces, it inspires a special interest in the spiritual development of our beliefs. Neptune harmonizes spiritual vibrations and represents intuition and higher feminine wisdom. While Neptune is retrograde, many of the spiritual issues that have come up in the last five to six months will reoccur. For the next five months, be aware of the frequency of escapist tendencies, and of the inclination to internalize deep-rooted spiritual matters. Being firm with your own spiritual center will allow for progressive spiritual growth. Be careful not to blindly disrupt the core of another's belief system, nor to become ensnared by someone else's blindness with regard to your own beliefs during Neptune's retrograde months.

June 4th Saturday

Moon in Cancer	PDT	EDT
Jupiter enters Taurus	6:56 AM	9:56 AM
Moon sextile Mars	10:48 AM	1:48 PM
Mercury sextile Uranus	12:57 PM	3:57 PM

Birthday: Angelina Jolie 1975

Mood Watch: Feelings are surfacing continuously with the Moon's travels through Cancer. Our instincts are hard at work as we take the time to nurture the heart, pamper the soul, and enjoy the best there is in a comforting home environment. In the privacy of the home, we can work out a number of kinks in our lives, and are at liberty to display a wider variety of moods and feelings. This is the time to work through those feelings and let them tell us what we need to know about those emotional planes of existence. Listen to your intuition; our instincts are powerful survival tools in these days of chaotic change and challenge.

Jupiter enters Taurus (Jupiter in Taurus: June 4, 2011 – June 11, 2012) An expanding era of advancement in banking and economic prosperity begins today with the planet of luck and fortune, Jupiter, newly entering the constellation Taurus. Also, we can expect to see a great deal of inflation.

Jupiter in Taurus is likely to bring high demands on such Taurus-like focuses as banking institutions, architectural feats, estate management, funding for the arts, beauty spas and resorts, and administrative management. Jupiter's influence brings enthusiasm, stimulates economy and focuses on prosperity. Jupiter's prosperity may be experienced through the hardworking, stabilizing drive of Taurus, with an emphasis on material security and sound investments. This often results in the necessity to find competent caretakers and create conservative management strategies. Jupiter is the expansive influence, while Taurus is the slow and steady practitioner of creating and obtaining material wealth. The single most credible outcome that these factors are likely to produce, especially after the past couple of years of digging ourselves out of a recession, is the predictable assurance of skyrocketing inflation. The key to success with Jupiter in Taurus comes with the proper management of goods and services. Since inflation is inevitable, it will be necessary for many folks to concentrate on what they have, and how they can readily make it grow to meet the mounting needs of future markets and the high cost of living.

JUPITER IN ARIES – A BRIEF HISTORY

Since January 22, 2011 and throughout portions of 2010, Jupiter has traveled through Aries, focusing the magic of great wealth and expense on such Aries-like things as new enterprise, competitive sports, metalworking, engineering, arms manufacturing, mechanics, and the automobile industry. Jupiter in Aries has brought a pioneering enthusiasm to world affairs and in international business endeavors. This has been a time of new discoveries and, for some, new ways of making a profit. Aries says: "I AM," and it is through our individual efforts that we establish our mark in unprecedented ways and a sense of advancement is achieved. Out of the newly established enterprises, while Jupiter has been in Aries, comes the financing of the banking industry, and the support of those enterprises will be determined, as Jupiter now passes from Aries ("I Am") to Taurus ("I Have").

JUPITER IN TAURUS

As for our future with Jupiter in Taurus, the traits of Taurus are somewhat conservative by nature, and this requires the flow of prosperity to be steady, attainable, applicable, substantive, and controllable. The wise or conservative investment is one that will stand the test of time, but while inflation is so rampant, the necessity to spend will be quite demanding. The joy found in Jupiter's prosperous returns through the sign of Taurus must have a comforting and reassuring quality of value. The old Taurus adage, "I Have," implies that capital gains will be hard won and wages will be compromised. The more people hold on to their valuables and cash, the less likely the growth and stimulus of the overall economy will be. This is why the government pumps so much taxpayer money into the banks whenever there is a financial crisis. Fiscal spending is encouraged for the sake of economic growth. Those who have the money and resources for economic growth will be the attraction magnets that will control the way economic gains are processed. This is nothing new in the banking and corporate industry, so the common clichés of financial advancement will be more obvious then ever in this time of Jupiter in Taurus.

Apart from the common emphasis on fortunes and the material world, Jupiter's influences also emphasize the ways in which we develop and maintain our sense of joy and happiness. The overall morale of the people will have its ups and downs as we will become ever so aware of who is living a privileged or prosperous life and who isn't. Through this challenging and exciting time, the diminishing middle class will more swiftly take their stand on either side of the wheel of fortune. That's why it's essential that those who struggle with financial matters learn the art of maintaining an enthusiastic and optimistic hope for the future. Jupiter represents luck, and good luck is more likely to be viable when we invest in the development of our skills, and maintain an attractive, positive and upbeat attitude, despite the rising inflation and apparent selectiveness of employers. Taurus is ruled by Venus, the planet of love and attraction. If we keep our eye on the ball of what we love and desire, and if we maintain a steady positive attitude, we are more likely to attract the right kind of employment and the most acceptable level of income, and we will stay ahead of the monster of inflation.

Jupiter expansively provides, while Venus (the ruler of Taurus) attracts and receptively accepts. Jupiter gloats over wealth, skill, and abundance and so does Taurus. Jupiter's social appeal represents prosperous growth, valuable talents, fascination, joy, joviality, and the spreading of happiness. When Jupiter traverses through the Venus ruled domain of Taurus, the act of prospering emphasizes the need for security, practicality, beauty, and comfort. Here, there are no hidden mysteries to the ways and means of attainment, and it is usually measured through the fixed earth sign's mastery of the earth plane – through material substance and valued possessions, as opposed to the unpredictable risks of chancy, unbridled investments. This will be a time of a busy marketplace filled with recalled goods and second hand luxury items. For the sake of keeping up with inflation, many folks are likely to sell their wares at bargain prices. That makes this a buyer's paradise filled with opportunities and a chance to find rare collectables. Wise investors are likely to do well in this kind of environment, but this will not be a time of easy liquidation. Those who can afford to be patient would do best to hang on to prize materials and real estate until the flow of our economy evens out.

Throughout the year to come, it will be the Taurus people who will be able to identify with some abundant opportunities and joyous personal experiences while Jupiter crosses over their natal Sun. They will also have a strong influence on the wave of the economic future, and since many of them are prone to seeking sound investments, their sage advice may have some merit during this time. However, it is always wise to stick with the investors who have a proven track record. The other earth signs of the zodiac, Capricorn and Virgo, will enjoy the fruits of Jupiter being trine to their natal Sun signs. This will bring the potential for financial boons and accounting opportunities for Capricorn and Virgo people. Scorpio folks would be wise to use their perceptive sensibilities and take precautions with their expenditures while Jupiter opposes their natal Sun. They may also find that the effort to handle massive volumes of business – or a large inheritance – may be overwhelming at times in the next year. Some Scorpios will find themselves in a pickle of a financial crisis, and this would be a good time for them to carefully readdress their methods of handling money. Aquarius and Leo people may discover that it will be especially difficult to keep up with expenses and opportunities in their lives while Jupiter squares to their natal Sun signs. They would be wise to proceed cautiously in business and to avoid compulsive buying and unnecessary use of credit. Pisces and Cancer people's natal Sun signs will be in the sextile position to Jupiter this year, and this will bring the potential for business or career opportunities in those areas of life where these people have already been working hard, or where they have made some genuine effort to succeed over time. These are only opportunities, and they must be recognized and seized upon in order for Pisces and Cancer people to prosper.

Despite the downside of the competitive and often greedy corporate attitude, efficient and well organized frontiers of economic growth are bound to persist in this pending year of Jupiter in Taurus. Economic shifts are likely to have some weight to them, and this would be an especially useful year to take note of exactly who is prospering – and why. Now more than ever, Jupiter's massive growth patterns will be seen in a progressive stabilization of the economy's vast crisis points. Those who take diligent measures to act wisely and practically with their efforts to prosper will surely see the fruits of their labors.

Mercury sextile Uranus (occurring June 2 – 5) Mercury in Gemini sextile Uranus in Aries focuses talk, information, and news on unusual occurrences. Sensationalism may be played up in the news during this time. While Uranus is in Aries, chaos will be stirred up in such Aries-like things as new enterprises and mechanical engineering. Mercury sextile Uranus gives us the opportunity to freely speak our minds and to address the turmoil that exists in our lives. This aspect last occurred on February 2.

June 5th Sunday

Moon in Cancer / Leo	PDT	EDT
Moon enters Leo	8:03 AM	11:03 AM
Moon square Jupiter	8:26 AM	11:26 AM
Moon trine Uranus	3:20 PM	6:20 PM
Moon sextile Mercury	8:04 PM	11:04 PM
Venus square Neptune begins (see June 10)		

Birthday: Bill Moyers 1934

Mood Watch: Out of the moody haze of an overnight void-of-course Cancer Moon, the Leo Moon brings a courageous show of liveliness. This morning's Moon square Jupiter may be a time when people feel challenged by a lack of means, or there may be a lack of confidence in certain kinds of investments. Despite everyone's personal struggles, Leo Moon encourages us to strive for the best and not to short change ourselves. Moon trine Uranus brings bold and exciting expressions of mood. Later, Moon sextile Mercury is a good time to review the details of day.

June 6th Monday

Moon in Leo	PDT	EDT
Moon sextile Saturn	2:36 AM	5:36 AM
Moon sextile Sun	11:48 AM	2:48 PM
Moon square Mars	7:00 PM	10:00 PM

Birthday: Alex Saunders 1926

Mood Watch: Be they predators or prey, all wild beasts rise in the morning with the inherent awareness that at some point they will have to hustle, fly, chase, or run like mad in order to survive. The waxing Leo Moon puts us in touch with our inner beast and gives us the impetus to do what we have to do to keep fit, strong, courageous, and in touch with the integral parts of the self. Tonight's Moon square Mars may be the time to temper the beast with care, as this aspect is often a challenging time to test one's strength. Overall, Sun in Gemini and Moon in Leo brings a healthy formula for joy and contentment.

June 7th Tuesday

Moon in Leo / Virgo	PDT	EDT
Moon square Venus goes v/c	8:26 AM	11:26 AM
Moon enters Virgo	12:33 PM	3:33 PM
Mercury trine Saturn	1:40 PM	4:40 PM
Moon trine Jupiter	1:42 PM	4:42 PM
Sun conjunct Mercury begins (see June 12)		
Jupiter trine Pluto begins (see July 7)		

Birthday: Tom Jones 1940

Mood Watch: For a time this morning, the Moon in Leo goes void-of-course. It's hard to get satisfaction or to feel harmonious with others with Moon square Venus. Laziness may be evident, and delays may also be prevalent. As the Moon enters

144

Virgo, our moods are likely to be more attentive. A much more conscientious spirit of interaction allows us to focus on work, cleaning up, and all sorts of practical matters. The afternoon is slated for some positive aspects. Moon trine Jupiter encourages our sense of progress and growth, and puts us in touch with our need for joy and prosperity. Virgo Moon assists us to find joy in simplicity.

Mercury trine Saturn (occurring June 4 – 8) Mercury is in Gemini where talk is easily generated, and where news, media focuses, and information opens up many possibilities for the way we think. Saturn is in Libra where new laws are forged, and there is a strong emphasis on the need to protect ourselves and our civil rights. Mercury trine Saturn brings favorable dialogue concerning where to draw the lines. Timely information and important news represent a gift or blessing. News concerning the end of a long and arduous task brings relief. This is a great time to study or practice memorization skills. Mercury trine Saturn last occurred on February 14.

June 8ᵗʰ Wednesday

FIRST QUARTER MOON in VIRGO	PDT	EDT
Moon trine Pluto	12:02 AM	3:02 AM
Moon square Mercury	9:31 AM	12:31 PM
Moon square Sun	7:10 PM	10:10 PM
Jupiter sextile Neptune	7:39 PM	10:39 PM

Birthday: Frank Lloyd Wright 1867

Mood Watch: There is a strong investigative curiosity at work with the Sun in Gemini and the Moon in Virgo. This is the **First Quarter Moon in Virgo** (Moon square Sun). Both of these Mercury ruled signs (Gemini and Virgo) emphasize the need to keep things flowing both on a logical and practical level of application, especially when passing on information. This particular Virgo Moon comes to us during a very busy time of spring when the "quickening" of summer is upon us.

Jupiter sextile Neptune (occurring May 20 – June 18) Jupiter directs our senses to prosperity, and brings expansion and new realms of fulfillment and discovery. Neptune brings the unknown and life's great mysteries into a place in the human spirit where they can be felt and experienced. Jupiter in Taurus sextile Neptune in Pisces provides us with opportunities for successful business, and the spirit may be newly empowered with divine intuition.

Jupiter represents wealth and commerce, while Neptune represents spiritual movements, addictive substances, the sea, and all those things dredged up from the sea, such as petroleum – North America's most widely consumed addiction. The fishing industry and the Navy may appear to prosper during this time of Jupiter sextile Neptune. There is also a chance for prosperity to flourish (Jupiter) in the arts and in the world of music (Neptune). This sextile of Jupiter and Neptune gives us the illusion that gas prices couldn't possibly go any higher and that (maybe) a shortage doesn't really exist. These are the dwindling glory days of a gas guzzling culture. While we are currently finding insightful ways to believe in our economy, and to try to explore further to meet our growing expenditures

(Jupiter in Taurus), we cannot continue to build our fortunes and our dependencies on petroleum products alone. The North American economy may well step over the ultimate boundaries of sensible oil consumption, which will lead us to heartily examine some vital efforts to replace our petroleum demands with something more environmentally acceptable.

Jupiter sextile Neptune gives us the awareness of the chance for abundance, but we must not be fooled by a false sense of permanent abundance. The spirit of humankind will eventually be challenged by its dependencies. Income and a large line of credit do not mean there's money in the bank, but while we have the means to avoid the truth, we tend to assume that it will always be there for us. Are we really prospering (Jupiter) or have we come to depend on a Neptunian illusion? For some folks, this aspect brings the ability to perceive beyond the unknown, and that's good because it allows us to see beyond our current situation and to search for solutions to the big energy crisis scenarios of the future. Jupiter's workings appeal to our nature as consumers. When the planet of expansion (Jupiter) is sextile to the planet of spirituality (Neptune) discoveries may occur, showing us how to stretch out our spiritual experience of life, and to empower our beliefs with something that brings us pure joy and fulfillment.

As long as one is working with a meditative process or is focusing on a spiritual quest of some nature, this aspect gives the believer the opportunity to expand to great heights and empower his or her imagination and personal realms of intuition. Jupiter sextile Neptune allows us to expand our beliefs and to take on a more uplifting viewpoint of life. This aspect brings a better understanding of the play of Spirit in our daily lives. It will to begin to reoccur, for the second time this year, on November 22 and will reach a non-exact peak (within two degrees) on December 26.

June 9th Thursday

Moon in Virgo / Libra	PDT	EDT	
Moon trine Mars goes v/c	1:12 AM	4:12 AM	
Venus enters Gemini	7:23 AM	10:23 AM	
Moon enters Libra	3:30 PM	6:30 PM	
Moon trine Venus	4:15 PM	7:15 PM	
Moon opposite Uranus	10:34 PM	1:34 AM	(Jun 10)
Venus sextile Uranus begins (see June 12)			

Birthday: Johnny Depp 1963

Mood Watch: Before dawn, the Virgo Moon goes void-of-course and remains void until late in the day. Perhaps the single most distracting thing about today's moods is the tendency towards non-productive doubt. There may be too much of an emphasis on why a thing isn't working and less emphasis on what it will take to fix it. This can be frustrating at times, particularly if there is a continual difference of opinions and not enough collaboration. For some, it may be more ideal to spend time alone, but when this is not possible, it may be more rewarding to cast some humor on a subject than to argue it into extinction. Later, Moon in Libra turns everything around, and there will be a great deal more effort towards collaboration and cooperation.

Venus enters Gemini (Venus in Gemini: June 9 – July 3) Venus, the influence of love, magnetism and attraction now enters Gemini, the personification of duality. Love desires may be split and suffer from ambivalence and schisms. Gemini people will focus more intently on personal attractions and love related matters, while Sagittarius folks may be overwhelmed by love concerns as Venus opposes their natal Sun. Virgo and Pisces people are also likely to feel affection related challenges or difficulties in their lives as Venus squares their natal Sun positions. Librans and Aquarians will find that love related matters will be a little easier while Venus is in the trine position to their natal sun signs. With Venus in Gemini, there is an attraction to writing, speaking about, and recording extraordinary love experiences and stories. Gossip and talk about love matters will be especially prevalent. Venus in Gemini shows us the two sides of love – the giving and the taking. As attractions appear more diverse, concerns may arise among those with a jealous nature. Love related changes are rampant – to some it's a challenge, while for others, it's a breath of fresh air.

June 10ᵗʰ Friday

Moon in Libra	PDT	EDT	
Venus square Neptune	1:23 AM	4:23 AM	
Moon square Pluto	2:38 AM	5:38 AM	
Moon conjunct Saturn	9:00 AM	12:00 PM	
Moon trine Mercury	9:01 PM	12:01 AM	(Jun 11)

Birthday: Judy Garland 1922

Mood Watch: The Moon in Libra brings forth moods focused on harmony and the decision making process, which will no doubt tug at us all day. The Sun and the Moon are in air signs, emphasizing the need to apply logic and mental clarity to the things we do. Sun in Gemini keeps us keen on the two sides to everything we observe, allowing us to be more open and adaptable in our decision making process. Be sure to get the better part of your decision making process done today; tomorrow's long void-of-course Moon is likely to put a stress on our ability to make clear and decisive choices.

Venus square Neptune (occurring June 5 – 12) Venus in Gemini square Neptune in Pisces brings diverse pleasures, love, and expressions of beauty and femininity into a place where they run up against the obstacles represented by the higher, more refined goddess image. A conflict of beliefs about womanhood is common with this aspect, and sometimes women, artists, and very attractive people are placed on high pedestals. Despite this, the human element usually leads them to certain error and they suffer great delusions. It is here that beauty suffers a spiritual conflict. The expectation and conditioning of others has created a false image of beauty, and the person on whom it is imposed is likely to be suffocated by the beliefs of others. With Venus square Neptune, what we want is challenged by what we know is best for us. Consequently, it may be difficult for some people to make a personal connection with spiritual attractions. Beliefs concerning love matters may be tested. Despite the conflicts, this is a time to rise to the challenge of believing in love and loving your own choice of spiritual path. As for the art of love, the influences of this aspect are not as harsh for those who understand that true beauty is found in the core of feminine wisdom, and that magnetic attraction goes beyond temporal beauty. This aspect last occurred on January 4, and will reoccur on October 31.

June 11ᵗʰ Saturday

Moon in Libra / Scorpio	PDT	EDT
Moon trine Sun goes v/c	1:03 AM	4:03 AM
Moon enters Scorpio	5:33 PM	8:33 PM
Moon trine Neptune	7:03 PM	10:03 PM
Moon opposite Jupiter	8:04 PM	11:04 PM

Birthday: Hugh Laurie 1959

Mood Watch: Before dawn, the waxing Libra Moon goes void-of-course, and this is likely to create a lot of waffling, uncertainty, and indecision throughout the day. Libra Moon is a time to make adjustments and to attempt to create harmony whenever possible, even though that may take some extra time. Tonight as the Moon enters Scorpio, a more decisive expression of moods gives us the impetus to act on our volition. Sun in Gemini and Moon in Scorpio brings detail filled excitement and a daring quality of interaction.

June 12ᵗʰ Sunday

Moon in Scorpio	PDT	EDT
Moon sextile Pluto	4:31 AM	7:31 AM
Sun conjunct Mercury	4:44 PM	7:44 PM
Venus sextile Uranus	7:35 PM	10:35 PM
Saturn goes direct	8:51 PM	11:51 PM
Venus trine Saturn begins (see June 17)		

Birthday: Chick Corea 1941

Mood Watch: During a waxing Scorpio Moon in the days of Gemini, we tend to face challenges, find solutions, keep active, and we're likely to empower our moods with a fair dollop of passion. It is the Gemini in us that goes about the detail of placing the cherry on the top of that dollop of passion, and it is the Scorpio in us that snatches it away. With so much going on, there is always plenty to observe.

Sun conjunct Mercury (June 7 – 15) This conjunction will create a much more thoughtful, communicative and expressive year ahead for those Gemini folks celebrating birthdays June 7 – 15. This is your ruling planet and it's your time (birthday Gemini) to record ideas, relay important messages, and pay close attention to your imaginative thoughts as they are touched by Mercury, creating the urge to speak and be heard. Birthday Gemini, your thoughts will reveal a great deal about who you are, now and in the year to come.

148

Venus sextile Uranus (occurring June 9 – 14) Venus in Gemini is sextile to Uranus in Aries. Our love for communication devices takes on a radical or unusual kind of expression. Radically serious kinds of love and aesthetics can be very uplifting at this time, particularly while extreme types of tests are occurring and being stretched beyond the limits in love related matters. Eccentric love may erupt with this aspect. This is the time to work on pent up frustrations with loved ones and to reconcile differences by loving and accepting variation, giving freedom and slack to our loved ones. Venus sextile Uranus can encourage us to break useless tendencies and habits, and also may bring an opportunity for love related matters to transcend the restriction of unmet personal needs. Venus sextile Uranus last occurred March 1 and it will reoccur on December 20.

Saturn goes direct (Saturn direct: June 12, 2011 – Feb. 9, 2012) Saturn, which represents time, restriction, responsibility, and disciplinary acts, has been retrograde since January 25 and will go direct today until February 9 next year. Saturn retrograde often requires us to backtrack on many previous, as yet unfulfilled obligations and disciplines. Since January, Saturn retrograde has been a time of implementing, testing and correcting various types of security measures in our lives, and many sacrifices were made in order for us to feel a sense of completion and accomplishment. Today Saturn goes direct at the 10 degree mark of Libra and will remain in Libra until October 5, 2012 when it enters Scorpio for the first time this century. This is a good time to regenerate the discipline of our senses, to end destructive habits, particularly bad relationship practices, as well as to make new lifestyle choices and changes. As Saturn begins to move forward, this may be the time for Libra folks to move forward towards positive endings and new beginnings as Libra related focuses become society's priority. Certainly, one priority has been the act of restructuring the use of our court systems, libraries, and marital practices. Saturn in Libra focuses on the power of marriage, schools, scholarship programs, team management, judicial practices, mental health, and the logic and balance of the mind.

June 13th Monday

Moon in Scorpio / Sagittarius	PDT	EDT	
Moon opposite Mars goes v/c	10:43 AM	1:43 PM	
Moon enters Sagittarius	7:38 PM	10:38 PM	
Moon square Neptune	9:08 PM	12:08 AM	(Jun 14)
Mars square Neptune begins (see June 21)			

Birthday: William Butler Yeats 1865

Mood Watch: Pressure mounts as the week begins with a heavily waxing Scorpio Moon. As the Moon goes void-of-course, be careful not to place yourself in a particularly vulnerable position, as victimization may run rampant. Diligence is often what it takes to overcome the intense kinds of pressures that are currently demanding our attention. Tonight, as the Moon enters Sagittarius, the spirit of the pending Full Moon, set to take place Wednesday afternoon, gears us up for adventure, strong activity, and a lot of food for thought.

June 14th Tuesday

Flag Day, USA

Moon in Sagittarius	PDT	EDT
Moon trine Uranus	2:53 AM	5:53 AM
Moon opposite Venus	5:46 AM	8:46 AM
Moon sextile Saturn	1:18 PM	4:18 PM
Mercury trine Neptune begins (see June 16)		

Birthday: Harriet Beecher Stowe 1811

Mood Watch: The Full Sagittarius Moon eve accentuates the mood with the need for a full grasp of the facts, as well as a sense of knowing where we're headed. This is an excellent time for us to explore, seek adventure, and contemplate or participate in travel. Global awareness is sparked, and philosophical views are running strongly. Sagittarius says: "I see." Seek vision! Tomorrow's lunar eclipse is likely to bring a somewhat ominous feeling of change and rapid movement. The Full Sagittarius Moon often gives us the sense that various matters have gone past the usual boundaries and into completely new territory. Everything is going according to plan; go with the flow.

June 15th Wednesday

FULL MOON in SAGITTARIUS– *Total Lunar Eclipse*

Moon in Sagittarius / Capricorn	PDT	EDT	
Moon opposite Sun	1:13 PM	4:13 PM	
Moon opposite Mercury goes v/c	8:30 PM	11:30 PM	
Moon enters Capricorn	10:58 PM	1:58 AM	(Jun 16)
Mercury sextile Jupiter begins (see June 17)			
Mercury square Uranus begins (see June 18)			

Birthday: Jim Belushi 1954

Mood Watch: The **Full Moon in Sagittarius** (Moon opposite Sun) brings fulfilling insights about life, and emotional energy runs very high. For many, there is a tendency to go way out beyond the usual bounds and discover new territory as a matter of circumstance. How we chose to perceive and develop our understanding of this new territory has a lot to do with what stage in our life we have come to, and what kind of philosophy best suits our own individual needs.

Lunar Eclipse in Sagittarius: A lunar eclipse occurs when the Earth moves between the moon and the sun, blocking the light that reflects off the moon's surface back to Earth. Some believe that eclipses bring darker than average moods. Some see this as mere superstition while others may base this belief on their personal experiences. A lunar eclipse with the Moon in Sagittarius may bring some unexpected natural disasters, or some other kinds of earth shattering events. There may also be a death of a notable figure. Sagittarius says: "I see;" this is an important time to beware of intuitive hunches and predictions. This may also be a challenging time to make progress with a tight schedule.

June 16th Thursday

Moon in Capricorn	PDT	EDT	
Moon sextile Neptune	12:31 AM	3:31 AM	
Moon trine Jupiter	3:04 AM	6:04 AM	
Moon square Uranus	6:35 AM	9:35 AM	
Moon conjunct Pluto	10:22 AM	1:22 PM	
Mercury enters Cancer	12:08 PM	3:08 PM	
Moon square Saturn	5:24 PM	8:24 PM	
Mercury trine Neptune	9:51 PM	12:51 AM	(Jun 17)
Sun trine Neptune begins (see June 22)			

♊

Birthday: Alice Bailey 1880

Mood Watch: It's the day after a somewhat intense Full ecliptic Sagittarius Moon. Capricorn Moon is a good time to focus on making a workable, steady pace. Sun in Gemini and Moon in Capricorn is an excellent time to multi-task with precision and focused effort. Here we are rarely hindered by uncertainty or emotionality. This is a time to make progress and to get some business done. Our moods will be purposeful and relatively serious throughout the day.

Mercury enters Cancer (Mercury in Cancer: June 16 – July 1) Mercury governs communications. The shift in communications turns our attention from an emphasis on details and logic (Mercury in Gemini) to a focus on feelings and senses (Mercury in Cancer). This is a time when many people will appear to intuit their way through conversations. Thoughts may blend with mood as the emphasis on emotional expression takes the stage. As Mercury goes through the sign of Cancer, take special note of a tendency for people to talk more specifically about their feelings, defenses, and the need to be nurtured. Mercury in Cancer makes some people more intuitive to the thoughts of others, and this may be an easier time to interpret people's thoughts by observing their emotional body language. Through Cancer, thoughts and communications are shaped by the course of our complex world of emotions.

Mercury trine Neptune (occurring June 14 – 18) Mercury just made the transition from Gemini to Cancer and it is currently located at the zero degree mark of Cancer, where it is trine to Neptune at the zero degree mark of Pisces. This favorable aspect brings thoughtful and engaging discussions and intuitive knowledge and perception. Communicate about spiritual needs with helpful counsel and receive gifts of renewed faith in your own beliefs. Accept that some messages are there to spiritually uplift you. Spiritual affirmations and important messages may seem complex while these planets are trine at the cusps, but they are designed to ease the mind and comfort the heart. This is a superb aspect for discussing personal philosophies and metaphysical subjects. Confessions and spiritual confidentialities will be beneficial and easier to relay at this time. Mercury trine Neptune brings gifts of encouraging news from Spirit. This aspect will reoccur on October 12.

June 17th Friday

Moon in Capricorn	PDT	EDT	
Mercury sextile Jupiter	5:35 PM	8:35 PM	
Venus trine Saturn	9:30 PM	12:30 AM	(Jun 18)

Birthday: M.C. Escher 1898

Mood Watch: The Moon, although waning, is still rather full. Capricorn Moon encourages us to keep a steady head, and to handle the emotional process professionally; it also gives us the impetus to complete projects and stay on track.

Mercury sextile Jupiter (occurring June 15 – 18) This aspect offers the potential for good news of growth and prosperity, especially for those who are open to broadening their awareness. Mercury brings news and talk, while Jupiter brings wealth and prosperous advancement. The money flows where our attention goes. It may be an advantageous time to ask for a job or a loan. Mercury in Cancer sextile Jupiter in Taurus allows us to communicate our feelings and our emotional needs (Mercury in Cancer), while it brings opportunities and the potential for success (the sextile aspect) in typical Taurus endeavors. These include the growth of funds and investments, the expansion of practical needs and luxurious comforts, and advancements in banking, farming, and horticulture (Jupiter in Taurus). Opportunity exists for both the employer and the employee. Mercury sextile Jupiter brings joyful and mind expanding conversations. This aspect last occurred on February 5.

Venus trine Saturn (occurring June 12 – 20) When Venus interacts with Saturn it brings a very timely quality to relationships, and raises the questions of commitment and devotion with regard to our active love connections. Fortunately, the trine aspect brings probabilities that are more positive in nature when it comes to the law of attraction. Venus trine Saturn implies that there is a good possibility here for a happy ending. Venus in Gemini trine Saturn in Libra brings an intelligent and interesting expression of love and commitment to love. Venus in Gemini emphasizes the need for versatility and intelligence in matters of love. Here is where we easily devote ourselves to the thing(s) that attract us most. This aspect last occurred on March 14.

June 18th Saturday

Moon in Capricorn / Aquarius	PDT	EDT
Moon trine Mars goes v/c	1:07 AM	4:07 AM
Moon enters Aquarius	4:47 AM	7:47 AM
Moon square Jupiter	9:54 AM	12:54 PM
Moon sextile Uranus	12:54 PM	3:54 PM
Mercury square Uranus	1:11 PM	4:11 PM
Mercury square Saturn begins (see June 21)		
Mercury-opposite-Pluto-non-exact begins (see June 19)		

Birthday: Paul McCartney 1942

Mood Watch: Sun in Gemini and Moon in Aquarius is a great time to be innovative, clever, and to tap into some rich intelligence. That said, this may not

152

be the day to make headway with friends, while the Moon is square to Jupiter, and while Mercury square Uranus reaches its peak (see below). Try to work matters out with others as best you can. Aquarius Moon puts us in touch with the many needs and foibles of humanity. Sometimes we must set emotions aside and address the real problems, the long term disruptions, and not just the immediate emotional responses and symptoms. If there is ever a time to sort through the details of our human dilemmas, Sun in Gemini and Moon in Aquarius is it. Meanwhile, try to have some fun too – we are, after all, only human.

Mercury square Uranus (occurring June 15 – 19) Mercury in Cancer square Uranus in Aries creates explosive mental states and causes some people to speak abrasively or to promote overly radical ideas. Tact and diplomacy are likely to go right out the door when religion is discussed. Communications with regard to some very emotional topics may come up against unusual or explosive reactions. Harmony is always best achieved when we exercise discretion – nonetheless, there are times when we must speak our minds. This really is a time to watch what you say: communications have the potential to shake matters up considerably. This aspect last occurred on January 10.

June 19ᵗʰ Sunday

Father's Day

Moon in Aquarius	PDT	EDT
Moon trine Saturn	12:18 AM	3:18 AM
Moon trine Venus	3:07 AM	6:07 AM
Mercury-opposite-Pluto-non-exact (see below)		
Sun square Uranus begins (see June 26)		

Birthday: Paula Abdul 1962

Mood Watch: Moon in Aquarius turns our moods towards a thoughtful mode of expression, and emphasizes the role of science, technology, and integrated systems. Moods are directed towards finding the most knowledgeable source available to save oneself a lot of time and trouble getting important projects off the ground.

Mercury-opposite-Pluto-non-exact (occurring June 18 – 20) For a short time, Pluto comes within a three degree orb of reaching an exact opposition, but before it can reach that opposition, Mercury quickly moves forward while Pluto falls back from our geocentric perspective. Pluto is the planet – so far away – that has scientists arguing whether it's a planet or not. It takes a long time to go through a process, and in astrology, Pluto is aptly represented as the planet of transformation and the shift of the generations. Mercury moves so quickly that its "non-exact" encounters with other planets are much more common. Mercury in Cancer in its near opposition to Pluto in Capricorn gives the impression that one might wish to speak up before the powers that be, to make an important and vital statement at a crucial time. This may be quickly followed by a heavy hearted hesitance. Matters with regard to Pluto always take time. There isn't a full aspect here – perhaps this may not be the time to speak out to the course of destiny.

June 20th Monday

Moon in Aquarius / Pisces	PDT	EDT
Moon trine Sun	12:01 PM	3:01 PM
Moon square Mars goes v/c	1:22 PM	4:22 PM
Moon enters Pisces	1:45 PM	4:45 PM
Moon conjunct Neptune	3:24 PM	6:24 PM
Mars enters Gemini	7:49 PM	10:49 PM
Moon sextile Jupiter	8:02 PM	11:02 PM
Sun sextile Jupiter begins (see June 25)		

Birthday: Lionel Richie 1949

Mood Watch: The Aquarius Moon wanes, and this is a good time to internalize knowledge and to focus the mind on the things that will be useful when the time comes to make an impact on something that's important to humanity. This afternoon, the Moon makes its shift into Pisces, and our moods will be more inclined to observe the artistic side of our thoughtful endeavors. Sun in Gemini and Moon in Pisces brings playful, intuitive, and imaginative moods.

Mars enters Gemini (Mars in Gemini: June 20 – Aug.3) Mars, the planet of war, energy, action, and force will focus its attention through Gemini, the sign of thinking, communicating, and duality. Gemini people will experience heated thoughts, challenges with anger and fevers, and will most likely endure extended surges of energy and strength. When the energy is harnessed, action manifests as oral or written communications – and all of these expressions will have a fiery and inspired flare. As a general rule, Mars in Gemini helps to stimulate and activate dual perspectives, making it easy to see and understand both sides of a heated discussion while making it more difficult to take sides. Forces may seem scattered and restless for some people at this time. Other people will find that Mars in Gemini sharpens the perception and insight, and these people will stand out through their clear outspokenness. This is a good time to avoid being talked into fighting other people's battles – watch out for smooth talking recruiters.

CANCER

Key Phrase: "I FEEL"

Cardinal Water Sign

Ruling Planet: Moon

Symbol: The Crab

June 21th through

July 21st PDT/July 23nd EDT

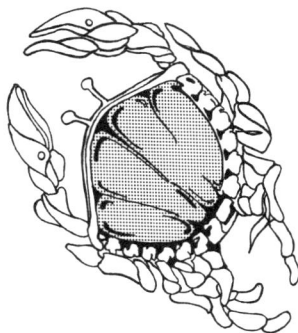

June 21st Tuesday

Summer Solstice

Moon in Pisces	**PDT**	**EDT**	
Moon sextile Pluto	2:15 AM	5:15 AM	
Moon trine Mercury	10:08 AM	1:08 PM	
Sun enters Cancer	10:16 AM	1:16 PM	
Mercury square Saturn	11:42 AM	2:42 PM	
Moon square Venus goes v/c	7:50 PM	10:50 PM	
Mars square Neptune	11:44 PM	2:44 AM	(Jun 22)
Sun opposite Pluto begins (see June 27)			
Mars sextile Uranus begins (see June 27)			

Birthday: Prince William of Wales 1982

Mood Watch: Throughout the day, waning Pisces Moon tests the weak links in the human spirit. It is often a time when we contend with our illusions, and struggle with our dreams while we review our beliefs. Repetitively escaping from troubles does not make them any easier, but at times like this, escapism is the highly likely theme. Most of the things we do must be put into perspective and into the proper context, but in dreams, anything is possible. Pisces Moon brings a very meaningful – but subtle – journey for the soul. Don't put off important things today; tomorrow's endless void-of-course Moon will not be a day for much progress.

Sun enters Cancer (Sun in Cancer: June 21 – July 22/23) Around this time, Summer Solstice enthusiasts are out celebrating old traditions and creating new ones while thanking the Sun for life and light. The dominion of the sign of Cancer is expressed by cardinal water, affecting people in deep and unconscious ways. Cancer people are extremely intuitive and often very psychic or perceptive. Cancers value their deep emotional attachments, their treasured memories and feelings. Cancer is a home oriented sign, and making the home a well-loved place calls out to us. Barbeques, home improvements, and other home based events are the focuses of many folks during the days of Sun in Cancer. This morning's commencement of Summer Solstice encompasses the solar qualities of Gemini and Cancer, and this phenomenon could be referred to as a "spri-sum" day (part spring/part summer). This will be a long day of solar light, also known as the longest day of the year. It is rather auspicious for the British monarchy to have a significant family member, an heir to the throne – Prince William – whose birthday falls on Summer Solstice. The concept of the archetype of the solar king has been avidly celebrated in many cultures throughout world history and in numerous mythology novels.

Mercury square Saturn (occurring June 18 – 22) Mercury in Cancer square Saturn in Libra creates tension in relationships. Under the influence of this aspect, the battle to maintain accurate or precise information may be strongly evident. There may also be a tendency for "foot-in-mouth disease" as people may say the wrong things at the wrong time. It is wise to use caution when attempting communications during Mercury square Saturn, especially concerning matters of time and timing. It is also wise to be careful not to misinterpret court data, binding contracts and general information. While Mercury is square to Saturn, beware of the tendency for people to make uninformed assumptions about the conclusion or outcome of important matters. This aspect last occurred on January 26.

Mars square Neptune (occurring June 13 – 26) Heated activities run into obstacles concerning the work of Great Spirit and the fulfillment of spiritual harmony. Mars is in Gemini and there may be some thought provoking disruptions that intrude on or impede our spiritual level of experience. Martial forces are bursting through temples, belief systems, and holy moments. Active aggression occurs around spiritual groups and religious institutions, often targeting the belief systems of others. Mariners at sea may run into challenging storms. This aspect also brings the potential for accidents and temper tantrums, especially with regard to opinions about substance abuse and sacred matters. It is important not to get so wrapped up in the spiritual side of things that physical world realities, such as fire, are overlooked. Angry outbursts are likely to affect sacred land or the personal territory of spiritual sentiment. While Mars square Neptune occurs, it is best to anticipate confrontations concerning moral or spiritual issues. As this aspect passes, it will be easier to put spiritual beliefs and practices back on course without too much conflict or interference. Meanwhile, stay aware and ready to deal with whatever comes along.

June 22nd Wednesday

Moon void-of-course in Pisces	**PDT**	**EDT**
Sun trine Neptune	7:06 AM	10:06 AM

Birthday: Todd Rundgren 1948

Mood Watch: The long void-of-course Moon in Pisces wanes and it is likely that very little will get done today. This is not to say that completing tasks will be impossible, but it is certainly true that various kinds of interruptions and distractions will be the cause of many delays and postponements. This is a splendid time to focus on art, music, creative writing, leisurely endeavors, and spirituality. Beware of the tendency for many people to indulge in substance abuse, depression, denial, or negligence.

Sun trine Neptune (occurring June 16 – 25) This occurrence of Sun trine Neptune particularly affects Gemini and Cancer people celebrating birthdays from June 16 – 25. These birthday folks are experiencing the favorable trine aspect of Neptune to their natal Sun, bringing gifts of spiritual encounters and awareness, as well as a calming effect on life. This serves as a good time (particularly for these birthday folks) to seek visions, apply prayer and meditation, and to explore spiritual avenues and beliefs that are being presented. Sun trine Neptune ensures that the compulsory passive and kindly qualities of Neptune's influence will lead these birthday people to be easily encouraged by spiritually uplifting practices and sanctuaries. Birthday folks, the trine of Neptune to your natal Sun will assist you in finding the calm space in the eye of the storm. This aspect will reoccur on October 21.

June 23rd Thursday
LAST QUARTER MOON in ARIES

Moon in Pisces / Aries	PDT	EDT
Moon enters Aries	1:23 AM	4:23 AM
Moon square Sun	4:48 AM	7:48 AM
Moon sextile Mars	4:48 AM	7:48 AM
Moon conjunct Uranus	10:23 AM	1:23 PM
Moon square Pluto	2:08 PM	5:08 PM

Birthday: Milt Hinton 1910

Mood Watch: We now come to the **Last Quarter Moon in Aries** (Moon square Sun). In some cases, obstacles appear between one's emotions and one's sense of personal identity due to the square aspect. This Moon in Aries expression of mood has very little trouble manifesting new energies. Last Quarter Moon requires disengaging from intensified emotional energy. Dropping problems with the ego becomes the key to this moon. One cannot change the stubbornness and selfishness of others, but one can make a difference by setting the right example individually. Be true to yourself.

June 24th Friday

Moon in Aries	PDT	EDT
Moon square Mercury	10:29 AM	1:29 PM
Moon sextile Venus goes v/c	3:06 PM	6:06 PM

Birthday: Jeff Beck 1944

Mood Watch: Today's waning Moon in Aries sets the tone for many people to push their way through traffic and shopping lines, and to focus on themselves and their own interests. While some are assured they know exactly what they want, others seem baffled at the tenacity and the fortitude behind the push and drive of selfish desires. Selfhood is okay to sport around and we are a self-oriented culture, feeling our way through to find our identities and maintain our egos with some sort of pride. We're doing okay as long as we are not completely oblivious to the needs of others. This is indeed a time when selfhood is touched upon, and our general moods are based on our own personal needs, as well as those pushy or powerful enough to come first! Avoid butting heads if that's not what you're looking for, since it's very easy to do during an Aries Moon.

June 25th Saturday

Moon in Aries / Taurus	PDT	EDT	
Moon enters Taurus	1:52 PM	4:52 PM	
Moon sextile Neptune	3:27 PM	6:27 PM	
Sun sextile Jupiter	4:54 PM	7:54 PM	
Moon conjunct Jupiter	10:06 PM	1:06 AM	(Jun 26)
Moon sextile Sun	10:28 PM	1:28 AM	(Jun 26)

Birthday: George Orwell 1903

Mood Watch: Throughout the morning, the void-of-course Aries Moon tends to create a lot of impatience and pushiness in our attitudes. Sometimes it is less time consuming to be observant and politely persistent than to be blatantly demanding or just plain rudely offensive. Later, Moon in Taurus gives us a practical edge and allows us to be resourceful as well as thrifty.

Sun sextile Jupiter (occurring June 20 – 28) Gemini/Cancer people celebrating birthdays this year from June 20 – 28 are now being brought into a favorable natal Sun position to Jupiter. It's a time of opportunity and expansion for these birthday folks if they act on their desires and work towards their goals. Skills learned throughout this year will support their overall plans for career advancement and fortune building. It's a good time to make the most of it Gemini/Cancer folks! This aspect last occurred on January 19.

June 26th Sunday

Moon in Taurus	PDT	EDT
Moon trine Pluto	2:21 AM	5:21 AM
Sun square Uranus	3:13 AM	6:13 AM
Sun square Saturn begins (see July 2)		

Birthday: Peter Lorre 1904

Mood Watch: What a splendid day to get in tune with nature! A waning Taurus Moon focuses our attention on the things we have, the things we hope to have, and those things that must go. Purge and clean the physical world for a livable, practical, comfortable environment. Hold on to, care for, and empower your treasures. Seek beauty and bring it into your life!

Sun square Uranus (occurring June 19 – 29) This occurrence of Sun square Uranus particularly affects Gemini and Cancer people celebrating birthdays June 19 – 29. The square of Uranus to these birthday folks' natal Sun brings a strong dose of unrestrained chaos and challenging events. This may be the year

158

for you, birthday folks, to surrender to those aspects of life that are truly out
of your control, and to concentrate more rationally on those facets of life over
which you do have control. Sometimes the aftermath of Uranus's influence is an
improvement, but with the square aspect at work, it is likely these people will feel
personally challenged. Birthday people, if your life has no foundation, there is
no point in holding on to the illusion of stability at this juncture of your sojourn.
Albeit slowly, this aspect will pass. Try to be detached from chaotic events as they
occur, and the outcome will seem less costly. It is vital not to give rapid change too
much resistance, lest you be subject to the reversals of trying to fight chaos with
logic at a time when resistance is futile. Project the picture of peace and it will be
there for you at the other end. This aspect will reoccur on December 22.

June 27ᵗʰ Monday

Moon in Taurus	PDT	EDT	
Mars sextile Uranus	3:26 AM	6:26 AM	
Moon sextile Mercury goes v/c	9:23 AM	12:23 PM	
Sun opposite Pluto	10:19 PM	1:19 AM	(Jun 28)
Mars trine Saturn begins (see July 6)			

Birthday: Tobey Maguire 1975

Mood Watch: The day starts out pleasantly enough, but it isn't long before the
waning Taurus Moon goes void-of-course. Many people may be preoccupied by
their physical needs, especially with regard to money and money management. A
void-of-course Taurus Moon can be a lazy or stubborn time for our moods. Keep
a keen eye on the money, and be careful not to get caught up in impulse shopping
or large scale financial decisions. This is a good time to clean and organize.

Mars sextile Uranus (occurring June 21 – 30) Mars in Gemini is sextile to Uranus
in Aries. The polarized forces of combat (Mars in Gemini) have the potential (the
sextile aspect) to create bold and courageous kinds of chaos in swift and incisive
ways (Uranus in Aries). Mars governs all activities and forces of action. Uranus
governs the element of surprise, change, and liberation. The sextile aspect brings
opportunity, and puts this dualistic and premeditated Mars energy into a position
of arousing and igniting the explosive, unpredictable and chaotic energies of
Uranus. Both of these planets are charged with forceful energy and vitality as
well as being violent and unsettled at times. Masculine forces are forging ahead
abruptly and loudly right now. The overall qualities of Mars sextile Uranus are
very fiery, although not necessarily completely destructive. It is important to look
for the opportunity and potential in all sources of raw masculine energy. This
aspect last occurred on January 12.

Sun opposite Pluto (occurring June 21 – 30) Sun in Cancer opposes Pluto in
Capricorn. Summer solstice cusp born Gemini people and early born Cancer folks
having birthdays from June 21 – 30 are undergoing the effects of Pluto being in a
lengthy opposition to their natal Sun sign. Birthday folks, with Pluto in opposition
to your identity, this is the time to accept transition, however overwhelming the
circumstances. Persist in recognizing the empowering differences each generation

embodies. Gemini folks born near the Cancer cusp – here's the good news: it won't be that much longer for Pluto to be in opposition to your natal Sun position. Since 1995, Pluto has been opposite to Gemini, teaching Gemini people about the necessity of regeneration, and the shifting of the powers that be. Sun in Cancer opposite Pluto in Capricorn particularly affects early born Cancer birthday people, and they must begin to face the awakening challenges of transformation. These challenges may appear threatening and are often perceived as a painful process of loss and destruction. Late Gemini and early born Cancer birthday folks, do not get hung up on high expectations of life or you are likely to burn out. These lessons are meant to be, so open up to the need for endurance and perseverance during this time – use wisdom as your guide. Survival counts! Use your senses and your sensibilities well, but do not resist the forces of great change. Surviving all this means the best of life is yet to come, as you will grow to appreciate life in a delightfully transformed way. This is also true for your opposites, the late born Sagittarians and early born Capricorns, who are feeling the conjunction of Pluto to their natal Sun.

June 28th Tuesday

Moon in Taurus / Gemini	PDT	EDT	
Moon enters Gemini	12:55 AM	3:55 AM	
Moon square Neptune	2:23 AM	5:23 AM	
Moon sextile Uranus	9:35 AM	12:35 PM	
Moon conjunct Mars	11:21 AM	2:21 PM	
Moon trine Saturn	9:16 PM	12:16 AM	(Jun 29)

Birthday: Stewart Farrar 1916

Mood Watch: Gemini Moon puts the focus of our moods on communicating and receiving information. Activities revolve around writing, speeches, conversations, and secretarial duties. On the surface, a lot of the information sifts past our ears, through seemingly meaningless detail, and eventually more significant, more useful and practical information is attained.

June 29th Wednesday

Moon in Gemini / *No Exact Aspects*
Venus trine Neptune begins (see July 4)
Birthday: Antoine de Saint-Exupéry 1900

Mood Watch: Gemini Moon brings curious, talkative, and communicative moods. The Moon also wanes darkly, which brings depth and profoundness to our moods. This is a good time to collect encouraging thoughts, positive affirmations, and clever ideas. In a problematic world there is no end to all the reasons why our lives can be so complex. Gemini Moon gives us the incentive to filter through tons of meaningless or irrelevant information in order to spot the significant data that will serve our most important needs.

June 30th Thursday

Moon in Gemini / Cancer	PDT	EDT
Moon conjunct Venus goes v/c	12:32 AM	3:32 AM
Moon enters Cancer	9:12 AM	12:12 PM
Moon trine Neptune	10:32 AM	1:32 PM
Moon square Uranus	5:27 PM	8:27 PM
Moon sextile Jupiter	6:11 PM	9:11 PM
Moon opposite Pluto	8:07 PM	11:07 PM

Birthday: Michael Phelps 1985

Mood Watch: The void-of-course Gemini Moon starts off the day with a myriad of distractions and interruptions. As the Moon enters Cancer, our moods are magnified with the potential for irritability and the need for reassurance. It's the New Moon eve as well as the eve of a solar eclipse. People may seem withdrawn at times or just plain moody. Some patience will be required and a little bit of sympathy can go a long way towards improving the general mood.

July 1st Friday

Canada Day
NEW MOON IN CANCER – *Partial Solar Eclipse*

	PDT	EDT	
Moon conjunct Sun	1:53 AM	4:53 AM	
Moon square Saturn goes v/c	4:37 AM	7:37 AM	
Mercury enters Leo	10:37 PM	1:37 AM	(Jul 2)
Mercury square Jupiter begins (see July 5)			
Mercury trine Uranus begins (see July 4)			

Birthday: Princess Diana 1961

Mood Watch: The **New Moon in Cancer** (Moon conjunct Sun) beckons to our moods to tune into newly emerging feelings about ourselves. The New Cancer Moon invites new desires to nurture the child within and build up a fresh outlook on our home life. Cancer focuses on the nurturing strength of the mother. This is a good time to bring new things to the home and brighten up one's outlook with nurturing and uplifting moods and feelings.

Solar Eclipse in Cancer This Solar Eclipse brings an emphasis on controversies rooted in our feelings and emotional core. For some, the ability to have clear feelings may seem overshadowed, but it must be remembered that this is only a brief shadow. Eclipses are believed to threaten the lives and liberty of leaders and special figures in society. The cardinal water sign of Cancer in the ecliptic state often influences hurricanes, floods, storms, and drought. This is the time to reassure those who are undergoing emotional dramas and to be patient with emotional outbursts. Every time there is a Solar Eclipse, there is usually a Lunar Eclipse within two weeks. This Eclipse duo will have another Eclipse pair at the opposite time of year. Although this may not feel like a particularly easy time for starting anew, the Solar Eclipse touches our lives with a fluid and accepting assertiveness to move through the greatest obstacles. Beware of the tendency for some people to lean towards substance abuse, depression, and emotional instability.

Mercury enters Leo (Mercury in Leo: July 1 – 28) Mercury in Leo is an excellent time to effectively write or perform screenplays and comedy. When Leo the lion speaks, it's a penetrating sound! Mercury in Leo puts the focus of information, news and discussions on entertainment, personal interests, and connection with families. This is the time when many kids are turning to – or away from – family in an effort to find answers. They seek answers they can live with, answers about determining self-identity as well as survival skills. Mercury in Leo is a time when the mind establishes, reaffirms and maintains a self-created identity. Connections with Leos will come easily as expressed thoughts become more colorful and dramatic, and communications shift toward charismatic interplay. Self-expression and soulful fortitude will be more evident in our communications while Mercury is in Leo. On August 8, the retrograde Mercury (Aug. 2 – 26) will reenter Leo for another round of Mercury in Leo (Aug. 8 – Sept. 8). For more information on Mercury retrograde through Leo, see the introduction in this book on *Mercury retrograde periods*.

July 2nd Saturday

Moon in Cancer / Leo	PDT	EDT	
Moon enters Leo	2:42 PM	5:42 PM	
Moon conjunct Mercury	4:55 PM	7:55 PM	
Sun square Saturn	5:16 PM	8:16 PM	
Moon trine Uranus	10:37 PM	1:37 AM	(Jul 3)
Moon square Jupiter	11:55 PM	2:55 AM	(Jul 3)
Venus square Uranus begins (see July 7)			

Birthday: Jerry Hall 1956

Mood Watch: The morning brings a void-of-course Cancer Moon, and there is likely to be a prevalence of defensiveness and moodiness throughout this time. Later the Leo Moon brings both the expression of playfulness and the need to keep life entertaining, particularly after all the emotional purging our moods have undergone recently. A newly waxing Leo Moon on a summer Saturday is a good time to enjoy picnics and barbeques with family and friends.

Sun square Saturn (occurring June 26 – July 5) This occurrence of Sun in Cancer square Saturn in Libra especially affects Cancer people who are celebrating birthdays June 26 – July 5. These folks may experience personal challenges of impatience, loss of control, a poor sense of timing, or difficulty identifying with current obligations. The challenge is to overcome obstacles that intrude on one's discipline and accuracy. This may be a time of sacrifice, loss or compromise, and may also be a time of complexity and insecurity for these birthday folks. Saturn represents those things in life we are willing to work for and maintain. It also represents our sense of discipline and our application of effort and focus, and helps us learn about our limitations and where our strengths can be realized. This is a good time for Cancer birthday folks to conserve energies and take losses

162

and difficulties in stride. Through the tests of this time, a stronger human being emerges to take on future tests with greater confidence and ability. Avoiding responsibilities or hardships now will only make life more difficult later. This aspect last occurred on January 7, affecting the Capricorn birthday folks of that time.

July 3rd Sunday

Moon in Leo	PDT	EDT	
Moon sextile Mars	6:00 AM	9:00 AM	
Moon sextile Saturn goes v/c	9:25 AM	12:25 PM	
Venus enters Cancer	9:16 PM	12:16 AM	(Jul 4)
Venus opposite Pluto begins (see July 9)			

Birthday: Montel Williams 1956

Mood Watch: Playfulness of moods allows for jovial encounters with the youthfully waxing Leo Moon. Early in the day, the Leo Moon goes void-of-course making this a good time for leisurely exploits, time for oneself, and simple endeavors. If the lion does not sleep or play, his hunger leads him into the most serious venture of stalking. Keep your bellies full and your spirits light and there won't be much trouble keeping peace on the plains tonight.

Venus enters Cancer (Venus in Cancer: July 3 – 28) Venus now enters the nurturing sign of Cancer, an appropriate place for the expression of love and affection. It invites those with rocky love relationships to patch things up, and to do so with more heart and less uncertainty. Venus in Cancer encourages our affections and affinities to be carefully placed and nurtured. When attractions occur, they will have a lasting impression and will seem very strong and emotionally sound. Venus in Cancer brings out a love for such things as the ocean, leisurely aquatic sports, motherly care and expression, and all varieties of nurturing. While Venus travels over their natal Sun, those folks born in the sign of Cancer will be especially aware of their love life and their needs for pleasure.

July 4th Monday

Independence Day, USA

Moon in Leo / Virgo	PDT	EDT
Venus trine Neptune	10:26 AM	1:26 PM
Mercury trine Uranus	5:47 PM	8:47 PM
Moon enters Virgo	6:15 PM	9:15 PM
Moon opposite Neptune	7:22 PM	10:22 PM
Moon sextile Venus	8:14 PM	11:14 PM

Birthday: Gina Lollobrigida 1927

Mood Watch: The long void-of-course Leo Moon day brings a tendency for people to be preoccupied, self involved, and there is likely to be a hankering for some recognition and encouragement. Tonight's Moon in Virgo is a good time for outdoor recreation and celebration, with a strong emphasis placed on safety and precaution. Moon opposite Neptune is a firm reminder to be aware of human

163

beings' propensity towards substance abuse and escapism. Moon sextile Venus brings the potential for kindly affections.

Venus trine Neptune (occurring June 29 – July 6) Neptune just entered Pisces this year (see April 4), and for the first time in our lifetime, Venus in Cancer is trine Neptune in Pisces. This brings nurturing and motherly feminine love right in harmony with intuitive kinds of spiritual expression. Artistic endeavors will shine with spiritual adeptness. This aspect brings calmness and tranquility that are vitally needed, particularly in love related matters. When coming from a place of love, it is easier to draw down a spiritual enhancement of that love with Venus trine Neptune. Enjoying beauty is a way to acquire gifts of the spirit world. This is a good time to actively engage in peaceful, pleasurable, and spiritual love. This aspect will reoccur on October 7.

Mercury trine Uranus (occurring July 1 – 6) Mercury, emphasizing the transmission of news and information, is now in the favorable trine position to Uranus, representing disruption and chaos. This aspect brings news of disorder and calamity which (through the trine aspect) represents a gift, probably one of freedom or a break in the mundane routine. There are many premature or radical breakthroughs waiting in the wings, and Mercury trine Uranus often brings news of these discoveries. Mercury is in Leo trine to Uranus in Aries. Talk will be generated about radical changes that occur among friends and family. Catch phrases or radical concept statements and ideas, are often born under this aspect, and are more easily absorbed. Mercury trine Uranus also allows for brilliant concepts to shine through and be worded in a way that radically makes sense. This is a good time to record thoughts and appreciate brilliant thinking. This aspect will reoccur November 3, and it will also come to a non-exact position on December 14.

July 5th Tuesday

Moon in Virgo	PDT	EDT
Moon trine Jupiter	3:48 AM	6:48 AM
Moon trine Pluto	4:27 AM	7:27 AM
Mercury square Jupiter	11:08 AM	2:08 PM
Moon square Mars	11:50 AM	2:50 PM
Moon sextile Sun goes v/c	5:19 PM	8:19 PM
Venus sextile Jupiter begins (see July 8)		

Birthday: Huey Lewis 1951

Mood Watch: The waxing Virgo Moon encourages our moods to keep main aspirations in sight so that details are put into perspective. Virgo Moon keeps us sensitive to our dietary needs and digestive cycle. Cleanliness, order, and precision will keep us feeling comfortably productive. Be careful not to get caught in the crossfire of Moon square Mars. Tough as it may seem, today will be the better day to attempt to make some progress with work. Tonight's void-of-course Moon brings a good time to relax and take it easy. It will remain void throughout most of tomorrow.

Mercury square Jupiter (occurring July 1 – 7) Mercury in Leo is square to Jupiter in Taurus; this may be a tough time to communicate a sense of reassurance, particularly with regard to individual's personal livelihoods and personal savings. It may also be a difficult time to raise money for charities. During this aspect, it may be best to hold off on a job request, asking for a raise, buying a new business, or signing any binding contracts concerning long term investment and payment schedules. This aspect may bring discussions or complaints which revolve around the difficulties of getting funds or capital to grow, and it has a tendency to create expensive misunderstandings when it comes to large scale investments. This aspect last occurred on January 11.

July 6th Wednesday

Moon in Virgo / Libra

	PDT	EDT
Mars trine Saturn	5:15 AM	8:15 AM
Moon enters Libra	8:53 PM	11:53 PM
Mercury sextile Saturn begins (see July 9)		
Mercury sextile Mars begins (see July 11)		

Birthday: His Holiness the 14th Dali Lama 1935

Mood Watch: A long void-of-course Moon day in Virgo often brings tired or withdrawn moods. People may tend to be a little bit more on the skeptical side, and there is a strong emphasis on the need to be precise, practical, and discerning. Today, gentleness, patience, and kindness will go far in remedying people's cautious ways. Later, the waxing Libra Moon sets a harmonious tone to our moods.

Mars trine Saturn (occurring June 27 – July 10) Mars in Gemini trine Saturn in Libra brings positive – although somewhat fluctuating – breakthroughs in expediting the will to accomplish certain goals. Large scale projects can expect to move ahead. Our actions bring gifts with this aspect, provided there is an application of discipline and timing. At best, Mars trine Saturn provides a sense of good timing. Action will be greatly influenced by the powers of persuasion and thoughtful intent. This is a favorably effective time to take action with words (Mars in Gemini) and to take control with the law and in court (Saturn in Libra). This may be a good time to apply diligent practice with one's favorite sport, especially those activities which demand precision and perfect timing. The timely gifts of willpower and discipline bring rewards and positive results. To fully benefit from this aspect, one must use the energy (Mars) responsibly (Saturn). This is usually a time of harmonious transitions, when endings and new beginnings are easily merged. This aspect last occurred on February 6.

July 7th Thursday

FIRST QUARTER MOON in LIBRA

	PDT	EDT	
Moon square Venus	3:37 AM	6:37 AM	
Moon opposite Uranus	4:34 AM	7:34 AM	
Moon square Pluto	6:56 AM	9:56 AM	
Jupiter trine Pluto	7:06 AM	10:06 AM	
Moon sextile Mercury	11:36 AM	2:36 PM	
Venus square Uranus	2:43 PM	5:43 PM	
Moon conjunct Saturn	3:20 PM	6:20 PM	
Moon trine Mars	4:59 PM	7:59 PM	
Moon square Sun goes v/c	11:29 PM	2:29 AM	(Jul 8)
Venus square Saturn begins (see July 13)			

Birthday: Ringo Starr 1940

Mood Watch: The Sun is in Cancer emphasizing activities of the home (the world of our feelings) and the need to preserve our emotional attachments; the **First Quarter Moon in Libra** (Moon square Sun) encourages us to harmonize with our partners and friends. This Moon brings a focus on the need to create balance in various relationships, particularly those of a close nature. Throughout today we cannot help but notice that it's time to make adjustments! Compromise is a two way street. Stand up for what you need, but be prepared to put out some effort towards the needs of others. It is best to create as much organization, harmony, and balance as you can today; tomorrow's long void-of-course Libra Moon will be a difficult time to get much done or to coordinate well with others.

Jupiter trine Pluto (occurring June 7 – Nov. 16) Jupiter in Taurus is trine Pluto in Capricorn. Expansion of a material nature is bound to go well for those in positions of power. Jupiter represents expansion, prosperity, social advancement, and opportunities towards growth, just to name a few of its qualities. Pluto represents transformation, power, fate, and the transfer of lifestyles from one generation to the next. Through this aspect, various power structures will be taking their fill of advancement in the world. This aspect is likely to bring an economic shift which will bestow many gifts of opportunity, and promote advancement towards some novel form of power for some of those hard working folks among us. Strong power plays and shifts in the economy are likely to become more prominent over the long term in international market at this time; take note of companies making strong advancements. This aspect brings some relief and greater ease when facing up to the troubles left by the previous generations. Jupiter trine Pluto aids us in a powerful way when we are advancing beyond an old standard of life towards something more prosperous. There are likely to be powerfully influential gifts bestowed with regard to an inheritance during this aspect of Jupiter trine Pluto. This long winded aspect occurs with two peaks – today and again on October 28 before it ends on November 16.

Venus square Uranus (occurring July 2 – 10) Venus, the planet that governs love and magnetism, is square to Uranus, the planet of chaos and disruption. It may be difficult for love (Venus) to flourish in a spontaneous and carefree fashion. Venus in Cancer is square to Uranus in Aries. Some folks are likely to become too easily affronted by radical or explosive kinds of magnetism. Those who are directly affected by the complexity of this aspect may encounter an emotional meltdown; for them it's an important time to get help and support. Find the calm place in the eye of the storm and support those you love. This influence may be testing the power of love to withstand the chaos of extremes and sudden change. This aspect last occurred on February 2 and will reoccur on November 26.

July 8th Friday

Moon in Libra / Scorpio	PDT	EDT	
Venus sextile Jupiter	11:05 PM	2:05 AM	(Jul 9)
Moon enters Scorpio	11:31 PM	2:31 AM	(Jul 9)

Birthday: Kevin Bacon 1958

Mood Watch: The period of the waxing Libra Moon emphasizes harmony, justice, and a collaborative spirit. However, the void-of-course phase of the Moon dominates the hours of the day and the night with a continual process of deliberation, vacillation, and the need for compromises with others. The pendulum swings both ways, but for some who are in need of decisive action, the perpetual state of flux can be unnerving today. Indecision and hesitance are some of the most common symptoms of the void Libra Moon. Patience is a wise and wonderful Libran trait that can be most endearing in a time of uncertainty.

Venus sextile Jupiter (occurring July 5 – 10) Venus is in Cancer, the place of pure and nurturing love play. Jupiter is in Taurus, bringing a practical outreach for fulfillment and a joyful effort towards getting in touch with the things we love. Heartfelt – as well as endearing – attractions and pleasures (Venus in Cancer) lead us to prosperous opportunities in nature related focuses, farming, landscaping, banking, accounting, and architecture (Jupiter in Taurus). This is an excellent time to shower loved ones with gifts and compliments. A lovers' getaway may be just the ticket to recapture some romance. This is the time to allow expansion to occur in love matters, and to take the next step towards enlivening and enhancing the beauty of life. A greater opportunity for increasing skills or augmenting your livelihood is available, especially if your focus remains on doing what you love most. This aspect last occurred on March 10.

July 9th Saturday

Moon in Scorpio	PDT	EDT
Moon trine Neptune	12:31 AM	3:31 AM
Mercury sextile Saturn	1:18 AM	4:18 AM
Venus opposite Pluto	1:32 AM	4:32 AM
Moon sextile Pluto	9:33 AM	12:33 PM
Moon opposite Jupiter	10:10 AM	1:10 PM
Moon trine Venus	11:06 AM	2:06 PM
Uranus goes retrograde	5:34 PM	8:34 PM
Moon square Mercury	8:05 PM	11:05 PM

Birthday: Tom Hanks 1956

Mood Watch: Today our moods enter into a phase of dramatic awareness. The waxing Scorpio Moon puts us in touch with our passions. Sun in Cancer and Moon in Scorpio often create a somewhat watery and emotional kind of mood setting. This is an excellent time to work on remedies for pain, encourage yourself and others to face important problems and issues, and to indulge in creative and revitalizing activities. This evening's Moon square Mercury may cause some awkwardness when communicating difficult subjects. Beware of the tendency for thoughtless remarks to cause resentfulness.

Mercury sextile Saturn (occurring July 6 – 10) Mercury in Leo is sextile Saturn in Libra. Mercury in Leo emphasizes the need to communicate about personal matters as well as family and friends. Meanwhile, Saturn in Libra demands balanced and harmonious measures with regard to setting up perimeters and implementing rules. This tends to be a time when struggles and difficulties are discussed, and people draw collective conclusions on how best to handle their problems or responsibilities. This is an opportunistic aspect for communicating work skills. Make use of it while the opportunity is here.

Venus opposite Pluto (occurring July 3 – 11) Venus in Cancer opposes Pluto in Capricorn. The love we feel for home – and those places from which we draw a nurturing spirit (Venus in Cancer) – will be diametrically opposed to those elements and conditions of life that transform our homes and home-life into something more career based (Pluto in Capricorn). Matters concerning love, beauty, and affection may be overwhelmed by powerful forces or unforeseeable twists of fate. These fateful forces may be intruding somehow on the objects or people we love and admire. This could include just about any kind of scenario – from being shattered over the loss of a loved one, to a terminal disease, to the process of learning how to fully accept and support some kind of total transformation of a loved one. Some people find it difficult to support loved ones through severe kinds of hardship, yet now is the time to offer support to them, despite the opposing forces that appear too harsh or overwhelming. This aspect may well bring on an acute awareness of the desire that some have for power, and the need to have power over loved ones. No one, no matter how powerful, can justifiably tell us what we love, who we love, or how we are to love. Deep in our hearts dwells the truth. When the going gets tough, look to your heart!

Uranus goes retrograde (Uranus retrograde: July 9 – Dec. 9) Uranus, the outer planet representing revolution, chaos, explosive energy, and big changes, is currently at the four degree mark of Aries. Symbolically, this is the cusp of the zodiac where the orobus serpent bites its own tail and begins to consume itself, and it represents the amalgamation of the ending and beginning energies of the universe. Uranus, an outer planet, first entered Aries last year on May 27. Outer planets move slowly, and this one will take five months to backtrack only 4 degrees before it moves forward once again at the zero degree mark of Aries. Uranus influences chaos and volatile or abrupt energies, and inspires the need for change and breakthroughs in the pursuit of freedom. When retrograde, the influence of Uranus teaches us to handle uncertainty, particularly internal chaos.

168

Many aspects of chaos tend to be sporadically repeated until the boundaries of restriction loosen enough so we can move more freely. Uranus retrograde is a time when humanity as a whole must backtrack over their revolutionary practices in order to make breakthroughs in the long run. Uranus liberates, although for some people the retrograde process may seem to be excessively inhibiting, particularly if one's surroundings do not allow for much freedom. For rebels, contemplation and internalization bring greater inner strength. While Uranus is retrograde, be sure to set a standard for a certain degree of freedom in your life, so that you can stop and smell the flowers this summer and into the days of autumn. Don't let this valuable time of the year slide by without allowing your inner rebel to kick up his or her heels once in awhile. Freedom is a worthy thing to claim.

July 10th Sunday

Moon in Scorpio

	PDT	EDT
Moon trine Sun goes v/c	6:05 AM	9:05 AM

URANUS-SQUARE-PLUTO-NON-EXACT (see below)

Birthday: Jessica Simpson 1980

Mood Watch: Sun in Cancer and Moon in Scorpio creates a watery, fluid, intuitive, sensitive, and strongly emotional expression of moods. There are a lot of reasons why we can be emotional; our sense of humanity is threatened all the time in these challenging days of the New Aeon. Scorpio Moon puts us in touch with the many ways we are individually, and collectively, suffering. The best way to activate this sensitive and empowering realm of emotionality is to internally reinforce positive affirmations in the evolutionary process of humanity. Scorpio Moon puts us in tune with our struggles to peacefully coexist and to do the right things.

URANUS-SQUARE-PLUTO-NON-EXACT (occurring April 7 – Oct. 9) Due to Uranus retrograde (see yesterday), from around this time through mid-September, this square aspect comes within a one degree orb; that's the closest we come to it reaching its peak this year. It began occurring on April 7 and has been looming ever closer until this period we have now reached. After mid-September, these two planets will begin to separate again, causing this near square aspect to completely dissipate by October 9.

This aspect is not your run-of-the-mill common occurrence! Oh no – it has an irregular cycle of every 50 to 80 years, depending on the retrograde cycles of Uranus and Pluto. This major aspect involves two of the three outer planets, which are among the slowest moving in our solar system. Their interaction with each other affects *all* of humankind, bringing unfathomable – and unpredictable – acts of chaos, transformation and complex changes, usually of historical proportions.

In 2009 we got the first glimpse (from June 7 – 23, 2009) of the affects of Uranus square Pluto, which takes years to develop, and will take another year to reach its ominous peak. Last year, Uranus square Pluto showed itself for the second time this century (May 6 – August 11, 2010), and the events during this occurrence period provided us with some major clues for the types of dramatic changes we can expect to encounter over the next decade.

169

Uranus is the outer planet that represents revolution, chaos, explosive energy, and big changes. Pluto is known as the underworld god, the one who tests and evaluates the stability of all things, and where there is weakness, Pluto removes or annihilates weakness with illness, famine, decay, and putrefaction. Pluto purifies or cleans away that which is dead and gone. Where Pluto traverses, permanent change occurs. Out of this transformation, an entirely different perspective will affect our understanding of how things work on the physical plane. In the square position, these two planets are a force to be reckoned with – and then some.

Uranus in Aries square Pluto in Capricorn brings explosive new beginnings and a highly disciplined world of industrious transformation. False starts will go up in smoke as fast as old institutions will crumble. Competition is stiff in the world at large. This is the time of hard work towards establishing systems that must function for generations to come. The square aspect represents the stumbling blocks – as well as the stepping stones – to overcome complexity, destruction, and the struggles of life.

This aspect last occurred in the early 1930s (the classic depression), and it won't return – after this next phase – until the early 2070s. The signs of the times are unable to hide while the mighty Uranus-square-Pluto-non-exact debacle continues. Next year this aspect will return full swing for a very illuminating realization of exactly what types of trials will come of Uranus in Aries square Pluto in Capricorn. The exact peak occurrence dates for Uranus square Pluto are June 24, 2012, September 19, 2012, May 20, 2013, November 1, 2013, April 21, 2014, and March 17, 2015. When it's all over, very little will ever seem the same; Uranus square Pluto guarantees the most radical kind of transformation for all. This is the time to start paying attention to the signs.

July 11th Monday

Moon in Scorpio / Sagittarius	PDT	EDT	
Moon enters Sagittarius	2:46 AM	5:46 AM	
Moon square Neptune	3:44 AM	6:44 AM	
Moon trine Uranus	10:39 AM	1:39 PM	
Mercury sextile Mars	8:28 PM	11:28 PM	
Moon sextile Saturn	10:04 PM	1:04 AM	(Jul 12)

Birthday: Lon Milo DuQuette July 11, 1948
"Now there's a man with an open mind – you can feel the breeze from here." – Groucho Marx (1890 – 1977)

Mood Watch: Out of the fixed, emotional realm of the dream world, the void-of-course Scorpio Moon shakes the skeletons loose from our proverbial closets. As the waxing Moon enters Sagittarius, we are given the incentive to explore, to investigate, and to engage in a little adventure. There are many ways to do this – internally, externally, or through a particular method or medium. There are many tools from which to choose – a specific book, a computer program, or a game of strategy. The important thing is to keep an open mind. A closed mind cannot expand. Sagittarius is ruled by Jupiter, the planet of expansion, prosperity, and joviality.

170

Mercury sextile Mars (occurring July 6 – Sept. 30) This aspect will occur for longer than usual due to the retrograde cycle of Mercury (Aug. 2 – 26). Mercury in Leo sextile Mars in Gemini brings charismatic messages and carefully premeditated actions. Enthusiastic responses to discussions are sure to keep our communications buzzing along swiftly. This aspect ensures that communications will move quickly. Mercury sextile Mars presents opportunities which can be received, recognized, communicated and acted upon. News or information may lead to immediate action. It's an advantageous time to apply one's word with a full backing of action for a very favorable outcome. This aspect will reach two more peaks – for the second and third time during this occurrence period – on August 4 and September 29.

July 12th Tuesday

Moon in Sagittarius	PDT	EDT
Moon opposite Mars	4:55 AM	7:55 AM
Moon trine Mercury goes v/c	5:20 AM	8:20 AM

Birthday: Buckminster Fuller 1895

Mood Watch: Moon opposite Mars puts a burst of energy into our early morning. Moon trine Mercury brings a natural inclination for us to reach out to others. The Sagittarius Moon goes void-of-course early in the day, which tends to create delays with things like traffic, travel plans, and transportation. A lot of patience will be required today, as the endless void-of-course Sagittarius Moon often brings spacey moods, and there's commonly a strong preoccupation with the need to get back on track and moving in a positive, progressive direction.

July 13th Wednesday

Moon in Sagittarius / Capricorn	PDT	EDT
Venus square Saturn	12:35 AM	3:35 AM
Moon enters Capricorn	7:13 AM	10:13 AM
Moon sextile Neptune	8:08 AM	11:08 AM
Moon square Uranus	3:20 PM	6:20 PM
Moon conjunct Pluto	5:33 PM	8:33 PM
Moon trine Jupiter	7:31 PM	10:31 PM

Birthday: John Dee 1527 / Papus (Gérard Encausse) 1865

Mood Watch: It may seem like a disaster zone of uncertainty early this morning, but the void-of-course Sagittarius Moon soon enters Capricorn. The Full Moon eve is upon us and while the Moon is full in Capricorn, David Bowie's lyrical term "serious moonlight" describes it all. After all, David Bowie is a Capricorn! Full Capricorn Moon activities tend to be serious, profound, goal conscious, astute, and enterprising. Capricorn Moon reminds us to act in a conscientious way, to be practical and aware, particularly when it comes to knowing one's limitations. This is quite odd to think about when the Full Moon is so often associated with lunacy and craziness. Capricorn is in the opposite position to the Moon's home base, Cancer, and yet, sometimes opposites create the perfect balance. Capricorn tests the edge of emotional clamor with a serious drive to excel, and to succeed, without the hindrance of emotional indulgence or distraction. This Capricorn Moon brings a serious need for clarity, pragmatism, stability, perfect timing, and responsibility. This rockin' energy will continue to build through tomorrow evening when the Full Moon reaches its peak. As Bowie says:*"Let's Dance!..."*

Venus square Saturn (occurring July 7 – 15) Venus in Cancer is square to Saturn in Libra. It may be difficult to engage in pleasures, romance, or to adequately protect the ones you love, particularly when complex obligations and responsibilities are involved. It may seem as if something is always getting in the way of basic pleasures. Perhaps it is best not to get bent out of shape over some people's need to create restrictions in order to protect their own sense of security while love related troubles are being worked out. No matter how much one prioritizes a focus on love, it is still likely to be misinterpreted on some level during Venus square Saturn. Love related dramas may be taken too seriously. Give it your best – keep singing the praises of love and applying the law of attraction, but expect some challenges and high demands for discipline nonetheless. This aspect last occurred on February 18 and it will reoccur on December 18.

July 14th Thursday

FULL MOON in CAPRICORN	PDT	EDT	
Moon square Saturn	3:19 AM	6:19 AM	
Moon opposite Venus	5:55 AM	8:55 AM	
Moon opposite Sun goes v/c	11:39 PM	2:39 AM	(Jul 15)

Birthday: Bebe Buell 1953

Mood Watch: The **Full Moon in Capricorn** (Moon opposite Sun) reaches its peak at the close of the evening. All through the day, serious energy builds and intensifies. For starters, in the early hours of the morning, Moon square Saturn brings the harsh reminder of the complexity of our work, and there are things we may find ourselves grappling over. As the Moon opposes Venus, we are deeply inspired to seek beauty, and to empower the attraction magnet – wherever we need it to work. The Full Moon always suggests a time of celebration, and the earthy Capricorn expression focuses on the achievement of goals through the application of persistence and diligence. The gold is in your integrity and work. It's a key time to focus on setting and accomplishing important goals that will eventually bring satisfaction. It is also the time to *celebrate* your accomplishments!

July 15th Friday

Moon in Capricorn / Aquarius	PDT	EDT	
Moon enters Aquarius	1:29 PM	4:29 PM	
Moon sextile Uranus	9:55 PM	12:55 AM	(Jul 16)

Birthday: Linda Ronstadt 1946

Mood Watch: For a considerable stretch of time, the void-of-course Capricorn Moon may encumber our sensibilities. The post full Moon time can be very tiring to many folks. It is wise to keep a cool pace, while also remembering to take little breaks along the way. As the Moon enters Aquarius, an exciting charge of energy infuses our moods. A full, but waning, Aquarius Moon brings thought provoking insights.

July 16th Saturday

Moon in Aquarius	PDT	EDT	
Moon square Jupiter	2:53 AM	5:53 AM	
Moon trine Saturn	10:40 AM	1:40 PM	
Moon trine Mars	11:55 PM	2:55 AM	(Jul 17)

Birthday: Ginger Rogers 1911

Mood Watch: The Moon wanes in Aquarius. Today we will be more inclined to seek knowledgeable solutions to labor intensive troubles. Once we've worked our way through the various duties, more exciting ideas and interesting thoughts will occupy our minds. The summertime Aquarius Moon is an excellent time to explore innovative outdoor activities and new or spontaneous kinds of leisurely hobbies.

July 17th Sunday

Moon in Aquarius / Pisces	PDT	EDT	
Moon opposite Mercury goes v/c	5:23 AM	8:23 AM	
Moon enters Pisces	10:12 PM	1:12 AM	(Jul 18)
Moon conjunct Neptune	11:01 PM	2:01 AM	(Jul 18)

Birthday: Vince Guaraldi 1928

Mood Watch: The day begins with the waning Aquarius Moon going void-of-course for the remainder of the day and well into this evening. People may seem either very ingenious or downright moronic. Brilliance and foolishness take all forms and shapes. This is no time to shut down and give into human stupidity. Knowledge is a responsibility; it is important to correct ignorance in a non-confrontational manner. Not everyone will succumb to common sense, but sometimes a simple suggestion can assist to alter the destructive behavior of another. Never underestimate the power of suggestion.

July 18th Monday

Moon in Pisces	PDT	EDT
Moon sextile Pluto	9:16 AM	12:16 PM
Moon sextile Jupiter	12:51 PM	3:51 PM

Birthday: Hunter S. Thompson 1937

Mood Watch: Throughout the day, waning Pisces Moon tests the weak links in the human spirit. It is often a time when we contend with our illusions, and struggle with our dreams while we review our beliefs. Repetitively escaping from troubles does not make them any easier, but at times like this, escapism is the highly likely theme. Most of the things we do must be put into perspective and into the proper context, but in dreams, anything is possible. Pisces Moon brings a very meaningful – but subtle – journey for the soul.

July 19th Tuesday

Moon in Pisces	PDT	EDT
Moon trine Venus	11:42 AM	2:42 PM
Moon square Mars	1:44 PM	4:44 PM

Birthday: Arthur Rackham 1867

Mood Watch: The waning Pisces Moon is an excellent time to seek a comfortable space, to daydream, and let the mind wander. Moon trine Venus starts off our day with a strong attraction to beauty and the things we love, and this makes it an inviting time to harmonize with ease. As the day continues, the Pisces Moon envelops our moods with instinctive inclinations, a deep curiosity, and a subtle quality of perception. This afternoon's waning Pisces Moon brings a penchant for hypersensitivity, especially while Moon square Mars makes it difficult for some folks to manage their aggressions. Pisces Moon is famous for opening up our spiritual interests and it is wise to share these interests in a safe, encouraging, uplifting environment.

July 20th Wednesday

Moon in Pisces / Aries	PDT	EDT
Moon trine Sun goes v/c	4:14 AM	7:14 AM
Moon enters Aries	9:25 AM	12:25 PM
Moon conjunct Uranus	6:29 PM	9:29 PM
Moon square Pluto	8:45 PM	11:45 PM

Birthday: Carlos Santana 1947

Mood Watch: Early this morning, the waning Pisces Moon goes void-of-course. For a time, people may tend to appear incredibly wishy-washy, vague, and unclear. As the Moon enters Aries, we experience the need to engage with others in a much more direct and self-assured fashion. Aries Moon puts us in touch with our need for purpose, action, and clear direction. Later tonight, the dramas and the power-plays thickly coat the atmosphere of our moods, while Moon square Pluto reminds us of the difficulties of fate's unyielding transitions. The waning Aries Moon keeps us busy as we charge into – and out of – the bold and intrepid urgency of life itself.

July 21st Thursday

Moon in Aries	PDT	EDT
Moon opposite Saturn	8:53 AM	11:53 AM
Sun trine Uranus begins (see July 27)		

Birthday: Ernest Hemingway 1899

Mood Watch: The Aries Moon puts us in touch with the need to act swiftly on our responsibilities, particularly while Moon opposite Saturn brings a strong sense of urgency for us to get a handle on our sense of control. Aries Moon brings out self-awareness and self-assertiveness, and focuses our attention on pushing forward with force and vigor, with strength and intent. Aries Moon often inspires us to focus on something new or delve into our work with a new spirit of determination. It calls to us to get motivated, however small the cause.

LEO

Key Phrase: "I WILL"

Fixed Fire Sign

Ruling Planet: Sun

Symbol: The Majestic Lion

July 22nd PDT / 23rd EDT

through August 23rd

July 22nd Friday
LAST QUARTER MOON in TAURUS

Moon in Aries / Taurus	PDT	EDT	
Moon sextile Mars	5:45 AM	8:45 AM	
Moon square Venus	6:57 AM	9:57 AM	
Moon trine Mercury goes v/c	2:34 PM	5:34 PM	
Sun enters Leo	9:11 PM	12:11 AM	(Jul 23)
Moon enters Taurus	9:57 PM	12:57 AM	(Jul 23)
Moon square Sun	10:01 PM	1:01 AM	(Jul 23)
Moon sextile Neptune	10:35 PM	1:35 AM	(Jul 23)

Birthday: Danny Glover 1946

Mood Watch: The **Last Quarter Moon in Taurus** (Moon square Sun) focuses the general course of our moods on creating some sense of order in our financial situations, and encourages the need for creature comforts and esthetically pleasing or luxurious surroundings. There is often a focus on cleaning up and/or selling various useful artifacts that have collected in our lives. The Last Quarter Taurus Moon frequently inspires the activities of yard sales, auctions and flea markets. This is a good time to transform one's atmosphere into a more useful and practical working order. Letting go of attachment to material things that have bogged one down with too much maintenance or disruptive costs may very well be the best move. Certain kinds of sacrifice produce some very remedial freedom.

Sun enters Leo (Sun in Leo: July 22/23 – Aug. 23) Leo, the sign ruled by the Sun, fills the season with strong, instinctive fervor and deep, fiery desire. Leo focuses on will, identity, truth, selfhood, integrity, pride, and strength. Yours is a lustful time of year, Leo, and your totem, the lion, is one of the most self-assured of the zodiac's symbols. Sun in Leo focuses our attention on Sun related frolic and play, outdoor activities for children and families, and the entire entertainment industry.

This is the time for self-development and fulfillment. Leo says, "I Will," and it is important for a Leo to be expressive in the act of will. The Leo part within us must remember with a true affirmation of will we can have *anything* we want – we just can't have *everything*. Choose what is true to the self!

July 23rd Saturday

Moon in Taurus	PDT	EDT
Moon trine Pluto	9:11 AM	12:11 PM
Moon conjunct Jupiter	2:19 PM	5:19 PM

Birthday: Daniel Radcliffe 1989

Mood Watch: The waning Taurus Moon puts us in touch with our physical needs. This morning's Moon trine Pluto gives us the insight on how to combat pain and disruption, and especially, how to accelerate healing and recuperation. Moon in Taurus is also an excellent time to search for good deals, practical goods, and a pleasing and comfortable environment. This afternoon's Moon conjunct Jupiter brings an excellent time to seek joy, prosperity, and adventure.

July 24th Sunday

Moon in Taurus – No exact aspects	PDT	EDT

Birthday: Emelia Earhart 1897
Mercury opposite Neptune begins (see August 8)

Mood Watch: The waning Taurus Moon brings continued efforts to perfect our surroundings and to enjoy luxurious pleasures. Not only do many have to assess their material possessions, sometimes the physical body and the vitality of one's health are in question; it is vitally important to make healthy choices and apply the labor or rest necessary to keep the body, the beloved temple of our life, in good working order.

July 25th Monday

Moon in Taurus / Gemini	PDT	EDT
Moon sextile Venus	1:44 AM	4:44 AM
Moon square Mercury goes v/c	6:11 AM	9:11 AM
Moon enters Gemini	9:34 AM	12:34 PM
Moon square Neptune	10:04 AM	1:04 PM
Moon sextile Sun	2:37 PM	5:37 PM
Moon sextile Uranus	6:12 PM	9:12 PM
Sun conjunct Venus begins (see August 16)		
Sun square Jupiter begins (see August 1)		
Mars trine Neptune begins (see August 3)		

Birthday: Maxfield Parrish 1870

Mood Watch: The waning Taurus Moon goes void-of-course for a few hours this morning and this may be a time of stubbornness, forgetfulness, and delays. We may also be somewhat argumentative or doubtful as Moon square Mercury occurs. As the Moon enters Gemini, people will be a great deal more observant, detail oriented, and interactive. However, Moon square Neptune is known to bring a time of uncertainty and there may be a focus placed on people's conflicting beliefs. By afternoon, Moon sextile Sun tempers our moods with an emphasis on some of the more positive things occurring that pertain to the summer season. Later, Moon sextile Uranus opens up our minds to the things that give us a sense of freedom and intelligence.

July 26th Tuesday

Moon in Gemini	**PDT**	**EDT**
Moon trine Saturn	8:35 AM	11:35 AM

Birthday: George Bernard Shaw 1856

Mood Watch: It's a positively upbeat Sun in Leo, Moon in Gemini day. This is a good time to seek fun. Moon trine Saturn starts off the day with a good sense of timing and firm perception of things. This waning Gemini Moon is here to assist us in getting our thoughts and communications more evenly aligned. Gemini is a Mercury ruled sign and now that Mercury is about to go retrograde next week (August 2 – 26), this is the time to organize, finish important projects, and to prepare future plans carefully while the flow of our communications can be experienced with greater ease. All of this is particularly so while the Moon is in Gemini, reminding us how to mediate, interpret, deliberate, and negotiate in all those areas of life where discernment and forethought are needed most.

July 27th Wednesday

Moon in Gemini / Cancer	**PDT**	**EDT**
Moon conjunct Mars	9:55 AM	12:55 PM
Sun trine Uranus	12:43 PM	3:43 PM
Moon sextile Mercury goes v/c	5:35 PM	8:35 PM
Moon enters Cancer	6:11 PM	9:11 PM
Moon trine Neptune	6:33 PM	9:33 PM
Venus trine Uranus begins (see July 31)		
Mercury sextile Mars begins (see August 4)		

Birthday: E.A. Wallis Budge 1857

Mood Watch: The Gemini Moon picks up our moods with a lot more chatter and talk. Gemini Moon brings curious moods and a more lively level of interest in the world of unending trivia. Early in the day, Moon conjunct Mars brings a great deal of activity, motion, and heat. This evening, Moon sextile Mercury stirs our thoughts as the Gemini Moon goes void-of-course for a little while. Idle chatter and idle traffic swiftly change to a focus on the hunger for domestic comforts. The waning Moon in Cancer is a good time to seek tranquility, especially while Moon trine Neptune invites us to relax.

Sun trine Uranus (occurring July 21 – 30) This occurrence of Sun trine Uranus favorably affects our Cancer and Leo friends celebrating birthdays July 21 – 30. It puts the radical forces of Uranus in the favorable trine position to the natal Sun of these Cancer and Leo folks. This is the time for these birthday people to make the breakthrough. Don't hold back, birthday folks; chaos is here to stay for awhile, and the apparent madness occurring in your lives is there for a reason. Let the experience be positive as long as this aspect brings gifts. Expect restless desires for freedom and a heartfelt need to break out of your personal prison. These challenges are a necessary part of these folks' growth patterns, and the resultant changes are positive in nature, though on the surface they may seem harsh and overbearing. Freedom knocks loudly and the course of change for these people is inevitable in the next year. The trine aspect bestows gifts of triumph, and this could be a good time to let chaos be the force that brings freedom. This aspect will reoccur November 23, affecting the Scorpio and Sagittarius birthday people of that time.

July 28th Thursday

Moon in Cancer	PDT	EDT
Moon square Uranus	2:14 AM	5:14 AM
Venus enters Leo	7:58 AM	10:58 AM
Moon sextile Jupiter	9:50 AM	12:50 PM
Mercury enters Virgo	10:58 AM	1:58 PM
Moon square Saturn	4:03 PM	7:03 PM

Birthday: Beatrix Potter 1866

Mood Watch: The waning Cancer Moon has its ups and downs today. Although we are likely to be somewhat temperamental at times, this is quite understandable, as our moods are the defense mechanism that keeps us guarded from the periodically indulgent moods of others. Sometimes we are moved to share our emotional quandaries, and sometimes we endure our own emotional shifts silently. Cancer Moon shows us how to go with the flow.

Venus enters Leo (Venus in Leo: July 28 – Aug. 21) Venus in Leo brings out the more playful side of love. It also brings out the desire for more sophisticated and elaborate types of art and aesthetics. Venus represents the expression of love and affection; it is the influence of magnetism, beauty, and of feminine refinement. In the sign of Leo, Venus brings out desires and needs for personal attention. Magnetism is one of Leo's most endearing traits, and it is this magnetism that brings what Leos want most: loving attention. The entertainment industry will be highlighted as music, poetry, art, singing and acting are all enhanced with heartfelt expression. Leos will be more aware of their need for love. The love of looking good, having the best, and being the best is alluring to the ego. Wild lust will abound and the love of fantasies will be enhanced. Leo demands a lot of affection and, when Venus comes into play, the need for attention sometimes outweighs the need to reciprocate that attention. It is always wise not to have expectations in love matters and to be sure that the joys of exchanging love are balanced.

Mercury enters Virgo (Mercury in Virgo: July 28 – Aug. 8) Virgo is a most advantageous place for Mercury – the place where it both rules and is exalted. Mercury in Virgo brings clarity to our plan for the coming events of autumn. It also puts the focus of talk on such issues as computers, budgets, systems analysis, harvesting, accounting, filing, and organizing. Mercury in Virgo brings out the skeptical and analytical side of every argument and topic of discussion, keeping us on our toes. Overall, this is a great time for communications, research, and strategic planning. Mercury is about to go retrograde (Aug. 2 – 26); while it is retrograde, it will reenter Leo on August 8, and once Mercury is direct (Aug. 26), it will reenter Virgo on September 8. For more information on Mercury retrograde through the sign of Virgo, see the introduction on *Mercury retrograde periods*.

July 29ᵗʰ Friday

Moon in Cancer / Leo	PDT	EDT	
Moon opposite Neptune goes v/c	4:46 PM	7:46 PM	
Moon enters Leo	11:15 PM	2:15 AM	(Jul 30)

Birthday: Stanley Kunitz 1905

Mood Watch: The waning Cancer Moon commonly brings introspective exploration over emotional matters. Cancer Moon puts us in touch with the need to care for and nurture ourselves – but, of course, it's always darkest before the dawn, and this may seem like a time when it becomes necessary to weed out bad habits and poor judgment that trigger negative emotional responses. A New Moon eve with the Moon in Cancer is prominently one of those times when we are reminded of the need overcome temptation and do the right thing. Later today, the darkly waning Cancer Moon goes void-of-course. This is the time to take it easy, but beware of people's tendencies to overeat, wallow in self-pity, or engage in worrisome behavior.

July 30ᵗʰ Saturday

NEW MOON in LEO	PDT	EDT
Moon conjunct Venus	3:03 AM	6:03 AM
Moon trine Uranus	6:47 AM	9:47 AM
Moon conjunct Sun	11:39 AM	2:39 PM
Moon square Jupiter	2:22 PM	5:22 PM
Moon sextile Saturn	8:09 PM	11:09 PM
Venus square Jupiter begins (see August 4)		

Birthday: Henry Ford 1863

Mood Watch: The **New Moon in Leo** (Moon conjunct Sun) is a time of personal discovery. Leo is the optimist, and the New Leo Moon brings positive new perspectives to personal goals, as well as inspiring a fresh outlook on one's image. Some may be strongly touched by the need to get a new lease on life. The desire for the latest fashion and a focus on hair is commonplace for this sort of mood setting. A new pattern of positive self-image and dignity can be created while the old beastly pattern will have to be tempered and corrected. Image comes from within and is generated by the sheer magnitude of one's will. Everyone has room to grow if they take the time to apply self-worth, self-respect, and discipline. Leo also represents family and friends, and this may be just the time to initiate a new lease on an old friendship, or to enjoy a favorite hobby with the family.

July 31st Sunday

Moon in Leo	PDT	EDT	
Venus trine Uranus	9:08 PM	12:08 AM	(Aug 1)
Moon sextile Mars goes v/c	11:19 PM	2:19 AM	(Aug 1)
Sun sextile Saturn begins (see August 5)			
Mars square Uranus begins (see August 9)			

Birthday: J.K. Rowling 1965

Mood Watch: It's a Leo Moon day, bringing forth both the expression of playfulness and the need to keep life interesting and entertaining, particularly after all the emotional purging our moods have undergone recently. A newly waxing Moon in Leo invites us to enjoy family gatherings, personal hobbies and projects, and to engage in fun and exciting summer activities with friends.

Venus trine Uranus (occurring July 27 – Aug. 3) Venus in Leo is trine Uranus in Aries. Playful and romantic kinds of love and attraction (Venus in Leo) will bring positive breakthroughs (the trine aspect) through radical self-expression (Uranus in Aries). This is a time of freedom fighters and rebel love, and youth is easily attracted to the spirit of rebellion. Dangerous love and taking chances become common occurrences. This aspect creates an attraction to the unusual, yet it allows a harmony to exist in love related matters while chaotic occurrences are taking place. Love at first sight is explosive at this time, but not necessarily long lasting. This aspect last occurred on January 4 and it will occur again on November 3.

August 1st Monday

Lammas (Lughnassad) / Civic Holiday, Provincial Day, Canada

Moon in Leo / Virgo	PDT	EDT
Moon enters Virgo	1:41 AM	4:41 AM
Moon conjunct Mercury	3:28 AM	6:28 AM
Sun square Jupiter	7:41 AM	10:41 AM
Moon trine Pluto	10:35 AM	1:35 PM
Moon trine Jupiter goes v/c	4:37 PM	7:37 PM

Birthday: Jerry Garcia 1942

Mood Watch: While the youthfully waxing Moon is in Virgo, cautious and attentive attitudes pervade the atmosphere. Virgo Moon brings a general attitude of cautious resourcefulness, and we often lean towards the more practical method of satisfying our needs. The Virgo Moon prepares us for tomorrow's commencement of Mercury retrograde. This is the time to refrain from strenuous jobs and commitments. Today brings us to the solar holiday of *Lammas*, and we have now reached the halfway mark of summer. The word *Lammas* comes from the term loaf-mass and it traditionally represents the first harvest of corn. The Druids call this festival holiday Lughnasadh, a time dedicated to Lugh, the Celtic

Sun god whose name means "shining one." Just as the first crops are cut, this time represents a sacrifice, for Lugh was killed, but he came back to life. After Summer Solstice (June 21) the Sun's light begins to die, and rebirth occurs at Winter Solstice (December 21). Lammas takes place when the crops are thirsty and the green traces of spring have long gone. The fields become strawlike and golden. The Green Man of spring (May 1/Beltane) has been transformed, and he now appears to us as a straw figure popularly known as The Wicker Man or Jack Straw. Although the Sun's light dies away, the life of the Sun is retained in the living harvest. Let unwanted worries and fears die with the Sun King, and reaffirm the picture of self with the promise of the life contained in the harvest of seeds. Collect seeds of wisdom and contemplate in the heart of summer what part of you must die, and what part must be sustained through the impending autumn and winter until it can be reborn at Solstice. Celebrate life in the bounty of the summer harvest.

Sun square Jupiter (occurring July 25 – Aug. 4) This occurrence of Sun square Jupiter will particularly affect those Leo people celebrating birthdays July 25 – August 4. This includes U.S.A. President Barack Obama, whose birthday is on August 4. This aspect creates difficulties and obstacles to the personal joy and prosperous welfare of these birthday folks. Getting ahead financially or just staying on top of current trends or financial shifts may be personally challenging right now, requiring persistence and determination. Leo folks who are doing well financially may find this aspect is challenging their sense of what makes them happy, or that advancement in the world brings too much complexity and requires a lot of management. They may find it difficult to identify with the things they thought would make them happy or bring satisfaction. Though not all Leos are living as prosperously as they may desire, they do have the ability to come through this and be much better for it. Obstacles create challenges, but do not necessarily dictate an end to efforts to improve our welfare. It is the Leo personality (Sun) that is being challenged (square aspect) in matters of advancement (Jupiter), requiring them to make do with less assistance than they had anticipated. This may be a time to redefine and redirect personal goals. These birthday folks must reexamine what truly brings prosperity for them in their lives. This aspect last occurred on December 16, 2010 affecting some of the birthday Sagittarius folks (Dec. 15 – 19, 2010) of that time.

August 2nd Tuesday

Moon void-of-course in Virgo	PDT	EDT
Mercury goes retrograde	8:50 PM	11:50 PM
Mars opposite Pluto begins (see August 11)		

Birthday: Peter O'Toole 1932

Mood Watch: The void-of-course Moon in Virgo reminds us that we have entered a phase of watchfulness and resourcefulness. Skepticism and doubt are contributing factors to delays and disagreements throughout today. Virgo Moon calls to us to be sensible, smart, and precise about our facts during this challenging time of Mercury retrograde. Purity and cleanliness are the keys to enjoying a newly waxing Virgo Moon. Our moods will tend to be cautious, careful, and, for some, perhaps shy and retiring. This is a good time for us to review our assets, to check on our earth-friendly green footprint, and to work towards preventing a wasteful or expensive course of action. Virgo says: "I analyze," but this is no time to jump to conclusions!

Mercury goes retrograde (Mercury retrograde: Aug. 2 – 26) Hold on to your thinking caps – for the next little while (until August 8), Mercury will be retrograde in one of the primary places it rules, Virgo. On August 8, Mercury will continue to be retrograde through Leo until it completes this retrograde cycle on August 26. Mercury retrograde in Virgo (Aug. 2 – 8) is likely to bring disruption to our attempts to accurately analyze matters, and there are likely to be numerous misunderstandings over all kinds of data. Mercury retrograde in Leo (Aug. 8 – 26) is likely to bring a great deal of communication disruption to issues with regard to family affairs and friendships. Be on the lookout for frequent bouts of dyslexia and other communication mistakes, particularly in such Virgo and Leo related activities as research, analytical sciences, health matters, accounting, family endeavors, screenplays and scripts, and overall communications among colleagues and friends. During this time it will be best to attempt communications more than once or twice, and to be persistent as well as patient. At first it may be difficult to sit through everyone's excuses and misinformation, but eventually there will be a logical explanation to Mercury related setbacks. For more information on Mercury retrograde, see the section in the introduction about *Mercury retrograde periods.*

August 3rd Wednesday

Moon in Virgo / Libra	PDT	EDT	
Mars enters Cancer	2:21 AM	5:21 AM	
Moon enters Libra	3:04 AM	6:04 AM	
Moon square Mars	3:06 AM	6:06 AM	
Mars trine Neptune	3:53 AM	6:53 AM	
Moon opposite Uranus	10:12 AM	1:12 PM	
Moon square Pluto	11:53 AM	2:53 PM	
Moon sextile Venus	3:56 PM	6:56 PM	
Moon sextile Sun	10:04 PM	1:04 AM	(Aug 4)
Moon conjunct Saturn	11:53 PM	2:53 AM	(Aug 4)

Birthday: Tony Bennett 1926

Mood Watch: Waxing Libra Moon focuses our moods on the need to create harmony and beauty in our lives, and to get on with the necessity to create some order with our sense of progress. Friends and partners often become the highlights of our focuses during the waxing Libra Moon. This may be a good time to initiate a new friendship or rediscover a sense of newness with an old friend.

Mars trine Neptune (occurring July 25 – Aug. 7) Mars in Cancer trine Neptune in Pisces at the zero degree mark brings exhilarating emotional indulgences, spiritually enhanced acceptance, and uplifting as well as moving types of energy.

182

This aspect creates an active trend to empower our beliefs. This will be an active time of obtaining spiritual gifts and helpful guidelines from the spirit world. Mars guarantees activities will occur, and with Neptune in the trine position, these activities will be favorably stirred up with spiritual and psychic awareness. This serves as a good time to initiate creative and imaginative spiritual practices and ceremonies, and to empower the personal outlook and spiritual wellbeing.

August 4th Thursday

Moon in Libra	PDT	EDT	
Mercury sextile Mars	4:19 PM	7:19 PM	
NEPTUNE ENTERS AQUARIUS	7:53 PM	10:53 PM	
Venus square Jupiter	9:34 PM	12:34 AM	(Aug 5)
Venus sextile Saturn begins (see August 7)			

Birthdays: Louis Armstrong 1901/ Barack Obama 1961

Mood Watch: The Libra Moon places the emphasis of our moods on the joyous company of good friends, loving companions, and supporters. Libra Moon also focuses our sights on carrying out important objectives, and on harmonizing teamwork. It additionally emphasizes the importance of law and justice.

Mercury sextile Mars (occurring July 6 – Sept. 30) This aspect will occur for longer than usual due to the retrograde cycle of Mercury (Aug. 2 – 26). Mercury in Leo sextile Mars in Gemini brings charismatic messages and carefully premeditated actions. Enthusiastic responses to discussions are sure to keep our communications buzzing along swiftly. This aspect ensures that communications will move quickly. Mercury sextile Mars presents opportunities which can be received, recognized, communicated and acted upon. News or information may lead to immediate action. It's an advantageous time to apply one's word with a full backing of action for a very favorable outcome. This aspect last occurred on July 11, and it will reach one more peak – for the third time during this occurrence period – on September 29.

Neptune enters Aquarius (Neptune in Aquarius: Aug. 4, 2011 – Feb. 3, 2012) On April 4, Neptune entered Pisces and on June 3, Neptune went retrograde and it will remain retrograde until November 9, which is why it is re-entering the tail end of Aquarius today. Neptune was initially in Aquarius from January 28, 1998 to April 4, 2011. Neptune is currently entering into the last phase of its travels in Aquarius.

Neptune puts us in touch with inner peace and spiritual release. Spirituality (Neptune) once again focuses awareness through human issues and concerns (Aquarius). Liberation comes when we learn to place our belief in ourselves. Neptune was last in Aquarius between 1834 – 1847. There was much in the way of revolutions at that time; the revolution was really occurring in the diversity of our belief systems. Now with Neptune in Aquarius once again, scientific and religious views are taking a strong stand as Neptune wends its way through its final journey in Aquarius. It is through Neptune that we learn to surrender completely and take control of our senses by letting go completely. This is when our dreams take us beyond the things we cannot control. This realm of expression is the higher and more spiritually tuned parts of the self, the "inner self" that is connected to the Holy Spirit or The Holy Guardian Angel. Some of our greatest challenges concerning our beliefs will now take place with science and technology issues. Neptune's influence provides vision and understanding of the spiritual growth of all things. Neptune in Aquarius focuses on the essential need for belief to be placed in humankind; that is, we must believe in ourselves and our own capabilities in order to survive spiritually. For more information on this subject, see the section on "Neptune in Aquarius" in the *April 4th essay on Neptune enters Pisces*.

Venus square Jupiter (occurring July 30 – Aug. 7) This aspect brings love and attraction (Venus) into difficulty or hard work (the square aspect) over the need for prosperity, growth and jubilation (Jupiter). Venus in Leo square Jupiter in Taurus brings a love for friends, family and entertainment at a pressing time when the need to handle escalating economic obligations or banking debts may be difficult. Some folks may be experiencing challenges with their sense of appreciation, enjoyment, or fulfillment. Our experiences of beauty and affection may be tested by the difficulty of attracting or acquiring prosperity and joy. Some might say that the act of appreciating beauty is a form of prosperity in itself, but at times like this, a great deal more effort and support is required. This aspect may create an obstacle to acknowledging the expenses incurred by our attractions and love-needs. It reminds us that something more than love's blindness is required in order for us to fully realize our riches and the value of what we care about most. This aspect last occurred on February 6 and it will reoccur on December 20.

August 5th Friday

Moon in Libra / Scorpio	PDT	EDT	
Sun sextile Saturn	3:47 AM	6:47 AM	
Moon trine Neptune goes v/c	4:55 AM	7:55 AM	
Moon enters Scorpio	4:56 AM	7:56 AM	
Moon sextile Mercury	6:32 AM	9:32 AM	
Moon trine Mars	7:26 AM	10:26 AM	
Moon sextile Pluto	1:54 PM	4:54 PM	
Moon opposite Jupiter	8:51 PM	11:51 PM	
Moon square Venus	10:57 PM	1:57 AM	(Aug 6)

Birthday: Neil Armstrong 1930

Mood Watch: Ever so swiftly this morning, the Libra Moon goes void-of-course then enters Scorpio. The energy intensifies and our moods will be more prone to seek excitement, thrills, and stimulation – waxing Scorpio Moon is never dull and it invites us to get a handle on the great shifts in energy.

Sun sextile Saturn (occurring July 31 – Aug. 5) This occurrence of Sun sextile Saturn particularly affects Leo people who are celebrating birthdays between July 31 – August 5, helping them focus their energy and disciplines with greater clarity throughout the year. As Saturn enters the sextile aspect to the natal Sun of these Leo people, they will have a greater sense of making progress through

184

discipline, and they may very well begin to see the rewards of their diligent labor in the coming year. This is only true, however, as long as they apply themselves to their work and maintain a vigilant and persistent effort to master personal discipline and training. Greater control comes with genuine effort. This aspect will reoccur on December 19, affecting the lives of some Sagittarians and solstice born Capricorns.

August 6th Saturday

FIRST QRTR MOON in SCORPIO

	PDT	EDT
Moon square Sun	4:08 AM	7:08 AM

Birthday: Andy Warhol 1928

Mood Watch: The **First Quarter Moon in Scorpio** (Moon square Sun) arouses our moods in deep and impassioned ways. Get in touch with your creative and perceptive side. It is often true that emotional damage can be greater than physical damage. What heals on the outside cannot be hidden as what does – or doesn't – heal on the inside. This is a time to address internal wounds with reassurance and care to mend emotional scars with love and encouragement.

August 7th Sunday

Moon in Scorpio / Sagittarius

	PDT	EDT
Moon square Neptune goes v/c	8:13 AM	11:13 AM
Moon enters Sagittarius	8:20 AM	11:20 AM
Moon square Mercury	8:53 AM	11:53 AM
Moon trine Uranus	3:45 PM	6:45 PM
Venus sextile Saturn	7:18 PM	10:18 PM

Birthday: Alan Leo 1860

Mood Watch: For a short time this morning, our moods may seem disoriented as the Scorpio Moon goes void-of-course and then swiftly enters Sagittarius. Moon square Mercury brings a time to be especially cautious about miscommunications or misinformation, a common trend during Mercury retrograde. Sun in Leo and Moon in Sagittarius bring an outgoing, aspiring, and promising outlook. Moods are backed by an energetic and enthusiastic spirit. Lively, resilient, and athletic types of energy abound. Inspired perspectives help to uplift the overall mood, and this is a great time to spread hope, good cheer, and positive sensations. Put some life force into each step. Harness the good vibrations.

Venus sextile Saturn (occurring Aug. 4 – 9) Venus in Leo sextile Saturn in Libra brings compelling and affectionate expressions of love which are well balanced, and amicably controlled. Venus emphasizes the vibrations of love, magnetism, and beauty, and while in Leo, it brings the need for pleasure and entertainment between lovers and friends. Saturn's influence focuses on the awareness of time, responsibility, and dedication; while this planet is in Libra, it inspires the need for harmony and peace. Saturn reminds us that beauty is temporary but with proper maintenance, it can also be preserved. Venus sextile Saturn last occurred on January 23 and will reoccur on November 22.

August 8th Monday

Moon in Sagittarius	PDT	EDT
Mercury enters Leo	2:46 AM	5:46 AM
Moon sextile Saturn	7:06 AM	10:06 AM
Moon trine Venus	8:12 AM	11:12 AM
Moon trine Sun	12:21 PM	3:21 PM
Mercury opposite Neptune	4:38 PM	7:38 PM

Birthday: Dustin Hoffman 1937

Mood Watch: The Sagittarius Moon brings very active and creative events and scenarios for us to choose from and enjoy. The Sun and Moon are in fire signs, encouraging outgoing, creative, and entertaining activities. Today's lunar aspects are positive in nature. Summer vacation trips may be successfully carried out at this time, but it is wise to double check travel schedules and appointments while Mercury is retrograde (Aug. 2 – 26). Sagittarius Moon is a time of discovery and exploration.

Mercury enters Leo (Mercury in Leo: Aug. 8 – Sept. 8) Retrograde Mercury (Aug. 2 – 26), re-enters the tail end of Leo today, where it will complete its cycle in Leo for the year. This is the second time Mercury has entered Leo this year; for more information on Mercury in Leo, *see July 1*, when it first entered Leo back while it was direct. For more information on Mercury's current retrograde status in Leo, see the introduction in this book on *Mercury retrograde periods*.

Mercury opposite Neptune (July 24 – Sept. 10) Due to the retrograde motion of both these planets, this opposition is occurring for a longer than average period. There is a rather confusing and erratic dance that occurs here, as these two planets have been frequently and briefly going into and out of opposition over the course of the above noted occurrence period. Mercury opposite Neptune makes us acutely aware of discussions concerning religious beliefs. Mercury in Leo brings gregarious communications, while Neptune in Aquarius focuses spiritual matters upon the whole of humanity. Beliefs go beyond the physical to the metaphysical realms, where information is accessed and spiritual fortification occurs. It is wisest to be clear on one's own beliefs, and not to put oneself in a position of having to expose or defend those beliefs before a pack of merciless critics. Spiritual growth and enlightenment are not easy things to relay in conversation, and during this aspect it may seem particularly overwhelming for some folks to try to communicate effectively – or to comprehend what others are trying to communicate about spiritual matters. This is especially true while Mercury is retrograde (Aug. 2 – 26). Another exact peak for this aspect will occur on September 8.

August 9th Tuesday

Moon in Sagittarius / Capricorn	PDT	EDT
Mars square Uranus	9:33 AM	12:33 PM
Moon trine Mercury	12:20 PM	3:20 PM
Moon sextile Neptune goes v/c	1:24 PM	4:24 PM

	PDT	EDT	
Moon enters Capricorn	1:37 PM	4:37 PM	
Moon square Uranus	9:12 PM	12:12 AM	(Aug 10)
Moon opposite Mars	9:51 PM	12:51 AM	(Aug 10)
Moon conjunct Pluto	11:06 PM	2:06 AM	(Aug 10)

Birthday: Sam Elliott 1944

Mood Watch: The waxing Sagittarius Moon brings an upbeat message, while Moon trine Mercury opens up an advantageous time to sort out details and correct miscommunications more swiftly. This afternoon Moon sextile Neptune brings relaxed, open, and explorative moods. The Moon goes void-of-course, and in what may seem like the blink of an eye, spacey and disoriented moods turn to decisive clarity as the Moon enters Capricorn. Serious intent fills our moods. Tonight's Moon square Uranus and Moon opposite Mars bring complex disruption and strongly defensive – or offensive – types of moods.

Mars square Uranus (occurring July 31 – Aug. 13) Mars square Uranus is sometimes tyrannical, and is never an aspect to be underestimated. Masculine fortitude and the enigmatic force of chaos are in an especially volatile and difficult phase of expression when Mars is square to Uranus. This aspect was suspiciously present when the December 26, 2004 tsunami tidal wave disaster of the century swept the Indian Ocean. Today, Mars is in Cancer and, while it squares to Uranus, the resulting tensions may create excessively emotional responses and could also cause extensive damage in the forces of offensive and defensive action. While Uranus is in Aries, chaos abounds in the area of new enterprise and self-made empires. The events of Mars square Uranus do not always predictably yield natural disasters, but unfortunately they are often the catalyst for difficult human trials and tension. This aspect is like a pressure cooker; it may seem dormant at first, but if not carefully handled, the aftermath can be a real mess! It is wise to completely avoid extremely risky undertakings that may rock the boat of fiery activity during Mars square Uranus. This is no time to step into the eye of the storm! Fortunately, this is the only time this aspect will occur this year.

August 10ᵗʰ Wednesday

Moon in Capricorn	**PDT**	**EDT**
Moon trine Jupiter	7:16 AM	10:16 AM
Moon square Saturn goes v/c	1:33 PM	4:33 PM

Birthday: Antonio Banderas 1960

Mood Watch: For starters, Moon trine Jupiter brings positive, optimistic, and generous moods. However, it is best to take action with the things that need to be done as early as possible today, preferably before the Moon goes void-of-course in Capricorn. A waxing Moon in Capricorn is a good time to reaffirm goals and objectives. This is often done by setting a deadline, then making some serious effort to complete the goal on time. Once the Moon goes void-of-course, Moon square Saturn places obstacles in our time frame, and hinders our sense of control. This evening, it may take an extra long time to work through remaining tasks. Prepare to pace yourself; tomorrow's long void-of-course Capricorn Moon could be grueling at times.

August 11th Thursday

Moon in Capricorn / Aquarius

	PDT	EDT
Mars opposite Pluto	2:32 AM	5:32 AM
Moon enters Aquarius	8:47 PM	11:47 PM
Mars sextile Jupiter begins (see August 18)		

Birthday: Alex Haley 1921

Mood Watch: People may seem somewhat indifferent towards – or unwilling to get too excited about – numerous things today. It's a long void-of-course Capricorn Moon day, and while there's a great deal of attention paid to the essential need for labor and assistance, many people are hesitant to provide either. Drop your expectations, relax, and try again tomorrow. Constant work and no play will make this a very dull day. Later, Moon in Aquarius brings charitable and sympathetic moods.

Mars opposite Pluto (occurring Aug. 2 – 15) Mars in Cancer opposes Pluto in Capricorn, stirring up emotional activities in the home over career related transformations. Oppositions have a strong impact. Combine that fact with two strong planetary influences, Mars and Pluto – the outcome often involves swift, martial transformation. This aspect may create conflict between generations, and between those with diametrically opposed cultures. Now that Pluto is in Capricorn, a serious transformation directly affects leaders and those who have an effect on the economy. This is a time to be vigilant and guarded. Expect swift, permanent changes during this time of Mars opposite Pluto. This aspect last occurred during the last two weeks of August 2009 (Aug. 26, 2009), a time of major economic disruption and havoc.

August 12th Friday

Moon in Aquarius

	PDT	EDT	
Moon sextile Uranus	4:32 AM	7:32 AM	
Moon square Jupiter	3:19 PM	6:19 PM	
Moon trine Saturn	9:57 PM	12:57 AM	(Aug 13)

Birthday: Madame H. P. Blavatsky 1831

Mood Watch: Moon in Aquarius is waxing towards fullness, and the energy at this time is busy and strong. Aquarius Moon puts the focus on the need to apply knowledge. A hunger for knowledge and investigation brings a surge of social gatherings. The Full Aquarius Moon eve has been known to bring unusual kinds of thoughts, scientific anomalies, and extraordinary discoveries. Some folks may seem overly idealistic, while others may be especially brilliant – perhaps even hard to follow. Aquarius Moon brings out the absurd in some folks. On the other hand, this may be a time of amazing breakthroughs, rebel rousing fun, or deep thought. This kind of energy is worth tapping into, especially if it can in some way help humanity. Go with the flow – it's the Full Moon Eve!

August 13th Saturday

♌

FULL MOON in AQUARIUS	PDT	EDT	
Moon opposite Venus	10:22 AM	1:22 PM	
Moon opposite Sun	11:57 AM	2:57 PM	
Moon opposite Mercury	10:29 PM	1:29 AM	(Aug 14)
Sun conjunct Mercury begins (see August 16)			
Mercury conjunct Venus begins (see August 16)			

Birthday: Alfred Hitchcock 1899

Mood Watch: The **Full Moon in Aquarius** (Moon opposite Sun) enlivens our senses with the need to apply clarity and definition. The mood of the day is likely to be blanketed in bizarre and unusual occurrences, and it's often focused on modern technological breakthroughs and inventions. People may seem idealistic and generous in some respects of this lunar expression, or out-of-hand and downright unrealistic in others. This is a good time to investigate, play around with ideas, seek answers, invent, reinvent, and celebrate knowledge. Humanitarian issues and breakthroughs are often the focal points of the Full Aquarius Moon.

August 14th Sunday

Moon in Aquarius / Pisces	PDT	EDT	
Moon conjunct Neptune goes v/c	5:25 AM	8:25 AM	
Moon enters Pisces	5:54 AM	8:54 AM	
Moon sextile Pluto	3:54 PM	6:54 PM	
Moon trine Mars	9:06 PM	12:06 AM	(Aug 15)
Mars square Saturn begins (see August 25)			

Birthday: Steve Martin 1945

Mood Watch: What just happened? An indescribable phenomenon known as the Full Aquarius Moon – that's what! This morning, the impact of last night's full moon can still be felt, and mutably so. As the Moon conjuncts with Neptune, the ruler of Pisces and the place of the mutable waters, there is a very spacey and tranquil lull for a short time, and then the Moon enters Pisces. Hypersensitivity runs strongly as our moods move through a wide spectrum of emotional responses to this weekend's full moon activity. Later, Moon sextile Pluto is an opportunistic time to get in tune with ways to improve – or remedy – harsh transitions or fateful conditions. Much later, Moon trine Mars is an ideal time to envision strength and to empower courage. Tomorrow will bring especially spacey moods as the long void-of-course Moon day will have a timeless quality.

August 15th Monday

Moon in Pisces	PDT	EDT
Moon sextile Jupiter goes v/c	1:21 AM	4:21 AM

Birthday: Oscar Peterson 1925

Mood Watch: The long void-of-course Pisces Moon day indicates that we will still need to do some emotional processing to overcome the taxing qualities of the recent Full Aquarius Moon weekend. People will tend to go into, and out of, a series of time-warps throughout the day and night. This is the time to take it easy and be patient with others while delays, distractions, and escapist tendencies are the likely reasons for a nonproductive start to a new workweek. Be watchful for the potential of people's susceptibility to temptation or substance abuse. This is a positively wonderful time to indulge in leisurely and calming pleasures, meditation, art, crafts, music, and any creative process that helps to ease tension and overcome depression.

August 16th Tuesday

Moon in Pisces / Aries

	PDT	EDT
Sun conjunct Venus	5:07 AM	8:07 AM
Mercury conjunct Venus	4:20 PM	7:20 PM
Moon enters Aries	5:01 PM	8:01 PM
Sun conjunct Mercury	6:03 PM	9:03 PM
Venus opposite Neptune begins (see August 21)		
Sun opposite Neptune begins (see August 22)		

Birthday: Madonna 1958

Mood Watch: Much of today brings the continuance of yesterday's long void-of-course Pisces Moon. It is difficult enough working through communications while Mercury is retrograde (Aug. 2 – 26), and a waning void-of-course Pisces Moon can be disastrously disruptive and unaccommodating at times. This Moon reminds us that our beliefs can be very challenging. Despite our greatest efforts, there are a lot of delusional pitfalls that can deeply affect us or bring us down if we let them. When faith is tested, a positive attitude will do wonders. Tonight's Aries Moon brings bolder and braver moods to strengthen our outlook on life.

Sun conjunct Venus (occurring July 25 – Aug. 27) The Sun and Venus are conjunct in Leo. This conjunction particularly affects the love lives of those Leo and Virgo people celebrating birthdays from July 25 – August 27. These birthday folks are being filled with the need to have or to express love as best as they can, and this is the year for them to address the love matters in their lives. There is an attraction which draws us to beauty, romance, and love when Venus connects with the natal solar degrees. The issue of love is unavoidable, and these birthday folks' love needs become evident whether they wish to acknowledge them or not. It is through the attraction magnet of Venus that the personality (Sun sign) is assured of that with which they choose to identify, be affected by, and attracted to. Sometimes sheer magnetism is unavoidable and an event or relationship cannot be chosen – it just happens. This can encompass not only love matters, but also other areas such as the arts, aesthetics or appreciation of beauty. This will be a year of love, birthday Leo and Virgo people.

Mercury conjunct Venus (occurring Aug. 13 – 18) When these two planets are conjunct, the energy suggests the need to communicate love. Today's conjunction of Mercury and Venus takes place in the courageous realm of Leo. This is often a time when intimate and loving thoughts are shared with assertive playfulness. Mercury is currently retrograde (Aug. 2 – 26) which makes this an important

190

time to be careful what we say, and to carefully consider the feelings of others when speaking. For some folks, there may be a tendency for love-related communication to seem somewhat reserved or overly internalized, although the need to communicate love is definitely there. It would be best to communicate love without getting too hung up on emotional issues, and there will be a lot of talk about our commitment to love. Hold no expectations in the expression of love, and take no offense if your own attempts to express your love are poorly interpreted. Mercury conjunct Venus last occurred on May 9 and May 16. This conjunction will come close to reoccurring (non-exact) on November 1, with Mercury and Venus in Scorpio.

Sun conjunct Mercury (occurring Aug. 13 – 18) This conjunction will create a much more thoughtful, communicative and expressive year ahead for those Leo folks celebrating birthdays August 13 – 18. This is your time (birthday Leo) to record ideas, relay important messages, and pay close attention to your imaginative thoughts as they are touched by Mercury, creating the urge to speak and be heard. Birthday Leo, your thoughts will reveal a great deal about who you are, now and in the year to come.

August 17th Wednesday

Moon in Aries	PDT	EDT	
Moon conjunct Uranus	1:03 AM	4:03 AM	
Moon square Pluto	3:16 AM	6:16 AM	
Moon square Mars	12:11 PM	3:11 PM	
Moon opposite Saturn	8:48 PM	11:48 PM	

Birthday: Robert DeNiro 1943

Mood Watch: The summer heat is on with Moon in Aries and Sun in Leo. This is a great time to be creative and enjoy outdoor activities, but be especially careful to avoid accidents, or overly hot attitudes, during Moon square Mars. It's also an especially important time to keep watch over the potential for starting forest fires during this hot and dry season of the year in many parts of North America. Aries Moon reminds us to build on self confidence and to seek opportunities.

August 18th Thursday

Moon in Aries	PDT	EDT	
Mars sextile Jupiter	9:49 AM	12:49 PM	
Moon trine Mercury	2:02 PM	5:02 PM	
Moon trine Sun	9:12 PM	12:12 AM	(Aug 19)
Moon trine Venus	10:52 PM	1:52 AM	(Aug 19)

Birthday: Patrick Swayze 1952

Mood Watch: Sun in Leo and Moon in Aries emphasize the power of selfhood. This is indeed a time when selfhood is touched upon, and our general moods are based on our own personal needs, as well as the needs of those who are pushy or powerful enough to come first! Positive lunar aspects make this a great day to get things done, clear up problems and misunderstandings, and to maximize strength and confidence. Avoid butting heads if that's not what you're looking for, since it's very easy to do on a waning Aries Moon. That said, a bit of head butting in jest can be a superb outlet between friends.

Mars sextile Jupiter (occurring Aug. 11 – 21) This aspect brings the opportunity for action to be endowed with reward. Those who act on certain urges and impulses, and take action towards achieving their heart's desire, are very likely to make a breakthrough with this aspect. Mars in Cancer is sextile to Jupiter in Taurus. Actions taken towards making improvements in the home not only adds value, but will bring rewarding comfort and prosperous joy in the long run. This is a time to activate true effort towards increasing career skills – or enhancing a career move – with an affirmative act of will. Remember *action* is required, mere good intentions will get you nothing while this aspect is in full force. This is a good time to seek opportunities towards making improvements in life. This aspect last occurred on January 13.

August 19ᵗʰ Friday

Moon in Aries / Taurus	PDT	EDT	
Moon sextile Neptune goes v/c	4:49 AM	7:49 AM	
Moon enters Taurus	5:36 AM	8:36 AM	
Moon trine Pluto	3:53 PM	6:53 PM	

Birthday: Bill Clinton 1946

Mood Watch: For a short time this morning, the Moon is void-of-course in Aries. This brings impatient moods, and it may not be conducive to get the early part of the morning started productively. However, the Moon enters Taurus early enough to ensure plenty of recovery time to make the morning fruitful. Waning Taurus Moon is a good time to review finances, get the physical world in order, and to tend to practical needs and personal comforts.

August 20ᵗʰ Saturday

Moon in Taurus	PDT	EDT	
Moon conjunct Jupiter	2:13 AM	5:13 AM	
Moon sextile Mars	4:26 AM	7:26 AM	
Moon square Mercury	11:12 PM	2:12 AM	(Aug 21)
Venus trine Pluto begins (see August 25)			

Birthday: H.P. Lovecraft 1890

Mood Watch: This is the time to appreciate the beauty and the comforts all around us. The waning Moon in Taurus brings to our moods a bullish determination to control those money related woes. This Moon activates our moods to handle material matters succinctly. A truthful, resolute mentality brings resilience to our moods as we steadily take care of business throughout the day and move on swiftly towards evening comforts. Taurus Moon puts us in touch with the need for physical and sensual comforts.

August 21st Sunday
LAST QUARTER MOON in TAURUS

♌

Moon in Taurus / Gemini	PDT	EDT
Venus opposite Neptune	6:38 AM	9:38 AM
Moon square Sun	2:54 PM	5:54 PM
Venus enters Virgo	3:10 PM	6:10 PM
Moon square Neptune goes v/c	4:59 PM	7:59 PM
Moon enters Gemini	5:52 PM	8:52 PM
Moon square Venus	6:11 PM	9:11 PM

Birthday: Aubrey Beardsley 1872

Mood Watch: The **Last Quarter Moon in Taurus** (Moon square Sun) focuses the general course of our moods on creating some sense of order in our financial situations, and encourages the need for creature comforts and esthetically pleasing or luxurious surroundings. There is often a focus on cleaning up and/or selling various useful artifacts that have collected in our lives. The Last Quarter Taurus Moon frequently inspires the activities of yard sales, auctions and flea markets. This is a good time to transform one's atmosphere into a more useful and practical working order. Letting go of attachment to material things that have bogged one down with too much maintenance or disruptive costs may very well be the best move. Certain kinds of sacrifice produce some very remedial freedom. Tonight's Moon in Gemini brings curious and talkative moods.

Venus opposite Neptune (occurring Aug. 16 – Aug. 23) Venus in Leo is opposing retrograde Neptune in Aquarius. What we are attracted to may be opposed to what we (or others) believe in. Selfishness conflicts with philanthropy. Wild and instinctual expressions of love and beauty are at odds with universal beliefs. This aspect brings an awareness of the dichotomy between fashion's feminine archetypes versus a natural or spiritual expression of femininity. The feminine spirit needs to be free and connect with a more divine image of womanhood; however, the goddess that lives within may seem distant or hard to reach. Nonetheless, the feminine parts of the spirit (Venus) are being made acutely aware of the divine parts of the spirit (Neptune) in one way or another. The opposition of Venus to Neptune may seem like an overwhelming time to try to make a spiritual connection with large groups of people, especially through the mediums of art, music, and theater. There may be a desire to create a spiritual refuge or retreat – an attractive, sensual, and aesthetically pleasing sanctuary. This opposition is occurring with Venus at the cusp of Leo/Virgo and Neptune retrograde at the cusp of Aquarius/Pisces. Dynamic, and sometimes trying, attempts are at work in an effort to get in tune with the feminine spirit.

Venus enters Virgo (Venus in Virgo: Aug. 21 – Sept. 14) Venus now enters the sign of Virgo, where love and attraction are highlighted with such Virgo-like traits as shyness, prudence, purity, and virginal beauty. While Venus is in Virgo, the expression of love and beauty will be analyzed and reflected upon, and love related activities are more often reserved or calculated than they are acted upon. Venus in Virgo is referred to as "the fall," a less ideal position for Venus and a time when disappointment in love matters may be felt by some folks. Keep faith in your affections, despite the cooling of passions.

August 22ⁿᵈ Monday

Moon in Gemini	PDT	EDT	
Moon sextile Uranus	1:29 AM	4:29 AM	
Sun opposite Neptune	4:35 PM	7:35 PM	
Moon trine Saturn goes v/c	9:46 PM	12:46 AM	(Aug 23)
Sun trine Pluto begins (see Aug. 28)			

Birthday: John Lee Hooker 1917

Mood Watch: The waning Gemini Moon often brings helpful or interesting information for each of us, individually, to internalize. It can also be a good Moon to work through communication problems, review the details of a given situation, and to talk about what's on our minds, especially while Mercury is retrograde (Aug. 2 – 26). Gemini Moon is a revealing time to look at the two sides of a story.

Sun opposite Neptune (occurring Aug. 16 – 25) This occurrence of Sun opposite Neptune especially affects Leo and cusp born Virgo people celebrating birthdays from August 16 – 25. Neptune in opposition to these folks' natal Sun brings a strong awareness of Spirit, the spiritual path, and the acknowledgment of one's beliefs. The challenge facing these birthday folks is to confront and overcome all disruptive personal doubts that cause them to question the practice of believing. These people will be imminently aware this year of the vast shifts in spiritual beliefs, and they may feel quite overwhelmed by the confusion and fluctuations of their own spiritual awareness. This is no surprise – it is occurring for numerous people at this time – our birthday friends will just experience it more directly.

Seek your favorite sanctuary and tune into Spirit.

VIRGO

Key Phrase: " I ANALYZE "

Mutable Earth Sign

Ruling Planet: Mercury

Symbol: The Virgin

August 23ʳᵈ through

September 23ʳᵈ

August 23ʳᵈ Tuesday

Moon in Gemini	PDT	EDT
Sun enters Virgo	4:20 AM	7:20 AM
Moon sextile Mercury	7:33 AM	10:33 AM

Birthday: Barbara Eden 1934

Mood Watch: The waning Gemini Moon keeps us busily communicating and thinking through various expressions of mood. While the Sun is still in Leo, our Gemini Moon moods are playful and frivolous, but it's more probable that our moods will be sleepy, especially since it will be rather early this morning when the Sun enters Virgo. Moon in Gemini and Sun in Virgo emphasize the need for careful attention to detail, precision, and thoroughness. Gemini and Virgo are Mercury ruled signs that yield a lot of nervous energy. Such energy needs to be channeled and given a proper outlet. This morning's Moon sextile Mercury can be a very beneficial time to reaffirm facts, double check figures, and hammer out the details of a busy and productive day.

Sun enters Virgo (Sun in Virgo: Aug. 23 – Sept. 23) Virgo's key phrase is, "I analyze," and the pragmatic spirit of Virgo examines all avenues of life. It is just like Virgo to pick everything apart, detail by detail, and yet Virgo strives to get as much of an overview of the whole picture as possible. Virgo questions, Virgo doubts, and Virgo demands proof. The Mercury ruled mutable sign of earth is keen, sharp-witted, and not so quick to believe any sort of random information, unless it's painstakingly researched by some reputable sources. Virgo will question the source every time. Virgos are famous for their ability to count, calculate, and measure everything that must be accounted for, which is why Virgo is chosen to watch over the vital and bountiful harvest season.

August 24th Wednesday

Moon in Gemini / Cancer	PDT	EDT	
Moon trine Neptune goes v/c	2:33 AM	5:33 AM	
Moon enters Cancer	3:30 AM	6:30 AM	
Moon sextile Sun	5:22 AM	8:22 AM	
Moon sextile Venus	9:52 AM	12:52 PM	
Moon square Uranus	10:30 AM	1:30 PM	
Moon opposite Neptune	10:02 PM	1:02 AM	(Aug 25)
Moon sextile Jupiter	10:24 PM	1:24 AM	(Aug 25)

Birthday: Steven Frye 1957

Mood Watch: Waning Moon is the time to work through and let go of negative feelings, but we must first experience these feelings before disposing of them. The Moon represents moods, and when the Moon is in her native sign, Cancer, there is a tendency for all ranges of mood to be richly felt. Cancer Moon is a good time to review our lives with an element of maternal care and attention. Sun in Virgo and Moon in Cancer is the time to nurture emotional needs while taking care to see to it that nutritional requirements are being met. It is also good to check that personal concerns are carefully addressed. Reassurance is there for those who are vigilant to do the right thing. What would mother do?

August 25th Thursday

Moon in Cancer	PDT	EDT
Mars square Saturn	3:46 AM	6:46 AM
Moon square Saturn	5:58 AM	8:58 AM
Moon conjunct Mars	6:04 AM	9:04 AM
Moon opposite Pluto goes v/c	12:28 PM	3:28 PM
Venus trine Pluto	4:12 PM	7:12 PM
Venus trine Jupiter begins (see Aug. 29)		

Birthday: Elvis Costello 1954

Mood Watch: The morning may be trying at first while Moon square Saturn challenges us with limitations. Moon conjunct Mars brings active and full tempered expressions of mood, and this is a good time to get motivated. This afternoon, the void-of-course Cancer Moon commences, and it will continue throughout the day and into the evening; this is a recipe for spacey, withdrawn, and possibly even grumpy moods. Try not to let your worries get the best of you, and remember, moodiness is inevitable with the void-of-course Cancer Moon.

Mars square Saturn (occurring Aug. 14 – 30) Mars is in Cancer and Saturn is in Libra; emotional difficulties or threats may be especially trying as attempts at creating harmony in the workplace – or in the judicial system – may be troublesome. In general, this aspect brings abrupt endings. It is also known for creating confrontations between offensive and defensive forces, and is usually not a good time to start a new enterprise. When deploying forces in battle, this aspect often brings fiery and sometimes tragic endings. It is wise to proceed with extra caution. This may be an especially difficult time to muster the strength to finish up projects, or to end affairs amicably. Hang in there; it won't be long before this aspect passes. Fortunately, this is the only time that Mars will square Saturn this year.

Venus trine Pluto (occurring August 20 – 28) Venus trine Pluto is certainly exciting – with fate, power, love, and intensity at work! This aspect represents a love or fascination occurring with regard to the work of fate as well as power. Venus in Virgo emphasizes our love for cleanliness, purification, and good health practices, and while Venus is trine to Pluto, there is a strong appeal among the various generations – and among influential powers – to apply more care and effort to organize and implement greater health practices. Venus trine Pluto allows a breakthrough to occur for those who have trouble accepting the work of fate. This aspect allows loving energy to flow more easily between generations. Love triumphs over all, especially with Venus trine Pluto. This is a great time to let love cure the pain. This aspect last occurred on May 21.

August 26ᵗʰ Friday

Moon in Cancer / Leo

	PDT	EDT
Moon enters Leo	9:08 AM	12:08 PM
Mercury goes direct	3:02 PM	6:02 PM
Moon trine Uranus	3:30 PM	6:30 PM

Birthday: Mother Teresa 1910

Mood Watch: The early hours bring a void-of-course Cancer Moon, and it may take a little while to shake ourselves from an emotional morning haze. Mercury will go direct today, but this transition remains challenging, particularly during a void Moon. As the Moon enters Leo, we are poised to get a handle on the heartbeat of our willpower. The waning Leo Moon is a good time to look within and energize personal willpower and integral strength.

Mercury goes direct (Mercury direct: Aug. 26 – Nov. 23) Since August 2, Mercury has been retrograde in the signs Virgo and Leo, commonly causing communication glitches and confusion when relaying information. Mercury retrograde in Virgo caused important information and data to undergo a tailspin, and while retrograde in Leo, it has placed a lot of communication mix-ups in the affairs of friends and family. Now we can breathe a greatly needed sigh of relief as Mercury, the planet governing the realms of communication, becomes stationary and will soon begin to move forward. Take note that our faculties and manner of communicating will definitely improve within the next few days. Although perhaps not today, when the stationary Mercury often freezes communication efforts, but very soon our communications will run more smoothly; this will be a good time to begin clearing up various misunderstandings occurring over the past few weeks. For more on Mercury retrograde patterns throughout this year, see the introduction on *Mercury retrograde periods.*

August 27ᵗʰ Saturday

Moon in Leo

	PDT	EDT
Moon square Jupiter	2:44 AM	5:44 AM
Moon sextile Saturn	10:06 AM	1:06 PM
Moon conjunct Mercury goes v/c	4:48 PM	7:48 PM
Sun trine Jupiter begins (see September 2)		

Birthday: Paul "Pee-wee Herman" Reubens 1952

Mood Watch: The waning Leo Moon brings playful and feisty moods. No one knows you better than you do, and if someone does, perhaps it's time you paid some more attention to your own personal character development. The waning Leo Moon makes us introspective, and this is a good time to make some improvements on personal development. As the Leo Moon goes void-of-course, be sure to take it easy on yourself and others, as this is a time when inconveniences create impatience, and laziness leads to a lot of complaints. Be sure to take care tonight and to eat on time. A hungry lion is a beastly creature.

August 28th Sunday

NEW MOON in VIRGO

Moon in Leo / Virgo	PDT	EDT
Sun trine Pluto	8:12 AM	11:12 AM
Moon enters Virgo	11:13 AM	2:13 PM
Moon trine Pluto	7:17 PM	10:17 PM
Moon conjunct Sun	8:04 PM	11:04 PM

Birthday: Jack Black 1969

Mood Watch: The **New Moon in Virgo** (Moon conjunct Sun) invites us to start all over again with the development process of our feelings. This Moon calls to us to apply enthused methods of discernment, a new way of analyzing, and to apply caution. How about a new way of accounting or applying health practices? Finding fresh resources is often a common practice during the New Virgo Moon. This is the time to organize and prepare for the autumn season, a time when making adjustments is essential. New Virgo Moon assists us to prepare for the changes that occur in the physical world. This is the time of the harvest, and this Moon will help us make the most of this fruitful time with thrifty ingenuity.

Sun trine Pluto (occurring Aug. 22 – 31) Positive, life-altering changes are occurring in the lives of Leo and Virgo cusp born people celebrating birthdays this year from August 22 – 31. They are currently undergoing the favorable trine aspect of Pluto to their natal Sun, bringing out experiences that involve transformation and encounters with greater powers and fate. Have no fear; this is a time to get in touch with your power, birthday Leos and Virgos! Pluto moves slowly in our cosmos, and powerful encounters that seem deadly or harsh are actually a necessary part of the process. Matters involving fate can be positive, and the trine aspect does represent a gift being bestowed – however unlikely it may seem. Be grateful this trine brings power issues into your life in a more positive fashion, leading to positive transformation. Finding out how to benefit from this power is a big part of discovering Pluto's gifts. This aspect last occurred April 27, affecting some of the Taurus cusp born folks.

August 29th Monday

Moon in Virgo	PDT	EDT	
Moon conjunct Venus	2:10 AM	5:10 AM	
Moon trine Jupiter	3:57 AM	6:57 AM	
Moon sextile Mars goes v/c	3:14 PM	6:14 PM	
Venus trine Jupiter	11:46 PM	2:46 AM	(Aug 30)

Birthday: Michael Jackson 1958

Mood Watch: New feelings about organization and making important connections persistently emerge with the freshly waxing Virgo Moon. This is the time to enjoy the fruits of summer and take in healthy foods as well as implementing more thorough health practices. Astute thoughts and feelings blend together to create a mood of resourcefulness and caution. Today's thriftiness and persistence bring great end-of-the-month deals. However, take it easy on the deals after the

Moon goes void-of-course; skepticism, doubt, and hesitance are some of the most common reasons for minor evening setbacks.

♍

Venus trine Jupiter (occurring Aug. 25 – Sept. 1) Valuable and inspiring gifts of love and affection come with this aspect. Love (Venus) is harmoniously placed with prosperity and opportunity (Jupiter). Venus in Scorpio trine Jupiter in Pisces brings intense and ecstatic expressions of love and affection, which may lead to enterprising and elaborate displays of richness and prosperity. This is a great time to give gifts of love, and for many, it offers an expansive outlook of love's power. Getting ahead in life, in this case, has everything to do with appreciating and loving those areas of life in which we want to expand and prosper. A positive outlook can help make this happen. This aspect last occurred on January 4 and will reoccur on November 27.

August 30th Tuesday

Moon in Virgo / Libra	PDT	EDT
Jupiter goes retrograde	2:17 AM	5:17 AM
Moon enters Libra	11:25 AM	2:25 PM
Moon opposite Uranus	5:08 PM	8:08 PM
Moon square Pluto	7:21 PM	10:21 PM

Birthday: Cameron Diaz 1972

Mood Watch: Throughout morning, the void-of-course Virgo Moon brings a nervous quality to our moods. There is a hesitance in the air as delays and minor setbacks occur. As the Moon enters Libra, our moods shift over to a much more amicable and harmonious expression. The youthfully waxing Libra Moon gears our moods toward wrapping up the affairs of the month and preparing for the autumn season ahead in these busy final weeks of summer. This is a good time to review decisions that have to be made and to work towards making adjustments and compromises with others. Tonight, Moon opposite Uranus brings chaotic moods, and later on this evening, Moon square Pluto brings profound moods. We may not be able to save the whole world from its troubles, but we can work on healing and helping ourselves and those around us. Libra Moon emphasizes the need for peace and harmony.

Jupiter goes retrograde (Jupiter retrograde: Aug. 30 – Dec. 25) The planet of expansion and prosperity now begins to recede back through the early degrees of Taurus today through December 25. Jupiter in Taurus brings prosperity and expansion to such areas of life as banking, investing, and business in general. This is a time when marketing strategies often employ such Taurus-like themes as spas, esthetics, farming, horticulture, landscaping, building, architecture, real estate sales, and surveying. Jupiter retrograde is not the best time for the growth of large scale funds and investments, but it is a good time to meditate on – and to observe carefully – what truly makes us happy in the realms of fortune seeking. A clearer sense of growth will occur through internal processing and through personal skill development. While Jupiter is retrograde, it is important to apply wisdom and caution in the economic area of our lives, and in our livelihood, so we may see future growth. Although Jupiter in Taurus represents banking investment, this is

199

not necessarily the best time to invest heavily; however, creating new business incentives and meditating upon the direction of business will be very revealing during Jupiter retrograde in Taurus. On Christmas this year, Jupiter will go direct at the zero degree mark of Taurus. Remember – less is more. Let go of the old matter and build anew from a firm foundation.

August 31ˢᵗ Wednesday

Moon in Libra	PDT	EDT
Moon conjunct Saturn	11:43 AM	2:43 PM
Moon square Mars	5:27 PM	8:27 PM
Moon sextile Mercury	8:24 PM	11:24 PM

Birthday: Richard Gere 1949

Mood Watch: Moon conjunct Saturn brings serious and productive moods today. A newly waxing Libra Moon allows us to approach the day with an open and informed mind. It's time to build on a more balanced and amicable bond of trust with the Moon in Libra. Cooperation and teamwork are essential themes that give us the edge to make important breakthroughs. That said, this evening's Moon square Mars is probably the worst time for harmonious interaction. As we work together, it will become quickly apparent what we must do to make things go more smoothly. Later, Moon sextile Mercury is a good time to think matters through. Waxing Libra Moon is generally a good time to make decisions.

September 1ˢᵗ Thursday

Moon in Libra / Scorpio	PDT	EDT
Moon trine Neptune goes v/c	10:34 AM	1:34 PM
Moon enters Scorpio	11:47 AM	2:47 PM
Moon sextile Pluto	7:54 PM	10:54 PM

Birthday: Edgar Rice Burroughs 1875

Mood Watch: This new month and day begins well with the waxing Libra Moon. However, as the Moon goes void-of-course, there will be a short interlude of indecision, delays, and minor setbacks. As the Moon enters Scorpio, our moods are noticeably more sensitive and perceptive. Scorpio Moon often guides us through challenges and teaches us about stabilizing our emotional core in the midst of handling intensity or stress. Moon in Scorpio, a fixed water sign, reminds us that the psyche requires house cleaning now and then. When this occurs, we need to face our fears and to confront worry or paranoia with brave certainty.

September 2ⁿᵈ Friday

Moon in Scorpio	PDT	EDT
Moon sextile Sun	3:40 AM	6:40 AM
Moon opposite Jupiter	4:50 AM	7:50 AM
Moon sextile Venus	12:08 PM	3:08 PM
Sun trine Jupiter	8:59 PM	11:59 PM

| Moon trine Mars | 9:10 PM | 12:10 AM | (Sep 3) | ♍ |

Birthday: Salma Hayek 1968

Mood Watch: The waxing Scorpio Moon sets the tone of mood with a sense of urgency and drama. Scorpio Moon opens up such rich emotional issues as birth, sex, death, and transformation. Regenerative forces are at work to bring forth change and adjustment. Scorpio Moon reminds us that life is a struggle in the process of coming and going, from a state of the impermanent to the permanent, and back again. We are reminded on some level of the importance and significance of certain events in our life, and how those events have shaped us through the year.

Sun trine Jupiter (occurring Aug. 27 – Sept. 5) This aspect brings those Virgo people celebrating a birthday from August 27 – September 5 to a favorable natal solar position with relation to Jupiter. This will be a time of gifts and expansion for these birthday folks, and there are good times ahead for them in the coming year. Despite Jupiter retrograde (see August 30), this aspect will bring a better sense of what it means to expand and attain one's personal desire. Be sure to take the time right now, birthday people, to enjoy and appreciate life, which will definitely improve for you, despite other trials you may be facing. This aspect brings the gift of joy, so make use of it and be sure to look for the silver lining in your life! Sun trine Jupiter will reoccur December 22 with the Sun in Capricorn, affecting some of the Sagittarius and Capricorn birthday people of that time.

September 3rd Saturday
Moon in Scorpio / Sagittarius

	PDT	EDT
Moon square Mercury	1:03 AM	4:03 AM
Moon square Neptune goes v/c	12:41 PM	3:41 PM
Moon enters Sagittarius	2:03 PM	5:03 PM
Moon trine Uranus	7:58 PM	10:58 PM

Birthday: Liz Greene 1946

Mood Watch: Instinctive urges and intuitive observations are running strongly this morning with the waning Moon in Scorpio. This afternoon, as the Moon goes void-of-course, it may be easy to get distracted, become dazed, or to find it difficult to pay attention. This is the time to stay guarded, watch for thievery, and to avoid dubious or suspicious behavior. As the Moon enters Sagittarius, our moods will be much more accommodating, generous, and adventurous. Tonight, Moon trine Uranus brings the urge for people to kick up their heels a little, and to have some good ole mischievous, fun loving enjoyment.

September 4th Sunday
FIRST QUARTER MOON in SAGITTARIUS

	PDT	EDT
Moon square Sun	10:39 AM	1:39 PM
Moon sextile Saturn	5:17 PM	8:17 PM
Moon square Venus	8:53 PM	11:53 PM
Venus sextile Mars begins (see September 10)		

Birthday: Damon Wayans 1960

Mood Watch: The **First Quarter Moon in Sagittarius** (Moon square Sun) allows our moods to be adaptable and responsive to the situations that arise. Likely interests include sports events, adventure, vision quests, and philosophical perspectives. While the Virgo Sun reminds us to budget our resources for the changing season ahead, the Sagittarius Moon reminds us to reach out there while the brilliant beauty of summer is still occurring. Adventure and hope abound. Sagittarius says: "I see" – make use of the vision and take the time to *see beyond*.

September 5th Monday

Labor Day, USA / Labour Day, Canada

Moon in Sagittarius / Capricorn	PDT	EDT
Moon trine Mercury	10:04 AM	1:04 PM
Moon sextile Neptune goes v/c	5:30 PM	8:30 PM
Moon enters Capricorn	7:03 PM	10:03 PM

Birthday: Freddie Mercury 1946

Mood Watch: A waxing Moon in Sagittarius brings out the adventurous side of our moods. Early in the day, Moon trine Mercury is a splendid time to work on plans, schedules, and communications. Curious and explorative thoughts captivate our moods, particularly while the influence of Moon sextile Neptune entices our imagination and our insightfulness. However, the Moon also goes void-of-course and this could be costly, as many folks will be thrown off by a complex dispersion of energies. For awhile during the evening, it may seem difficult for us to get our bearings and to maintain a sense of staying on course. No fear! Discoveries made at this time will open us up to a richer perspective on life. A different perspective may just be what is needed in order to carry our energies over into the swiftly changing force of the pending season. Tonight, the Moon enters Capricorn, and our serious moods will add some importance – and perhaps, a sense of accomplishment to the tempo of the day.

September 6th Tuesday

Moon in Capricorn	PDT	EDT	
Moon square Uranus	1:08 AM	4:08 AM	
Moon conjunct Pluto	4:00 AM	7:00 AM	
Moon trine Jupiter	1:49 PM	4:49 PM	
Moon trine Sun	9:07 PM	12:07 AM	(Sep 7)

Birthday: Roger Waters 1943

Mood Watch: The Capricorn Moon brings clear and decisive interactions between people. The Sun is in Virgo, and with the Moon waxing in Capricorn, this is a very earthy time. It's a good time to get some business done and to focus on money related matters. This afternoon's Moon trine Jupiter brings jovial and generous moods. Strong ambitions are at work today, and it may be necessary to be careful not to get stepped on by anyone, particularly while in the process of trying to get your own work done. Capricorn Moon, notoriously, brings serious demands.

September 7ᵗʰ Wednesday

♍

Moon in Capricorn	PDT	EDT	
Moon square Saturn	12:11 AM	3:11 AM	
Moon trine Venus	9:20 AM	12:20 PM	
Moon opposite Mars goes v/c	1:35 PM	4:35 PM	

Birthday: Buddy Holly 1936

Mood Watch: While the Moon waxes in Capricorn, some very practical and easy-going moods make this a good time to get things done. Sun in Virgo and Moon in Capricorn is a superb time to clean up your surroundings, tend to unfinished business, and to catch up in those areas of life where the physical world needs some extra work. There is always something that needs to be done, even if that means taking the time to rest and relax. This will be especially true once the Capricorn Moon has gone void-of-course, and the evening will be a time of slow progress and time warps. Practical and stoic moods can bring dry humor.

September 8ᵗʰ Thursday

Moon in Capricorn / Aquarius	PDT	EDT	
Moon enters Aquarius	2:42 AM	5:42 AM	
Mercury opposite Neptune	8:17 AM	11:17 AM	
Moon sextile Uranus	8:53 AM	11:53 AM	
Moon square Jupiter	10:06 PM	1:06 AM	(Sep 9)
Mercury enters Virgo	10:58 PM	1:58 AM	(Sep 9)
Mercury trine Pluto begins (see September 11)			

Birthday: Peter Sellers 1925

Mood Watch: The waxing Moon in Aquarius brings a focus on knowledge and learning new skills. This is a time of fairs, social endeavors, and conventions, as well as philanthropic and fund raising events. Aquarius Moon puts us in touch with our human side, particularly with the ups and downs in today's lunar aspects. While we often fall back on the awareness that we are simply human, the waxing Aquarius Moon also puts us in touch with the fact that we are – sometimes – superhuman or extraordinary. Reaching out to others in a brotherly or sisterly fashion enhances our chances of being extraordinary. Keep your eyes and ears peeled for the unique opportunity to experience – or perpetrate – a human gesture that is nothing shy of astonishing!

Mercury opposite Neptune (occurring July 24 – Sept. 10) Due to the retrograde motion of both these planets, this opposition is occurring for a longer than average period. Mercury in Leo brings gregarious communications, while Neptune in Aquarius focuses spiritual matters upon the whole of humanity. For a recap on the story of this lengthy rendition of Mercury opposite Neptune, *see August 8*, when this aspect last reached its peak.

Mercury enters Virgo (Mercury in Virgo: Sept. 8 – 25) Due to the last retrograde period of Mercury (Aug. 2 – 26), Mercury is now entering Virgo for the second time this year. This is an excellent place for Mercury; for a recap of the story of why it's good, *see July 28*, back when Mercury first entered Virgo. For a refresher on last month's Mercury retrograde through the sign of Virgo (Aug. 2 – 8), see the introduction on *Mercury retrograde periods*.

September 9ᵗʰ Friday

Moon in Aquarius   **PDT**   **EDT**
     Moon trine Saturn   9:30 AM   12:30 PM

Birthday: Otis Redding 1941

Mood Watch: The day begins favorably with Moon trine Saturn. The general mood on this Aquarius Moon day is positive, outgoing, and eccentric. Thoughts and ideas will be unusual and inspired. This is a good time to enjoy social outings and appreciate the late summer with our most inspired friends and comrades. Human rights issues or debates are taking place all the time, and it is often the Aquarius Moon influence that gives us the chance to collectively share special human interests and promote humanitarian causes. This is also a good time to work on finding solutions to pressing problems. Let the ingenuity and insightfulness of this Aquarius Moon time guide you to find some brilliant answers.

September 10ᵗʰ Saturday

Moon in Aquarius / Pisces   **PDT**   **EDT**
     Moon conjunct Neptune goes v/c   10:31 AM   1:31 PM
     Moon enters Pisces   12:26 PM   3:26 PM
     Moon opposite Mercury   6:05 PM   9:05 PM
     Venus sextile Mars   9:21 PM   12:21 AM   (Sep 11)
     Moon sextile Pluto   10:01 PM   1:01 AM   (Sep 11)

Birthday: Dan "Homer Simpson" Castellanetaeta 1958

Mood Watch: A strongly waxing Aquarius Moon starts off our day with a focus on the need to obtain some tangible information. Moon conjunct Neptune occurs as the Moon goes void-of-course. At this point we may find it difficult to concentrate or to agree on clear terms. This spacey mid-afternoon is probably a good time to focus on relaxing and resting the mind, particularly while the technical world seems to be messing with our heads. As the Moon enters Pisces our moods will appear considerably more dreamy, imaginative, and interactive. A wide range of moods can occur with the influence of the mutable waters of Pisces. We are embarking upon a very magical and mystical Full Moon time.

Venus sextile Mars (occurring Sept. 4 – 14) Calculating, analytical, and cautious kinds of affection are evident while Venus in Virgo is sextile to Mars in Cancer. Despite the fact that Venus and Mars are not positioned in particularly advantageous signs, playfulness and multifaceted attractions will be evident through this aspect. It is here that feminine (Venus) and masculine (Mars) forces have an opportunity (the sextile aspect) to support each other. The Mars influence emphasizes the awareness and application of action, movement, involvement, and also harnesses strength and energy. Venus reminds us to draw towards ourselves the pleasures we desire. Here we have the incentive to apply action with love. This is the only time this aspect will occur this year.

204

September 11th Sunday

Grandparent's Day

Moon in Pisces

	PDT	EDT	
Moon sextile Jupiter	8:16 AM	11:16 AM	
Mercury trine Pluto	10:27 PM	1:27 AM	(Sep 12)
Mercury trine Jupiter begins (see September 14)			

Birthday: D.H. Lawrence 1885

Mood Watch: Full Moon Eve is upon us and this is a great time to count blessings and express kindness. Myth, mysticism, folklore, and magic will always have a strong appeal in modern culture, particularly as our world cultures and global communities become more intertwined and complex. The tarot trump card entitled *MOON* is attributed to the zodiacal sign, Pisces. It is here that our moods reflect some of the deepest parts of our soul. The Full Pisces Moon gives us what it takes to pass through the troubled waters of the soul.

Mercury trine Pluto (occurring Sept. 8 – 13) Mercury in Taurus trine Pluto in Capricorn brings resourceful thoughts and communications that will have powerful results. This aspect brings hope like a gift, and the myth of Pandora's Box shows us that hope regenerates our senses and fills us with the potential for triumph over difficulties. Mercury in Taurus gives a very practical and logical quality to our methods of communicating. This would be a good time to share tales of triumph, spreading those miraculous stories that remind us of the great potential of winning against all odds. This positive aspect aids communication about struggles with fate, trouble, major financial losses, and fatal illnesses. Mercury trine Pluto last occurred on May 20.

September 12th Monday

FULL MOON in PISCES

Moon in Pisces / Aries

	PDT	EDT	
Moon opposite Sun	2:26 AM	5:26 AM	
Moon trine Mars	4:17 PM	7:17 PM	
Moon opposite Venus goes v/c	6:45 PM	9:45 PM	
Moon enters Aries	11:49 PM	2:49 AM	(Sep 13)
Venus opposite Uranus begins (see September 17)			

Birthday: Maria Muldaur 1943

Mood Watch: The **Full Moon in Pisces** (Moon opposite Sun) brings out the psychic in everyone. People can be very sensitive, and as a result, some people express themselves in very artistic or perhaps nonsensical ways. Enchantment sets the stage for Full Pisces Moon activity early in the day. Dance, music, and art are often activities of the Full Pisces Moon. Imaginations will run wild today and anything is possible. Pisces says: "I believe," and while the Moon is full in Pisces, it is vitally important to carry our beliefs wisely, as destructive tendencies may bring us down if we're not careful. This will also be a time to watch out for low self-esteem or substance abuse. Tonight, the Pisces Moon will go void-of-course, and this often brings exceedingly spacey and easily distracted moods. Beware of the tendency for many folks to overextend themselves, or to be particularly susceptible to their vulnerabilities. The Aries Moon will later bring a positive time to reinforce our personal confidence levels.

September 13ᵗʰ Tuesday

Moon in Aries	PDT	EDT
Moon conjunct Uranus	5:59 AM	8:59 AM
Moon square Pluto	9:38 AM	12:38 PM
Venus square Pluto begins (see September 18)		
Mars trine Uranus begins (see September 23)		

Birthday: Jacqueline Bisset 1944

Mood Watch: The morning might be a bit dicey and explosive at times with the Moon conjunct Uranus. We may also find there's a bit of drama occurring with Moon square Pluto. Life gets better as the day progresses. The post-full Moon wanes in Aries, bringing out a sense of urgency and evoking the warrior in all of us. This is a time when new projects are developing. This kind of lunar expression brings out a reflection of the self, and urges one to look toward their own sense of importance, guidance, and leadership. Self-respect is an essential practice for the seasoned warrior.

September 14ᵗʰ Wednesday

Moon in Aries	PDT	EDT
Moon opposite Saturn	9:26 AM	12:26 PM
Mercury trine Jupiter	6:43 PM	9:43 PM
Venus enters Libra	7:40 PM	10:40 PM

Birthday: Sam Neil 1947

Mood Watch: Early in the day, Moon opposite Saturn brings an intense time for handling matters and keeping things under control. The Aries Moon brings out self-awareness and self-assertiveness, and focuses our attention on pushing forward with force and vigor, with strength and intent. A waning Aries Moon reminds us to be cautious of other people's needs to assert themselves. This is not a time to get into a pushing match, though such behavior may be rather common.

Mercury trine Jupiter (occurring Sept. 11 – 16) Despite the fact that Jupiter is retrograde (Aug. 30 – Dec. 25), this is a most favorable aspect that brings good news of expansion and prosperity to those who are open to broadening their awareness. Ask and you shall have! Mercury in Virgo trine Jupiter in Taurus inspires thorough and confident communication which can lead to career breakthroughs, adventure, great achievements, happiness and wellbeing. This is an excellent time to learn new skills which will improve one's livelihood and better one's outlook. Mercury brings news, while Jupiter brings wealth and prosperous change. Mercury trine Jupiter is often considered to be an advantageous time to advertise and put information out there, and to ask for a job or a loan. Look openly for opportunity when sharing information, and promote yourself and your capabilities.

Venus enters Libra (Venus in Libra: Sept. 14 – Oct. 8) Today, Venus enters Libra, and the course of love, magnetism, affection and feminine perception begins to focus on harmonizing and balancing relationships, marriages, and friendships. Venus in Libra stimulates our Libra friends with a strong sense of affection, and of focusing our love relationships towards the goal of creating a more harmonized and balanced state of being. Venus is at home in Libra, and brings out a love of libraries, of scholarly works, and there is a greater attraction to large bodies of information. Venus in Libra emphasizes the love of books, education, law and order, friends and loved ones, and particularly a love and desire for balance wherever possible. As for the delicacy of love matters, in order to settle on the best choices and decisions possible, Libra strives hard to apply a great wealth of knowledge, common law, history, and helpful information with regard to relationships. Attraction is a mystery; Libra seeks to decode the mystery.

September 15th Thursday

Moon in Aries / Taurus

	PDT	EDT	
Moon square Mars	8:06 AM	11:06 AM	
Moon sextile Neptune goes v/c	10:10 AM	1:10 PM	
Moon enters Taurus	12:24 PM	3:24 PM	
Moon trine Pluto	10:20 PM	1:20 AM	(Sep 16)

Birthday: Tommy Lee Jones 1946

Mood Watch: This morning's Moon square Mars is a particularly important time to exercise caution and to be careful to avoid accidents and hot blooded attitudes. The heat is eased and we have the potential to apply a much more calming affect on life with Moon sextile Neptune. This is also the time when the Moon goes void-of-course for a couple of hours. Spacey moods contribute to the fact that only a few people are paying attention to what's going on. This afternoon, as the Moon enters Taurus, our moods will become considerably more grounded. Progress occurs as our efforts to take care of business are swiftly rewarded.

September 16th Friday

Moon in Taurus

	PDT	EDT
Moon conjunct Jupiter	8:26 AM	11:26 AM
Pluto goes direct	11:23 AM	2:23 PM
Moon trine Mercury	3:34 PM	6:34 PM

Birthday: David Copperfield 1956

Mood Watch: Today's waning Taurus Moon stirs a heartfelt awareness of what we have, what we have lost, and what we hope to gain. Moon conjunct Jupiter brings hopefulness and a prosperous spirit to our outlook on matters. When the Moon is in Taurus, it is said to be "exalted," an ideal aspect to get in tune with the earth and our bodies. Taurus Moon reminds us to take thorough care of our worldly possessions, before the damaging elements of time and neglect take care of them first. Sun in Virgo and Moon in Taurus demand prudent and practical measures towards gaining satisfaction. Today will be a good day to tackle physical tasks and to move with ease.

Pluto goes direct (Pluto direct: Sept. 16, 2011 – April 11, 2012) After the long – but common – retrograde period of Pluto (April 9 – September 16), the planet of transformation now moves into a smooth, direct pattern for the rest of the year. Since April 9, Pluto has been going back through the early degrees of Capricorn. Now that it is direct, with Pluto at the four degree mark of Capricorn, we can better acknowledge the evolution of humankind's condition in order to survive and adapt to the challenges that are occurring on planet Earth. This transformation emphasizes consciousness, without which we would not be. This is not a time to take life for granted; rather, it is a time to participate in making life better by consciously transforming fear into determination and despair into belief in oneself. Pluto in Capricorn (since 2008) inspires a new journey where we build a new world for ourselves and for the generations to come.

September 17ᵗʰ Saturday

Moon in Taurus	PDT	EDT	
Venus opposite Uranus	4:05 AM	7:05 AM	
Moon trine Sun	2:19 PM	5:19 PM	
Moon square Neptune	10:45 PM	1:45 AM	(Sep 18)

Birthday: John Ritter 1948

Mood Watch: The Taurus Moon in the closing days of summer is a splendid time to focus on acquiring essential and practical goods. Waning Taurus Moon brings on a cool pace of rummaging through piles of material goods. What we put off doing all summer now needs to be addressed. This is the time to focus on cleaning up the homestead. Earthy focuses are the key today, as the physical realities of this time of year urge us to collect what we need and get to work on making our surroundings comfortable and secure.

Venus opposite Uranus (occurring Sept. 12 – 19) Venus in Libra opposite Uranus in Aries brings many possibilities while Venus and Uranus counteract each other near the equinoxes of the zodiac. The polarity of Libra and Aries tests the harmony of relationships. The balance of love is challenged by unusual enterprises and radical warfare. Conflict may surface as love relationships are tested by fundamental differences over extraneous new developments and extraordinary circumstances. On the up side, exciting and unusual kinds of pleasure bring radical new awareness. On the down side, this type of love is explosive in nature, creating radical obsessions – some healthy and some not. Although they are often short lived, this aspect allows for unusual, exciting, and torrid love affairs. This is a good time for artists to make breakthroughs and for eccentric expressions of affection. Issues of freedom are likely to be raised in love related disputes. No matter how you look at it, issues of love are surely being activated with a broadening sense of awareness. This is the only time this aspect will occur this year.

208

September 18th Sunday

Moon in Taurus / Gemini

	PDT	EDT
Moon sextile Mars goes v/c	12:08 AM	3:08 AM
Moon enters Gemini	1:06 AM	4:06 AM
Moon sextile Uranus	6:51 AM	9:51 AM
Moon trine Venus	10:02 AM	1:02 PM
Moon opposite Pluto	12:45 PM	3:45 PM
Venus square Pluto	6:07 PM	9:07 PM
Mars enters Leo	6:50 PM	9:50 PM

Birthday: Greta Garbo 1905

Mood Watch: The Sun is in Virgo and the Moon is in Gemini, and this brings a strong emphasis on communications, organization, and resources. This is the time to make connections with others. Many folks will keep busy planning and calculating their pending autumn activities. Moon guides us to think matters through intelligently.

Venus square Pluto (occurring Sept. 13 – 21) Venus in Libra is square Pluto in Capricorn. The diplomatic, peaceable, cooperative and naturally harmonious side of our affections (Venus in Libra) is likely to take a pretty good beating, while a seemingly major transformation is occurring on a physical level (Pluto in Capricorn). Our concepts of beauty may be challenged as the corruption of superpowers prompts action which threatens or alters the beauty and pleasure in our lives. Venus square Pluto usually involves such difficulties as loss or death of a loved one, the obstacles of rejection, and general oppression for those aspects of life to which we are undeniably attached and which we hold dear. If something of this nature is occurring for you, it is best to recognize that love will triumph in every dimension, despite the pain of separation, or the disease and strife of the beloved. Be both strong and gentle in matters of love. Let the obstacles of love's pain become the building blocks of a better outlook, and a stronger love will supersede these current trials of the heart. This aspect is a little more merciful at this time, with Venus in its home sign, Libra; that is, it's much more merciful than it was earlier this year, with Venus in the detrimental position of Aries on April 27.

Mars enters Leo (Mars in Leo: Sept. 18 – Nov. 10) Leo is a fearless place for the planet Mars; sheer action is stimulated and animated here. Leo people will have a lot of extra energy and some of them will be forced to reckon with their temper while Mars passes through Leo's natal sun sign. Leo folks, be creative with this extra energy while you have it. In the meantime, while traveling through Leo, Mars will go into the square position to the signs Taurus and Scorpio. Taurus and Scorpio people may have an exhausting – or accident prone – time. They may also need to steer clear of heated disputes, particularly with Leos. Aquarius people may be overwhelmed by brazen activity in their lives while Mars opposes their natal Sun. Mars in Leo generally brings positive and fortifying energy to the scope of all action. It's a good time to get in touch with one's instincts and to activate personal willpower.

September 19th Monday

Moon in Gemini	PDT	EDT
Moon trine Saturn	11:20 AM	2:20 PM
Moon square Mercury	2:29 PM	5:29 PM
Sun opposite Uranus begins (see September 25)		
Sun sextile Mars begins (see September 29)		

Birthday: Leslie "Twiggy" Lawson 1949

Mood Watch: The waning Gemini Moon brings the need for change. Moon trine Saturn is a useful lunar aspect for getting a handle on responsibilities. The sun and moon are in the Mercury-ruled signs Gemini and Virgo. It's a good time to clean up and simplify the office space, to organize papers, and to eliminate superfluous matter. The Gemini Moon is a good time to diligently shuffle through unsorted details and task lists. Many folks will be inclined to catch up on communications, enjoy word games, puzzles, and casual conversations. That said, it may be wise to steer clear of complicated subjects as the Moon squares to Mercury.

September 20th Tuesday
LAST QUARTER MOON in GEMINI

Moon in Gemini / Cancer	PDT	EDT	
Moon square Sun	6:38 AM	9:38 AM	
Moon trine Neptune goes v/c	9:33 AM	12:33 PM	
Moon enters Cancer	11:53 AM	2:53 PM	
Moon square Uranus	5:09 PM	8:09 PM	
Moon opposite Pluto	9:09 PM	12:09 AM	(Sep 21)

Birthday: Ferdinand "Jelly Roll" Morton 1885

Mood Watch: The **Last Quarter Moon in Gemini** (Moon square Sun) brings talkative moods and informative interaction. People will have a lot on their minds this morning while intellectual pursuits are considered. As the Moon goes void-of-course, our attention to detail could become so involved that many folks may start to miss the point of their conversations. It is so easy to get distracted during the void-of-course Gemini Moon. As the Moon enters Cancer, our emotional attachments will begin to surface, and our focuses will be aimed at what feeds and nourishes our complex emotional needs.

September 21st Wednesday

Moon in Cancer	PDT	EDT
Moon square Venus	2:38 AM	5:38 AM
Moon sextile Jupiter	5:51 AM	8:51 AM
Moon square Saturn	8:37 PM	11:37 PM
Sun conjunct Mercury begins (see September 28)		
Sun square Pluto begins (see September 28)		

Birthday: H.G. Wells 1866

Mood Watch: The Moon is in Cancer, and the entire day gears up our senses with deep emotional expressions and focuses our attention on nurturing and instinctual

210

urges. This serves as a good time to brighten up the home and make it feel more comfortable. Later tonight, Moon square Saturn brings a challenge to keep things under control, and this is a good time to take it easy on high expectations and difficult jobs. Waning Cancer Moon promotes pampering and puts the focus on relaxing and letting go of the tendency to worry about things.

September 22nd Thursday

Moon in Cancer / Leo

	PDT	EDT	
Moon opposite Saturn	7:45 AM	10:45 AM	
Moon sextile Mercury	8:17 AM	11:17 AM	
Moon sextile Sun goes v/c	6:22 PM	9:22 PM	
Moon enters Leo	6:55 PM	9:55 PM	
Moon conjunct Mars	11:24 PM	2:24 AM	(Sep 23)
Moon trine Uranus	11:38 PM	2:38 AM	(Sep 23)

Birthday: Joan Jett 1960

Mood Watch: This morning, Moon opposite Saturn brings serious attitudes, and there may be the feeling that there's just too much to do. It's no problem if we apply ourselves wisely, and fortunately, Moon sextile Mercury is an opportunistic lunar aspect for delegating jobs and asking for assistance. Today's waning Cancer Moon is a superb time to reassure people with loving care and a hopeful attitude. This evening's Moon in Leo means many folks will be seeking some entertainment and a lively spirit.

LIBRA

Key Phrase: "I BALANCE"

Cardinal Air Sign

Ruling Planet: Venus

Symbol: The Scales

September 23rd through October 23rd

September 23rd Friday

Autumnal Equinox

Moon in Leo

	PDT	EDT
Sun enters Libra	2:04 AM	5:04 AM
Mars trine Uranus	4:23 AM	7:23 AM
Moon square Jupiter	11:14 AM	2:14 PM
Moon sextile Venus	1:49 PM	4:49 PM
Mercury opposite Uranus begins (see September 26)		

Birthday: Heinrich Cornelius Agrippa 1486

Mood Watch: The waning Leo Moon brings good-natured and energetic moods. If you're holding onto emotional stuff, the waning Leo Moon is a good time to lean on friends and family, or to work on fulfilling your personal needs. Leo Moon often reminds us of our individual desires, and this is an excellent time to work on self-development and to appease the beastly side of our nature with some good, clean fun. Leo Moon also brings out our elaborate and sophisticated qualities. Celebrate the Autumnal Equinox in style!

Sun enters Libra (Sun in Libra: Sept. 23 – Oct. 23) It's the magical time of Autumnal Equinox. This time of year calls to us to reach out to one another and to create a support system of helpful friends to prepare for the busy season ahead and the darker and colder days yet to come. The Sun now enters Libra, a Venus ruled sign that focuses our attention on the power of teamwork and partnership. The key phrase for Libra is, "I balance," and the key to Libra's happiness comes with a sense of balance. Another factor to take into account for our Libran friends is the perpetual state of adjustment required to meet that balance. Libra could therefore easily say, "I adjust." The cornucopia of life is full of expressions of harmony and beauty. Libra focuses on libraries and accesses data and knowledge, particularly in the area of law. May this new autumn season be pleasurable and fruitful for you and all your loved ones!

Mars trine Uranus (occurring Sept. 13 – 27) Mars in Leo trine Uranus in Aries brings positive, but very heated and chaotic activities. Personal projections are likely to be blown way out of proportion. However, the trine aspect brings a positive interaction between these two extremely fiery planets that are currently in fire signs. This may be a good time to stir things up in order to get noticed or to get some dramatic results. The radical tendencies that are seen in people's desires and needs aren't likely to pass by quietly with this aspect. This is the time positive breakthroughs may occur. Be careful what you stand for or you'll fall for anything in this atmosphere of active yet favorable destruction. This is a good time to tackle the breakdown of unwanted barriers that stifle the human spirit from evolving in chosen ways. Mars trine Uranus is bound to create fire somewhere and the heat can be worked to our advantage. In the triumph mode, Mars trine Uranus creates fireworks of celebration, and there is a certain sense of truly being alive with regard to the demand for independence and freedom. Strike while the iron is hot; this is the only time this aspect will occur this year.

September 24th Saturday

Moon in Leo / Virgo	PDT	EDT	
Moon sextile Saturn	1:36 AM	4:36 AM	
Moon opposite Neptune goes v/c	7:39 PM	10:39 PM	
Moon enters Virgo	9:49 PM	12:49 AM	(Sep 25)
Mercury square Pluto begins (see September 28)			
Venus conjunct Saturn begins (see September 29)			
Mars square Jupiter begins (see October 2)			

Birthday: Jim Henson 1936

Mood Watch: The Leo Moon reminds us of our need for creature comforts, inspiration, and optimism. Leo Moon activities emphasize the need for family interaction, hobbies, and special interests. Events involving theater and the fine arts are excellent focuses on a Leo Moon day. Lazy and leisurely moods are common during the void-of-course Leo Moon. Later, Moon in Virgo brings a great deal of introspection.

Ω

September 25th Sunday

Moon in Virgo	PDT	EDT
Moon trine Pluto	5:49 AM	8:49 AM
Moon trine Jupiter goes v/c	12:47 PM	3:47 PM
Mercury enters Libra	2:08 PM	5:08 PM
Sun opposite Uranus	5:14 PM	8:14 PM

Birthday: Christopher Reeve 1952

Mood Watch: Waning Virgo Moon activity stresses the need to prepare and organize for the colder months ahead. There is a strong emphasis on making decisions and preparing schedules. The Virgo Moon also emphasizes the need for good health practices and proper physical hygiene. This afternoon, as the waning Virgo Moon goes void-of-course, our moods will be somewhat withdrawn and subdued. Skepticism runs strongly throughout the evening. It is time to brace ourselves for the long void-of-course Moon day tomorrow.

Mercury enters Libra (Mercury in Libra: Sept. 25 – Oct. 13) Mercury in Libra aligns us with diplomacy, tact, and the need to connect with friends and loved ones. Libra is the cardinal autumn sign that emphasizes balance and adjustment. Today through October 13, Mercury in Libra will bring a focus on harmonizing with others and preparing for the change of the seasons. This is a good time for people to communicate by gathering important information, as our decision making process kicks into high gear.

Sun opposite Uranus (occurring Sept. 19 – 28) This occurrence of Sun opposite Uranus particularly affects Virgo and Libra people celebrating birthdays September 19 – 28. The opposition of Uranus creates an acute awareness of the revolutionary forces in one's life. There will undoubtedly be a lot of chaos, and the challenge (in part) may be to accept the rebel within you, and to persevere through the drastic and edgy discord. This is the time to go with the flow of unusual and unpredictable occurrences. It's also a good time to learn the Tao of chaos, and to understand that this awakening force is enlivening a sense of freedom. The only alternatives are to break through, or to break down if one resists. Survival counts; use your senses and your sensibilities well but do not resist the forces of great change. In its opposition to Virgo and Libra, Uranus will both challenge and strengthen our Virgo and Libra (birthday) friends to live a life of freedom. This will be an exciting and, at times, exhausting year ahead for these birthday folks. Uranus is currently at the two degree mark of Aries. We have come to the end of the cycle of Uranus in Pisces (2003 – 2010/2011), and this is also the end of the Uranus opposition to Virgo. This aspect has been annually teaching Virgo people the value in allowing for a greater range of possibilities. In the years to come, it will be Libra people's turn to ride the big waves of chaos while Uranus opposes their natal sun.

September 26th Monday

Moon in Virgo / Libra

	PDT	EDT	
Moon enters Libra	9:50 PM	12:50 AM	(Sep 27)
Mercury opposite Uranus	11:29 PM	2:29 AM	(Sep 27)

Birthday: T.S. Eliot 1888

Mood Watch: As the darkly waning Virgo Moon progresses through the day, it is also void-of-course, and there may be a tendency for people to doubt, to be skeptical, and to be slow to respond to matters, much to the extent that not much progress will occur. This is a day to pace ourselves and to resolve the idea that answers to our questions won't come quickly, and they may not come at all. The New Moon eve is upon us and it's time for a renewal! The Libra Moon will bring harmony.

Mercury opposite Uranus (occurring Sept. 23 – 28) Mercury in Libra opposes Uranus in Aries. Explosive events under discussion are testing our ability to maintain a sense of balance in the chaos of the battle. Extraordinary diplomacy handles volatile energy with immaculate grace. Radical thinking springs up with this aspect. Ideas may seem bigger than life, and talk seems to focus on concepts which have not been fully grasped, but appear to be presented with assured confidence. Shocking or liberating statements tend to come out with this aspect. There is an acute awareness of the need to speak out for freedom, and the dialogue may appear sharp; radical and sometimes vulgar language may erupt. Outrageous claims and verbal presumptions made at this time may bring fiery or irrational flare-ups in discussion groups and chat rooms. This is a really good time to watch your mouth. This is the only time this aspect occurs this year.

September 27th Tuesday

NEW MOON in LIBRA

	PDT	EDT	
Moon opposite Uranus	1:48 AM	4:48 AM	
Moon conjunct Mercury	2:08 AM	5:08 AM	
Moon conjunct Sun	4:08 AM	7:08 AM	
Moon square Pluto	5:34 AM	8:34 AM	
Moon sextile Mars	5:54 AM	8:54 AM	
Moon conjunct Venus	11:33 PM	2:33 AM	(Sep 28)

Birthday: Gwyneth Paltrow 1972

Mood Watch: The **New Moon in Libra** (Moon conjunct Sun) is a time of reaffirming and harmonizing our relationships with friends and partners, as well as a time of initiating friendships while autumn activities create a fresh working environment for many people. New rules also set the standard for how to create a more harmonious environment in the days of autumn. This Moon places an emphasis on laws, the courts, the litigation process, custody battles, and the like. Justice comes when there is peace, but this is not always found in the courts. The

214

rest of the world will pretty much do what it has always done since the beginning of time, and not all matters are individually controllable. In order to begin anew, the New Libra Moon reminds us to seek peace within.

♎

September 28th Wednesday

Moon in Libra / Scorpio	PDT	EDT	
Sun square Pluto	2:36 AM	5:36 AM	
Moon conjunct Saturn	2:36 AM	5:36 AM	
Mercury square Pluto	7:26 AM	10:26 AM	
Sun conjunct Mercury	1:15 PM	4:15 PM	
Moon trine Neptune goes v/c	6:51 PM	9:51 PM	
Moon enters Scorpio	9:04 PM	12:04 AM	(Sep 29)

Birthday: Brigitte Bardot 1934

Mood Watch: Libra Moon, which is ever so new, now opens the porthole to autumn moods. Throughout this past week, the solar light has dipped its rays aggressively through our windows and casts prismatic lights through the crystals that are there to capture them. This is the time to place ourselves in the equilibrium of the forces, to put balance into our lives. Tonight's Scorpio Moon is a good time to focus on protection and emotional security.

Sun square Pluto (occurring Sept. 21 – Oct. 1) This occurrence of Sun square Pluto particularly affects those Libra people celebrating birthdays from September 21 – October 1. For them, Pluto squaring their natal Sun brings disruptive changes and many challenges to overcome, such as the pain of loss and the severity of transformation. These tests often involve illness, irreparable damage, and dramatic life and death changes. This is the time to persevere through the obstacles of hardship. The hardships that are taking place now will resurface again in time, and that necessitates finding methods of release and of attitude adjustment in order to survive the anxiety and stress. Take it one day at a time, and do not let fear and worry rule you, birthday folks. Move steadily through the required transformation, as stagnation and fear will only bring extended suffering. Pluto tests are hard, but not impossible. This aspect last occurred on March 28, affecting the March born Aries people of that time.

Mercury square Pluto (occurring Sept. 24 – 30) Mercury in Libra is square to Pluto in Capricorn. Attempts at communicating the need for balance may be difficult with regard to dominant powers that are fatefully at work creating permanent changes that will affect the generations to come. Procrastinating and vacillating thoughts make it especially difficult to communicate with those of another generation, or to discuss hardships and matters of fate in a constructive manner. This is a particularly hard time to deal with burdensome issues and discuss them in a manner that relieves tension. Mercury square Pluto often brings harsh and sometimes fatal news. Talk revolves around the corruption of superpowers. This may be an especially difficult time to discuss matters involving permanent change. This aspect last occurred on March 13 and there was also a non-exact occurrence of Mercury square Pluto on April 20.

Sun conjunct Mercury (occurring Sept. 21 – Oct. 2) This conjunction will create a much more thoughtful, communicative and expressive year ahead for those Libra folks celebrating birthdays September 21 – October 2. This is your time (birthday Libra) to record ideas, relay important messages, and pay close attention to your imaginative thoughts as they are touched by Mercury, creating the urge to speak and be heard. Birthday Libra, your thoughts will reveal a great deal about who you are, now and in the year to come.

September 29th Thursday

Rosh Hashanah

Moon in Scorpio	PDT	EDT	
Mercury sextile Mars	12:27 AM	3:27 AM	
Moon sextile Pluto	4:55 AM	7:55 AM	
Moon square Mars	7:12 AM	10:12 AM	
Moon opposite Jupiter	11:12 AM	2:12 PM	
Venus conjunct Saturn	4:47 PM	7:47 PM	
Sun sextile Mars	11:43 PM	2:43 AM	(Sep 30)

Birthday: Madeline Kahn 1942

Mood Watch: Instinctive urges and intuitive observations are running strongly now. Scorpio Moon reminds us that life is a struggle in the process of coming and going, from a state of the impermanent to the permanent, and back again. We are reminded on some level of the importance and significance of certain events in our life, and how those events have shaped us through the year. Sometimes change happens faster than we are able to process. Scorpio Moon is a vital and swift processor of emotional expression. It is through this procedure that we are able to work through an extraordinary build-up of awareness and pressure. Scorpio Moon helps us to find creative ways to accept those unfathomable mysteries of life's twists of fate, which deeply affect us all from time to time.

Mercury sextile Mars (occurring July 6 – Sept. 30) This aspect has been stretched out for a longer than usual period due to the retrograde cycle of Mercury (Aug. 2 – 26). This is the third time Mercury sextile Mars has reached its peak during this occurrence period – the first one occurred on July 11, and the second one occurred on August 4, when Mercury was retrograde. Today's Mercury in Libra sextile Mars in Leo brings thought provoking and harmonizing messages as well as ambitious actions. Enthusiastic responses to discussions are sure to keep our communications buzzing along swiftly. This aspect ensures that communications will move quickly. Mercury sextile Mars presents opportunities which can be received, recognized, communicated and acted upon. News or information may lead to immediate action. It's an advantageous time to apply one's word with a full backing of action for a very favorable outcome.

Venus conjunct Saturn (occurring Sept. 24 – Oct. 2) Venus and Saturn are conjunct in Libra. This creates subtly affectionate, communicative, and serious bonding between loved ones. This conjunction brings a favorable time to apply discipline in the arts and in love related matters. Venus conjunct Saturn represents

216

our commitment and responsibility to the people and things we love and care about. It may also indicate there is a strong, timely quality about love matters taking place, or that love matters are undergoing a restriction, or possibly even closure of some kind. This conjunction of Venus and Saturn can go either way on the positive-negative scale, since the loving attraction of Venus can be either encouraged or thwarted by the responsible, serious, and limiting discipline of Saturn's energy. This is the only time Venus will be conjunct with Saturn this year.

Sun sextile Mars (occurring Sept. 19 – Oct. 5) Sun sextile Mars brings a surge of favorable energy and activity into our lives, particularly enlivening the lives of those Libra people celebrating a birthday from September 19 – October 5. There are opportunities at work, which must be acted upon in order for all of this extra energy to pay off. There may also be a lot of anguish or pressure with regard to self-image, and the heat stirred up by this experience requires direction and assertiveness. Now is the time for Libra birthday folks to take action, to get in shape, and to build up their energy and strength. This is the only time this solar aspect will occur with Mars this year.

September 30ᵗʰ Friday

Moon in Scorpio / Sagittarius	**PDT**	**EDT**	
Moon square Neptune goes v/c	7:17 PM	10:17 PM	
Moon enters Sagittarius	9:41 PM	12:41 AM	(Oct 1)

Birthday: Truman Capote 1924

Mood Watch: Today's Scorpio Moon reminds us of the necessity to transform ourselves. Wherever passions exist, we will be drawn to them. There is willpower – and there is extraordinary willpower which is invariably fueled by passion and deep desire. Scorpio Moon is a good time to remember what's really important to us, and to stay on track with current events. As the Moon goes void-of-course, it may be difficult to stay focused and to keep up with the strong feelings that are being circulated. Strict caution, vigilance, and moderation in the use of addictive substances are good ways to combat the potential for trouble.

October 1ˢᵗ Saturday

Moon in Sagittarius	**PDT**	**EDT**
Moon trine Uranus	1:38 AM	4:38 AM
Moon trine Mars	10:29 AM	1:29 PM
Moon sextile Sun	11:30 AM	2:30 PM
Moon sextile Mercury	3:57 PM	6:57 PM

Birthday: Isaac Bonewits 1949

Mood Watch: The waxing Sagittarius Moon kicks off this month with upbeat lunar aspects, a positive attitude, and there is also a visionary process in the making. Sagittarius says, "I see," and with this outlook there is a strong desire to travel, explore, and investigate possibilities. Optimism and enthusiasm inspire friendly and uplifting moods. If we are astute and willing to watch for the signs, a vision of the month ahead illuminates our senses. A picture or a vision can be magnified with a positive affirmation. Perfect and empower the vision.

October 2ⁿᵈ Sunday

Moon in Sagittarius	PDT	EDT	
Moon sextile Saturn	5:36 AM	8:36 AM	
Moon sextile Venus	11:02 AM	2:02 PM	
Mars square Jupiter	10:20 PM	1:20 AM	(Oct 3)
Moon sextile Neptune goes v/c	10:37 PM	1:37 AM	(Oct 3)
Mercury conjunct Saturn begins (see October 6)			
Venus trine Neptune begins (see October 7)			

Birthday: Groucho Marx 1890

Mood Watch: Fascination and adventure call to us with Sun in Libra and Moon in Sagittarius. The waxing Sagittarius Moon brings adaptable, creative, versatile, and enterprising moods. All of today's lunar aspects are sextile and this means there are many possibilities in the works, but only as long as we act on them. Sagittarius Moon gives us the flexibility to adapt to a number of moods as they come. A more philosophical approach to life gives us the feeling that we can handle whatever comes along. Sagittarius points the way with insightfulness.

Mars square Jupiter (occurring Sept. 24 – Oct. 7) With this aspect various activities are met with the obstacles of economic oppression and shortfall. This is a difficult time to excel in business endeavors, especially in actively trading markets. This aspect warns us that there will be complications and stiff competition when approaching the job market aggressively. Trying to make progress using headstrong attitudes and unwarranted self-confidence might impede progress. This aspect brings no-nonsense demands or increases in our workload. Mars in Leo suggests the need for aggressive business tactics in personal banking adjustments, which are likely to become expensive while Mars is square to Jupiter. Additionally, the expenses of the entertainment industry may be particularly high. Jupiter is in Taurus, focusing on the expansion of wealth through banking and financial investments. The square aspect of these two planets creates a challenging dynamic in the struggle to grow economically. Expect to work a lot harder and perhaps a lot longer in order to smooth the rough edges of the financial empire while Mars in Leo squares Jupiter in Taurus. Fortunately, this is the only time this aspect occurs this year.

October 3ʳᵈ Monday

FIRST QUARTER MOON in CAPRICORN

Moon in Sagittarius / Capricorn	PDT	EDT
Moon enters Capricorn	1:15 AM	4:15 AM
Moon square Uranus	5:19 AM	8:19 AM
Moon conjunct Pluto	10:07 AM	1:07 PM
Moon trine Jupiter	4:23 PM	7:23 PM
Moon square Sun	8:15 PM	11:15 PM

♎

Mood Watch: The **First Quarter Moon in Capricorn** (Moon square Sun) strongly emphasizes the need for serious labor. Some staunch determination is required. There is a steadily mounting concern to achieve a notable level of accomplishment or completion in projects. The harvest ripens and the physical labor force of the world is hard at work. People's moods are greatly moved by the acknowledgement of merits. The need to hunt for a steady job, a marketing edge, or a secure investment keeps us vigilant and focused. Punctuality in business is stressed. Some may feel isolated by constant work and no play. No one likes feeling rushed, particularly when high standards must be met.

October 4th Tuesday

Moon in Capricorn	PDT	EDT	
Moon square Mercury	4:47 AM	7:47 AM	
Moon square Saturn	11:52 AM	2:52 PM	
Moon square Venus goes v/c	10:57 PM	1:57 AM	(Oct 5)

Birthday: Susan Sarandon 1946

Mood Watch: Morning efforts to communicate will have their ups and downs with Moon square Mercury. It's important to be persistent, but not pushy, when communicating. Later, Moon square Saturn brings a lot of pressure, obstacles, and additional responsibilities. The Capricorn Moon leads to serious moods, particularly when things aren't going smoothly. Fortunately, Capricorn Moon also gives us the impetus to be persistent and practical. Steady does it.

October 5th Wednesday

Moon in Capricorn/ Aquarius	PDT	EDT	
Moon enters Aquarius	8:17 AM	11:17 AM	
Moon sextile Uranus	12:26 PM	3:26 PM	
Moon square Jupiter	11:51 PM	2:51 AM	(Oct 6)

Birthday: Kate Winslet 1975

Mood Watch: The earliest part of the day brings sobering moods and attitudes while the Moon is void-of-course in Capricorn. As the Moon enters Aquarius, our outlook on the day will be much more luminous. The Sun is in Libra, the Moon is in Aquarius, and this is a time of officiating over and clarifying the terms of our life with education, law, documentation, and research. A busy shuffle rustles through the halls of large institutions. Waxing Aquarius Moon puts the spotlight on such focuses as science, charities and humanitarian based causes and issues. Unusual and unconventional people are spurred towards exposing their creative genius.

October 6th Thursday

Moon in Aquarius	PDT	EDT	
Moon opposite Mars	4:08 AM	7:08 AM	
Moon trine Sun	9:13 AM	12:13 PM	
Mercury conjunct Saturn	3:01 PM	6:01 PM	
Moon trine Saturn	9:25 PM	12:25 AM	(Oct 7)
Moon trine Mercury	10:21 PM	1:21 AM	(Oct 7)
Sun conjunct Saturn begins (see October 13)			

Birthday: George Westinghouse 1846

Mood Watch: Another lively day with Moon in Aquarius keeps us active and interested in the technical world of development. The general mood is outgoing and eccentric. Moon in Aquarius brings on a full day of inspired moods and openness towards learning and exploring new views of the people around us. Aquarius Moon focuses our moods on seeking knowledge as well as innovative and unusual avenues of thought.

Mercury conjunct Saturn (occurring Oct. 2 – 8) Mercury conjunct Saturn will bring talk about the need to put an end to the useless or unwanted components of our lives. It will focus our thoughts on the areas of life that have reached limitations, or where timely new beginnings – or endings – are occurring. When occurring in Libra, this conjunction implies that strong rules or guidelines will be established with regard to social conduct, court cases, and relationships. There is a discerning quality at work with Mercury conjunct Saturn, making this conjunction a very good one for speakers and writers to inspire, initiate and capture vital thoughts. News concerning the end of a cycle is likely to occur. Examples include retirement announcements, job loss, and possibly even the news of a notable death. Overall, Mercury conjunct Saturn tends to bring out a strong tone of seriousness in communications. There is a restriction, a discipline, a carefully considered emphasis of thoughts placed on our communications; it's a serious intent to get the word across in no uncertain terms. There is the strong implication at work that we must be seriously responsible for what we say, particularly around authority and in official public statements. "Anything you say can and will be used against you..." This is the only time this conjunction of Mercury and Saturn will occur this year.

October 7th Friday

Moon in Aquarius / Pisces	PDT	EDT
Moon trine Venus	2:58 PM	5:58 PM
Moon conjunct Neptune goes v/c	3:07 PM	6:07 PM
Venus trine Neptune	4:27 PM	7:27 PM
Moon enters Pisces	6:13 PM	9:13 PM

Birthday: John Cougar Mellencamp 1951

Mood Watch: The Aquarius Moon in the first part of the day brings an active interest in the technological process, human interest stories, and creative inventions. Moon trine Venus is a splendid time to enjoy favorite pleasures and art. While the Moon is void-of-course in Aquarius for a few hours, the world will appear considerably more crowded, slow moving, and there may be a lot of mindless mistakes slowing down our progress. This evening's Moon in Pisces brings artistic, calming, and intuitive moods.

Venus trine Neptune (occurring Oct. 2 – 10) Venus in Libra trine Neptune in Aquarius enhances spiritual love. This aspect brings well balanced and generous kinds of love into harmony with a very ingenious kind of spiritual expression. Neptune, now at the cusp of Aquarius and Pisces, is a slow moving planet currently completing its trine cycles to Venus in the air signs, Gemini and Libra. Our feminine and spiritual awareness completes a cycle of communicating and harmonizing a more divine sense of feminine wisdom. Well into the future, 2011/2012 to 2026, Neptune in Pisces (see April 4) will be forming a trine to Venus through the water signs, Cancer and Scorpio. This aspect, combined with these two planets in the water signs of the zodiac, brings feminine wisdom into a place where it can be readily absorbed and accessed for divine healing and nurturing. Venus trine Neptune delivers a calmness and tranquility that are vitally needed, and there is a greater potential to create a spiritually enhanced atmosphere. Wherever there is spiritual turmoil, Venus trine Neptune helps to ease our woes with a support network of feminine kindness. Visiting or meditating upon sacred places and favorite sanctuaries brings visions and inner wisdom. Peaceful, pleasurable, and spiritual love is possible with this aspect, which last occurred on July 4.

October 8th Saturday

Yom Kippur

Moon in Pisces	**PDT**	**EDT**	
Moon sextile Pluto	4:05 AM	7:05 AM	
Moon sextile Jupiter	9:50 AM	12:50 PM	
Moon opposite Saturn goes v/c	1:38 PM	4:38 PM	
Venus enters Scorpio	10:49 PM	1:49 AM	(Oct 9)
Mercury trine Neptune begins (see October 12)			

Birthday: Chevy Chase 1943

Mood Watch: The Pisces Moon brings busily shifting moods and attitudes. Our moods drift into and out of a series of flowing and changing images and impressions. As the Moon travels through Pisces, a mystical and timeless element of perception captivates our moods. Bubbly, artistic, enchanting, and dreamy moments allow us to access a hidden sanctuary where the soulful or prayerful part of ourselves is unleashed. Today many folks will be drawn towards the need to seek out a favorite space or refuge – something far from the mundane. Let this be the place that recharges the batteries and allows faith to be renewed. While the Pisces Moon is void-of-course, expect delays, misunderstandings, overindulgence, and sheer laziness. This is likely to carry over throughout the entire day tomorrow.

Venus enters Scorpio (Venus in Scorpio: Oct. 8 – Nov. 2) Venus, which influences love, beauty, art, and attraction, now moves through Scorpio, bringing out deep and passionate levels of love's expression. We may feel preoccupied with themes of birth, sex, death and rebirth, and transformation. Magnetism runs strong with Venus in Scorpio, and love affairs are often torrid and well hidden. Sometimes the dark side of our love and our hidden fears surface while Venus is in Scorpio; this forces us to come clean about these feelings, and to take strong measures to ensure the power of our love. Venus is in detriment in the sign of Scorpio. This may be a time to work out anxiety, fear, mourning, and emotional stress relating to love. Love with passion is an empowering thing, but it is wise to ensure the experience does not hinder the wellbeing of those who are close to you. The intensity of Scorpio love can sometimes overwhelm loved ones. Love shines best when it is mutually expressed.

October 9th Sunday

Moon void-of-course in Pisces   **PDT**   **EDT**
    Venus sextile Pluto begins (see October 13)
Birthday: John Lennon 1940

Mood Watch: The strongly waxing Pisces Moon draws many people to the heart of their beliefs. Addictive tendencies bring the risk of overindulgence. While the Pisces Moon is void-of-course throughout the entire day and night, moodiness and the desire to escape from reality will lead many people to indulge their fantasies and dreams. No one's paying attention today, and it may be particularly difficult to concentrate and stay focused through tedious jobs or meetings. This is really not a good time to attempt to keep order and clarity among people – relax, enjoy some good entertainment, and go easy on the brain.

October 10th Monday

Columbus Day, USA / Thanksgiving Day, Canada
Moon in Pisces / Aries   **PDT**   **EDT**
"Of course, America had often been discovered before Columbus, but it had always been hushed up." – Oscar Wilde (1854 – 1900)

Moon enters Aries	5:57 AM	8:57 AM
Moon conjunct Uranus	9:58 AM	12:58 PM
Moon square Pluto	4:05 PM	7:05 PM

    Venus opposite Jupiter begins (see October 14)
Birthday: Thelonious Monk 1917

Mood Watch: In the early hours of the morning, while the Moon is void-of-course in Pisces, spacey and uncertain moods keep us occupied in a dreamlike state. As the Moon enters Aries, our moods will swiftly become considerably more restless, eager, and bold. Moon conjunct Uranus in Aries brings chaotic energy to the forefront of our responses to life. People will tend to react more quickly, decisively, and expediently than usual. Later today, Moon square Pluto brings confrontational energies that often deal with matters of fate and permanent change. This is the Full Moon Eve of October. This energy is loud, harmoniously discordant, over the top, thrilling and exasperating – kind of like a Thelonious

Monk composition.

Ω

October 11th Tuesday

FULL MOON in ARIES	PDT	EDT
Moon trine Mars	9:02 AM	12:02 PM
Moon opposite Sun	7:05 PM	10:05 PM
Mercury-conjunct-Venus-non-exact begins (see November 1)		

Birthday: Eleanor Roosevelt 1884

Mood Watch: The **Full Moon in Aries** (Moon opposite Sun) inspires action as the momentum of its influences charges our spirits with an extra dose of energy. All the high pomp and hype of this time comes to a crescendo and is marked with the burning and willful force of Aries Moon activity. A warrior spirit touches us all, particularly with regard to the personal challenges in our lives. Be prepared for headstrong attitudes and potential rudeness. Avoid hastiness and impetuosity. There will also be a great deal of confidence, enthusiasm, and a pioneering spirit. This is a good time to celebrate and to enjoy the fruits of our labors. Shine on, Harvest Moon!

October 12th Wednesday

Moon in Aries / Taurus	PDT	EDT
Mercury trine Neptune	3:10 AM	6:10 AM
Moon opposite Mercury	1:35 PM	4:35 PM
Moon sextile Neptune goes v/c	3:14 PM	6:14 PM
Moon enters Taurus	6:34 PM	9:34 PM

Birthday: Aleister Crowley 1875

Mood Watch: The day begins with the fullness of the Aries Moon and it's nothing shy of spectacular and striking. The dramatic character of the Aries ram charges through the morning like a stark, shining beacon of light. After the battles of the Full Moon night, we are sure footed, and we are still here. We maintain our course with steadfast diligence. This afternoon, Moon opposite Mercury may be a busy and trying time to keep up with communications or general mental acuity. Moon sextile Neptune brings subdued moods while the Moon goes void-of-course for a few hours. Those who have been overworked will stand out, and they must have rest. Impatience, short temperedness, traffic, and delays – these are the typical signs of a void post-full Aries Moon. Tonight's Moon in Taurus will bring a grounding spirit which will be much more conducive for rest.

Mercury trine Neptune (occurring Oct. 8 – 13) Mercury in Libra trine Neptune in Aquarius brings diplomacy in speech, and it also brings intuitive and uplifting knowledge. Communicate about spiritual needs with helpful counsel and receive gifts of renewed faith in your own beliefs. Recognize that some messages are there to spiritually uplift you. Neptune is currently retrograde (June 3 – Nov. 9) as it backtracks through its final transit in Aquarius (Neptune in Aquarius: Aug. 4, 2011 – Feb. 3, 2012). It's a good time to internalize important spiritual messages, particularly positive thoughts for humanity. This is the last time in our lifetime that Mercury will be trine to Neptune in Aquarius. This aspect last occurred on June 16 when Neptune began its first baby steps in Pisces. In the long run, Neptune will be in Pisces February 3, 2012 – January 26, 2026.

October 13th Thursday

Moon in Taurus	PDT	EDT
Venus sextile Pluto	12:42 AM	3:42 AM
Mercury enters Scorpio	3:51 AM	6:51 AM
Moon trine Pluto	4:52 AM	7:52 AM
Moon opposite Venus	5:23 AM	8:23 AM
Moon conjunct Jupiter	9:24 AM	12:24 PM
Sun conjunct Saturn	2:12 PM	5:12 PM
Mercury opposite Jupiter begins (see October 17)		
Mercury sextile Pluto begins (see October 16)		

Birthday: Paul Simon 1941

Mood Watch: Stable and practical security calls to us on this waning Taurus Moon day. In order to feel balance in our life and to make adjustments in this Libra time of year, we must address money related matters and take care of practical concerns. Taurus Moon puts us in touch with our sensibilities and lets us know what we will need to outfit ourselves for the season.

Venus sextile Pluto (occurring Oct. 9 – 14) Venus is in Scorpio focusing on the need for swift, passionate, attentive, and urgent responses in love matters. Pluto is in Capricorn changing the structure of power, fate, and career advancement. This aspect is most useful for those who command an element of love and passion for their work or career, and it allows them to optimize beauty in the course of their efforts. Opportunity knocks, and here, true beauty bridges the gap between generations. It is here that love may triumph over death. Venus sextile Pluto may bring exceptional breakthroughs in relationships. Sometimes this aspect helps us to recognize the devotion of our loved ones, to see the acceptance of the difficulty and hardship that comes with their devotion. Now is a good time to recognize and acknowledge the efforts of loved ones. This aspect may allow someone to find true love by virtue of some unexpected twist of fate. This aspect last occurred on April 2.

Mercury enters Scorpio (Mercury in Scorpio: Oct. 13 – Nov. 2) Mercury in Scorpio is often a time when communications are veiled in secrecy, and talk revolves around matters of intensity and sensitivity. Passionate issues are communicated with creativity and intuition. This is also a time to be aware that a sharp tongue may easily cause a violent or challenging reaction. It is through this medium of Mercury in the sign of Scorpio that the expression of communications is seemingly fearless, obstinate, reckless, and passionate. From indecent babble to the subtle perfection of clear articulation, discussions frequently deliver a powerful punch. Not only our words but also our appearance, mannerisms and attitudes all send out the message of who we are. The mask we choose for the grand masquerade of autumn's darkening days teaches us much about ourselves.

Sun conjunct Saturn (occurring Oct. 6 – 17) This occurrence of Sun conjunct Saturn especially affects those Libra people celebrating birthdays October 6 - 17. These birthday people are being reminded to take charge of their lives more responsibly, and to recognize the importance of their limitations. This year, it may be best for these birthday Libras to incorporate a balanced lifestyle by applying routines that contribute to their sense of harmony. Maybe it's time for an overhaul, Libra – at least until certain areas of your life become more comfortable again. Saturn is urging you to connect with a sound dose of responsibility that fits your lifestyle and energy level. This may be the time to tune into your sensibilities and make some serious decisions that you've needed to make. Don't be so hard on yourself, Libra; reward yourself throughout this year with each measure of your progress – it's good for the soul. Make up for lost time, and apply some self-love and nurturing to your renewed self-discipline. Hang in there and keep up the work, birthday folks, and don't be so glum; the tedious work in which you are now immersed will bring you genuine rewards later on.

October 14th Friday

Moon in Taurus	**PDT**	**EDT**
Moon square Mars	12:54 AM	3:54 AM
Venus opposite Jupiter	4:53 PM	7:53 PM

Birthday: e e cummings 1894

Mood Watch: The Moon is in Taurus and the Sun is in Libra. Both Taurus and Libra are ruled by the planet Venus. This emphasizes the need for the security and balance of love. It also puts the emphasis on the need for pleasure, kindness, and beauty. It may be overwhelming to tap into Venus-like affections while Venus opposite Jupiter reaches its peak (see below). Taurus Moon puts us in touch with the sensibility and practicality of our moods.

Venus opposite Jupiter (occurring Oct. 10 – 16) Love and the arts (Venus) are undergoing the tests and imperative need (the opposition) for fortune and expansion (Jupiter). Venus in Scorpio brings a love for passion as well as the desire for transformation in relationships. Meanwhile, Jupiter in Taurus focuses on the need for financial security and stable growth towards prosperity. Venus opposite Jupiter brings on a significant awareness of the dynamics of attraction and wealth. Custody battles are hard fought under these circumstances. The process of overcoming personal loss requires a great deal of effort to attain the healing power of love. Money related tests and troubles in relationships are often a factor under this aspect. Venus opposite Jupiter increases awareness of the need for joy in relationships. This is the only time this aspect will occur this year.

October 15th Saturday

Moon in Taurus / Gemini	PDT	EDT
Moon square Neptune goes v/c	3:51 AM	6:51 AM
Moon enters Gemini	7:14 AM	10:14 AM
Moon sextile Uranus	10:52 AM	1:52 PM
Sun trine Neptune begins (see October 21)		

Birthday: P.G. Wodehouse 1881

Mood Watch: The waning Taurus Moon goes void-of-course early this morning and our day is likely to start out lazily and with quite a bit of stubbornness. As the Moon enters Gemini, our moods will appear more inquisitive, interactive, and mindful of details. Sun in Libra and Moon in Gemini bring an interesting time of intellectual pursuits, witty humor, and congenial interaction. This is an excellent time to strategize and socialize.

October 16th Sunday

Moon in Gemini	PDT	EDT
Mercury sextile Pluto	9:57 AM	12:57 PM
Moon sextile Mars	4:05 PM	7:05 PM
Mars sextile Saturn begins (see October 26)		

Birthday: Oscar Wilde 1854

Mood Watch: Gemini Moon with the Libra Sun is a good time to engage in teamwork, focus on research, and to make inquiries. A lot can be learned today. Why not choose some interesting people to interact with and get some helpful ideas? Everyone needs support. Give a little, inquire, and learn something! Moon sextile Mars is a positive time to take action.

Mercury sextile Pluto (occurring Oct. 13 – 17) This aspect brings an opportunity for us to get the message across to people in strong positions of power and authority. Mercury is in Scorpio, focusing discussions on matters of birth, sex, death, and transformation. Pluto in Capricorn is forcing us to acknowledge our resources and to use them wisely. Mass media may well be entranced by news concerning world superpowers and/or challenging power issues. This is an opportunistic time to reach out to those of another generation and make an attempt to communicate something vital. This aspect last occurred on February 25.

October 17th Monday

Moon in Gemini / Cancer	PDT	EDT	
Moon trine Saturn	12:15 AM	3:15 AM	
Moon trine Sun	6:36 AM	9:36 AM	
Mercury opposite Jupiter	11:55 AM	2:55 PM	
Moon trine Neptune goes v/c	3:17 PM	6:17 PM	
Moon enters Cancer	6:37 PM	9:37 PM	
Moon square Uranus	9:57 PM	12:57 AM	(Oct 18)
Venus square Mars begins (see October 26)			

Birthday: Rita Hayworth 1918

Mood Watch: The waning Gemini Moon keeps us on the up and up. Gemini Moon is always a time to assess the details of life. Later in the day, the Gemini Moon goes void-of-course for a few hours, and there may be lots of traffic, minor set-backs and general mix-ups. Complexity forces us to mull things over. As the Moon enters Cancer, intuitive moods remind us to take care of ourselves. Here, our feelings begin to surface in more affirmative ways. Change brings different feelings. Emotional responses to recent events begin to surface.

Mercury opposite Jupiter (occurring Oct. 13 – 19) Mercury in Scorpio is opposite to Jupiter in Taurus, bringing overwhelming tenacity and poignant observations about the true market value of our economic future. We may find ourselves bartering for things that cannot be sold. An economic shift brings notable financial or political awareness, and the incessant chatter which fills the airwaves has a further effect on the sharp movements occurring in the stock market. This aspect also focuses news on the opulent lifestyles of the rich and famous, as people find themselves unable to stop talking about their financial situation or their need for advancement, a raise, or an income. Wealth is highlighted, and there is considerable debate as to what wealth really represents. Most of the time wealth is an illusion, and people really don't know what they're talking about when they make assumptions about the apparent wellbeing of others. As class separation continues, it is a time of acute concern in this realm. This short-lived aspect only occurs once this year.

October 18ᵗʰ Tuesday

Moon in Cancer	**PDT**	**EDT**
Moon opposite Pluto	4:34 AM	7:34 AM
Moon sextile Jupiter	7:31 AM	10:31 AM
Moon trine Mercury	10:30 AM	1:30 PM
Moon trine Venus	5:59 PM	8:59 PM

Birthday: Chuck Berry 1926

Mood Watch: The waning Cancer Moon is a good time to apply cleansing practices, particularly emotional cleansing, and to make the home sparkle with beautiful accents and inviting specialty foods. Be careful not to indulge unduly – overeating is a common way to combat feelings of not being loved and to drown out personal troubles or family conflicts. Feed the hunger, nurture the soul.

October 19ᵗʰ Wednesday

LAST QUARTER MOON in CANCER	**PDT**	**EDT**
Moon square Saturn	10:21 AM	1:21 PM
Moon square Sun goes v/c	8:30 PM	11:30 PM

Birthday: John Lithgow 1945

Mood Watch: The **Last Quarter Moon in Cancer** (Moon square Sun) often brings emotional concerns that require an extra bit of nurturing and understanding. This is an excellent Moon to boldly examine and courageously drop emotional baggage, resentments, grudges, and any other types of emotional complications that are no longer serving a purpose. This is a good time to practice patience and to lend a listening ear. However, don't get caught up in allowing others to bend your ear if you feel like they are being manipulative or wasting your precious time. In group situations, it is wise to be patient, and to practice a kind and cool composure. Later, the void-of-course Cancer Moon is a good time to rest, as our moods tend to be withdrawn or especially hypersensitive.

October 20th Thursday

Moon in Cancer / Leo	PDT	EDT
Moon enters Leo	3:05 AM	6:05 AM
Moon trine Uranus	6:03 AM	9:03 AM
Moon square Jupiter	2:37 PM	5:37 PM

Birthday: Viggo Mortensen 1958

Mood Watch: The Moon in Leo encourages our moods in more playful and uplifting ways. This morning's Moon trine Uranus invites us to exercise our sense of freedom and wild abandon. Leo Moon moods are based on the need for affection and attention. People like to seek out their personal choice of entertainment, and often express the need to be acknowledged or noticed. Waning Leo Moon serves as a time of introspection and self-reflection. Moon square Jupiter may be a challenging time to feel generous, outgoing, or explorative.

October 21st Friday

Moon in Leo	PDT	EDT
Moon square Mercury	12:57 AM	3:57 AM
Moon square Venus	6:25 AM	9:25 AM
Moon conjunct Mars	1:11 PM	4:11 PM
Moon sextile Saturn	4:36 PM	7:36 PM
Sun trine Neptune	4:57 PM	7:57 PM
Mercury square Mars begins (see October 28)		

Birthday: Dizzy Gillespie 1917

Mood Watch: Waning Leo Moon is a good time to encourage the people around us by acknowledging them with compliments and praise for their recent accomplishments. A small compliment can go a long way to reassure people their efforts are not in vain. Credit where credit is due, but by all means, give credit! This morning, Moon square Venus may be a difficult time to share affections and interact with loved ones. This afternoon's Moon conjunct Mars will bring a very active time when the beastly side of the self kicks over into warrior-mode. Moon sextile Saturn could be a useful time to begin to wind down and get a handle on things. Leo Moon brings out our most basic instincts.

Sun trine Neptune (occurring Oct. 15 – 24) This occurrence of Sun trine Neptune particularly affects those Libra and Scorpio people celebrating birthdays October 15 – 24. These birthday folks are experiencing the favorable trine aspect of Neptune to their natal Sun. This brings gifts of spiritual encounters and awareness, as well as a calming effect on one's life. It also serves as a good time

228

(particularly for these birthday folks) to seek visions, apply prayer and meditation, and to explore spiritual avenues and beliefs that are being presented. This aspect last occurred on June 22.

October 22nd Saturday

Moon in Leo / Virgo	PDT	EDT
Moon opposite Neptune	4:40 AM	7:40 AM
Moon sextile Sun goes v/c	5:34 AM	8:34 AM
Moon enters Virgo	7:40 AM	10:40 AM
Moon trine Pluto	4:26 PM	7:26 PM
Moon trine Jupiter	5:54 PM	8:54 PM

Birthday: Timothy Leary 1920

Mood Watch: The Leo Moon goes void-of-course for a couple of hours this morning, bringing out our lazy and leisurely side. As the Moon enters Virgo, there is a distinct level of conscientious focus that may be detected in our moods. The waning Virgo Moon brings out our meticulous side, and there is a nervous quality to our demeanor. Here on the last day of Sun in Libra, the Virgo Moon reminds us of our need to be pragmatic, observant, and efficient.

SCORPIO

Key Phrase: " I CREATE " or "I DESIRE"

Fixed Water Sign

Ruling Planet: Pluto

Symbol(s): The Scorpion,

The Eagle, and The Phoenix

October 23rd through

November 22nd

October 23rd Sunday

Moon in Virgo	PDT	EDT
Moon sextile Mercury	9:48 AM	12:48 PM
Sun enters Scorpio	11:30 AM	2:30 PM
Moon sextile Venus goes v/c	1:47 PM	4:47 PM
Sun opposite Jupiter begins (see October 28)		

Birthday: Nicholas Stuart Gray 1922

Mood Watch: The waning Virgo Moon brings a spirit of communication and curiosity, and many will be analyzing their feelings. Virgo Moon is a time when we tend to deliberate, and try to put things into perspective. This afternoon, the Moon goes void-of-course for the remainder of the day and evening. This is a good time to explore the gentle qualities of Virgo; seek relaxing hobbies, apply thorough physical hygiene, enjoy healthy and nutritious foods, and spread the virtues of kindness, gentleness, altruism, subtlety, and discernment.

Sun enters Scorpio (Sun in Scorpio: Oct. 23 – Nov. 22) This time of year, like the Scorpio personality, creates an air of mystery and mysticism. This is a time when people are more likely to focus on their hidden agendas and their need to get in touch with their own passion. Scorpio focuses our attention on the most important events of life: birth, sex, death and regeneration or transformation, as this sign is ruled by the underworld god known as Pluto. Scorpio represents the powers of hidden meaning, the need for secrecy, and the deeper psychologically ensnaring struggles with the self-destructive nature of humans and beasts. The totem of the sign of Scorpio is classically the desert arachnid known as the scorpion. The scorpion sting can kill; this is the violent or criminal side of the Scorpio personality. There are other totems – the Eagle and the Phoenix. These higher aspects of the Scorpio personality relate to the eagle's ability to observe from very far away, and see a larger and more objective picture of life while noting all the details essential to life itself. The Phoenix totem represents the ability to rise above the burning rays of the sun as a transformed and enlightened being. Pushing through and surviving the perilous difficulties and dangers of life is practically a personality trait of the sign of Scorpio. The Scorpio archetype demands some respect. Scorpios are often stereotyped for having a desire to live richly and often dangerously. There is always the vast and more esoteric version, too – the way of spirit, the mystical and spiritual path, or the acknowledgment of one's own truth.

October 24th Monday

Moon in Virgo / Libra	PDT	EDT
Moon enters Libra	8:49 AM	11:49 AM
Moon opposite Uranus	11:11 AM	2:11 PM
Moon square Pluto	5:11 PM	8:11 PM
Sun sextile Pluto begins (see October 28)		

Birthday: Kevin Kline 1947

Mood Watch: There may be some grouchy morning moods with the Moon void-of-course in Virgo. By the time the Moon enters Libra, the spirit of our moods will be considerably more accommodating. Libra says: "I balance," and there is no point in waiting for the imbalances of your life to bring you down; take measures to secure a firm sense of stability. Moon opposite Uranus brings high energy and there may be some clean up required. Later, Moon square Pluto may test our stamina and strength. We are reminded of the necessity to be prepared for the change in weather and the transformation process of autumn.

October 25th Tuesday

Moon in Libra

	PDT	EDT
Moon sextile Mars	6:50 PM	9:50 PM
Moon conjunct Saturn	7:03 PM	10:03 PM

Birthday: Pablo Picasso 1881

♏

Mood Watch: Waning Libra Moon focuses our moods on the need for peace and forgiveness. Relationships that need mending at this time require structure and some ground rules in order to generate trust. This is the time to banish those moods and emotions that prevent us from harmonizing and generating good feelings with others. This evening's Moon sextile Mars brings positive vitality to our moods. Moon conjunct Saturn brings a good time to review our accomplishments and to empower our goals and aspirations.

October 26th Wednesday

NEW MOON in SCORPIO – *Hecate's Moon*

Moon in Libra / Scorpio

	PDT	EDT
Mars sextile Saturn	2:37 AM	5:37 AM
Moon trine Neptune goes v/c	5:18 AM	8:18 AM
Moon enters Scorpio	8:08 AM	11:08 AM
Moon conjunct Sun	12:55 PM	3:55 PM
Venus square Mars	3:23 PM	6:23 PM
Moon sextile Pluto	4:28 PM	7:28 PM
Moon opposite Jupiter	4:53 PM	7:53 PM
Venus square Neptune begins (see October 31)		

Birthday: Hillary Rodham Clinton 1947

Mood Watch: For a few hours in early morning, the darkly waning void-of-course Libra Moon brings confusion and indecision. It isn't long before the **New Moon in Scorpio** (Moon conjunct Sun) reaches its regenerative point – and the sign of Scorpio just happens to represent the phenomenon of regenerative force and transformation. The New Moon in Scorpio focuses on a rebirthing process for our emotional body, and this is the time when we are sure to address the proverbial skeletons in our emotional closet. New Moon in Scorpio encourages us to regenerate our hopes while transforming our fears into a courageous and renewed outlook for ourselves. This is the time to take bold steps to defeat undesirable emotional patterns and fear mechanisms. New Scorpio Moon casts new light on our ability to overcome pain and suffering.

Hecate's Moon: Hecate is the Wiccan goddess of the underworld who leads us through death towards a cycle of rebirth. She guides the lost souls to their final destiny, and can be called on at this time to guide those who have passed on, especially those who have met their end in a demeaning and challenged way, such as violent death or suicide. Hecate cures the ills that surround death.

Mars sextile Saturn (occurring October 16 – 30) Mars in Leo sextile Saturn in Libra is an active time for establishing personal strengths in the realm of careers, particularly careers that emphasize or influence law and justice. During this aspect, actions create opportunities, provided there is an application of discipline and timing. Those who are affected by this aspect may feel noticed now. Diligently practice your favorite sport, especially those physical activities that demand precision and perfect timing. Movement and the application of energy (Mars), plus responsibility and awareness of limitation (Saturn) allow the timely qualities of completion and new beginnings to occur. Those who are weak may find greater strength through relationships, particularly while Saturn is in Libra. This would be the time to end a bad habit or to work to accomplish a goal. This is the only time this aspect will occur this year.

Venus square Mars (occurring Oct. 17 – 30) Venus in Scorpio is square to Mars in Leo. Beware of the jealousy and the fierce competition that these planets in these signs will tend to create. Venus square Mars creates tension and obstacles between the forces of love and the forces of defense. The archetypal images of Venus and Mars are largely that of feminine and masculine counterparts, and this aspect may bring stress between people in love relationships. The pain of separation or the sorrow of unrequited love may be a symptom of this time, as the rocky boat of romance is due to have some notable ups and downs. On the other hand, the difficulties of these tests may strengthen the power of love and, although it is sometimes very difficult to endure love related conflicts, it is also a necessary process to ensure the authenticity of our love experience.

October 27th Thursday

Moon in Scorpio	PDT	EDT	
Moon conjunct Mercury	7:08 PM	10:08 PM	
Moon square Mars	7:56 PM	10:56 PM	
Moon conjunct Venus	9:23 PM	12:23 AM	(Oct 28)
Mars opposite Neptune begins (see November 7)			
Mercury square Neptune begins (see November 1)			

Birthday: Theodore Roosevelt 1858

Mood Watch: The Moon is still dark, still new, although now waxing in Scorpio. This is a time for regeneration and for many, a place to come to new terms with regard to transformation. There is an initiation process of the soul taking place for those who are open to rebirth. Mystery and intrigue ring strongly throughout the day. New Moon in Scorpio is a splendid time to drop autumn seeds expected to rise next spring. There are also seeds of dreams and seeds of the heart. This could be the day to accomplish something new – something that feels right. Meanwhile, the fruition of the harvest is still with us; the Great Pumpkin has outgrown all the other pumpkins!

October 28th Friday

Moon in Scorpio / Sagittarius	PDT	EDT
Moon square Neptune goes v/c	4:48 AM	7:48 AM
Moon enters Sagittarius	7:45 AM	10:45 AM
Mercury square Mars	8:07 AM	11:07 AM

Jupiter trine Pluto	9:29 AM	12:29 PM
Moon trine Uranus	9:57 AM	12:57 PM
Sun opposite Jupiter	6:41 PM	9:41 PM
Sun sextile Pluto	8:10 PM	11:10 PM

♏

Birthday: Bill Gates 1955

Mood Watch: The morning's void-of-course Scorpio Moon is a good time to be vigilant, awake, and cautious. Those who are not on the ball are likely to have the ball snatched away. Soon enough, the Moon enters Sagittarius and our moods are likely to be positive and outgoing throughout the remainder of the day. As autumn continues, the Sagittarius Moon keeps our sights open to all the visionary possibilities. This may seem trite, but it isn't; in order to reap the rewards of something worthwhile, we must first conceive of the possibilities.

Mercury square Mars (Oct. 21 – 31) Mercury in Scorpio is reaching an exact square to Mars in Leo. Those who are undergoing conflict with others may find that such activities as secrecy, verbal abuse and deceptive chatter will lead to certain destruction and complex kinds of discord. Refrain from making risky comments, and be careful not to misinterpret information as being hostile or personal. This is not a good time to lose one's temper. Be especially careful to watch what you say, preferably thinking before you speak; words can be easily taken the wrong way. This aspect stimulates arguments and mental blocks concerning people's actions, and it may lead to verbal abuse and destruction Remember, during this complex time of Mercury square Mars, not to shoot the messenger. This aspect will repeat again on December 4 and December 31.

Jupiter trine Pluto (occurring June 7 – Nov. 16) For the second time since July 7, this long winded aspect is reaching a second peak during this long occurrence period. For a recap on the story of how Jupiter in Taurus trine Pluto in Capricorn affects us, *see July 7*, when it last reached a peak.

Sun opposite Jupiter (occurring Oct. 23 – 31) Libra birthday people, celebrating birthdays from October 23 – 31, are experiencing the opposition of Jupiter to their natal Sun. This brings an acute awareness of the shifts in personal economic conditions, for better or worse. There is a strong personal acknowledgment, or perhaps an obsession, at work to obtain a sense of wealth, joy, and wellbeing. Use your best techniques, birthday folks, to persevere through financial trials. Governing your expenditures with wisdom instead of impetuosity will assuredly bring you around to the place you know you need to be. This aspect only occurs once this year.

Sun sextile Pluto (occurring Oct. 24 – 30) The Sun in Scorpio sextile Pluto in Capricorn brings opportunities that appear both vast and demanding to Scorpio born people who are celebrating birthdays October 24 – 30. These birthday people are experiencing the sextile aspect of their natal sun to Pluto, giving them opportunities to take charge, to step into positions of power, and to accept and embrace permanent change in their lives. These are powerful transformations which provide opportunities to embody what has been learned from the personal trials of the past. Go thee forth and conquer, master Scorpions! Persist with diligence to resolve the conflicts of your life with self-respect and assurance. Your time to triumph is always available when your will to achieve is balanced by knowledge and hard work. This holds true for all signs of the zodiac. This aspect last occurred on February 25, affecting some of the Pisceans experiencing birthdays around that time.

October 29th Saturday

Moon in Sagittarius

	PDT	EDT	
Moon sextile Saturn	8:17 PM	11:17 PM	
Moon trine Mars	11:03 PM	2:03 AM	(Oct 30)
Venus trine Uranus begins (see November 3)			
Saturn-trine-Neptune-non-exact begins (see below)			

Birthday: Kate Jackson 1948

Mood Watch: Sagittarius Moon brings optimism and resilience to the challenges of our moods, and it also invites us to explore various philosophical perspectives. Sun in Scorpio and Moon in Sagittarius focus our energies on the necessity to work under challenging conditions, and to overcome darkness with creativity and vision. The darkening days of autumn require resolute strength and warmth of spirit. The Sagittarius Moon newly waxes, bringing hope, an expanding outlook, and encouragement to move forward. This is a good time to travel or plan a trip.

Saturn-trine-Neptune-non-exact begins (occurrence range: Oct. 29, 2011 – March 13, 2012) Today begins the earliest effects of a trine between Saturn and Neptune. The closest point at which this aspect reaches a peak will be on January 21, 2012. This little non-exact trine dance between Saturn and Neptune kicks off a favorable commitment on the part of many people to embrace their spiritual needs. Saturn represents commitment, control, the limits we place upon ourselves and other people, and the discipline required to get our specific objectives and goals accomplished. Neptune represents our beliefs, our spiritual path, the places where there is least resistance for us, and it also represents the arts – the Muse that exists within each of us. The trine aspect is the peace maker, particularly while Saturn is in Libra, the sign of the peace maker. This is a great time to get in touch with our spiritual needs and to manifest them on the physical plane. Build your temple of light, find your sanctuary, get in touch with your beliefs and learn how to guard them. Saturn is the guard, or sentinel, at the temple door. Let no man enter who would sabotage your beliefs! How do we make this possible? It occurs through our commitment to find our true selves, to realize our truth, and to protect that truth with a commitment to what we believe. This is a favorable aspect that will assist us to make this happen. This is also a time when drug addiction centers will begin to make sweeping progress, as more and more people will find it within themselves to address their compulsive behavior and commit to the effort of becoming clean. This trine aspect is currently occurring in the air signs, as Saturn in Libra is trine to Neptune in Aquarius. It ensures that our first attempts

234

to experience and approach this long winded aspect are done intelligently. This is the time to stand up for what you believe, and to assist others in your relationships to do the same. ♏

October 30ᵗʰ Sunday

Moon in Sagittarius / Capricorn	PDT	EDT	
Moon sextile Neptune goes v/c	6:30 AM	9:30 AM	
Moon enters Capricorn	9:38 AM	12:38 PM	
Moon square Uranus	11:52 AM	2:52 PM	
Moon trine Jupiter	6:19 PM	9:19 PM	
Moon conjunct Pluto	6:58 PM	9:58 PM	
Moon sextile Sun	10:33 PM	1:33 AM	(Oct 31)
Mercury trine Uranus begins (see November 3)			

Birthday: Ezra Pound 1885

Mood Watch: The day may seem to start off rather spacey with the void-of-course Moon in Sagittarius. As the Moon enters Capricorn, our moods tend to be more practical, grounded, and on the level. Moon square Uranus may bring chaotic conflict. This evening's Moon trine Jupiter inspires the need to splurge and have fun. Later, Moon conjunct Pluto suggests a grueling level of tolerance may be required. Capricorn Moon doesn't give us much time to mull over our feelings.

October 31ˢᵗ Monday

All Hallows (Halloween) / Samhain / Witches' New Year

Moon in Capricorn	PDT	EDT
Venus square Neptune	2:19 PM	5:19 PM

Birthday: Dan Rather 1931

Mood Watch: The waxing Capricorn Moon brings a refined sense of duty to the tradition of Halloween. The drive of the mountain goat is determined, loyal, and stoic. However, there are better points to consider. Capricorn Moon is generally a serious time, but under the circumstances, the serious minded qualities of this lunar expression can be fascinating, astounding to behold, and quite amusing. Capricorn's humor is subtle and simple, but hilarious once you get the joke. If you stop to observe carefully, there is a distinguished, profound, and entertaining quality to our moods. Success brings long lasting happiness.

Venus square Neptune (occurring Oct. 26 – Nov. 3) This may be a difficult – or extra busy – time to be drawn to or to meditate on spiritual matters or activities. Love matters could be rocky due to a conflict of beliefs. Venus is in Scorpio, where the art of attraction often occurs on the emotional plane, while the retrograde Neptune is in Aquarius, formulating a new spiritual outlook for humankind, and giving us much to think about. When these two planets are in conflict, it is a time when women are being sent mixed messages about how to live up to a higher standard of the self. This aspect last occurred on June 10 and January 4.

November 1st Tuesday

All Saints Day / Day of the Dead

Moon in Capricorn / Aquarius	PDT	EDT	
Moon square Saturn	1:14 AM	4:14 AM	
Mercury square Neptune	1:37 AM	4:37 AM	
Moon sextile Mercury	12:55 PM	3:55 PM	
Moon sextile Venus goes v/c	1:59 PM	4:59 PM	
Moon enters Aquarius	3:07 PM	6:07 PM	
Moon sextile Uranus	5:24 PM	8:24 PM	
Moon square Jupiter	11:53 PM	2:53 AM	(Nov 2)
Mercury-conjunct-Venus-non-exact (see below)			

Birthday: Larry Flynt 1942

Mood Watch: The *Day of the Dead* is a superb time to call upon the spirits of our ancestors, and the wisdom of those folks who have passed before us. Honor and celebrate their wisdom today, and it will assist you to make wise decisions. Today will feel as if many of us are on a roll. Great feats of accomplishment have been occurring while the Moon has been waxing in Capricorn these past couple of days. There's no harm in continuing to take big strides while many of us are busily tending to our responsibilities and our goals in life. The waxing Capricorn Moon is a handy time to do this, and even though some folks may feel tired at this stage of the season, the sense of making some headway feels good to most of us. Capricorn's old adage, "I use," is not always helpful to the sensitive folks among us. It's a use-and-be-used world sometimes. If we were able to be entirely independent, we wouldn't have Capricorns around. There is nothing wrong with creating structure and stability that will benefit others as well as yourself. Later today, the Aquarius Moon takes the adage one step further: "I know." With knowledge, we can do anything – we can even break down the structure of faulty legislation, false hopes, and the pretentious abuses of misuse. Every sign of the zodiac creates a balance in its own way.

Mercury square Neptune (occurring Oct. 27 – Nov. 3) Mercury in Scorpio is square to Neptune in Aquarius. Difficult subjects may be particularly tough to relay, especially when there are so many unknown factors involved. This aspect often brings a struggle to communicate with regard to the spirit world and human spirituality. Efforts to explain our beliefs may be especially challenging. Neptune is in Aquarius for the last stretch, until February 3, 2012, and it's stirring up issues around human divinity and humanity's beliefs in this confusing and changing period of the dawning age. While Mercury in Scorpio is squaring Neptune, dramatic types of thought will be generated, particularly with respect to issues that concern divine experience (birth, sex, death); relaying this information may seem all the more difficult with this aspect. Anticipate the possibility of religion related arguments and disputes. Deep subjects must not be treated lightly while Mercury squares Neptune. This aspect last occurred on June 3. This aspect will begin to reoccur from December 11 – 17, in what is called a non-exact aspect; see December 15, Mercury-square-Neptune-non-exact.

236

Mercury-conjunct-Venus-non-exact (occurring Oct. 11 – Nov. 19) Mercury and Venus have come very close to a near exact conjunction in Scorpio. In fact, it is extremely difficult to pinpoint just where this near conjunction comes closest, as there is an ongoing one degree orbital conjunction which began around October 25 and extends throughout this week. This means that Mercury and Venus are in a neck and neck race to reach an *exact* conjunction that never occurs. This ongoing (near) conjunction happens at the tail end of Scorpio and extends into Sagittarius. Does love's sting come repeatedly through words and gestures? Perhaps some kind of melodrama may be occurring around efforts to obtain the object of one's desire, particularly through negotiations. Topsy-turvy communications may lead to some travel efforts as this conjunction dance goes from Scorpio to Sagittarius. There may be close encounters with words of affection, as the crucial element of the message may be missing the mark somehow. There's no telling just exactly how this trickster dance with love will manifest, particularly with no exact interlude of a spot-on conjunction in sight. Whatever the reason for your love spats, it is best not to attach too much significance to the things that are, or are not, said. Watch the actions, not the words, and the law of attraction will work itself out. This conjunction of Mercury and Venus has already reached three exact peaks this year, on May 9, May 16, and August 16.

November 2ⁿᵈ Wednesday
FIRST QUARTER MOON in AQUARIUS

	PDT	EDT
Venus enters Sagittarius	1:51 AM	4:51 AM
Moon square Sun	9:38 AM	12:38 PM
Mercury enters Sagittarius	9:54 AM	12:54 PM

Birthday: k.d. lang 1961

Mood Watch: We have now reached the **First Quarter Moon in Aquarius** (Moon square Sun). Waxing Aquarius Moon puts the spotlight on eccentric and unusual breakthroughs of humankind. Controversial subjects are strongly at work. At this time, we are often aware of great shifts of energy and change in consciousness. The Aquarius Moon will assist our moods to meet and formally address humanity's newest challenges. Whenever we take strides to improve our world, the ramifications of our actions – and our experiments – are not always fully realized, but now we're taking broader measures to consider the impact our actions have on the environment. Aquarius Moon directs our attention to the vitally important focuses of humanity.

Venus enters Sagittarius (Venus in Sagittarius: Nov. 2 – 26) What goes around, comes around, and for the second time this year, Venus enters Sagittarius. This month Venus will remain in Sagittarius until the 26ᵗʰ. For a recap of the story on how Venus in Sagittarius works, *see January 7*, when Venus began this circle of love.

Mercury enters Sagittarius (Mercury in Sagittarius: Nov. 2, 2011 – Jan. 7, 2012) Mercury, the planet of communication, information, and news is traveling through Sagittarius. New perspectives are bound to come up. News is always more philosophical and visionary when Mercury is in this sign. Word travels fast and further than expected. Sagittarius is the challenging "detrimental" place for Mercury, and this is a time when Mercury's greatest weapon – words – are best communicated with carefully considered diplomacy. The longer a message is passed on, the more misconstrued it can become from its original source. Be sure to go straight to the source if you want to know the truth about something. People will be increasingly curious to know what is happening in the world, and to be more aware of global perspectives. Mercury in Sagittarius offers an opportunity to share your vision of a better world with others, and also brings adventure to the world of communications. Mercury will go retrograde (Nov. 23 – Dec. 13) causing the planet of communications to remain in Sagittarius for an extended period of time. For more information on Mercury retrograde in Sagittarius, see the section in the introduction about *Mercury retrograde periods*.

November 3rd Thursday

Moon in Aquarius	PDT	EDT
Venus trine Uranus	12:54 AM	3:54 AM
Mercury trine Uranus	6:57 AM	9:57 AM
Moon trine Saturn	10:05 AM	1:05 PM
Moon opposite Mars	5:05 PM	8:05 PM
Moon conjunct Neptune goes v/c	8:40 PM	11:40 PM

Birthday: Benvenuto Cellini 1500

Mood Watch: The waxing Aquarius Moon inspires, fortifies, and uplifts our knowledge, and there is usually a greater emphasis on the necessity for humanitarianism. Progressive, open minded, and truthful attitudes will keep us inspired as the Moon waxes in Aquarius.

Venus trine Uranus (occurring Oct. 29 – Nov. 5) Venus in Sagittarius is trine Uranus in Aries. Adventurous and versatile kinds of love and attraction (Venus in Sagittarius) will bring positive breakthroughs (the trine aspect) through radical self-expression (Uranus in Aries). This is a time of freedom fighters and rebel love, and youth is easily attracted to the spirit of rebellion. Dangerous love and taking chances become common occurrences. This aspect creates an attraction to the unusual, yet it allows a harmony to exist in love related matters while chaotic occurrences are taking place. Love at first sight is explosive at this time, but not necessarily long lasting. This aspect last occurred on January 4 and July 31.

Mercury trine Uranus (occurring Oct. 30 – Nov. 5) Mercury in Sagittarius is trine to Uranus in Aries. This combination stirs up an adventurous, resilient, and philosophical thought process, one that is radically enterprising. This is a good time to record your thoughts and delight in brilliant thinking and information. Much of this brilliant thinking may seem like propaganda or information with a radical twist. Catch phrases, radical concept statements and ideas are often born under this aspect. Sensationalism, or matters of censorship, may be emphasized. Mercury in Sagittarius dredges up topics such as global awareness, the visionary process of seeing the future, athletic achievements, and the exploration of new concepts. Uranus is in Aries, creating radical change in areas of new enterprise, mechanical engineering, competitive sports, and fire fighting techniques. This aspect last occurred on July 4, and it will also come to a non-exact position on December 14.

November 4th Friday

Election Day, USA

Moon in Aquarius / Pisces	PDT	EDT
Moon enters Pisces	12:17 AM	3:17 AM
Moon square Mercury	5:01 AM	8:01 AM
Moon square Venus	5:32 AM	8:32 AM
Moon sextile Jupiter	8:55 AM	11:55 AM
Moon sextile Pluto	11:05 AM	2:05 PM

Birthday: Will Rogers 1879

Mood Watch: Early morning may start off with some difficulty as the Moon squares to Mercury and Venus; we must be careful how we communicate with loved ones, or we may find that we will have to let go of something that was treasured. However, Moon sextile Jupiter gives us the incentive to add a jovial spirit to the morning moods. Lastly, Moon sextile Pluto opens up our capacity to accept permanent changes. Pisces Moon gets us into the imaginative joys and pleasures of the arts. A waxing Pisces Moon arouses our intuition, dreams, and beliefs. It may be best to bundle up as Sun in Scorpio and Moon in Pisces invite deeply penetrating, wet weather, and patterns of wicked weather may sweep the country.

November 5th Saturday

Moon in Pisces	PDT	EDT
Moon trine Sun goes v/c	1:04 AM	4:04 AM

Birthday: Vivien Leigh 1913

Mood Watch: A long void-of-course Pisces Moon day brings spacey and easily distracted moods. The symptoms of this void Moon are generally uncertainty, laziness, and a tendency to escape from reality in whatever way presents itself. Today our moods drift into and out of a series of flowing and changing images and impressions. As the Moon travels through Pisces, a mystical and timeless element of perception captivates our moods. Bubbly, artistic, enchanting, and dreamy moments allow us to access some hidden sanctuary where the soulful or prayerful part of ourselves is revealed.

Daylight Saving Time ends tomorrow. Don't forget to turn all clocks and timepieces back one hour this evening before hitting the sack. Tomorrow we begin Standard Time; at 2:00 a.m. on November 6th Daylight Saving Time ends coast to coast in North America.

November 6ᵗʰ Sunday

DAYLIGHT SAVING TIME ENDS

Turn clocks back one hour at 2:00 a.m.

Moon in Pisces / Aries	PST	EST	
Moon enters Aries	11:02 AM	2:02 PM	
Moon conjunct Uranus	1:14 PM	4:14 PM	
Moon square Pluto	10:15 PM	1:15 AM	(Nov. 7)
Moon trine Mercury	11:15 PM	2:15 AM	(Nov. 7)
Moon trine Venus	11:25 PM	2:25 AM	(Nov. 7)

Birthday: Maria Shriver 1955

Mood Watch: A spacey quality of mood continues as the void-of-course Pisces Moon carries on throughout morning. It is no surprise that many folks will be easily fooled by the recent change of Daylight to Standard North American time. As the Moon enters Aries, our moods appear much more determined. A brisk new mood is in the air, as the waxing Moon in Aries invites us to take charge and get in tune with leadership and self-reliance.

November 7ᵗʰ Monday

Moon in Aries	PST	EST
Mars opposite Neptune	4:44 AM	7:44 AM
Mars trine Jupiter begins (see November 16)		

Birthday: Joni Mitchell 1943

Mood Watch: Aries Moon brings a headstrong and rambunctious expression of moods. Nonetheless, a waxing Aries Moon is a great way to start off the work week. Aries says: "I am," and a much more self-assertive, self-motivated, and self-involved phase of moods can be expected. Once in awhile, certain individuals need to assert their independence. They need to know that they can do things on their own. Although we often depend on each other, there are times when we must learn how to rely solely on ourselves. The waxing Aries Moon time is a prime candidate for those, once in awhile, realizations.

Mars opposite Neptune (occurring Oct. 27 – Nov. 13) Individual integrity (Mars in Leo) is challenged by or opposed to (opposite) humanity's belief in science (Neptune in Aquarius). Mars activates and stirs up action, while Neptune calms and dissolves all concern. When in opposition these two planets create an acute awareness of our spiritual beliefs and the manner in which those beliefs are acted upon and absorbed. For some, this aspect can create a spiritual breakthrough, while for others, it may be that events are forging a strong spiritual awareness challenging personal beliefs. Sometimes we lash out at the world for draining so much of our energy. Perhaps this is a healthy sign that we need to restructure our priorities, to take action towards finding a peaceful sanctuary where we can recharge our batteries. With Mars in Leo and Neptune in Aquarius, actions which relate to the self and the family are sometimes at odds with outside beliefs or beliefs imposed by society. Establishing a more healthy attitude towards defending the self and one's own beliefs is the best remedy for the opposing outbursts that affect our spiritual wellbeing. This is the only time this aspect will occur this year.

November 8th Tuesday

Moon in Aries / Taurus	PST	EST	
Moon opposite Saturn	10:09 AM	1:09 PM	
Moon sextile Neptune	7:58 PM	10:58 PM	
Moon opposite Venus	9:01 PM	12:01 AM	(Nov 9)
Moon trine Mars goes v/c	9:45 PM	12:45 AM	(Nov 9)
Moon enters Taurus	11:45 PM	2:45 AM	(Nov 9)

Birthday: Bonnie Raitt 1949

Mood Watch: Sun in Scorpio and Moon in Aries bring an enterprising spirit that is courageous and unstoppable. Many of the more impatient people among us are no longer putting up with inadequacy, and are now taking matters into their own hands. A competitive, confident, and enterprising level of productivity picks up our moods. Determined attitudes keep the energy levels up, as well as the fact that this is the Full Moon Eve, and energy is expected to run exorbitantly strongly. The Aries Moon gives us the wherewithal to do what we must do.

November 9th Wednesday

FULL MOON in TAURUS	PST	EST
Moon conjunct Jupiter	7:19 AM	10:19 AM
Moon opposite Sun	9:00 AM	12:00 PM
Neptune goes direct	10:53 AM	1:53 PM
Moon trine Pluto	11:07 AM	2:07 PM

Birthday: Carl Sagan 1934

Mood Watch: The **Full Moon in Taurus** (Moon opposite Sun) invites us to celebrate the beauty and the perfection of the valuable elements of the earth, and brings appreciation for the beauty in nature. The Moon is exalted in Taurus, bringing us rich, sensual, and vibrant expressions of mood. The Taurus totem is the bull, and in its splendor, the bull is a marvelous and classically stubborn

---

---

creature of habit. This Full Moon reminds us to take the time to enjoy and create beauty around us, and to indulge a little bit in some luxurious pleasures or leisure time. For those who realize the importance of celebrating planet Earth, now is the time to reflect on what you do have and how it is that these physical gifts of Earth can be enjoyed. Ask Mother Moon to bring you what you need and she will teach you how to sow for the harvest of your desire.

Neptune goes direct (Neptune direct: Nov. 9, 2011 – June 8, 2012) Neptune resumes a direct-moving course after five months (since June 3) of being retrograde. This will regenerate our spiritual and intuitive work and facilitate our development. Neptune is in Aquarius, influencing the flow of the Aquarian age and the evolutionary processes of belief systems. Neptune is the master of illusion, while Aquarius demands scientific proof. As Neptune proceeds further into the final degrees of Aquarius, we will learn to achieve a higher and freer sense of spiritual awareness – a sense that something divine is occurring, even though it cannot be explained in mortal terms. Since the late 20th century, Neptune has been in Aquarius filling our belief systems with a great deal of knowledge. On April 4th Neptune made its debut in its home base in Pisces, where our spiritual experience is infused with adaptable and inspiring believability. Neptune's calming and forgiving nature will help us to let go of malicious and non-productive thoughts, and will melt away cold-heartedness. A good meditation, when sincerely applied, helps to discharge our emotional baggage. Frequently invoke the spiritually uplifting meditations that work for you. This practice will lead you to a positive and regenerative place in your own spiritual evolution. Neptune direct allows us to move freely forward, using divine wisdom and our spiritual aspirations as guides.

November 10th Thursday

Moon in Taurus

	PST	EST
Mars enters Virgo	8:15 PM	11:15 PM
Mars trine Pluto begins (see November 23)		

Birthday: Theophrastus Paracelsus 1493

Mood Watch: The intensity of yesterday's Full Moon in Taurus is still with us. Sun in Scorpio and Moon in Taurus weigh out the polarity of the things that matter, and the things that matter *most*. Wherever there is closure in some process of life, there are the things that go and the things that remain. In those areas of our lives that have undergone great permanent change, the Full Taurus Moon puts us in touch with what's really important to us, especially with regard to worldly possessions. There comes a time when we must let go of things; ultimately, all things must go. This Taurus Moon brings to our hearts an appreciation for what remains. Post-full Taurus Moon brings sentimental moods.

Mars enters Virgo (Mars in Virgo: Nov. 10, 2011 – July 3, 2012) Mars, "the god of war," enters the cautious and skeptical realm of Virgo. Today through July 3, 2012, Mars in Virgo creates heat, energy, and activity in the lives of Virgos. Mars in Virgo, in general, causes the heat of our activities to be focused on such

Virgo-like tasks as communications, accounting, and nitpicking perfection. Resourcefulness and cleverness are emphasized. Thoughtfulness and care are applied to war strategies. Mars in Virgo may also be a time when many folks are prone to argue, so pick your arguments carefully. It is interesting to note that Barack Obama (whose Sun is in Leo) has Mars in Virgo (22 degrees) in his birth chart. He will undergo the second "Mars return" of this presidential term from December 17, 2011 – February 28, 2012. It makes sense that in these interesting times the President would undergo a prolonged Mars return, since Mars will be in Virgo for a longer than usual period due to its retrograde cycle in this sign. Mars will go direct on April 13, 2012, and the final round of his Mars return will occur in full from June 3 – 23, 2012. President Obama's last Mars return occurred from July 7 – 23, 2010, one of the most trying astrological months in decades. It is during this time that the President oversaw the tragic oil spill in the gulf, as well as signing a bill that, in his words, "represents the most sweeping reforms of Wall Street since the Great Depression." Some people claimed his big battle was corporate money influencing the elections. The Mars return brings big battles, and also great strength. Mr. Obama's Mars in Virgo indicates that he is more inclined to meticulously analyze and discuss war related scenarios before acting on them. It also means that he will cleverly strategize his course of actions in a well informed manner. Note: Mars will be retrograde in this cycle of Virgo from January 23, 2012 (23 degrees Virgo), through April 13, 2012 (3degrees Virgo).

November 11th Friday

Veteran's Day, USA / Remembrance Day, Canada

Moon in Taurus / Gemini	PST	EST
Moon square Neptune goes v/c	8:26 AM	11:26 AM
Moon enters Gemini	12:09 PM	3:09 PM
Moon square Mars	12:51 PM	3:51 PM
Moon sextile Uranus	2:06 PM	5:06 PM

Birthday: Kurt Vonnegut 1922

"I don't believe in astrology, I use it because it works"
– Antero Alli (born Nov. 11, 1952)

Mood Watch: Happy 11/11/11! The waning Taurus Moon goes void-of-course this morning, emphasizing such things as sentimentality and stubbornness, and there could be some bullish attitudes at times. Morning events are likely to get off to a slow start, and there may be some inconveniences along the way. As the Moon enters Gemini, the energy of the day picks up, although Moon square Mars could be a time of conflicting energies; people need to get some things off their chests. As the day progresses, there is the potential for some positive, liberating breakthroughs with Moon sextile Uranus. Gemini Moon keeps our minds active.

November 12ᵗʰ Saturday

Moon in Gemini	**PST**	**EST**
Moon opposite Mercury	1:21 PM	4:21 PM

Birthday: Neil Young 1945

Mood Watch: The waning Gemini Moon keeps our minds on the go. Thinking matters through and exploring a wide range of details gives adaptability and flexibility to our outlook. Communicating, investigating, and examining our choices will help us to think through our situations. Today's only lunar aspect, Moon opposite Mercury, saturates our minds with an overload of information and communication. Be careful not to lose the point in the midst of the hubbub. This would be a good time to keep various focuses – and topics of interest – as simple and to-the-point as possible.

November 13ᵗʰ Sunday

Moon in Gemini / Cancer	**PST**	**EST**	
Moon trine Saturn	11:22 AM	2:22 PM	
Moon trine Neptune goes v/c	7:42 PM	10:42 PM	
Moon enters Cancer	11:18 PM	2:18 AM	(Nov 14)

Birthday: Whoopie Goldberg 1955

Mood Watch: Throughout the day, the waning Gemini Moon keeps us busy making connections and weighing out the pros and cons of our decisions. This is a good time for writing, networking, secretarial organization, and communications. The nature of the Gemini Moon keeps us curious and inquisitive, as well as oriented towards collecting details and sharing ideas. Tonight's void-of-course Gemini Moon brings a time of mindless chatter, or perhaps, just a simple lack of concentration.

November 14ᵗʰ Monday

Moon in Cancer	**PST**	**EST**
Moon square Uranus	1:05 AM	4:05 AM
Moon sextile Mars	2:27 AM	5:27 AM
Moon sextile Jupiter	5:22 AM	8:22 AM
Moon opposite Pluto	10:27 AM	1:27 PM
Sun square Neptune begins (see November 20)		

Birthday: Claude Monet 1840

Mood Watch: Sun in Scorpio with Moon in Cancer is generally a very elusive, watery, emotional, and instinctual time. An emotional emphasis seems to jump out of every form of interaction, even the casual kinds. Mother Moon is at home in Cancer, and many folks associate the home with mother. The archetypical mother focuses on nourishment, contentment, comfort, and safety. Where these are not, the motherly instinct tends to gnaw at the subconscious part of the soul. It beckons us to show care and compassion.

November 15th Tuesday   ♏

Moon in Cancer   PST   EST
   Moon opposite Neptune   2:33 PM   5:33 PM
   Moon trine Sun   8:03 PM   11:03 PM
   Moon square Saturn goes v/c   9:22 PM   12:22 AM   (Nov 16)
Birthday: Georgia O'Keeffe 1887

Mood Watch: If there is ever a symbol to describe the moods of Sun in Scorpio with the Moon in Cancer, it would have to be the symbol of the mother pelican who feeds the flesh from her own breast to her hungry offspring. Like the mother pelican, in times of famine we are prone to sacrifice the core of our being to the children of our hopes and dreams. We are protective of the things we love, and defensive whenever we sense danger. It is okay to be devoted to loved ones and the like, as long as we place a reasonable limit on what we can give. It is pointless to be self-sacrificing to the point of irreversible self-destruction. We must remember to give of ourselves in rational increments. Waning Cancer Moon is a good time to let go, to trust that all we can give will be enough. An important step to self-preservation is to abolish worry and fear.

November 16th Wednesday

Moon in Cancer / Leo   PST   EST
   Moon enters Leo   8:17 AM   11:17 AM
   Moon trine Uranus   9:54 AM   12:54 PM
   Moon square Jupiter   1:33 PM   4:33 PM
   Mars trine Jupiter   2:07 PM   5:07 PM
Birthday: Diana Krall 1964

Mood Watch: In the early hours of the morning, the void-of-course Cancer Moon brings moodiness and an emotional start to the day. As the Moon enters Leo, it's a good time to connect with personal needs, family, and friends. Moon trine Uranus helps us to break down unnecessary barriers that impede on our sense of freedom. Later today, Moon square Jupiter may be a time when we are prone to cut corners and grapple over the use of our limited resources. Positive affirmations instill confidence. Leo Moon brightens our hearts in the darkening days of autumn.

Mars trine Jupiter (occurring Nov. 7 – 21) Mars is in Virgo activating a strong focus on such essential activities as communications, the analysis process, and resourcefulness. Jupiter is in Taurus, expanding our sense of growth through the creation of practical beauty and comforts, through the arts, and through sound financial investments and growth in banking which allows us to tap into our expansive potential. This is the most auspicious time to take action to develop and learn extraordinary types of skills. This aspect brings an all-around emphasis on the power of success. Act on opportunities as they arise, and set visions and dreams into a feasible plan that holds the potential for favorable actions to occur. Mars activates and stirs action in this direction, while Jupiter represents not only economy and advancement, but our sense of philosophic and visionary awareness as well. For some people this aspect brings gifts of inheritance; for most of us it brings opportunities for growth. Mars trine Jupiter allows us to activate a stronger, more intelligent grasp of our domain, and gives many folks the extra energy and spark to boost their sense of achievement. This most favorable aspect only occurs once this year, so it will be best to take advantage while the action is potent.

November 17th Thursday

Moon in Leo	PST	EST
Moon trine Mercury	4:08 PM	7:08 PM
Moon trine Venus	7:59 PM	10:59 PM
Sun trine Uranus begins (see November 23)		

Birthday: Israel Regardie 1907

Mood Watch: When the Moon is waning in Leo, it urges us to take special care of ourselves as well as the children in our life. Projects of interest are sometimes considered children, too. If there is a hobby of special interest to you, take the time to brighten and enliven this work which represents your own talent and self-reflection. Throughout the working (or playing) day, jokes will fly, toys will be admired, and moods will reflect childlike frolic and revel. If you're serious about not being distracted by such playfulness, perhaps a quiet workspace is the key. If you must work with others, allow the frivolity to flow; the work will get done, but the child in everyone has to play now and then – why not now? After all, tonight's positive lunar aspects are inviting us to play.

November 18th Friday

LAST QUARTER MOON in LEO

Moon in Leo / Virgo	PST	EST	
Moon sextile Saturn	4:27 AM	7:27 AM	
Moon square Sun goes v/c	7:09 AM	10:09 AM	
Moon enters Virgo	2:18 PM	5:18 PM	
Moon trine Jupiter	6:50 PM	9:50 PM	
Moon conjunct Mars	9:11 PM	12:11 AM	(Nov 19)
Venus sextile Saturn begins (November 22)			

Birthday: Owen Wilson 1968

Mood Watch: The day begins with the **Last Quarter Moon in Leo** (Moon square Sun), just as it is going void-of-course. Out of the drive for the perfection of the self comes a battle with the self in one form or another. The void-moon part of the morning may bring spacey moods as forgetfulness, preoccupation with the self, and general mindlessness cause some inconvenience. As the Moon enters Virgo, there is a stronger drive towards perfection, and our moods will be more inclined to pay attention to what's going on and to tidy up the loose ends of our lives.

November 19th Saturday

ʍ

Moon in Virgo

	PST	EST	
Moon trine Pluto	12:32 AM	3:32 AM	
Moon square Mercury	10:51 PM	1:51 AM	(Nov 20)

Birthday: Larry King 1933

Mood Watch: Virgo Moon is a good time to access resources, take inventory, and to review accounts. The waning Virgo Moon also appeals to our need for caution. Virgo taps into our disbelieving or questioning nature. We are reminded that we need to tend to and exercise those basic but important health practices that keep us safe from harm. The Sun in Scorpio with the waning Moon in Virgo brings out our guarded, suspicious, and skeptical qualities. In a world full of the dangers of illness – or possible death – we are often reminded to use safe hygiene practices, and to handle foods with a thorough and meticulous cleaning process. The energies of the waning Virgo Moon emphasize our need to apply sensible precautionary measures wherever there is the potential for danger.

November 20th Sunday

Moon in Virgo / Libra

	PST	EST
Moon square Venus	4:54 AM	7:54 AM
Sun square Neptune	12:42 PM	3:42 PM
Moon sextile Sun goes v/c	2:21 PM	5:21 PM
Moon enters Libra	5:16 PM	8:16 PM
Moon opposite Uranus	6:35 PM	9:35 PM

Birthday: Joe Biden 1942

Mood Watch: The waning Virgo Moon brings subtle, keen, and sometimes prudent – or guarded – attitudes. Today, people will be playing their cards close to their chest, and they may *appear* somewhat reluctant to bluff. As the Moon goes void-of-course, there's no use in trying to convince anyone of anything – people's minds will appear to be working at a sluggish pace for a few hours. As the Moon enters Libra, our moods are focused on the need for peace and forgiveness. This evening's Moon opposite Uranus will be a period of conflicting or chaotic messages. Radical breakthroughs can occur this evening.

Sun square Neptune (occurring Nov. 14 – 23) This occurrence of Sun square Neptune especially affects Scorpio and Sagittarius cusp born people who are celebrating birthdays November 14 – 23. Neptune in the square position to these birthday folks' natal Sun brings a sense of obstacles getting in the way of Spirit or the acknowledgement of spiritual beliefs. The challenge for these Scorpio and Sagittarius birthday folks is to overcome the interfering doubts and confrontations. This especially applies to overcoming those extremely dangerous and destructive addictive tendencies. Remember, birthday folks, spiritual lessons do not have to be life threatening! Over the next year, there will undoubtedly be some spiritual adjustments, and perhaps a change of belief is required. This aspect last occurred on May 22, affecting the lives and beliefs of some of our Taurus and early born Gemini friends.

November 21st Monday

Moon in Libra	PST	EST
Moon square Pluto	3:03 AM	6:03 AM
Venus sextile Neptune begins (see November 24)		
Venus square Uranus begins (see November 26)		
Sun square Mars begins (see December 2)		

Birthday: Goldie Hawn 1945

Mood Watch: The waning Libra Moon focuses our attention on the need for justice, truth, fair play, and balance. Our minds will be full of activity and ready to face some of the more serious aspects of what is occurring around us. This is a time when teamwork and calculated effort will bring some of the larger problems we face into a much more controllable level of tolerance. Sun in Scorpio and Moon in Libra rocks! You will find a lot less apathy on the battlegrounds of today's events as heartfelt collaboration brings relief.

SAGITTARIUS

Key Phrase: "I SEE" or

" I PERCEIVE "

Mutable Fire Sign

Ruling Planet: Jupiter

Symbol: The Centaur

November 22nd through

December 21st

November 22nd Tuesday

Moon in Libra / Scorpio	PST	EST	
Venus sextile Saturn	12:18 AM	3:18 AM	
Moon sextile Mercury	1:39 AM	4:39 AM	
Sun enters Sagittarius	8:07 AM	11:07 AM	
Moon conjunct Saturn	9:43 AM	12:43 PM	
Moon sextile Venus	10:29 AM	1:29 PM	
Moon trine Neptune goes v/c	3:03 PM	6:03 PM	
Moon enters Scorpio	5:58 PM	8:58 PM	
Moon opposite Jupiter	9:24 PM	12:24 AM	(Nov 23)
Jupiter-sextile-Neptune-non-exact begins (see Dec. 26 & June 8)			

Birthday: Jamie Lee Curtis 1958

Mood Watch: Today is a day of transitions, with both the Sun and the Moon entering

248

new signs, and also with so many lunar aspects at work. The morning begins with the Sun in Scorpio and the Moon in Libra – a time when we are preoccupied with the passion and the devotion of our relationships. Swiftly, however, the Sun enters Sagittarius and our Libra Moon moods will be a lot more focused on the necessity for balance in the course of so many shifting energies. Don't put off this morning what isn't likely to be done this afternoon; for awhile, the Libra Moon will be void-of-course, and with this comes a great deal of waffling and indecision. There will undoubtedly be some delays due to the need for making some adjustments. Tonight's Moon in Scorpio is a good time to explore dreams and insights.

Venus sextile Saturn (occurring Nov. 18 – 23) Venus is in Sagittarius sextile to Saturn in Libra. Venus in Sagittarius invites an attraction to traveling, adventurous love play, and uplifting social encounters. Venus sextile Saturn brings the opportunity for us to gain some control of our love relationships, and to better understand our boundaries and limitations. Saturn in Libra brings an even-tempered and civil-minded attempt to apply discipline in relationships. It is through this aspect that love relationships are given an opportunity for stronger levels of commitment and responsibility. This is the time to protect loved ones with guidance, and to teach them about discipline. Perfect timing brings pleasure. Venus sextile Saturn teaches us how to hold on to and maintain the things we love – those places, people, and things that matter to us. True love has a binding and lasting affect, and this aspect often shows us the ways in which love stands the test of time. This aspect last reoccurred on January 23 and August 7.

Sun enters Sagittarius (Sun in Sagittarius: Nov. 22 – Dec. 21/22) Sun in Sagittarius represents the final laps of autumn and the shortest days of the solar year. The Sagittarius expression, "I see," opens our eyes to some new discoveries during this time. This mutable fire sign achieves visionary awareness by reaching out into the world of possibilities, the stars, and beyond. The Sagittarius time of year sees to the closing of autumn by putting to sleep the last of the restless foliage in preparation for the pending winter's great slumber. Sun in Sagittarius days bring a focus on prosperity. Jupiter is the ruling planet of Sagittarius and inspires Sagittarians to excel, expand, and prosper. As the holidays begin and the Christmas season unfurls, the pressure to consume elaborate foods and purchase gifts, while keeping the great economic wheel turning, can be monumental for absolutely everyone. We are often required to pull together an outstanding number of social events and personal expenditures. The concept of prosperity has been tested to the extremes each time this season unfolds; it is, therefore, very important to get back to the basics of what one identifies as prosperous. The true challenge for many of us will be met when we finally reach out towards the higher vision of what prosperity really means. Sun in Sagittarius serves as a good time to direct the forces of vision and inspiration towards attaining a sense of wealth and wellbeing.

November 23rd Wednesday

Moon in Scorpio	PST	EST	
Sun trine Uranus	2:13 AM	5:13 AM	
Moon sextile Mars	3:30 AM	6:30 AM	
Moon sextile Pluto	3:34 AM	6:34 AM	
Mars trine Pluto	6:06 AM	9:06 AM	
Mercury goes retrograde	11:19 PM	2:19 AM	(Nov 24)
Venus trine Jupiter begins (see November 27)			

Birthday: Harpo Marx 1888

Mood Watch: Today's events may be laced with strong doses of emotion. A waning Scorpio Moon calls to us to let go of destructive tendencies, challenges us to cease hurting ourselves and others, and invites us to transform our lower impulses into higher aspirations. Under supportive circumstances, this is a good time to let go of the pain you've been concealing. Tonight's Moon in Scorpio marks the eve of the New Moon and this is always a good time to apply caution, and to beware of the possibility of violent outbreaks and possessive or melodramatic behavior. This is also a time to be careful not to get overworked or overstressed. Whether through purging, healing, or grieving, Sun and Moon in Scorpio are likely to bring stormy and torrential weather both to our emotions and throughout the northern hemisphere. Excitement abounds, and life just got a whole lot more complex with Mercury retrograde (see below).

Sun trine Uranus (occurring Nov. 17 – 26) This occurrence of Sun trine Uranus favorably affects our Scorpio and Sagittarius friends celebrating birthdays November 17 – 26. It puts the radical forces of Uranus in the favorable trine position to their natal Sun. It is time for these people to make a breakthrough. Don't hold back, birthday people; chaos is here to stay for awhile. Let the experience be positive as long as this aspect brings gifts. Expect restless desires for freedom and the need to break out of your personal prison. Freedom knocks loudly, and the course of change is inevitable in the coming year. Change is necessary for growth. These influential changes are positive in nature, though on the surface they may seem harsh. Birthday people, the apparent madness occurring in your life is there for a reason. You will find a clearer picture in the long run by keeping up the good fight to preserve your inspiration, intelligence, Scorpio passion and Sagittarius optimism. The trine aspect gives gifts of triumph, and this may be a good time to let chaos be the force that brings freedom. This aspect last occurred July 27, affecting the cusp born birthday Cancer and Leo folks of that time.

Mars trine Pluto (occurring Nov. 10 – 30) Mars is now in Virgo trine Pluto in Capricorn. Discerning, cautious, and practical action leads to positive, monumental, and powerful transformations. Actions taken now are more likely to have favorable results or to be influential with higher powers. This is a good time to resolve personal aggression directed towards the views and differences of another generation or established powers. This is also a good time for vital discoveries in the fight against diseases. Mars trine Pluto brings opportunity for favorable direct action that may well make a powerful and impressionable impact. Youthful or strong new influences will reach places of power. Mars, the god of

250

war, and Pluto, the underworld god (or hell raiser), may actually be reaching some favorable kind of truce. This aspect last occurred on May 20.

Mercury goes retrograde (Mercury retrograde: Nov. 23 – Dec. 13) While Mercury is retrograde in Sagittarius, we can expect to see a lot of frustration with regard to communications mishaps and misunderstandings over travel, travel schedules, delayed forms of transportation, and with regard to exploration, as well as philosophical viewpoints. This is the eve of the New Moon and Solar Eclipse in Sagittarius. This is a time when our visions may be strong and, perhaps, intense. While Mercury is retrograde in Sagittarius, it may be difficult to accurately relay the importance or the depth of our understanding and experience of life. Although challenging and, despite the fact that it will often leave us dissatisfied and tongue tied, it's not impossible to keep up with Mercury related setbacks. Establishing a clear understanding will be the most important part of engaging in various kinds of agreements. Expect to repeat yourself more than once or twice, and to be persistent as well as patient during this time. For more information on Mercury retrograde, see the section in the introduction about *Mercury retrograde periods.*

November 24ᵗʰ Thursday

Thanksgiving Day, USA
NEW MOON in SAGITTARIUS– *Partial Solar Eclipse*

Moon in Scorpio / Sagittarius	PST	EST	
Moon square Neptune goes v/c	3:03 PM	6:03 PM	
Venus sextile Neptune	5:51 PM	8:51 PM	
Moon enters Sagittarius	5:57 PM	8:57 PM	
Moon trine Uranus	7:08 PM	10:08 PM	
Moon conjunct Sun	10:09 PM	1:09 AM	(Nov 25)

Birthday: Scott Joplin 1868

Mood Watch: The Scorpio Moon wanes darkly and inspires us to focus on the transformational parts of our lives which are often fraught with sacrifice and the need for adjustment. The soul searching process may seem arduous at times, particularly as the Moon squares with Neptune and then goes void-of-course. Emotional challenges always have a breaking point and we must be sure to provide ourselves with the space and clarity to process, absorb, and recover from difficult transitions. The **New Moon in Sagittarius** (Moon conjunct Sun) inspires us to look at life in a whole new way. Early in the day a hopeful outlook is felt strongly as the Moon reaches the new mark. New Moon in Sagittarius encourages us to start exercise programs, look into original philosophies, and to explore new territory in our lives. Sagittarius says, "I see," so vision and insight are the primary incentives to explore fresh ground. Today is a good day to look ahead and get in touch with an innovative vision for the coming month and year.

Solar Eclipse in Sagittarius: Some believe that eclipses bring darker than average moods. Some see this as mere superstition while others may base this belief on their personal experiences. This is an important time to beware of the dangers of travel as well as those who might take advantage of unwitting victims.

251

Venus sextile Neptune (occurring Nov. 21 – 26) Venus in Sagittarius sextile Neptune in Aquarius brings inspirational and creative love to the art of spirituality. The sextile of Venus to Neptune brings the opportunity for us to find spiritual enhancement in the adventure of love, and to spread its healing power around for all to share. This serves as an excellent time to reach out spiritually to those we love as well as to our spirit guides. This aspect last occurred on May 16 and February 1.

November 25ᵗʰ Friday

Moon in Sagittarius	PST	EST
Moon square Mars	5:06 AM	8:06 AM

Birthday: Paul Desmond 1924

Mood Watch: The early morning hours may be tricky for mustering up some strength with Moon square Mars, and this is a good time to take precautions against the potential for accidents and temperamental flare-ups. Sagittarius Moon generally brings insightful, philosophical, and optimistic moods. Deep, profound, and exhilarating visions give us the incentive to move past the minor, but irritating set-backs of this time. This is a good time to internalize personal visions and to picture the things that will bring joy and happiness to you.

November 26ᵗʰ Saturday

Moon in Sagittarius / Capricorn	PST	EST	
Moon conjunct Mercury	2:02 AM	5:02 AM	
Venus enters Capricorn	4:36 AM	7:36 AM	
Moon sextile Saturn	11:12 AM	2:12 PM	
Moon sextile Neptune goes v/c	4:05 PM	7:05 PM	
Venus square Uranus	6:27 PM	9:27 PM	
Moon enters Capricorn	7:04 PM	10:04 PM	
Moon square Uranus	8:16 PM	11:16 PM	
Moon conjunct Venus	8:26 PM	11:26 PM	
Moon trine Jupiter	10:01 PM	1:01 AM	(Nov 27)
Venus conjunct Pluto begins (see December 1)			

Birthday: Tina Turner 1939

Mood Watch: The waxing Sagittarius Moon brings hope, despite the ups and downs of today's lunar aspects. Pensive moods give birth to rich insights. However, for awhile in the evening, the Sagittarius Moon goes void-of-course, and this is an easy time for one to be thrown off track or to get lost. As the Moon enters Capricorn, our moods are geared towards the necessity to stay focused and to concentrate. The newly waxing Capricorn Moon brings determination.

Venus enters Capricorn (Venus in Capricorn: Nov. 26 – Dec. 20) What goes around, comes around, and for the second time this year, Venus enters Capricorn. This time, Venus will remain in Capricorn until December 20. For a recap of the story on how Venus in Capricorn works, *see February 3*, when Venus began this circle of love.

Venus square Uranus (occurring Nov. 21 – Nov. 29) Venus and Uranus are in transitional points at the cusps of Sagittarius/Capricorn and Pisces/Aries. Venus in Capricorn square Uranus in Aries – at the zero degree mark – brings swift change in love matters. It may be difficult for love (Venus) to flourish in a spontaneous and carefree fashion (Uranus), and there may be obstacles or obligations placed on love and independent freedom. This is a difficult time for rebels and revolutionaries, as their causes may not be heard in the midst of so much chaos. People are changing at a rapid rate and it is essential to let love take its course where it relates to personal freedom. This aspect last occurred on July 7 and February 2.

November 27th Sunday

Moon in Capricorn	PST	EST
Moon conjunct Pluto	5:25 AM	8:25 AM
Moon trine Mars	8:22 AM	11:22 AM
Venus trine Jupiter	1:23 PM	4:23 PM
Venus trine Mars begins (see December 5)		

Birthday: Jimi Hendrix 1942

Mood Watch: Moon in Capricorn provides our moods with a steady persistence to meet important goals and make progress with our work. Let the progress of your work shine and take joy in your accomplishments. A very busy new month awaits us, and this is a good time to make some headway. Waxing Capricorn Moon is a great time to set goals and to assess personal progress and achievements.

Venus trine Jupiter (occurring Nov. 23 – 29) Love (Venus) is harmoniously placed with prosperity and opportunity (Jupiter). Venus in Capricorn trine Jupiter in Taurus brings engaging companionship and affection that inspires goal conscious and practical means for creating joy and prosperity. Under this influence, love may grow and expand in committed and determined ways. This is a great time to give gifts of love and, for many people, it offers an expansive outlook. Without love in your life and a love for what you are doing, an expanding empire will eventually lose its luster. Venus trine Jupiter reminds us fortune can be realized with simple aesthetics and quality moments. This aspect last occurred on August 29 and January 4.

November 28th Monday

Moon in Capricorn / Aquarius	PST	EST	
Moon square Saturn goes v/c	3:01 PM	6:01 PM	
Moon enters Aquarius	11:01 PM	2:01 AM	(Nov 29)

Birthday: William Blake 1757

Mood Watch: The Capricorn Moon waxes, and many folks will be too busy to stop and check how they, or the folks around them, are feeling. In fact, we may find we are so preoccupied that we may not notice that, at times, we will be running around in circles. The Capricorn Moon goes void-of-course this afternoon, and although many people will remain determined, it is very likely that the busy rush of traffic and hubbub will also slow down our sense of progress considerably. The effects of Moon square Saturn often pose limitations. This evening would be a very good time to drop all the grudges that go along with not being able to achieve certain goals. By tomorrow, a new set of moods will put us on the right path.

November 29th Tuesday

Moon in Aquarius	PST	EST
Moon sextile Uranus	12:16 AM	3:16 AM
Moon square Jupiter	1:49 AM	4:49 AM
Moon sextile Sun	12:08 PM	3:08 PM
Jupiter-opposite-Saturn-non-exact begins (see below)		

Birthday: C.S. Lewis 1898

Mood Watch: Sun in Sagittarius and waxing Moon in Aquarius generally bring insightful, brilliant, and inspired incentives. That said, we must remember to follow up on every important detail while Mercury is retrograde (Nov. 23 – Dec. 13). Despite the need for a careful follow up on communications and schedules, the Aquarius Moon is a superb time to plan social endeavors and charitable events. This is also a good time to share and discuss strategies and theories.

Jupiter-opposite-Saturn-non-exact (occurring Nov. 29 – Feb. 3, 2012) This aspect begins occurring today at a three degree orbital range. However, it never actually reaches a peak while it fluctuates between three to five degrees. This is the time we come closest to this non-exact aspect occurring – within three degrees of an opposition. For more details on Jupiter opposite Saturn, *see March 28*, when it last reached an exact peak. Back in March, Jupiter was in Aries opposite Saturn in Libra, but now, Jupiter is in the early degrees of Taurus while Saturn is finishing its cycle in Libra. Now, economic pressures are putting the demand on the need for the material goods (Jupiter in Taurus). This non-exact aspect will dissipate on February 3, 2012.

November 30th Wednesday

Moon in Aquarius	PST	EST	
Moon sextile Mercury	5:35 AM	8:35 AM	
Moon trine Saturn	10:36 PM	1:36 AM	(Dec 1)

Birthday: Mark Twain 1835

Mood Watch: Progressive, open-minded, and truthful attitudes will keep us inspired as the Moon waxes in Aquarius. There is a spark of political controversy in the air. Remember to enjoy the freedom we now have and hold precious. Protect and uphold your rights! The more our rights are exercised the stronger they become. The benefits of good deeds are said to increase one's good karma threefold.

December 1st Thursday

Moon in Aquarius / Pisces	PST	EST
Moon conjunct Neptune goes v/c	3:26 AM	6:26 AM
Venus conjunct Pluto	5:50 AM	8:50 AM
Moon enters Pisces	6:45 AM	9:45 AM
Moon sextile Jupiter	9:22 AM	12:22 PM
Moon sextile Pluto	6:53 PM	9:53 PM
Moon opposite Mars	7:35 PM	10:35 PM
Moon sextile Venus	8:18 PM	11:18 PM
Sun conjunct Mercury begins (see December 4)		
Mercury square Mars begins (see December 4)		

Birthday: Lou Rawls 1933

Mood Watch: The void-of-course Aquarius Moon starts off the early morning with a great deal of complexity. Nonetheless, this is an important time to be prepared for anything. It won't be too long before the Moon enters Pisces, and this will be a helpful time to use your intuition. The Pisces Moon assists us to read between the lines, particularly with regard to people's intentions and their capabilities. While Mercury is retrograde, this is no time to rely on the word of others; use your intuition and follow up on the facts.

Venus conjunct Pluto (occurring Nov. 26 – Dec. 3) For the second time this year, Venus and Pluto are conjunct in Capricorn. This conjunction often places affections and love right where they are needed most: the areas of life that are deeply challenging and sometimes traumatic. For a recap on the story of how Venus conjunct Pluto affects us, see February 9 when it last occurred.

December 2nd Friday

FIRST QUARTER MOON in PISCES	PST	EST
Moon square Sun	1:52 AM	4:52 AM
Moon opposite Mars	2:01 AM	5:01 AM
Sun square Mars	5:07 AM	8:07 AM
Moon square Mercury goes v/c	10:05 AM	1:05 PM

Birthday: Gianni Versace 1946

Mood Watch: The **First Quarter Moon in Pisces** (Moon square Sun) often brings our hearts and minds to a peaceful place. A spacey, dreamy sort of consciousness leads to strong psychic awareness. While the first quarter Moon is in Pisces, calming music, art, and poetry will fill us with inspiration, intuition, and hope. The Pisces Moon will go void-of-course as it squares with Mercury, and it may be best to avoid foot-in-mouth disease. In other words, watch what you say and don't be fooled by smooth talkers. Unhappy people are likely to turn to intoxicants to escape their troubles. Deep meditation and spiritual practices will empower the imagination. That which you are sensing today will reveal especially powerful indications of what is going on. Use your intuition attentively. Observe cautiously and strive as best you may to ease the senses whenever they seem to be overloaded.

Sun square Mars (occurring Nov. 21 – Dec. 7) This aspect particularly affects those late season Scorpios and those Sagittarius born people celebrating birthdays this year from November 21 – December 7. It creates the illusion that obstacles are constantly getting in the way of the actions (and will) of these people. Harnessing energy seems like a chore. Heated situations may seem particularly daunting for these birthday folks. This is a good time for these people to lighten up on their expectations of themselves for awhile, and not let such setbacks get in the way of enjoying life. Relax! In time, it will be easier once again to get your personal goals and your willpower into a state of action. This may be an accident prone time in the lives of these birthday folks. Since this year may bring the tendency for accidents and mistakes, this will be a good time for these birthday folks to learn a great deal about how to pace themselves and to work through the obstacles in order to perfect personal visions and goals. This is the only time this aspect will occur this year.

December 3rd Saturday

Moon in Pisces / Aries	PST	EST
Moon enters Aries	5:51 PM	8:51 PM
Moon conjunct Uranus	7:10 PM	10:10 PM

Birthday: Brendan Fraser 1968

Mood Watch: As if yesterday wasn't already trying enough, the void-of-course Pisces Moon continues to bring spacey and easily distracted moods throughout today. Beware of drunks, traffic delays, and emotionally taxing scenarios. This would be an ideal time to focus on creative themes, crafts, and artistic endeavors. This evening's Aries Moon brings a warrior spirit. Drive and determination are evident in our moods, especially while Moon conjunct Uranus stirs up the caldron of our feelings.

December 4th Sunday

Moon in Aries	PST	EST
Sun conjunct Mercury	12:52 AM	3:52 AM
Moon square Pluto	6:40 AM	9:40 AM
Moon square Venus	2:56 PM	5:56 PM
Mercury square Mars	3:18 PM	6:18 PM
Moon trine Mercury	3:59 PM	6:59 PM
Moon trine Sun	7:20 PM	10:20 PM

Birthday: Jeff Bridges 1949

Mood Watch: Waxing Moon in Aries activates our moods with ambitious gusto. Despite a couple of lunar squares to challenge us, the momentum and positive force of the energy around us picks up greatly as the days of Sagittarius keep us busily striving for prosperity and contentment. Sun in Sagittarius and Moon in Aries bring creative zeal and enthusiasm to the ways in which we express ourselves. Moon trine Mercury is a useful time to reiterate on the details of plans, and to communicate with a little more ease while Mercury is retrograde (Nov. 23 – Dec. 13). However, for the most part, communications are challenged, especially while Mercury square Mars brings heated words (see below).

Sun conjunct Mercury (occurring Dec. 1 – 5) This conjunction will create a much more thoughtful, communicative and expressive year ahead for those Sagittarius folks celebrating birthdays December 1 – 5. This is your time (birthday Sagittarians) to record ideas, relay important messages, and pay close attention to your imaginative thoughts as they are touched by Mercury, creating the urge to speak and be heard. Birthday Sagittarians, your thoughts will reveal a great deal about who you are, now and in the year to come.

Mercury square Mars (occurring Dec. 1 – 6) Due to Mercury retrograde (Nov. 23 – Dec. 13), Mercury square Mars is reaching its peak for the second time since October 28. Insults and verbal abuse are common with this aspect. It might not even be intentional while Mercury is retrograde – it could be a simple case of misunderstanding but be aware of what you say nonetheless; the cauldron is hot right now. Mercury is currently retrograde in Sagittarius and it is wise to ensure that precautions are taken to avoid travel delays and mishaps. Mars is in Virgo where activities are tricky or complex. It could be awhile, at least until Mercury goes direct (Dec. 13), before currently erupting conflicts caused by some people's words and actions are smoothed over. This aspect last occurred on October 28 and it will repeat for a third time on December 31.

December 5th Monday

Moon in Aries

	PST	EST
Venus trine Mars	7:06 AM	10:06 AM

Birthday: Robert Hand 1942

Mood Watch: It's a fiery, active, get-up-and-go sort of a day. Waxing Moon in Aries brings a comfortably active working pace to kick off a new work week. The Sun and Moon are in fire signs inspiring us to keep warm and active. This is a time to do things for the self as well as for others. As ever, Aries Moon moods often preoccupy us with the need to stand out and be on top, to notice who is in control of situations and just how they're handling it. There is an eagerness or aggression present at times, yet overall there is youthful inspiration and a drive to get things started.

Venus trine Mars (occurring Nov. 27 – Dec. 8) Venus in Capricorn is trine Mars in Virgo. Committed, loyal, and reliable expressions of affection will bring very determined and meticulously devoted interactions between loved ones. Venus trine Mars brings love in action. When Venus and Mars are well harmonized by this ideal aspect, there is a greater opportunity for peace and healing in relationships, and often gifts are exchanged. These are gifts which help people to understand how masculine and feminine expressions are harmonized. This is the only time Venus trine Mars will occur this year.

December 6th Tuesday

Moon in Aries / Taurus	PST	EST
Moon sextile Neptune goes v/c	3:12 AM	6:12 AM
Moon enters Taurus	6:34 AM	9:34 AM
Moon conjunct Jupiter	8:36 AM	11:36 AM
Moon trine Pluto	7:38 PM	10:38 PM

Birthday: Dion Fortune 1890

Mood Watch: In the earlier hours of the morning, the void-of-course Aries Moon brings impatient or irritated moods. However, swiftly the Moon enters Taurus and our moods will be much more grounded and at ease. Moon conjunct Jupiter will be very instrumental in boosting our morale. Taurus Moon is a good time to focus on finances, acquiring goods and services, and taking care of practical needs. As the holidays approach, the waxing Taurus Moon is often a time when we are preoccupied with money, resources, and our ways and means of facilitating our needs. Let the Taurus Moon be an aid in showing you the way to acquiring what you need and want.

December 7th Wednesday

Moon in Taurus	PST	EST
Moon trine Mars	7:02 AM	10:02 AM
Moon trine Venus	10:46 AM	1:46 PM

Birthday: Tom Waits 1949

Mood Watch: This morning's trine aspects of the Moon will bring good energy and strong attraction. Waxing Taurus Moon focuses our attention on the matter of what we do or don't have in order to get by. Of course, there is also the matter of what we *want* to have in order to make the pending holidays festive. Money management and money related issues are very strong this time of year, especially when the Moon is in Taurus. Sensible buyers do not waste their energy on overpriced gifts. Quality and value are important, but so are our imaginative capabilities – and our pocket-books. Simple and practical gifts are a time honored tradition. The strongly waxing Taurus Moon also sets the stage for a lot of concern with regard to the handling and movement of valuables and goods. Slowly and steadily, let the bull's consummate pace keep the labor from being overtaxing.

December 8th Thursday

Moon in Taurus / Gemini	PST	EST
Moon square Neptune goes v/c	3:39 PM	6:39 PM
Moon enters Gemini	6:52 PM	9:52 PM
Moon sextile Uranus	8:08 PM	11:08 PM
Mercury-trine-Uranus-non-exact begins (see Dec. 14)		

Birthday: David Carradine 1936

Mood Watch: The waxing Taurus Moon keeps our spirits grounded. This is a good time to gain some ground on establishing routines, reviewing security measures, and stabilizing unruly conditions. This evening, as the Moon enters Gemini, our moods will be dazzled by interesting details, stories, and various tidbits of news.

December 9th Friday

Moon in Gemini	PST	EST	
Moon opposite Mercury	6:06 AM	9:06 AM	
Moon square Mars	8:43 PM	11:43 PM	
Uranus goes direct	11:04 PM	2:04 AM	(Dec 10)

Birthday: John Milton 1608

Mood Watch: Today's waxing Gemini Moon will keep us busily fussing over the details of life. Mercury is the ruler of Gemini; it is currently retrograde (since Nov. 23) and this may cause many folks to be in a perpetual state of correcting, reiterating, and modifying. Gemini Moon brings determined efforts to think through matters and find logical answers to unsolved puzzles. It's the Full Moon Eve, and this can be particularly taxing on the brain, especially when we awaken to Moon opposite Mercury – often the cause of too much information. Important tasks must be followed up carefully during this time when misunderstandings can easily occur. This evening's Moon square Mars is a challenging time for one's temper. Nonetheless, it is not a good policy to go to bed while holding grudges and beefs against others.

Uranus goes direct (Uranus direct: Dec. 9, 2011 – July 12, 2012) Since July 9, Uranus, known for stirring up calamity, has been retrograde. Now the planet of chaos and rebellion moves steadily forward at the zero degree mark of Aries, awakening the pioneering spirit of humanity, perhaps even inspiring breakthroughs in courageousness, leadership, and self-motivation. The work of radical and revolutionary forces resumes course as Uranus moves direct until July, 2012. We all feel the need to break out of oppressing conditions of life. As Uranus moves forward, the volatile quality of its work demands the utmost intelligence and knowledge as each level of urgency is unveiled. Uranus is the ruler of Aquarius and teaches us to seek higher levels of intelligence through unusual, brilliant, and open minded measures. The next time the urge for unabashed rebellion makes you kick up your heels, remember to kindle the light of love for humankind's wisdom. This is, after all, the Age of Aquarius.

December 10th Saturday

FULL MOON in GEMINI – *Total Lunar Eclipse*

	PST	EST	
Moon opposite Sun	6:36 AM	9:36 AM	
Moon trine Saturn	11:05 PM	2:05 AM	(Dec 11)

Birthday: Emily Dickinson 1830

Mood Watch: The first lunar aspect of the day occurred in the wee small hours, and with it came the peak of the **Full Gemini Moon** (Moon opposite Sun). This peak brings the crescendo of an intense Full Gemini Moon expression, the **Lunar**

Eclipse. A lunar eclipse occurs when the Earth moves between the moon and the sun, blocking the light that reflects off the moon's surface back to Earth. Darkness is the key, as there tends to be the common belief that the casting of a shadow upon the Moon brings darker than average moods. Some view this as mere superstition, while others may base this belief on their personal experiences. The Gemini Moon often brings moods that may seem overwhelmed by mutable thoughts just when we are trying to make decisions. Gemini Moon, in all of its glorious fullness, brings amazing talk, speeches, mind games, and intellectual pursuits. People may tend to babble senselessly, and very few are able to keep their minds on what they're doing, thinking, or feeling for very long. Ideally, this is a good time astrologically to pace oneself and relax the mind at various intervals. It may also be a time when our minds are relentlessly active and difficult to calm or ease. Full Moon in Gemini goes straight to charging our nervous systems, and we quickly discover that quieting down or easing an overworked nervous system takes some extra time after it has been running at top speed. Take it easy on the caffeine.

December 11th Sunday

Moon in Gemini / Cancer

	PST	EST
Moon trine Neptune goes v/c	2:24 AM	5:24 AM
Moon enters Cancer	5:25 AM	8:25 AM
Moon square Uranus	6:39 AM	9:39 AM
Moon sextile Jupiter	6:48 AM	9:48 AM
Moon opposite Pluto	6:03 PM	9:03 PM

Mercury-square-Neptune-non-exact begins (see December 15)

Birthday: John Kerry 1943

Mood Watch: In the earliest hours there may be some confusion while the Gemini Moon is void-of-course, but soon enough, Moon in Cancer kicks off the day with strong emotions. Yesterday's Full Gemini Moon, coupled with the lunar eclipse, may have been very difficult for some people, and today's Cancer Moon will certainly be a reflection of that difficulty on the emotional planes of existence. This morning's Moon square Uranus brings the most chaotic turmoil; however, Moon sextile Jupiter will help us to smooth over the rough edges with a sense of hope. A post-full Cancer Moon is the time to let feelings flow, especially when we find ourselves no longer able to contain them. It is also the time to comfort, and be comforted. Tonight's Moon opposite Pluto makes us acutely aware of the things we call *fate*.

December 12th Monday

Moon in Cancer

	PST	EST
Moon sextile Mars	8:07 AM	11:07 AM
Moon opposite Venus	8:26 PM	11:26 PM

Birthday: Frank Sinatra 1915

Mood Watch: Today's Moon in Cancer leaves many folks feeling somewhat withdrawn, and they are likely to be absorbed in their feelings. Moods emphasize feelings, and mother moon now wanes as we seek refuge from the cold and harsh elements of the world. Nurturing care, restful spaces, and moments of peace are what many people feel like pursuing today, and wherever there is internal upheaval, there is a need to vent strong feelings. Remember – feelings pass. Troubled feelings flow best when they are properly expressed and released, as opposed to retained and dwelled upon.

December 13th Tuesday

Moon in Cancer / Leo

	PST	EST
Moon square Saturn goes v/c	8:05 AM	11:05 AM
Moon enters Leo	1:48 PM	4:48 PM
Moon square Jupiter	2:55 PM	5:55 PM
Moon trine Uranus	2:59 PM	5:59 PM
Mercury goes direct	5:42 PM	8:42 PM
Moon trine Mercury	8:53 PM	11:53 PM
Venus square Saturn begins (see December 18)		

Birthday: Dick Van Dyke 1925

Mood Watch: This morning's Moon square Saturn brings a strong sense of faulty timing, and there will probably be a lot of frustration over work and responsibilities. The Cancer Moon shifts our senses into an especially temperamental state of being while it is void-of-course. It may be difficult to stop worrisome, redundant, or unproductive moodiness. As the Moon enters Leo, our moods are drawn to the need for affection, entertainment, and warmth. Mercury is resuming its course (see below); however, the transition of Mercury going direct can be a confusing time, and it will be a few days before the confusion can be completely cleared up.

Mercury goes direct (Mercury direct: Dec. 13, 2011 – March 11, 2012) Since November 23, Mercury has been retrograde in the sign of Sagittarius, commonly causing communication mix-ups particularly with regard to travel arrangements, travel schedules, and travel delays. Now we can breathe a greatly needed sigh of relief as Mercury, the planet governing the realms of communication, becomes stationary and will soon begin to move forward. Take note that our faculties and manner of communicating will definitely improve within the next few days. Although perhaps not today – when the stationary Mercury often freezes communication efforts – but very soon our communications will run more smoothly; this will be a good time to begin clearing up various misunderstandings that have occurred over the past few weeks. For more information on this recently completed phase of Mercury retrograde, see November 23. For more on Mercury retrograde patterns throughout this year, see the introduction on *Mercury retrograde periods*.

December 14th Wednesday

Moon in Leo	PST	EST
Moon opposite Saturn	2:07 AM	5:07 AM

Birthday: Tycho Brahe 1546

Mood Watch: Fiery and entertaining showmanship will fill the atmosphere today. Waning Leo Moon is a good time to work on letting go of personal fears and on showing bravery and courage. The Sun and Moon are both in fire signs, inviting us to be creative, positive, and active. Moon in Leo emphasizes such things as personal strength, will, integrity, stamina and, of course, it emphasizes how we present and conduct ourselves. The Leo Moon will help to give us the courage to fight our own individual battles. Be strong!

Mercury-trine-Uranus-non-exact (occurring Dec. 8 – 14) Due to Mercury retrograde (Nov. 23 – Dec. 13), this is as close as we come – within a three degree orb – to Mercury trine Uranus. This aspect began on December 8 and dissipates today before it even gets a chance to reach its peak. For a recap on the story of how Mercury trine Uranus affects us, *see November 3* when it last reached its peak with Mercury in Sagittarius. It also occurred back on July 4.

December 15th Thursday

Moon in Leo / Virgo	PST	EST
Moon trine Sun	8:06 AM	11:06 AM
Moon sextile Saturn	2:49 PM	5:49 PM
Moon opposite Neptune goes v/c	5:19 PM	8:19 PM
Moon enters Virgo	7:58 PM	10:58 PM
Moon trine Jupiter	8:54 PM	11:54 PM
Mercury-square-Neptune-non-exact (see below)		
Sun sextile Saturn begins (see December 19)		
Venus square Jupiter begins (see December 20)		

Birthday: Don Johnson 1949

Mood Watch: The waning Leo Moon is an especially important time to work things out with personal needs. July 26th born Leo, Carl Jung, wrote: "Wholeness is not achieved by cutting off a portion of one's being, but by integration of the contraries." Sometimes the Leo Moon brings out our beastly side, and Dr. Jung made a very good point about the need to accept what's there as a whole, and to integrate it in a way that balances out that beastly part of our character. For awhile this evening, the void-of-course Leo Moon brings forgetfulness, restlessness, and general distractions. Virgo Moon brings a better time to concentrate, especially now that Mercury has gone direct (see Dec. 13).

Mercury-square-Neptune-non-exact (occurring Dec. 11 – 17) Due to the recently passed retrograde cycle of Mercury (Nov. 23 – Dec. 13), today is as close to Mercury square Neptune as it gets, within a wide orb of six degrees. In fact, the orb has remained stationary at six degrees the whole time since it began, which means that it hasn't been especially strong, but it's still accountable to some extent. For a review on what kind of energy this aspect brings, see November 1,

262

when it last occurred with the full peak.

December 16th Friday

Moon in Virgo	PST	EST	
Moon square Mercury	3:35 AM	6:35 AM	
Moon trine Pluto	7:55 AM	10:55 AM	
Moon conjunct Mars	11:34 PM	2:34 AM	(Dec 17)
Sun sextile Neptune begins (see December 20)			
Sun square Uranus begins (see December 22)			
Sun trine Jupiter begins (see December 22)			

Birthday: Ludwig van Beethoven 1770

Mood Watch: The Virgo Moon leads us to question what we are doing, to ponder, analyze, deliberate, and communicate about what's going on. This is a good time to be resourceful and thorough, or the boss is likely to decisively prod us in this direction. Why not beat 'em to it? Anticipate what needs to be done and do it! Today, sharpness and keenness will get you some good bonus points.

December 17th Saturday

LAST QUARTER MOON in VIRGO	PST	EST
Moon square Sun	4:47 PM	7:47 PM
Moon trine Venus goes v/c	6:28 PM	9:28 PM
Venus sextile Uranus begins (see December 20)		

Birthday: Arthur Fiedler 1894

Mood Watch: The **Last Quarter Moon in Virgo** (Moon square Sun) calls for the release of doubt. These are the days of Sun in Sagittarius; applying the vision of how one wants to see their future-self is not an easy task, especially if poisonous and debilitating addictions are involved. However, the Sagittarian outlook often projects selfhood in an outward fashion in order to envision the demands of an expanding spirit. That same Sagittarian awareness is just as capable of traveling inward and perceiving the needs of the inner self. Let the doubts and fears of your life be flushed away at this time so that, through clarity, you may achieve the benefits of your visionary picture of health, wealth, and wellbeing.

December 18th Sunday

Moon in Virgo / Libra	PST	EST
Moon enters Libra	12:06 AM	3:06 AM
Moon opposite Uranus	1:14 AM	4:14 AM
Venus square Saturn	6:18 AM	9:18 AM
Moon sextile Mercury	9:24 AM	12:24 PM
Moon square Pluto	11:45 AM	2:45 PM

Birthday: Keith Richards 1943

Mood Watch: Moon in Libra focuses our attention on the need to make decisions, and to create some balance in our lives wherever it is needed, particularly with regard to our loved ones and friends. Moon sextile Mercury brings active minds and thoughtful early morning moods – a good time to think matters over, and to focus on solving complex puzzles. Moon square Pluto challenges the use of our power and it may be especially difficult to take initiative to do things.

Venus square Saturn (occurring Dec. 13 – 20) Venus in Capricorn is square to Saturn in Libra. Romances may appear overly serious and the limitations or restrictions may appear to cost too high a price. It may seem as if something is always getting in the way of basic pleasures. Perhaps it is best not to get bent out of shape over some people's need to create restrictions in order to protect their own sense of security while love related troubles are being worked out. No matter how much one prioritizes a focus on love, it is still likely to be misinterpreted on some level during Venus square Saturn. Love related dramas may be taken too seriously. Give it your best – keep singing the praises of love and applying the law of attraction, but expect some challenges and high demands for discipline nonetheless. This aspect last occurred on February 18 and July 13.

December 19ᵗʰ Monday

Moon in Libra	PST	EST	
Sun sextile Saturn	8:24 AM	11:24 AM	
Moon conjunct Saturn	10:18 PM	1:18 AM	(Dec 20)
Moon sextile Sun	11:17 PM	2:17 AM	(Dec 20)

Birthday: Criss Angel 1967

Mood Watch: Peaceful and hopeful feelings bring pleasantries and kindness among people. Where these traits don't exist, the Libra Moon brings a desire for us to strive for the best, or to utilize the law to create and define such things as protection and cordial civil duty. Overall, Libra Moon energy focuses on harmony. This is a good time to work things out with loved ones and partners.

Sun sextile Saturn (occurring Dec. 15 – 21) This occurrence of Sun sextile Saturn particularly affects Sagittarius and Solstice born Capricorn people celebrating birthdays between December 15 – 21, helping them focus their energy and discipline with greater clarity throughout this year. As Saturn traverses the sextile aspect to the natal Sun of these Sagittarius and cusp born Capricorn people, there is a sense of making progress through discipline, and they may very well begin to see the rewards of their diligent labor in the coming year. This is only true as long as they apply themselves to their work, and maintain a vigilant and persistent effort to master personal discipline and training. Greater control comes with genuine effort. This aspect last occurred on August 5, presenting better opportunities and allowing more control in the lives of some Leo folks.

December 20ᵗʰ Tuesday

Moon in Libra / Scorpio	PST	EST
Moon trine Neptune	12:13 AM	3:13 AM
Moon square Venus goes v/c	1:48 AM	4:48 AM
Moon enters Scorpio	2:32 AM	5:32 AM
Moon opposite Jupiter	3:14 AM	6:14 AM

Venus enters Aquarius	10:26 AM	1:26 PM	
Sun sextile Neptune	12:46 PM	3:46 PM	
Moon sextile Pluto	2:01 PM	5:01 PM	
Venus square Jupiter	6:19 PM	9:19 PM	
Venus sextile Uranus	11:56 PM	2:56 AM	(Dec 21)

Birthday: Uri Geller 1946

Mood Watch: The waning Scorpio Moon brings out our survival instincts, and tunes us into the perceptivity necessary to move through intense situations and emotional concerns. Scorpio Moon assists us to face the big transitions in life. As autumn turns to winter, our instincts teach us how to let go of the things we can no longer control. Scorpio Moon can be a good time to address matters of grief, resentment, grudges, and things of this nature. For some, the shaking loose of emotional turmoil can be very liberating. Therapy is available in a wide range of options. Discover what *your* best therapy is and learn how to apply it.

Venus enters Aquarius (Venus in Aquarius: Dec. 20, 2011 – Jan. 13, 2012) What goes around, comes around, and for the second time this year, Venus enters Aquarius. This time Venus will remain in Aquarius until January 13, 2012. For a recap of the story on how Venus in Aquarius works, *see March 1*, when Venus began this circle of love.

Sun sextile Neptune (occurring Dec. 16 – 22) This occurrence of Sun sextile Neptune creates an opportunistic time for those Sagittarius and (cusp born) Capricorn people celebrating birthdays from December 16 – 22. These Sagittarius and Capricorn folks are experiencing an opportunity to awaken in the realm of spirituality and creativity. There is an awareness of the self that goes deep here, and these birthday people are likely to appear distracted and difficult to reach while this phenomenon of great depth is occurring. This will be your year, birthday folks, to explore personal opportunities of spiritual growth. It may be a time to get away from it all, and find a sanctuary in which to meditate and open up to some valuable answers to old questions. These folks are in a place that gives them an opportunity to better understand the work of their path, but this is probably only true if they act on their own intuitive sensibilities, without the influences of others. That shouldn't be too hard for the adventurous, open-minded, and outgoing Sagittarius natures among us. Cusp born Capricorns may need to focus on relaxing a great deal more in order for them to be adequately receptive to their intuitive faculties. This will be your year (Sagittarius/Capricorn birthday people) to enhance and strengthen your intuition and primal instincts by tapping into them while they are easily available. This may also be the time to overcome addictions and disruptive patterns. This aspect last occurred on April 20, affecting some of the Aries and Taurus (cusp born) people of that time.

Venus square Jupiter (occurring Dec. 15 – 23) This aspect brings love and attraction (Venus) into difficulty or hard work (the square aspect) over material growth and our sense of jubilation (Jupiter). Venus newly in Aquarius at the zero degree mark, square Jupiter, newly in Taurus, brings a love for intelligent care and affection which may be challenged by the need to handle escalating economic

265

obligations or banking debts. Some folks may be experiencing challenges with their sense of appreciation, enjoyment, or fulfillment. Our experiences of beauty and affection may be tested by the difficulty of attracting or acquiring prosperity. Some might say that the act of appreciating beauty is a form of prosperity in itself, but at times like this, a great deal more effort and support is required. This aspect may create an obstacle to acknowledging the expenses incurred by our attractions and love-needs. It reminds us that something more than love's blindness is required in order for us to fully realize our riches and the value of what we care about most. This aspect last occurred on August 4, and before that on February 6.

Venus sextile Uranus (occurring Dec. 17 – 22) Venus in Aquarius is sextile to Uranus in Aries. Our love for humanity takes on a radical or unusual kind of expression. Radically serious kinds of love and aesthetics can be very uplifting at this time, particularly while extreme types of tests are occurring and being stretched beyond the limits in love related matters. Eccentric love may erupt with this aspect. This is the time to work on pent up frustrations with loved ones and to reconcile differences by loving and accepting variation, giving freedom and slack to our loved ones. Venus sextile Uranus can encourage us to break useless tendencies and habits, and also may bring an opportunity for love related matters to transcend the restriction of unmet personal needs. Venus sextile Uranus last occurred on March 1 and June 12.

CAPRICORN

Key Phrase: " I USE "
Cardinal Earth Sign
Ruling Planet: Saturn
Symbol: The Goat
December 21st, 2011 through
January 20th, 2012

December 21st Wednesday

Winter Solstice / Hanukkah begins (ends December 28)

Moon in Scorpio	**PST**	**EST**	
Moon sextile Mars	6:56 AM	9:56 AM	
Sun enters Capricorn	9:30 PM	12:30 AM	(Dec 22)

Birthday: Frank Zappa 1940

Mood Watch: There is beauty, sensation, and an electrical field of awareness at work. This morning's Moon sextile Mars emphasizes the need for strength, and ♑ if it's excitement you're looking for, you won't have to go far. A waning Moon in Scorpio calls to us to let go of strong destructive tendencies, and challenges us to cease hurting ourselves and others by transforming our lower impulses into higher aspirations. Under amicable circumstances, this is a good time to let go of the pain you've been concealing. Shopping crowds are thick this time of year. If you're not up to the intensity, now is *not* the time to risk the potential for overstressing yourself. The waning Scorpio Moon has a way of leading us directly to the pulse-point of activity. *Happy Winter Solstice!*

Sun enters Capricorn (Sun in Capricorn: Dec. 21/22, 2011 – Jan. 20, 2012) Spark up the lights – it's **Winter Solstice**! Today the Sun King returns from the ashes of the longest night. This is the time of Saturn-ruled Capricorn. Sun in Capricorn is the time to step into success. Jack Frost is nipping at our heels, but the Sun King returns! The lengthening days of the Sun are finally here and a new season and cycle begins. The symbol of Capricorn is the mountain goat. The Capricorn goat consciousness is revealed to us through the high and lofty heights the goat commands. No mountain is too high for the true archetypal Capricorn, and the focus of this season is always placed on accomplishing the highest of goals and achievements. The working pace for the New Year is established here. Capricorn energy emphasizes corporate growth, the creation and maintenance of institutions, construction and development, and the use and control of industrial services and equipment. Many outstanding Capricorns are devoted to their careers and lifestyles with unyielding tenacity. Capricorn days of the Sun are splendid times to focus on goals, and to discipline one's nature to make daily tasks add up to something worth accomplishing. Although tedious and often predictable, the Capricorn nature makes sure the job is done – and done well.

December 22nd Thursday

Moon in Scorpio / Sagittarius	PST	EST
Moon square Neptune goes v/c	1:48 AM	4:48 AM
Moon enters Sagittarius	4:02 AM	7:02 AM
Moon trine Uranus	5:12 AM	8:12 AM
Sun trine Jupiter	6:32 AM	9:32 AM
Moon sextile Venus	7:53 AM	10:53 AM
Sun square Uranus	2:13 PM	5:13 PM
Moon conjunct Mercury	7:09 PM	10:09 PM
Sun conjunct Pluto begins (see December 28)		

Birthday: Lady Bird Johnson 1912

Mood Watch: Overnight, the waning Scorpio Moon brings imaginative and therapeutic dreams. Early this morning, the waning Moon enters Sagittarius, and our moods begin to explore inner space. An imaginative, curious, philosophical spirit gives glimpses of how the recent memories of 2011 will help to set the course of the newer visions of 2012. In our journey through Capricorn winter, day or night, through storm or slumber, Sagittarius Moon gives the impetus "to see" intuitively.

Sun trine Jupiter (occurring Dec. 16 – 25) Sagittarius and Capricorn people celebrating a birthday from December 16 – 25 are undergoing a favorable natal solar position with relation to Jupiter. This will be a time of gifts and expansion for these birthday folks, and there are good times ahead for them in the coming year. This aspect will bring a better sense of what it means to expand and attain one's personal desire. Be sure to take the time right now, birthday people, to enjoy and appreciate life, which will definitely improve for you, despite other trials that you may be facing. Sun trine Jupiter brings the gift of joy, so make use of it and be sure to look for the silver lining in your life! This aspect last occurred September 2, affecting some of the Virgo birthday folks of that time.

Sun square Uranus (occurring Dec. 16 – 25) This occurrence of Sun square Uranus particularly affects Sagittarius and Capricorn people celebrating birthdays December 16 – 25. The square of Uranus in Aries to these birthday folks' natal Sun brings about challenging events and a strong dose of unrestrained chaos. This may be the year for you birthday people to surrender to those aspects of life that are truly out of your control, and to concentrate more rationally on those facets of life over which you do have control. Sometimes the aftermath of Uranus's influence is an improvement, but with the square aspect at work, it is likely these people will feel personally challenged. It is important to understand that some types of personal challenges are best left alone, while others must be confronted directly without causing destructive damage, particularly to the self. On the other hand, birthday folks, if your life has no foundation, there is no point in holding onto the illusion of stability at this juncture of your sojourn. This aspect will pass, and it is vital not to give this rapid change too much resistance, lest you be bound to the reversals of trying to fight chaos with logic at a time when resistance is futile. Matters will settle down in due time; try to be detached from chaotic events as they occur, and the outcome will seem less costly. If you need it, project the picture of peace and it will be there for you at the other end. This aspect last occurred on June 26.

December 23rd Friday

Moon in Sagittarius

	PST	EST
Moon square Mars	9:30 AM	12:30 PM

Birthday: Harry Shearer 1943

Mood Watch: Our moods may flare up in complex ways while Moon square Mars is occurring early in the day; beware of the potential for accidents and temperamental attitudes. New Moon Eve is upon us and the dark balsamic Moon can bring some rather mysterious or shadowy feelings on the week of winter solstice. A dark Moon coupled with these long nights reminds us to take our rest. Winter's slumber may seem like aeons away while the hubbub of holiday furry continues. Nonetheless, the Sagittarius Moon brings optimism, courage, and some liveliness.

December 24th Saturday Christmas Eve

ᚷ

NEW MOON in CAPRICORN

Moon in Sagittarius / Capricorn	PST	EST
Moon sextile Saturn	2:02 AM	5:02 AM
Moon sextile Neptune goes v/c	3:35 AM	6:35 AM
Moon enters Capricorn	5:46 AM	8:46 AM
Moon trine Jupiter	6:23 AM	9:23 AM
Moon square Uranus	7:00 AM	10:00 AM
Moon conjunct Sun	10:06 AM	1:06 PM
Moon conjunct Pluto	5:42 PM	8:42 PM

Birthday: Howard Hughes 1905

Mood Watch: The **New Moon in Capricorn** (Moon conjunct Sun) brings down-to-earth determination to our moods. New beginnings occur on the physical plane with the Moon and the Sun in Capricorn. New Moon in Capricorn urges us to create fresh goals and to set new heights for ourselves. The Capricorn Moon brings a powerful defiance in the face of adversity, and we must not let dark feelings affect our sense of pragmatism and dignity. Go easy on people and use your protective emotional shields to combat the harsh attitudes of others. Beware of the tendency for employers and leaders to expect a lot. No matter what – be positive!

December 25th Sunday

Christmas

Moon in Capricorn	PST	EST
Moon trine Mars	1:11 PM	4:11 PM
Jupiter goes direct	2:07 PM	5:07 PM
Mercury square Mars begins (see December 31)		

Birthday: Cab Calloway 1907

" The trick is in what one emphasizes. We either make ourselves miserable, or we make ourselves happy. The amount of work is the same. " – Carlos Castaneda (born this day,1925 – 1998)

Mood Watch: The bright young Capricorn Moon may bring the feeling that our sense of perseverance is being tested or elevated. The afternoon brings favorably strong energy with the Capricorn Moon trine Mars. Perseverance and a keen sense of self-preservation are the hallmarks of a newly waxing Capricorn Moon. The customs and formalities of Christmas bring comfort to the traditionalists among us. This is a good time to focus on goals and to make plans for achieving success. This is also a time to count the blessings of what we have achieved.

Jupiter goes direct (Jupiter direct: Dec. 25, 2011 – Oct. 4, 2012) Since August 30, Jupiter has been retrograde in the sign Taurus. Let us celebrate as the planet Jupiter moves forward! Jupiter represents skill, fortune, luck, wealth, expansion, wellbeing, and joviality; it's also associated with advancement, prosperity, opportunity, fulfillment, and inheritance. The process of Jupiter retrograde is sometimes difficult for systems, and for the predictability of economic growth, such as business and market control. All of this has been particularly true since Jupiter has been in the business and banker oriented sign, Taurus. Jupiter engages one with a sense of happiness and fulfillment. Now that Jupiter goes direct, advancement goes from an internalized process to an externalized process, which is how Jupiter operates best.

December 26th Monday

Boxing Day, Canada & UK

Moon in Capricorn / Aquarius	PST	EST	
Moon square Saturn goes v/c	5:35 AM	8:35 AM	
Moon enters Aquarius	9:14 AM	12:14 PM	
Moon square Jupiter	9:52 AM	12:52 PM	
Moon sextile Uranus	10:34 AM	1:34 PM	
Moon conjunct Venus	11:32 PM	2:32 AM	(Dec 27)
Jupiter-sextile-Neptune-non-exact (see below)			

Birthday: Henry Miller 1891

Mood Watch: Early this morning, Moon square Saturn brings a sound reminder of our struggles for control. For awhile, the void-of-course Capricorn Moon brings that rushed feeling, like nothing is happening fast enough, or with enough care, seriousness, or astuteness. This is no time to get hung up on quality control – it is enough for us to keep matters as functional as possible. However, soon enough, the Aquarius Moon enlivens the spirit of humanitarian efforts. Moon square Jupiter may bring a conflict as to how much energy and money is being spent. Moon sextile Uranus influences the need for unconventional efforts to make the kind of breakthroughs we need. Later tonight, Moon conjunct Venus empowers our sense of esthetics and attraction. The Aquarius Moon keeps us strongly connected to everyone and everything that we as individuals attempt to emulate. Our true heroes empower us.

Jupiter-sextile-Neptune-non-exact (occurring Nov. 22 – Dec. 26) Today is as close as we come, within a two degree orb, to a full peak aspect between Jupiter and Neptune. For a recap on the story of how Jupiter sextile Neptune works, *see June 8*, when it last occurred in full.

December 27th Tuesday

Moon in Aquarius	PST	EST
Moon sextile Mercury	11:00 AM	2:00 PM

Birthday: Gérard Depardieu 1948

Mood Watch: Moon sextile Mercury brings an excellent opportunity to get the word across. Moon in Aquarius focuses our moods on the need to apply knowledge in order to cut corners through the congested systems of humanity. The newly waxing Moon in Aquarius focuses our moods on idealistic, inventive and humanitarian expression. Aquarius brings out the need to face ourselves and learn things about who we are.

December 28th Wednesday

♑

Moon in Aquarius / Pisces	PST	EST	
Moon trine Saturn	12:09 PM	3:09 PM	
Moon conjunct Neptune goes v/c	1:30 PM	4:30 PM	
Moon enters Pisces	3:45 PM	6:45 PM	
Moon sextile Jupiter	4:28 PM	7:28 PM	
Sun conjunct Pluto	11:42 PM	2:42 AM	(Dec 29)

Birthday: Denzel Washington 1954

Mood Watch: This morning's youthfully waxing Aquarius Moon encourages us to act on our intelligent sensibilities and to seek knowledge where it is needed. This afternoon, as the Moon goes void-of-course, we may find our resources for knowledge and technical advice are limited. Humanitarian efforts may backfire at times as these busy final days of the year press us onward to meet the challenges of the pending New Year. As the Moon enters Pisces, a wide range of moods can lead us to numerous things such as drunkenness, psychic impressions, and colorful artistic endeavors. Tonight it may be best to plan out some sensible and practical guidelines and stick to them.

Sun conjunct Pluto (occurring Dec. 22, 2011 – Jan. 1, 2012) This occurrence of Sun conjunct Pluto strongly affects Capricorns – most specifically, those who are celebrating birthdays December 22, 2011 – January 1, 2012. These Capricorn birthday folks will experience challenges of mind-altering proportions. Sun conjunct Pluto affects the core of the personality, and diminishes those parts of the self which are weak and no longer viable. Pluto's energy melds with the personality to bring out the strongest points of one's character, the very best that one can muster. Pluto removes all impurities by transforming the old self through unpredictable trials. Take this opportunity to make some personal breakthroughs, birthday folks, and find your power! Learn to harness your power willingly and responsibly while great transformation is occurring in your life.

December 29th Thursday

Moon in Pisces	PST	EST
Moon sextile Pluto	5:26 AM	8:26 AM
Moon sextile Sun	5:56 AM	8:56 AM

Birthday: Marianne Faithfull 1946

Mood Watch: It is often true that the imagination likes to roam on a Pisces Moon day. Pisces Moon puts us in touch with our belief systems and the personal trials we must endure concerning our individual beliefs. For some, there is a creative process unfolding; for others, there is a battle going on with addictive behavior or the need to escape. For most, the dreamlike quality of this time drifts in a timeless fashion connecting us with our past as well as showing us the future as we open ourselves up in the now.

December 30th Friday

Moon in Pisces		PST	EST
	Moon square Mercury	1:39 AM	4:39 AM
	Moon opposite Mars	5:37 AM	8:37 AM

Birthday: Rudyard Kipling 1865

Mood Watch: Abstract, bubbly, and artistic moods fill the air with the waxing Moon in Pisces. This Moon places an emphasis on our need for spiritual fortification. Many will seek to find some form of validation for their beliefs or their sense of intuition. Waxing Moon in Pisces is a great time to enjoy musical and artistic expressions as well as mystery and make-believe.

December 31st Saturday

New Year's Eve

FIRST QUARTER MOON in PISCES	PST	EST	
Mercury square Mars	10:05 PM	1:05 AM	(Jan 1)
Moon square ☾un goes v/c	10:14 PM	1:14 AM	(Jan 1)

Birthday: Noel Tyl 1936

Mood Watch: The **First Quarter Moon in Pisces** (Moon square Sun) often brings our hearts and minds to a peaceful place. A spacey, dreamy sort of consciousness leads to strong psychic awareness. While the first quarter Moon is in Pisces, calming music, art, and poetry will fill us with inspiration, intuition, and hope. It's obvious that this is where the New Year's celebration comes in.

Mercury square Mars (occurring Dec. 25, 2011 – Jan. 3, 2012) For the third time this year, Mercury square Mars brings conflict and heated action over communications. Insults and verbal abuse are common with this aspect. Be cautious, but don't sweat it. For a recap on the story of what's going on with this phase of Mercury square Mars, *see October 28 and December 4.*

Happy New Year Everyone!

Ephemeris 2011 Noon GMT
Longitudes based on Greenwich Mean Time (GMT) at Noon

JANUARY 2011

Date	☉	☽	☿	♀	♂	♃	♄	♅	♆	♇
1	10♑42	05♐58	19♐58	24♏02	18♑45	26♓37	16♎40	26♓58	26♒44	05♑20
2	11 43	19 16	20 21	25 00	19 32	26 45	16 43	26 59	26 46	05 23
3	12 45	02♑21	20 50	25 59	20 18	26 53	16 45	27 00	26 48	05 25
4	13 46	15 13	21 26	26 58	21 05	27 02	16 48	27 02	26 50	05 27
5	14 47	27 51	22 07	27 58	21 51	27 10	16 50	27 03	26 51	05 29
6	15 48	10♒15	22 54	28 58	22 38	27 19	16 52	27 05	26 53	05 31
7	16 49	22 28	23 45	29 58	23 24	27 28	16 54	27 07	26 55	05 33
8	17 50	04♓31	24 40	00♐59	24 11	27 37	16 56	27 08	26 57	05 35
9	18 52	16 27	25 38	02 00	24 58	27 46	16 58	27 10	26 59	05 38
10	19 53	28 19	26 40	03 02	25 45	27 56	17 00	27 12	27 01	05 40
11	20 54	10♈11	27 45	04 04	26 31	28 05	17 01	27 13	27 03	05 42
12	21 55	22 08	28 52	05 06	27 18	28 15	17 03	27 15	27 05	05 44
13	22 56	04♉15	00♑01	06 09	28 05	28 24	17 04	27 17	27 07	05 46
14	23 57	16 36	01 13	07 12	28 52	28 34	17 06	27 19	27 09	05 48
15	24 58	29 15	02 26	08 15	29 39	28 44	17 07	27 21	27 10	05 50
16	26 00	12♊17	03 41	09 19	00♒26	28 54	17 08	27 23	27 13	05 52
17	27 01	25 43	04 58	10 23	01 12	29 04	17 09	27 25	27 15	05 54
18	28 02	09♋34	06 16	11 27	01 59	29 15	17 10	27 27	27 17	05 56
19	29 03	23 48	07 35	12 32	02 46	29 25	17 11	27 29	27 19	05 58
20	00♒04	08♌21	08 56	13 37	03 33	29 36	17 11	27 31	27 21	06 00
21	01 05	23 06	10 18	14 42	04 20	29 46	17 12	27 34	27 23	06 02
22	02 06	07♍55	11 40	15 47	05 07	29 57	17 12	27 36	27 25	06 04
23	03 07	22 41	13 04	16 53	05 55	00♈08	17 13	27 38	27 27	06 06
24	04 08	07♎16	14 29	17 59	06 42	00 19	17 13	27 40	27 29	06 08
25	05 09	21 37	15 54	19 05	07 29	00 30	17 13	27 43	27 31	06 10
26	06 10	05♏39	17 20	20 11	08 16	00 41	17♎13	27 45	27 33	06 12
27	07 11	19 23	18 48	21 17	09 03	00 53	17 13R	27 48	27 36	06 14
28	08 12	02♐49	20 16	22 24	09 50	01 04	17 13	27 50	27 38	06 16
29	09 13	15 58	21 44	23 31	10 37	01 16	17 13	27 53	27 40	06 18
30	10 14	28 53	23 14	24 38	11 25	01 27	17 12	27 55	27 42	06 20
31	11 15	11♑36	24 44	25 46	12 12	01 39	17 12	27 58	27 44	06 22

FEBRUARY 2011

Date	☉	☽	☿	♀	♂	♃	♄	♅	♆	♇
1	12♒16	24♑07	26♑15	26♐53	12♒59	01♈51	17 11R	28♓00	27♒46	06♑23
2	13 17	06♒29	27 47	28 01	13 46	02 03	17♎10	28 03	27 49	06 25
3	14 18	18 42	29 20	29 09	14 34	02 14	17 09	28 06	27 51	06 27
4	15 18	00♓48	00♒53	00♑17	15 21	02 27	17 09	28 08	27 53	06 29
5	16 19	12 47	02 27	01 25	16 08	02 39	17 07	28 11	27 55	06 31
6	17 20	24 41	04 01	02 33	16 56	02 51	17 06	28 14	27 58	06 32
7	18 21	06♈32	05 37	03 41	17 43	03 03	17 05	28 17	28 00	06 34
8	19 22	18 23	07 13	04 50	18 30	03 16	17 04	28 19	28 02	06 36
9	20 22	00♉18	08 50	05 59	19 18	03 28	17 02	28 22	28 04	06 38
10	21 23	12 21	10 28	07 08	20 05	03 41	17 01	28 25	28 07	06 39
11	22 24	24 37	12 07	08 17	20 52	03 53	16 59	28 28	28 09	06 41
12	23 25	07♊11	13 46	09 26	21 40	04 06	16 57	28 31	28 11	06 42
13	24 25	20 07	15 26	10 35	22 27	04 19	16 55	28 34	28 14	06 44
14	25 26	03♋29	17 07	11 44	23 15	04 32	16 53	28 37	28 16	06 46
15	26 27	17 20	18 49	12 54	24 02	04 45	16 51	28 40	28 18	06 47
16	27 27	01♌40	20 32	14 03	24 49	04 57	16 49	28 43	28 20	06 49
17	28 28	16 25	22 16	15 13	25 37	05 11	16 47	28 46	28 23	06 50
18	29 28	01♍29	24 00	16 23	26 24	05 24	16 45	28 49	28 25	06 52
19	00♓29	16 41	25 46	17 32	27 11	05 37	16 42	28 52	28 27	06 53
20	01 29	01♎53	27 32	18 42	27 59	05 50	16 40	28 55	28 29	06 55
21	02 30	16 52	29 20	19 52	28 46	06 03	16 37	28 58	28 32	06 56

FEBRUARY 2011 (Cont'd)

Date	☉	☽	☿	♀	♂	♃	♄	♅	♆	♇
22	03♓30	01♏31	01♓08	21♑03	29♒34	06♈17	16 34R	29 02	28♒34	06♑57
23	04 30	15 45	02 57	22 13	00♓21	06 30	16♎32	29 05	28 36	06 59
24	05 31	29 34	04 47	23 23	01 08	06 44	16 29	29 08	28 39	07 00
25	06 31	12♐57	06 38	24 34	01 56	06 57	16 26	29 11	28 41	07 01
26	07 32	25 58	08 30	25 44	02 43	07 11	16 23	29 14	28 43	07 03
27	08 32	08♑41	10 22	26 55	03 31	07 24	16 20	29 18	28 45	07 04
28	09 32	21 09	12 16	28 06	04 18	07 38	16 17	29 21	28 48	07 05

MARCH 2011

Date	☉	☽	☿	♀	♂	♃	♄	♅	♆	♇
1	10♓32	03♒26	14♓10	29♑16	05♓05	07♈52	16 13R	29♓24	28♒50	07♑06
2	11 33	15 34	16 05	00♒27	05 53	08 05	16♎10	29 28	28 52	07 08
3	12 33	27 36	18 00	01 38	06 40	08 19	16 06	29 31	28 54	07 09
4	13 33	09♓34	19 56	02 49	07 27	08 33	16 03	29 34	28 57	07 10
5	14 33	21 28	21 51	04 00	08 15	08 47	15 59	29 37	28 59	07 11
6	15 33	03♈20	23 47	05 11	09 02	09 01	15 56	29 41	29 01	07 12
7	16 33	15 12	25 43	06 22	09 49	09 15	15 52	29 44	29 03	07 13
8	17 33	27 05	27 38	07 33	10 37	09 29	15 48	29 48	29 05	07 14
9	18 33	09♉01	29 32	08 45	11 24	09 43	15 44	29 51	29 08	07 15
10	19 33	21 05	01♈25	09 56	12 11	09 57	15 41	29 54	29 10	07 16
11	20 33	03♊19	03 17	11 07	12 59	10 11	15 37	29 58	29 12	07 17
12	21 33	15 49	05 07	12 19	13 46	10 25	15 33	00♈01	29 14	07 18
13	22 33	28 38	06 54	13 30	14 33	10 39	15 28	00 04	29 16	07 19
14	23 33	11♋52	08 39	14 42	15 20	10 54	15 24	00 08	29 18	07 19
15	24 33	25 35	10 21	15 53	16 08	11 08	15 20	00 11	29 20	07 20
16	25 33	09♌47	11 58	17 05	16 55	11 22	15 16	00 15	29 23	07 21
17	26 32	24 27	13 32	18 16	17 42	11 36	15 12	00 18	29 25	07 22
18	27 32	09♍31	15 00	19 28	18 29	11 51	15 07	00 22	29 27	07 22
19	28 32	24 50	16 24	20 40	19 16	12 05	15 03	00 25	29 29	07 23
20	29 31	10♎12	17 41	21 51	20 03	12 19	14 59	00 28	29 31	07 24
21	00♈31	25 26	18 53	23 03	20 50	12 34	14 54	00 32	29 33	07 24
22	01 30	10♏21	19 58	24 15	21 37	12 48	14 50	00 35	29 35	07 25
23	02 30	24 50	20 57	25 27	22 24	13 02	14 45	00 39	29 37	07 25
24	03 30	08♐50	21 48	26 39	23 11	13 17	14 41	00 42	29 39	07 26
25	04 29	22 21	22 33	27 51	23 58	13 31	14 36	00 46	29 41	07 26
26	05 28	05♑25	23 09	29 03	24 45	13 46	14 32	00 49	29 43	07 27
27	06 28	18 07	23 38	00♓15	25 32	14 00	14 27	00 52	29 45	07 27
28	07 27	00♒30	24 00	01 27	26 19	14 15	14 23	00 56	29 47	07 28
29	08 27	12 41	24 14	02 39	27 06	14 29	14 18	00 59	29 48	07 28
30	09 26	24 42	24 20	03 51	27 53	14 44	14 13	01 03	29 50	07 28
31	10 25	06♓37	24 19R	05 03	28 40	14 58	14 09	01 06	29 52	07 29

APRIL 2011

Date	☉	☽	☿	♀	♂	♃	♄	♅	♆	♇
1	11♈24	18♓30	24 11R	06♓16	29♓27	15♈13	14 04R	01♈09	29♒54	07♑29
2	12 24	00♈21	23♈56	07 28	00♈13	15 27	13♎59	01 13	29 56	07 29
3	13 23	12 14	23 35	08 40	01 00	15 42	13 55	01 16	29 58	07 29
4	14 22	24 08	23 08	09 52	01 47	15 56	13 50	01 20	29 59	07 30
5	15 21	06♉06	22 36	11 04	02 34	16 11	13 45	01 23	00♓01	07 30
6	16 20	18 09	21 59	12 17	03 20	16 25	13 41	01 26	00 03	07 30
7	17 19	00♊19	21 19	13 29	04 07	16 40	13 36	01 30	00 05	07 30
8	18 18	12 39	20 36	14 41	04 53	16 54	13 31	01 33	00 06	07 30
9	19 17	25 12	19 51	15 54	05 40	17 09	13 27	01 36	00 08	07 30R
10	20 16	08♋02	19 04	17 06	06 27	17 23	13 22	01 40	00 10	07♑30
11	21 15	21 12	18 18	18 19	07 13	17 38	13 17	01 43	00 11	07 30
12	22 14	04♌47	17 32	19 31	08 00	17 52	13 13	01 46	00 13	07 30

APRIL 2011 (Cont'd)

Date	☉	☽	☿	♀	♂	♃	♄	♅	♆	♇
13	23♈13	18♌47	16 48R	20♈43	08♈46	18♈07	13 08R	01♈49	00♓14	07 30R
14	24 12	03♍14	16♈06	21 56	09 32	18 21	13♎04	01 53	00 16	07♑30
15	25 10	18 04	15 27	23 08	10 19	18 36	12 59	01 56	00 17	07 29
16	26 09	03♎10	14 52	24 21	11 05	18 50	12 55	01 59	00 19	07 29
17	27 08	18 24	14 21	25 33	11 51	19 05	12 50	02 02	00 20	07 29
18	28 06	03♏34	13 54	26 46	12 37	19 19	12 46	02 05	00 22	07 29
19	29 05	18 31	13 32	27 58	13 24	19 33	12 41	02 09	00 23	07 28
20	00♉04	03♐06	13 14	29 11	14 10	19 48	12 37	02 12	00 24	07 28
21	01 02	17 14	13 02	00 23	14 56	20 02	12 33	02 15	00 26	07 28
22	02 01	00♑53	12 55	01 36	15 42	20 16	12 29	02 18	00 27	07 27
23	02 59	14 05	12 53D	02 49	16 28	20 31	12 24	02 21	00 28	07 27
24	03 58	26 52	12♈56	04 01	17 14	20 45	12 20	02 24	00 30	07 26
25	04 56	09♒18	13 03	05 14	18 00	20 59	12 16	02 27	00 31	07 26
26	05 55	21 30	13 16	06 26	18 46	21 14	12 12	02 30	00 32	07 25
27	06 53	03♓30	13 34	07 39	19 32	21 28	12 08	02 33	00 33	07 25
28	07 51	15 24	13 56	08 52	20 17	21 42	12 04	02 36	00 34	07 24
29	08 50	27 15	14 22	10 04	21 03	21 56	12 00	02 39	00 36	07 24
30	09 48	09♈07	14 53	11 17	21 49	22 10	11 56	02 42	00 37	07 23

MAY 2011

Date	☉	☽	☿	♀	♂	♃	♄	♅	♆	♇
1	10♉46	21♈01	15♈27	12♈30	22♈35	22♈25	11 52R	02♈45	00♓38	07 23R
2	11 45	03♉01	16 06	13 43	23 20	22 39	11♎49	02 48	00 39	07♑22
3	12 43	15 07	16 48	14 55	24 06	22 53	11 45	02 50	00 40	07 21
4	13 41	27 21	17 34	16 08	24 51	23 07	11 41	02 53	00 41	07 20
5	14 39	09♊44	18 24	17 21	25 37	23 21	11 38	02 56	00 42	07 20
6	15 37	22 18	19 16	18 34	26 22	23 35	11 34	02 59	00 43	07 19
7	16 35	05♋03	20 12	19 46	27 08	23 49	11 31	03 01	00 44	07 18
8	17 34	18 04	21 11	20 59	27 53	24 03	11 28	03 04	00 44	07 17
9	18 32	01♌20	22 13	22 12	28 38	24 16	11 24	03 07	00 45	07 16
10	19 30	14 55	23 18	23 25	29 24	24 30	11 21	03 09	00 46	07 16
11	20 28	28 50	24 26	24 37	00♉09	24 44	11 18	03 12	00 47	07 15
12	21 26	13♍04	25 36	25 50	00 54	24 58	11 15	03 14	00 47	07 14
13	22 23	27 35	26 49	27 03	01 39	25 11	11 12	03 17	00 48	07 13
14	23 21	12♎20	28 04	28 16	02 24	25 25	11 09	03 19	00 49	07 12
15	24 19	27 11	29 22	29 29	03 09	25 39	11 07	03 22	00 49	07 11
16	25 17	12♏02	00♉42	00♉41	03 54	25 52	11 04	03 24	00 50	07 10
17	26 15	26 44	02 05	01 54	04 39	26 06	11 01	03 27	00 51	07 09
18	27 13	11♐10	03 30	03 07	05 24	26 19	10 59	03 29	00 51	07 08
19	28 10	25 14	04 58	04 20	06 09	26 32	10 56	03 31	00 52	07 07
20	29 08	08♑55	06 27	05 33	06 53	26 46	10 54	03 34	00 52	07 05
21	00♊06	22 10	07 59	06 46	07 38	26 59	10 52	03 36	00 52	07 04
22	01 04	05♒02	09 34	07 59	08 23	27 12	10 50	03 38	00 53	07 03
23	02 01	17 33	11 10	09 11	09 07	27 25	10 47	03 40	00 53	07 02
24	02 59	29 48	12 49	10 24	09 52	27 39	10 45	03 42	00 54	07 01
25	03 57	11♓50	14 30	11 37	10 36	27 52	10 44	03 45	00 54	07 00
26	04 54	23 45	16 14	12 50	11 21	28 05	10 42	03 47	00 54	06 58
27	05 52	05♈37	17 59	14 03	12 05	28 17	10 40	03 49	00 54	06 57
28	06 49	17 31	19 47	15 16	12 49	28 30	10 38	03 51	00 55	06 56
29	07 47	29 29	21 37	16 29	13 34	28 43	10 37	03 52	00 55	06 55
30	08 45	11♉34	23 29	17 42	14 18	28 56	10 36	03 54	00 55	06 53
31	09 42	23 49	25 24	18 55	15 02	29 09	10 34	03 56	00 55	06 52

JUNE 2011

Date	☉	☽	☿	♀	♂	♃	♄	♅	♆	♇
1	10♊40	06♊17	27♉21	20♉08	15♉46	29♈21	10 33R	03♈58	00♓55	06 51R
2	11 37	18 56	29 19	21 21	16 30	29 34	10♎32	04 00	00 55	06♑49
3	12 35	01♋50	01♊20	22 34	17 14	29 46	10 31	04 02	00 55R	06 48

JUNE 2011 (Cont'd)

Date	☉	☽	☿	♀	♂	♃	♄	♅	♆	♇
4	13♊32	14♋56	03♊23	23♉47	17♉58	29♈59	10 30R	04♈03	00 55R	06 47R
5	14 30	28 17	05 27	25 00	18 42	00♉11	10♎29	04 05	00♓55	06♑45
6	15 27	11♌50	07 33	26 13	19 26	00 23	10 28	04 06	00 55	06 44
7	16 25	25 37	09 41	27 26	20 09	00 35	10 28	04 08	00 55	06 42
8	17 22	09♍35	11 50	28 39	20 53	00 47	10 27	04 10	00 55	06 41
9	18 19	23 45	14 00	29 52	21 37	00 59	10 27	04 11	00 55	06 40
10	19 17	08♎03	16 11	01♊05	22 20	01 11	10 27	04 12	00 54	06 38
11	20 14	22 27	18 23	02 18	23 04	01 23	10 26	04 14	00 54	06 37
12	21 11	06♏52	20 35	03 31	23 47	01 35	10 26	04 15	00 54	06 35
13	22 09	21 16	22 47	04 45	24 31	01 46	10 26D	04 16	00 53	06 34
14	23 06	05♐32	24 59	05 58	25 14	01 58	10♎26	04 18	00 53	06 32
15	24 03	19 37	27 10	07 11	25 57	02 09	10 26	04 19	00 53	06 31
16	25 01	03♑26	29 21	08 24	26 41	02 21	10 27	04 20	00 52	06 29
17	25 58	16 56	01♋30	09 37	27 24	02 32	10 27	04 21	00 52	06 28
18	26 55	00♒06	03 39	10 50	28 07	02 43	10 28	04 22	00 51	06 26
19	27 52	12 57	05 46	12 03	28 50	02 54	10 28	04 23	00 51	06 25
20	28 50	25 29	07 52	13 17	29 33	03 05	10 29	04 24	00 50	06 23
21	29 47	07♓46	09 56	14 30	00♊16	03 16	10 30	04 25	00 50	06 22
22	00♋44	19 50	11 58	15 43	00 59	03 27	10 31	04 26	00 49	06 20
23	01 41	01♈47	13 58	16 56	01 42	03 38	10 31	04 27	00 49	06 19
24	02 39	13 40	15 56	18 10	02 24	03 49	10 33	04 28	00 48	06 17
25	03 36	25 34	17 52	19 23	03 07	03 59	10 34	04 28	00 47	06 16
26	04 33	07♉34	19 46	20 36	03 50	04 10	10 35	04 29	00 47	06 14
27	05 30	19 44	21 38	21 49	04 32	04 20	10 36	04 30	00 46	06 13
28	06 28	02♊06	23 28	23 03	05 15	04 30	10 38	04 30	00 45	06 11
29	07 25	14 45	25 16	24 16	05 57	04 40	10 39	04 31	00 44	06 10
30	08 22	27 41	27 02	25 29	06 40	04 50	10 41	04 31	00 44	06 08

JULY 2011

Date	☉	☽	☿	♀	♂	♃	♄	♅	♆	♇
1	09♋19	10♋56	28♋45	26♊43	07♊22	05♉00	10♎43	04♈32	00 43R	06 07R
2	10 17	24 27	00♌26	27 56	08 04	05 10	10 45	04 32	00♓42	06♑05
3	11 14	08♌13	02 05	29 10	08 47	05 19	10 47	04 32	00 41	06 04
4	12 11	22 12	03 42	00♋23	09 29	05 29	10 49	04 33	00 40	06 02
5	13 08	06♍20	05 17	01 37	10 11	05 38	10 51	04 33	00 39	06 01
6	14 05	20 33	06 49	02 50	10 53	05 47	10 53	04 33	00 38	05 59
7	15 03	04♎48	08 19	04 03	11 35	05 57	10 56	04 33	00 37	05 58
8	16 00	19 03	09 47	05 17	12 17	06 06	10 58	04 33	00 36	05 56
9	16 57	03♏13	11 13	06 30	12 59	06 15	11 01	04 33	00 35	05 55
10	17 54	17 19	12 37	07 44	13 40	06 23	11 03	04 33R	00 34	05 53
11	18 51	01♐17	13 58	08 57	14 22	06 32	11 06	04♈33	00 33	05 52
12	19 49	15 06	15 17	10 11	15 04	06 40	11 09	04 33	00 32	05 50
13	20 46	28 44	16 33	11 25	15 45	06 49	11 12	04 33	00 31	05 49
14	21 43	12♑10	17 47	12 38	16 27	06 57	11 15	04 33	00 29	05 47
15	22 40	25 22	18 58	13 52	17 08	07 05	11 18	04 33	00 28	05 46
16	23 37	08♒20	20 07	15 05	17 50	07 13	11 21	04 32	00 27	05 44
17	24 35	21 02	21 13	16 19	18 31	07 21	11 24	04 32	00 26	05 43
18	25 32	03♓30	22 16	17 33	19 12	07 29	11 27	04 32	00 24	05 41
19	26 29	15 44	23 17	18 46	19 53	07 36	11 31	04 31	00 23	05 40
20	27 26	27 47	24 14	20 00	20 35	07 43	11 34	04 31	00 22	05 39
21	28 24	09♈43	25 09	21 14	21 16	07 51	11 38	04 30	00 21	05 37
22	29 21	21 36	26 00	22 27	21 57	07 58	11 42	04 30	00 19	05 36
23	00♌18	03♉29	26 48	23 41	22 38	08 05	11 45	04 29	00 18	05 35
24	01 15	15 28	27 33	24 55	23 18	08 12	11 49	04 28	00 17	05 33
25	02 13	27 39	28 14	26 09	23 59	08 18	11 53	04 28	00 15	05 32
26	03 10	10♊05	28 51	27 23	24 40	08 25	11 57	04 27	00 14	05 31
27	04 07	22 50	29 24	28 36	25 21	08 31	12 01	04 26	00 12	05 29

JULY 2011 (Cont'd)

Date	☉	☽	☿	♀	♂	♃	♄	♅	♆	♇
28	05♌05	05♋57	29♌53	29♋50	26♊01	08♉37	12♎05	04 25R	00 11R	05 28R
29	06 02	19 28	00♍18	01♌04	26 42	08 43	12 10	04♈24	00♓09	05♑27
30	07 00	03♌21	00 38	02 18	27 23	08 49	12 14	04 23	00 08	05 25
31	07 57	17 33	00 54	03 32	28 03	08 55	12 18	04 22	00 07	05 24

AUGUST 2011

Date	☉	☽	☿	♀	♂	♃	♄	♅	♆	♇
1	08 54	02♍00	01♍05	04♌46	28♊43	09♉00	12♎23	04 21R	00 05R	05 23R
2	09 52	16 34	01 10	06 00	29 24	09 05	12 27	04♈20	00♓04	05♑22
3	10 49	01♎10	01 11R	07 14	00♋04	09 11	12 32	04 19	00 02	05 21
4	11 47	15 40	01♍07	08 28	00 44	09 16	12 37	04 18	00 00	05 19
5	12 44	00♏01	00 57	09 42	01 24	09 20	12 41	04 17	29♒59	05 18
6	13 42	14 10	00 42	10 56	02 04	09 25	12 46	04 16	29 57	05 17
7	14 39	28 04	00 22	12 10	02 44	09 30	12 51	04 14	29 56	05 16
8	15 36	11♐45	29♌57	13 24	03 24	09 34	12 56	04 13	29 54	05 15
9	16 34	25 12	29 27	14 38	04 04	09 38	13 01	04 12	29 53	05 14
10	17 32	08♑27	28 52	15 52	04 44	09 42	13 06	04 10	29 51	05 13
11	18 29	21 31	28 13	17 06	05 23	09 46	13 11	04 09	29 49	05 12
12	19 27	04♒22	27 30	18 20	06 03	09 49	13 17	04 07	29 48	05 11
13	20 24	17♒03	26 44	19 34	06 43	09 53	13 22	04 06	29 46	05 10
14	21 22	29 32	25 56	20 49	07 22	09 56	13 27	04 04	29 45	05 09
15	22 19	11♓50	25 06	22 03	08 01	09 59	13 33	04 03	29 43	05 08
16	23 17	23 58	24 16	23 17	08 41	10 02	13 38	04 01	29 41	05 07
17	24 15	05♈58	23 26	24 31	09 20	10 04	13 44	04 00	29 40	05 06
18	25 12	17 51	22 37	25 45	09 59	10 07	13 49	03 58	29 38	05 05
19	26 10	29 42	21 50	27 00	10 38	10 09	13 55	03 56	29 37	05 05
20	27 08	11♉33	21 07	28 14	11 18	10 11	14 01	03 54	29 35	05 04
21	28 05	23 30	20 28	29 28	11 57	10 13	14 07	03 53	29 33	05 03
22	29 03	05♊38	19 54	00♍42	12 35	10 15	14 12	03 51	29 32	05 02
23	00♍01	18 03	19 26	01 57	13 14	10 16	14 18	03 49	29 30	05 02
24	00 59	00♋48	19 04	03 11	13 53	10 17	14 24	03 47	29 28	05 01
25	01 57	13 58	18 49	04 25	14 32	10 18	14 30	03 45	29 27	05 00
26	02 55	27 35	18 42	05 40	15 11	10 19	14 36	03 43	29 25	05 00
27	03 53	11♌41	18 43D	06 54	15 49	10 20	14 42	03 41	29 23	04 59
28	04 51	26 11	18♌51	08 08	16 28	10 20	14 49	03 39	29 22	04 58
29	05 49	10♍59	19 08	09 23	17 06	10 21	14 55	03 37	29 20	04 58
30	06 47	25 58	19 33	10 37	17 44	10 21R	15 01	03 35	29 18	04 57
31	07 45	10♎58	20 06	11 51	18 23	10 21	15 07	03 33	29 17	04 57

SEPTEMBER 2011

Date	☉	☽	☿	♀	♂	♃	♄	♅	♆	♇
1	08♍43	25♎50	20♌47	13♍06	19♋01	10 20R	15♎14	03 31R	29 15R	04 56R
2	09 41	10♏26	21 36	14 20	19 39	10♉20	15 20	03♈29	29♒14	04♑56
3	10 39	24 42	22 32	15 35	20 17	10 19	15 26	03 27	29 12	04 55
4	11 37	08♐37	23 36	16 49	20 55	10 18	15 33	03 24	29 10	04 55
5	12 35	22 11	24 46	18 04	21 33	10 17	15 39	03 22	29 09	04 55
6	13 33	05♑27	26 02	19 18	22 11	10 16	15 46	03 20	29 07	04 54
7	14 31	18 27	27 24	20 33	22 49	10 14	15 53	03 18	29 06	04 54
8	15 30	01♒12	28 51	21 47	23 26	10 13	15 59	03 16	29 04	04 54
9	16 28	13 46	00♍23	23 01	24 04	10 11	16 06	03 13	29 03	04 54
10	17 26	26 11	01 59	24 16	24 41	10 08	16 13	03 11	29 01	04 53
11	18 24	08♓26	03 39	25 30	25 19	10 06	16 19	03 09	29 00	04 53
12	19 23	20 34	05 21	26 45	25 56	10 04	16 26	03 06	28 58	04 53
13	20 21	02♈34	07 07	27 59	26 33	10 01	16 33	03 04	28 56	04 53
14	21 20	14 29	08 54	29 14	27 10	09 58	16 40	03 02	28 55	04 53
15	22 18	26 20	10 43	00♎28	27 47	09 55	16 47	02 59	28 54	04 53
16	23 16	08♉10	12 34	01 43	28 24	09 52	16 54	02 57	28 52	04 53
17	24 15	20 00	14 25	02 58	29 01	09 48	17 00	02 55	28 51	04♑53D

SEPTEMBER 2011 (Cont'd)

Date	☉	☽	☿	♀	♂	♃	♄	♅	♆	♇
18	25♍13	01♊56	16♍17	04♎12	29♋38	09 45R	17♎07	02 52R	28 49R	04♑53
19	26 12	14 02	18 09	05 27	00♌15	09♉41	17 14	02♈50	28♒48	04 53
20	27 11	26 23	20 01	06 41	00 52	09 37	17 21	02 47	28 46	04 53
21	28 09	09♋04	21 53	07 56	01 28	09 32	17 29	02 45	28 45	04 53
22	29 08	22 11	23 45	09 10	02 05	09 28	17 36	02 43	28 44	04 53
23	00♎07	05♌45	25 37	10 25	02 41	09 24	17 43	02 40	28 42	04 53
24	01 05	19 50	27 27	11 40	03 18	09 19	17 50	02 38	28 41	04 54
25	02 04	04♍23	29 18	12 54	03 54	09 14	17 57	02 35	28 40	04 54
26	03 03	19 20	01♎07	14 09	04 30	09 09	18 04	02 33	28 38	04 54
27	04 02	04♎32	02 56	15 23	05 06	09 03	18 11	02 31	28 37	04 55
28	05 01	19 49	04 44	16 38	05 42	08 58	18 18	02 28	28 36	04 55
29	06 00	04♏58	06 31	17 53	06 18	08 52	18 26	02 26	28 35	04 55
30	06 59	19 51	08 18	19 07	06 54	08 47	18 33	02 23	28 33	04 56

OCTOBER 2011

Date	☉	☽	☿	♀	♂	♃	♄	♅	♆	♇
1	07♎58	04♐22	10♎03	20♎22	07♌29	08 41R	18♎40	02 21R	28 32R	04♑56
2	08 57	18 27	11 48	21 36	08 05	08♉35	18 47	02♈19	28♒31	04 57
3	09 56	02♑05	13 31	22 51	08 40	08 29	18 55	02 16	28 30	04 57
4	10 55	15 20	15 14	24 06	09 16	08 22	19 02	02 14	28 29	04 58
5	11 54	28 15	16 56	25 20	09 51	08 16	19 09	02 11	28 28	04 58
6	12 53	10♒51	18 38	26 35	10 26	08 09	19 17	02 09	28 27	04 59
7	13 52	23 15	20 18	27 49	11 01	08 03	19 24	02 07	28 26	05 00
8	14 51	05♓28	21 58	29 04	11 36	07 56	19 31	02 04	28 25	05 00
9	15 51	17 32	23 36	00♏19	12 11	07 49	19 38	02 02	28 24	05 01
10	16 50	29 31	25 14	01 33	12 45	07 42	19 46	02 00	28 23	05 02
11	17 49	11♈26	26 52	02 48	13 20	07 35	19 53	01 57	28 22	05 02
12	18 48	23 17	28 28	04 03	13 55	07 27	20 00	01 55	28 21	05 03
13	19 48	05♉08	00♏04	05 17	14 29	07 20	20 08	01 53	28 20	05 04
14	20 47	16 59	01 39	06 32	15 03	07 12	20 15	01 51	28 19	05 05
15	21 47	28 52	03 14	07 46	15 37	07 05	20 22	01 48	28 18	05 06
16	22 46	10♊52	04 47	09 01	16 11	06 57	20 30	01 46	28 17	05 07
17	23 46	23 00	06 21	10 16	16 45	06 50	20 37	01 44	28 17	05 07
18	24 45	05♋22	07 53	11 30	17 19	06 42	20 44	01 42	28 16	05 08
19	25 45	18 01	09 25	12 45	17 53	06 34	20 52	01 40	28 15	05 09
20	26 44	01♌02	10 56	13 59	18 26	06 26	20 59	01 38	28 15	05 10
21	27 44	14 29	12 27	15 14	19 00	06 18	21 06	01 36	28 14	05 11
22	28 44	28 25	13 57	16 29	19 33	06 10	21 14	01 33	28 13	05 13
23	29 43	12♍48	15 26	17 43	20 06	06 02	21 21	01 31	28 13	05 14
24	00♏43	27 36	16 55	18 58	20 39	05 54	21 28	01 29	28 12	05 15
25	01 43	12♎43	18 23	20 12	21 12	05 46	21 35	01 27	28 12	05 16
26	02 43	28 00	19 50	21 27	21 45	05 38	21 43	01 25	28 11	05 17
27	03 43	13♏14	21 17	22 42	22 18	05 29	21 50	01 23	28 11	05 18
28	04 42	28 17	22 43	23 56	22 50	05 21	21 57	01 22	28 10	05 20
29	05 42	13♐00	24 09	25 11	23 23	05 13	22 04	01 20	28 10	05 21
30	06 42	27 17	25 34	26 25	23 55	05 05	22 12	01 18	28 10	05 22
31	07 42	11♑06	26 57	27 40	24 27	04 57	22 19	01 16	28 09	05 23

NOVEMBER 2011

Date	☉	☽	☿	♀	♂	♃	♄	♅	♆	♇
1	08♏42	24♑28	28♏21	28♏55	24♌59	04 49R	22♎26	01 14R	28 09R	05♑25
2	09 42	07♒26	29 43	00♐09	25 31	04♉41	22 33	01♈13	28♒09	05 26
3	10 42	20 03	01♐04	01 24	26 02	04 33	22 40	01 11	28 08	05 28
4	11 43	02♓23	02 24	02 38	26 34	04 25	22 47	01 09	28 08	05 29
5	12 43	14 31	03 43	03 53	27 05	04 17	22 54	01 08	28 08	05 30
6	13 43	26 30	05 01	05 08	27 36	04 09	23 01	01 06	28 08	05 32
7	14 43	08♈23	06 18	06 22	28 07	04 01	23 08	01 04	28 08	05 33
8	15 43	20 14	07 33	07 37	28 38	03 53	23 15	01 03	28 08	05 35

NOVEMBER 2011 (Cont'd)

Date	☉	☽	☿	♀	♂	♃	♄	♅	♆	♇
9	16♏43	02♉05	08♐46	08♐51	29♌09	03 45R	23♎22	01 01R	28♒08	05♑36
10	17 44	13 58	09 58	10 06	29 39	03♉38	23 29	01♈00	28 08D	05 38
11	18 44	25 55	11 07	11 20	00♍09	03 30	23 36	00 59	28 08	05 40
12	19 44	07♊57	12 15	12 35	00 39	03 22	23 43	00 57	28 08	05 41
13	20 45	20 06	13 19	13 49	01 09	03 15	23 50	00 56	28 08	05 43
14	21 45	02♋25	14 21	15 04	01 39	03 08	23 56	00 55	28 08	05 44
15	22 45	14 56	15 19	16 18	02 09	03 00	24 03	00 53	28 08	05 46
16	23 46	27 41	16 14	17 33	02 38	02 53	24 10	00 52	28 09	05 48
17	24 46	10♌44	17 04	18 47	03 07	02 46	24 17	00 51	28 09	05 49
18	25 47	24 08	17 50	20 02	03 36	02 39	24 23	00 50	28 09	05 51
19	26 47	07♍53	18 30	21 16	04 05	02 33	24 30	00 49	28 09	05 53
20	27 48	22 01	19 04	22 31	04 33	02 26	24 36	00 48	28 10	05 55
21	28 48	06♎31	19 32	23 45	05 02	02 19	24 43	00 47	28 10	05 57
22	29 49	21 18	19 52	25 00	05 30	02 13	24 49	00 46	28 10	05 58
23	00♐50	06♏16	20 04	26 14	05 58	02 07	24 56	00 45	28 11	06 00
24	01 50	21 17	20 07R	27 29	06 26	02 01	25 02	00 44	28 11	06 02
25	02 51	06♐13	20♐00	28 43	06 53	01 55	25 08	00 44	28 12	06 04
26	03 52	20 55	19 43	29 58	07 20	01 49	25 15	00 43	28 13	06 06
27	04 53	05♑17	19 15	01♑12	07 47	01 43	25 21	00 42	28 13	06 08
28	05 53	19 14	18 36	02 27	08 14	01 38	25 27	00 42	28 14	06 09
29	06 54	02♒45	17 46	03 41	08 40	01 33	25 33	00 41	28 14	06 11
30	07 55	15 51	16 47	04 55	09 07	01 27	25 39	00 40	28 15	06 13

DECEMBER 2011

Date	☉	☽	☿	♀	♂	♃	♄	♅	♆	♇
1	08♐56	28♒33	15 38R	06♑10	09♌32	01 22R	25♎45	00 40R	28♒16	06♑15
2	09 56	10♓56	14♐23	07 24	09 58	01♉18	25 51	00♈40	28 17	06 17
3	10 57	23 04	13 02	08 38	10 24	01 13	25 57	00 39	28 17	06 19
4	11 58	05♈02	11 39	09 53	10 49	01 09	26 03	00 39	28 18	06 21
5	12 59	16 54	10 17	11 07	11 14	01 04	26 09	00 39	28 19	06 23
6	14 00	28 43	08 58	12 21	11 38	01 00	26 15	00 38	28 20	06 25
7	15 01	10♉35	07 45	13 36	12 02	00 57	26 20	00 38	28 21	06 27
8	16 02	22 32	06 40	14 50	12 26	00 53	26 26	00 38	28 22	06 29
9	17 03	04♊36	05 45	16 04	12 50	00 49	26 31	00 38	28 23	06 31
10	18 04	16 50	05 00	17 18	13 13	00 46	26 37	00 38D	28 24	06 33
11	19 05	29 15	04 26	18 33	13 37	00 43	26 42	00♈38	28 25	06 35
12	20 06	11♋52	04 04	19 47	13 59	00 40	26 48	00 38	28 26	06 37
13	21 06	24 41	03 53	21 01	14 22	00 38	26 53	00 38	28 27	06 40
14	22 07	07♌44	03 52D	22 15	14 44	00 35	26 58	00 38	28 28	06 42
15	23 09	21 01	04♐01	23 29	15 05	00 33	27 03	00 39	28 29	06 44
16	24 10	04♍32	04 19	24 43	15 27	00 31	27 08	00 39	28 31	06 46
17	25 11	18 17	04 45	25 58	15 48	00 29	27 13	00 39	28 32	06 48
18	26 12	02♎17	05 19	27 12	16 08	00 27	27 18	00 40	28 33	06 50
19	27 13	16 29	05 59	28 26	16 29	00 26	27 23	00 40	28 34	06 52
20	28 14	00♏52	06 45	29 40	16 49	00 24	27 28	00 41	28 36	06 54
21	29 15	15 23	07 37	00♒54	17 08	00 23	27 33	00 41	28 37	06 56
22	00♑16	29 58	08 33	02 08	17 27	00 23	27 37	00 42	28 38	06 59
23	01 17	14♐31	09 33	03 22	17 46	00 22	27 42	00 42	28 40	07 01
24	02 18	28 56	10 36	04 36	18 04	00 22	27 46	00 43	28 41	07 03
25	03 19	13♑07	11 43	05 49	18 22	00 21	27 51	00 44	28 43	07 05
26	04 21	27 00	12 52	07 03	18 39	00 21D	27 55	00 45	28 44	07 07
27	05 22	10♒32	14 04	08 17	18 56	00♉22	27 59	00 46	28 46	07 09
28	06 23	23 41	15 18	09 31	19 13	00 22	28 03	00 47	28 47	07 11
29	07 24	06♓28	16 33	10 45	19 29	00 23	28 07	00 48	28 49	07 14
30	08 25	18 55	17 51	11 58	19 44	00 24	28 11	00 49	28 50	07 16
31	09 26	01♈06	19 10	13 12	19 59	00 25	28 15	00 50	28 52	07 18

CELESTIAL FORECASTER

2012

FEATURING:

- Daily forecasts based on planetary alignments
- Monthly overview of significant aspects
- Built-in ephemeris
- Daily graph of aspect influences
- Phases of the Moon chart
- Famous birthdays
- Lunar aspects guide

Release date September 21, 2011

ISBN 978-0-9731518-9-3 pbk. 280 pp.
US $17.95 + 5.00 s&h = US $22.95
(includes HST) CDN $25.70

ORDER DIRECT FROM THE PUBLISHER
Send check or international money order to
Loon Feather Publications
Box 47031, Victoria, BC, Canada V9B 5T2
or visit **www.metaphysical.ca/forecaster**
to order on the internet
Standard trade terms apply